W9-DFU-756

These two volumes, part of the Cambridge Monographs and Texts in Applied Psycholinguistics, present high level up-to-date reviews of research, theory, and practice in reading, writing, and language learning and in disorders of first-language development. Each review focuses, wherever possible, on the work of its author or authors. The *Advances* will help researchers, teachers, students, and practitioners in psychology, linguistics, education, and the speech sciences keep abreast of major developments in many subareas of applied psycholinguistics.

Volume 1. Disorders of First-Language Development
Leading researchers consider most of the problems in first-language development: specific language impairment (Laurence B. Leonard; Phil J. Connell), mental retardation (Leonard Abbeduto and Sheldon Rosenberg), deafness (Stephen P. Quigley and Peter V. Paul), learning disability (Mavis Donahue), brain damage and language development (Marcel Kinsbourne and Merrill Hiscock), and language dissolution in later life (Jennifer Sandson, Loraine K. Obler, and Martin L. Albert). The contributors discuss topics such as the origin of specific language impairment, the pragmatics of normal and disordered language acquisition, language and communicative intervention procedures, the neurological organization of language, and the dynamics of language functioning in dementia and healthy aging.

Volume 2. Reading, Writing, and Language Learning
Major issues in reading, writing, and language learning are treated: linguistics and reading ability (Frank R. Vellutino and Donna M. Scanlon), reading and mental retardation (Linda P. Blanton, Melvyn I. Semmel, and Sharyn S. Rhodes), linguistics in reading and writing (Charles A. Perfetti and Deborah McCutchen), writing processes (Marlene Scardamalia and Carl Bereiter; John R. Hayes, Linda Flower, Karen A. Schriver, James F. Stratman, and Linda Carey), second-language learning (Evelyn Hatch and Barbara Hawkins), and bilingualism (Kenji Hakuta, Bernardo M. Ferdman, and Rafael M. Diaz). Chapters address such cross-cutting concerns as phonological coding in good and poor readers, cognitive strategies in reading among mildly mentally retarded learners, schooled language competence, composing strategies in mature and immature writers, cognitive processes in revision, strategies of second-language acquisition, and the impact of bilingualism on cognitive development.

Cambridge Monographs and Texts in Applied Psycholinguistics

Advances in applied psycholinguistics, Volume 1
Disorders of first-language development

Cambridge Monographs and Texts in Applied Psycholinguistics

General Editor: Sheldon Rosenberg

Advances in applied psycholinguistics, Volume 1

Disorders of first-language development

Edited by

SHELDON ROSENBERG

University of Illinois at Chicago

The right of the
University of Cambridge
to print and sell
all manner of books
was granted by
Henry VIII in 1534.
The University has printed
and published continuously
since 1584.

CAMBRIDGE UNIVERSITY PRESS

Cambridge

New York   New Rochelle   Melbourne   Sydney

Published by the Press Syndicate of the University of Cambridge
The Pitt Building, Trumpington Street, Cambridge CB2 1RP
32 East 57th Street, New York, NY 10022, USA
10 Stamford Road, Oakleigh, Melbourne 3166, Australia

First published 1987

Printed in the United States of America

Library of Congress Cataloging-in-Publication Data
Advances in applied psycholinguistics.

(Cambridge monographs and texts in applied
psycholinguistics)
Published also in 2 v.
Includes index.
1. Psycholinguistics.   2. Language acquisition.
3. Language disorders.   4. Reading.   5. Writing.
I. Rosenberg, Sheldon.   II. Series.
P37.A33 1987   401'.9   87–10285

Advances in applied psycholinguistics.

(Cambridge monographs and texts in applied
psycholinguistics)
Published also in 1 v.
Includes indexes.
Contents: v. 1. Disorders of first-language
development – v. 2. Reading, writing, and language
learning.
1. Psycholinguistics.   2. Language acquisition.
3. Language disorders.   4. Reading.   5. Writing.
I. Rosenberg, Sheldon.   II. Series.
P37.A33 1987b   401'.9   87-13258

British Library Cataloguing in Publication Data
Advances in applied psycholinguistics –

(Cambridge monographs and texts in applied
psycholinguistics).
1. Psycholinguistics
I. Rosenberg, Sheldon
401'.9   BF455

ISBN 0 521 30027 4 hard covers (combined set)
ISBN 0 521 31732 0 v.1 : paperback
ISBN 0 521 31733 9 v.2 : paperback

To my brothers
NORMAN AND ALVIN

Contents

Preface

The present volume, *Advances in applied psycholinguistics: disorders of first-language development*, and its companion volume, *Advances in applied psycholinguistics: reading, writing, and language learning*, are part of the series entitled Cambridge Monographs and Texts in Applied Psycholinguistics, which began with the publication in 1983 of Ann M. Peters's *The units of language acquisition*. The general aim of this series is to bring together work from all of the subfields of applied psycholinguistics by authors who approach applied problems from the vantage point of basic research and theory in psycholinguistics and related areas of cognitive psychology. The aim of the present *Advances* is to make available high-level up-to-date reviews of research, theory, and practice in the two major areas of applied psycholinguistics: (1) disorders of first-language development and (2) reading, writing, and language learning, with each review focusing, wherever possible, on the published and ongoing work of its author or authors. Thus, the *Advances* should help researchers, teachers, students, and practitioners in the many areas of applied psycholinguistics – from fields such as psychology, speech-hearing-language sciences and pathology, applied linguistics, educational psychology, special education, neurology, psychiatry, foreign-language teaching, and English composition – keep abreast of major developments in their areas of interest.

Although the present chapters underwent editorial review for style, organization, and accuracy of content, the content, scope, and organization of a given manuscript was ultimately left to its author or authors.

The majority of the problem areas associated with disorders of first-language development are represented in the present volume: specific language impairment (Leonard, Connell), mental retardation (Abbeduto and Rosenberg), deafness (Quigley and Paul), learning disability (Donahue), brain damage and language development (Kinsbourne and Hiscock), and language dissolution in later life (Sandson, Obler, and Albert). As readers will observe, Leonard takes a bold stance on the issue of the origin of specific language impairment, a stance that takes it out of the realm of first-language development and into that of individual differences in normal language acquisition. The material in Abbeduto and Rosenberg's and Donahue's chapters reflects the intense current interest of the literature in the pragmatics of language acquisition. Quigley and Paul as well as Connell address vital issues in language and communicative intervention. Kinsbourne and Hiscock attempt to correct some strongly held misconceptions concerning the impact of brain damage on language development and the neurological organization of language. Finally, Sandson, Obler, and Albert bring us up to date on the dynamics of language functioning in dementia and in healthy aging.

Sheldon Rosenberg

Chicago, Illinois

Contributors

Leonard Abbeduto Box 512, Peabody College, Vanderbilt University, Nashville, Tennessee 37203

Martin L. Albert Behavioral Neurosciences, Department of Neurology, Boston University Medical School and Boston Veterans Administration Medical Center, 150 South Huntington Avenue, Boston, Massachusetts 02130

Phil J. Connell Program in Speech and Language Pathology, Department of Communication Sciences and Disorders, Northwestern University, Evanston, Illinois 60201

Mavis Donahue College of Education, University of Illinois at Chicago, P.O. Box 4348, Chicago, Illinois 60680

Merrill Hiscock Psychology Division, University Hospital, Saskatoon, Saskatchewan, Canada S7N 0X0

Marcel Kinsbourne Behavioral Neurology Department, Eunice Kennedy Shriver Center for Mental Retardation, 200 Trapelo Road, Waltham, Massachusetts 02254

Laurence B. Leonard Audiology and Speech Sciences, Purdue University, West Lafayette, Indiana 47907

Loraine K. Obler Department of Neurology, Boston Veterans Administration Medical Center, 150 South Huntington Avenue, Boston, Massachusetts 02130

Peter V. Paul Department of Human Services Education, Ohio State University, 356 Arps Hall, 1945 North High Street, Columbus, Ohio 43210

Stephen P. Quigley 110 Education, University of Illinois at Urbana-Champaign, 1310 South Sixth Street, Champaign, Illinois 61820

Sheldon Rosenberg Department of Psychology and Institute for the Study of

Developmental Disabilities, University of Illinois at Chicago, P. O. Box 4348, Chicago, Illinois 60680

Jennifer Sandson Neurology/127, Boston Veterans Administration Medical Center, 150 South Huntington Avenue, Boston, Massachusetts 02130

1   Is specific language impairment a useful construct?

Laurence B. Leonard

Children with specific language impairment exhibit significant limitations in language functioning that cannot be attributed to deficits in hearing, oral structure and function, or general intelligence. Papers concerned with these children often set forth two important qualifications. First, specifically language impaired (SLI) children constitute a heterogeneous group, differing markedly from one another in their language characteristics and other areas of weakness. Second, such children are identified by exclusion criteria. That is, although SLI children differ from one another, none exhibits the hallmark characteristics of other identifiable handicapped groups. As a consequence, they represent a type of miscellaneous "other" category. In the present contribution, I shall use these same points to argue that the notion of specific language impairment is of questionable value as a guiding principle for research aimed at uncovering a cause of SLI children's problems and that, furthermore, provision of the necessary educational and clinical services for these children is not dependent on this construct.

The chapter is divided into two major sections. In the first section I review the evidence pertaining to the three most prominent accounts of specific language impairment. I attempt to show that none of these divergent accounts offers a reasonable explanation for language impairment, although at least one of them provides compelling evidence that often these children's problems are not restricted to language. In the second section I argue that the limitations of current research are due not so much to our selection of the wrong causal factors to study as to our assumption that there are tangible causes in the first place. The argument is made that the notion of a disorder or disruption of the developmental process need not be invoked to explain the existence of children with limited language abilities. Rather, children can show the same range of abilities in language as they do in other areas that do not customarily have a threshold beyond which a defect is assumed.

Three accounts of specific language impairment

The accounts of specific language impairment reviewed here are those that have received the greatest investigative attention in recent years and are thought, at least

1

by their proponents, to apply to a good number of the children given this clinical label. Excluded from consideration, then, are accounts of the problems of smaller subgroups of language-impaired children (e.g., that of Cromer, 1978, 1983) who may have symptoms (e.g., convulsive disorders, electroencephalographic abnormalities) that set them apart from most other SLI children.

The communicative environment of SLI children

Because SLI children give the impression of being unremarkable with the exception of their language disability, researchers have considered the possibility that the communicative environment of these children contributes significantly to their difficulties with language. This suspicion was undoubtedly fueled by early writings on the sources of these children's problems (e.g., Wyatt, 1969).

These early works offered two possible accounts of the adverse nature of SLI children's communicative environment. One was that SLI children had little need or opportunity to talk because other members of the family talked for them. The second was that SLI children's communicative input was of insufficient quantity and/or quality to promote normal language development. The second account seemed particularly plausible given findings that children living in institutional settings show depressed language skills relative to other abilities. As a case in point, Lamesch (1982) described a French child who was abandoned and placed in an institution. When evaluated some time later the child showed appropriate developmental abilities except in language. Lamesch observed the child's linguistic environment and believed it to be a contributing factor. No individual played a role as primary interactant. Instead, various members of the institution's staff came into contact with the child, and their language was aimed primarily at provoking or preventing some behavior by the child.

Most of the investigations in recent years have explored hypotheses that are variations of the second account. Only the study by Wellen and Broen (1982), discussed later, clearly pertains to the first. Rather than organizing the evidence in terms of the two accounts of environmental influences, then, I shall adopt an organization based on the source of input and the type of comparison group used. Specifically, the studies reviewed here are organized according to whether the focus is on the input of parents of SLI children, of other adults, or of peers interacting with SLI children and whether the comparison dyads include age-matched or language-matched normal-language (NL) children.

Consideration of the comparison dyads is an important ingredient in drawing conclusions from this literature. Case reports may provide useful information about the general dynamics of an interaction involving an SLI child, but they are limited in allowing us to interpret the specific developmental appropriateness of the interaction. For example, Blank, Gessner, and Esposito (1979) describe a rather unusual SLI child whose main limitation was a problem with dialogue. An examination of parent–child interactions suggested that the parents provided appropriate responses to the child's comments and questions and themselves asked appropriate questions and made appropriate comments. It is unclear, however, whether their interaction patterns were tuned primarily to the child's age-appropriate knowledge of the world or to his more limited communicative ability.

Unfortunately, even with the addition of comparison dyads, the studies reviewed here suffer from the limitation that investigators have not agreed on the type of input that is optimal even for NL children. As a result, the interpretation of differences between dyads involving SLI and those involving NL children is hampered.

Parents of SLI and parents of age-matched NL children. Wulbert, Inglis, Kriegsmann, and Mills (1975) examined the home environments of 20 SLI children (ages 2;10 to 5;8) and 20 age-matched NL children. The chief measure was the Caldwell Inventory of Home Stimulation, which included items involving direct observations of the mother's behavior. The mothers of SLI children were found to interact less with their children than were mothers of NL children, and they were quicker to shout at or threaten their children than reason with them. However, these mothers also reported that interactions with their children were difficult, because the children often rejected their communicative attempts.

Mother–child interactions involving 12 SLI children (ages 3 to 5 years) and 12 age-matched NL children were examined by Siegel, Cunningham, and van der Spuy (1979). During a structured task the mothers of the SLI children were more directive, more likely to interrupt their child's play with a command, and more likely to respond with directness to their child's questions. In other respects the two groups of mothers were not different. For example, they showed the same likelihood of initiating interaction, they both facilitated independent play, and they did not differ in the percentage of failures to respond to their child's interactive attempts. There was also evidence that the SLI children were less responsive than the NL children. For example, during free play the SLI children showed a lower likelihood of responding to their mother's questions, and if the mother failed to respond to one of their own communicative bids, they were less likely to reestablish communication.

In other studies, observed cases of differences between the speech addressed to SLI and age-matched NL children have been described as an expected occurrence given the restricted language abilities of SLI children. Cramblitt and Siegel (1977) noted that a mother's and father's speech to their SLI child (age 4;7) was more fluent, showed a lower type/token ratio, a lower mean length of utterance (MLU), fewer incomplete sentences, fewer questions, and more imperatives than speech addressed to an age-matched NL child. Cramblitt and Siegel noted that the same differences could be seen in speech to younger versus older NL children. Stein (1976) also reported mothers' and fathers' speech to SLI children (ages 3;11 to 5;11) and to NL children of the same age range. Participating in this study were

14 SLI and 20 NL children. As in the preceding study, mothers' and fathers' utterance length and complexity seemed in keeping with their child's language level.

In one of three experiments reported by Cunningham, Siegel, van der Spuy, and Bow (1982), comparisons were made between the speech of 33 mothers and their SLI children (ages 2;9 to 5;6) and that of 27 mothers and their NL children of the same age range. The two groups of mothers interacted with their children in a similar manner during free play. Both groups responded to their child's initiations, and they were similar in both their controlling and their encouraging behavior when the child was playing alone. During structured activities, the mothers of NL children asked a greater number of questions, as seen as well in the Cramblitt and Siegel (1977) study. However, the two groups of mothers were similar in their commands and in their rewarding of the child's compliance with commands.

Bondurant, Romeo, and Kretschmer (1983) also compared mothers of SLI and mothers of NL children in structured as well as unstructured activities. Participating in this study were 14 SLI children ages 2 to 5 years, 14 age-matched NL children, and their mothers. Fourteen language measures were examined. In the structured situation, in which the mother was to help her child build a toy farm that matched hers, differences between the two groups of mothers were seen for three measures. The mothers of the NL children showed higher MLU, asked more questions, and produced a greater number of acceptance utterances. Differences favoring the mothers of the NL children were again seen for MLU and acceptance utterances in the unstructured situation. In addition, the mothers of the SLI children gave more directions.

Two studies by Friel-Patti (1976, 1978) focused on eye gaze behavior of mothers of SLI and NL children. Participating in the earlier study were six mothers and their SLI children (ages 3;6 to 5;4) and six mothers and their age-matched NL children. The cumulative duration of eye gaze behavior of each interactant was noted. On average, each mother of an SLI child looked at her child for approximately 102 of the 720 sec constituting the sampling period. Each mother of an NL child looked at her child for approximately 82 sec. Similar tendencies were not seen for the children; SLI and NL children looked at their mothers for approximately 15 and 35 sec, respectively.

In the later study by Friel-Patti, 12 SLI children (ages 3;8 to 5;9) and 12 age-matched NL children interacted with their mothers. The NL children looked more often at their mothers and combined gazing with speaking more often than the SLI children. In turn, the mothers of NL children looked more frequently both while speaking to their children and while listening to them speak than did the mothers of SLI children. The latter finding does not accord with the earlier Friel-Patti (1976) finding that mothers of SLI children looked at their children for longer durations than mothers of NL children. Possibly the earlier study included gazing when neither mother nor child was speaking.

Other adults interacting with SLI and age-matched NL children. Several studies have examined interactions between SLI children and other adults. In a study by Bruck and Ruckenstein (1978), nine SLI children and nine NL children in the same kindergarten classes interacted with their teachers. The teachers were asked to instruct each child in how to play a game involving pictures. Many of the measures of the teachers' speech revealed no differences as a function of whether the conversational partner was an SLI or NL child. However, certain differences were noted. When interacting with the SLI children, the teachers used fewer clauses per utterance, made more requests for information, repeated more utterances, and asked more naming questions. They were also more likely to accompany their explanations with pointing when speaking with the SLI children.

Fried-Oken (1981) examined teacher interactions with five SLI (ages 3;2 to 4;5) and five age-matched NL children. The teachers' use of several different types of questions was noted. Although the total number of questions asked was similar for the two types of children, questions designed to evoke one-word responses were asked more frequently of the SLI children, whereas requests for explanations were more frequently directed toward the NL children. The distribution of the yes–no questions asked of the two groups was also different. Those asked of the NL children often involved a *do*-insertion (e.g., *Do you think the lady's going to break the glass?*). In contrast, most of the questions asked of the SLI children involved auxiliary inversion or a rising terminal intonation.

In the Cramblitt and Siegel (1977) study described earlier, the speech of the SLI child's regular babysitter was also examined. Her speech to the SLI child differed from that to the age-matched NL child in the same ways seen for the SLI child's parents.

A central question to be asked about the preceding studies is whether the input of parents, teachers, and babysitters of SLI children contributes to the children's language difficulties or whether the nature of their input is natural given these children's limitations. This issue was addressed by Newhoff (1977). In this study, five SLI children (ages 3;4 to 3;11) and five age-matched children who were rather advanced in linguistic skill interacted with women with whom they were unfamiliar. Each of the women was a mother of a young child. The women's speech was examined for instances of conjoining (e.g., a sentence containing two independent clauses linked by *and* or *because*) and subordination (e.g., a sentence containing an independent and a relative clause). The women showed a lower percentage of subordinating segments with the SLI children than with the linguistically advanced children.

Robinson (1977) used Newhoff's data to examine the women's use of questions with the two types of children. Of the 17 question types examined, only one revealed a difference between the children, and this question appeared a total of only five times in the corpora.

Parents of SLI and parents of language-matched NL children. A logical extension of the question regarding the naturalness of simplified speech to SLI children is whether the speech to these children resembles that directed to younger NL children operating at the same level of language ability as the SLI children. The language measures selected to match the SLI and NL children are an important consideration in this regard. Most studies have used MLU as the basis of matching because of the long-standing use of this measure as a general index of language development. Other studies have used a measure of comprehension on the grounds that adult speech adjustments are made with the listener's understanding in mind. A final study used a language measure that considers both language production and comprehension ability.

Perhaps the first of these studies was conducted by Millet and Newhoff (1978). Comparisons involved nine mothers and their SLI children (ages 3;10 to 5;1 with MLUs of 1.40 to 3.60 words) and nine mothers and their MLU-matched NL children. Differences between the mothers were seen for two of the five language behaviors examined. Mothers of NL children produced a greater number of semantically related responses to their children's utterances, and mothers of SLI children produced a greater number of unintelligible utterances.

Macpherson and Weber-Olsen (1980) compared mother–SLI child and mother–NL child dyads in terms of semantic as well as conversational aspects of language. The four SLI children ranged in age from 3;0 to 3;4 and in MLU from 1.2 to 2.0 morphemes. The four NL children showed similar MLUs. The mothers of the two types of children did not differ in their use of self-repetitions, imitations, expansions, or semantic extensions. They were similar as well in their use of utterances expressing various semantic relations. However, the mothers of SLI children showed a higher proportion of utterances involving three-term relations, such as agent + action + object and agent + object + location.

Children operating at an earlier level of language development participated in a study by Messick and Prelock (1981). The five SLI (ages 2;8 to 4;2) and five NL children produced only single-word utterances. Expressive vocabularies of the two groups of children were comparable. Examination of the mother–child interactions revealed no differences between the mothers of the two types of children in the conversational measures of interest. These included number of conversational turns, communicative acts, and responsiveness to topic changes.

Conti-Ramsden and Friel-Patti (1983) also examined the conversational characteristics of mother–child dyads. In this study, 14 SLI children (ages 3;6 to 5;4, MLUs of 1.64 to 4.45 morphemes) and 14 MLU-matched NL children participated. The mothers of the two groups of children were similar in their use of requestives, directives, assertives, and regulatives (e.g., attention getters, requests for clarification). For two of the four types of responsives examined, however, higher frequencies were seen for the mothers of the NL children. These were choice answers and acknowledgments. The authors proposed that these particular differences may have been due to the fact that the NL children initiated conversational topics more frequently than the SLI children, and therefore the mothers of these children had greater opportunity to provide responses.

Additional analyses of the same data were presented in Conti-Ramsden and Friel-Patti (1984). It was found that, although SLI children initiated conversation and introduced new topics less often than the NL children, the mothers of the SLI children were not distinguishable from the NL children's mothers in the form and level of their initiations and in the adequacy of their responses to their children's questions and comments.

Father–child dyads were examined in a study by Silverman and Newhoff (1979). The participants were nine fathers and their SLI children (mean age 4;3, mean MLU 2.47) and nine fathers and their MLU-matched NL children. The five speech measures used by Millet and Newhoff (1978) were used here. In this case, however, no significant differences were observed.

Schodorf and Edwards (1981) examined three-party interactions involving the child and both parents. The 10 SLI children ranged in age from 2;11 to 5;5 and in MLU from 1.16 to 2.59 morphemes. The 10 NL children were matched according to MLU. In contrast to several of the studies reported above, Schodorf and Edwards observed a number of differences between the parents of the SLI and NL children that suggested that the former were not providing appropriate language input. These parents used fewer total words, expansions, models, ready-mades (verbal routines), and grammatically complete sentences, and they made more corrections than the parents of the NL children. The MLUs of the mothers as they interacted with these children were then examined. No difference was seen on this measure.

Laskey and Klopp (1982) examined mother–child interactions involving 7 mothers and their SLI children (ages 2;3 to 3;9) and 10 mothers and their NL children. The two groups of children showed comparable combined (receptive and expressive) language ages on the Receptive–Expressive Emergent Language Scale (Bzoch & League, 1970). Mean language ages were 1;6 and 1;9 for the SLI and NL children, respectively. A total of 38 behaviors were examined, including the mothers' MLU and use of self-repetitions, expansions, naming questions, and acknowledgments. No differences between the two groups of mothers were observed for any of the measures.

Other adults interacting with SLI and language-matched NL children. Nakamura and Newhoff (1982) examined the type of input that speech-language pathologists provide to SLI and NL children. The eight SLI children participating ranged in age from 4;1 to 5;10 and showed an MLU range of 3.10 to 5.20 morphemes. The eight NL children were matched according to MLU. Each speech-language pathologist interacted with one child from each group. No differences were seen for the six main adult-language measures selected. One of these, semantically related responses, was analyzed in greater detail. The speech-language pathologists were found to use more complete and incomplete expansions with the SLI children, and more exact and partial imitations and pronoun extensions with the NL children.

The influence of SLI children's comprehension level on adults' input was explored by VanKleeck and Carpenter (1978). Participating were four SLI children ages 4 to 5 years. All produced only single-word utterances. However, two of the children showed language comprehension that approached age level, whereas the other two children showed poor comprehension ability. Ten adults served as interactants; each interacted with one child from each comprehension group. The adults relied more heavily on nonlinguistic context with nonverbal cuing and restricting lexical diversity when interacting with the low-comprehension SLI children. However, many other measures (e.g., adult self-repetition, request for confirmation) revealed no significant differences. VanKleeck and Carpenter concluded that language comprehension level must not be the only variable that influences adults' speech adjustments when interacting with SLI children.

Parents of SLI children versus other adults with the same children. Given the hypothesis that parents of SLI children provide improper linguistic input, it is surprising that few studies have compared these parents and other adults in interaction with SLI children. The Cramblitt and Siegel (1977) study reviewed earlier did just that and found no differences in the manner in which SLI children's babysitters, mothers, or fathers spoke to them. In two other studies, comparisons were made between parents of SLI children and speech-language pathologists. Giattino, Pollack, and Silliman (1978) examined the speech addressed to two SLI children (ages 4;6 and 4;1). Each child interacted with the mother, an experienced speech-language pathologist, and a student in training to become a speech-language pathologist. The three adults were very similar in the percentage of their utterances that were requests. The mothers tended to request actions most often. Both speech-language pathologists used more requests for verbal information than did the mothers.

Olswang and Carpenter (1978) examined the input provided to five SLI children (ages 3;4 to 5;9) by their mothers and by speech-language pathologists. Few of the 10 measures used revealed differences. However, the mothers of the SLI children asked more questions about materials in the environment, whereas the speech-language pathologists produced more comments about materials that were present, and they were more likely to imitate the child. One caution must be provided concerning the interpretation of the findings of this study. The data were grouped with those from four mothers interacting with their mentally retarded children.

Peers' speech to SLI children. Parents, teachers, and other adults are not the only individuals whose input may influence the language of SLI children. Other children may also facilitate or hinder their language. Marinkovich, Newhoff, and MacKenzie (1980) examined the interaction of six normally developing 5-year-olds with SLI children of the same age (mean MLU 3.32 morphemes), six age-matched NL children (mean MLU 5.36), and six younger NL children (mean age 3;0, mean MLU 4.03). The dependent measures were utterances that could be classified in terms of semantic relation categories such as existence, attribution, and causality. The children were found to use a greater number of the later-developing semantic relations with same-age NL children than with either younger NL children or SLI children. Their speech to the two latter groups was highly similar. The authors also examined whether the children would alter their speech to the SLI children with additional opportunities to interact with them. Such was the case; across time fewer later-developing semantic relations and more early-developing relations were used with these children. Essentially the same findings were noted by MacKenzie, Newhoff, and Marinkovich (1981), who examined the same data in terms of the use of earlier- and later-developing requests.

Wellen and Broen (1982) examined the degree to which children interrupted the speech of SLI children. Specifically, the interruptions of three groups of four normally developing children were compared. The three groups were comparable in age and MLU. One group had younger SLI siblings (ages 3;5 to 3;11, MLUs 1.66 to 2.08 words). Another group had NL siblings who were even younger than the SLI children (ages 2;3 to 2;5, MLUs 2.26 to 3.56). The remaining group's younger siblings were somewhat older than the SLI children (ages 4;5 to 4;8, MLUs 4.86 to 5.82). Each of the younger siblings was read a story and was asked questions with the older siblings present. The older siblings' interruptions of the younger children were noted. Both the SLI and the youngest of the NL children were interrupted more frequently than the other group of NL siblings. For the two groups who were frequently interrupted, the interruptions most often occurred when difficult questions had been asked. Interruptions of the youngest NL children were typically rephrasings of the question or prompts. Interruptions of the SLI children were usually the answers to the questions. Of course, it should be noted that the language abilities of the youngest NL children exceeded those of the SLI children.

Interpretation. Several years ago, Lederberg (1980) reviewed the evidence concerning the language environment of children with language delays. The data up to that point led her to conclude that "parents of delayed children seem to be as sensitive to their child's abilities as parents of normal children" (p. 151) and that parents should "no longer be accused of 'retarding' their child's development" (p. 151).

There is little in the work appearing since 1980 to alter Lederberg's basic position. Parents of SLI children do not seem to interact with their children in the same way as parents of NL children of the same age. Instead, their interactions seem dictated by the language production and comprehension abilities of the children. Thus, few differences are seen between parents of SLI children and parents of NL children showing comparable language ability. (The findings of Schodorf and Edwards, 1981, are a notable exception.) Furthermore, it appears that other adults and older siblings also interact with SLI children in much the same way as they interact with NL children of similar language ability. Some of the speech adjustments made by parents of SLI children are not precisely the same as those made by speech-language pathologists with the same children. The speech of the former tends to be more assertive and action-focused, that of the latter more reactive and language-focused. However, this may be due as much to the philosophies behind the training of speech-language pathologists or these individuals' relative unfamiliarity with the SLI children as to anything unusual about the parents of these children.

It might be argued that because we do not know precisely how speech to SLI children should be tailored to facilitate their language development, we cannot yet conclude that the input of these children is not a contributing factor in their difficulties. This is the kind of reasoning that in fact was used by Silverman and Newhoff (1979) and Bondurant et al. (1983), reviewed earlier. For example, after finding no differences between the speech of fathers of SLI children and that of fathers of language-matched NL children, Silverman and Newhoff acknowledged that the fathers of the SLI children may have made appropriate speech adjustments given their children's limited language abilities. At the same time, they raised the possibility that had the fathers shown greater use of certain language behaviors their children's language abilities might have been closer to age level. Yet fathers and mothers of SLI children are not the only persons who adapt their speech to SLI children's language level; other adults and children do as well. It seems natural to make such adjustments. One could therefore provide the counterargument that had the fathers of the SLI children produced speech with greater complexity, which is not what other adults do, the fathers could have been criticized for using speech that was problematic for their children or perhaps for having hindered the children's chances of making significant advances in language development. In short, the evidence that communicative input factors contribute to language difficulties is weak and certainly not the stuff of which theories of specific language impairment should be made.

Perception of rapid acoustic events

During the 1960s and into the 1970s there were a number of claims that SLI children's problems were attributable to "auditory-processing deficits." The meaning of this term varied from investigator to investigator. Studies of auditory-processing ability included any one or more of the following: auditory discrimination, sequencing, memory, and synthesis. SLI children often performed poorly on these tasks relative to same-age NL children.

One of the problems with the work of this era was that the various skills tapped in these studies could not be integrated into a well-articulated theory of SLI children's difficulties. A second problem was that some of the tasks were clearly linguistic in nature and thus improper as gauges of abilities presumed to be more basic than language perception. Rees (1981) provides a description and critique of many of these tasks, so they will not be detailed here.

Discrimination, sequencing, and serial memory. A significant refinement in auditory-processing research occurred with the appearance of the studies of Tallal and her colleagues. The first such study involved 12 SLI children (ages 6;9 to 9;3) and 12 same-age NL peers (Tallal & Piercy, 1973a). The children were presented two different 75-msec tones composed of frequencies within the speech range. One tone's fundamental frequency was 100 Hz; that of the other tone was 305 Hz (see Tallal & Piercy, 1973b; the fundamental frequencies given in the 1973a paper were incorrect). For both tones the first, second, and third formants were 497, 750, and 1,500 Hz, respectively.

Initially, the children were taught to respond to each tone separately by pushing one of two panels for one tone, the other panel for the other tone. The children were then taught to respond to each of the four two-tone sequences presented (1–2, 2–1, 1–1, 2–2) with an intersound interval (ISI) of 428 msec by pushing the panels in the appropriate order. After receiving this training, the children were tested on the same two-tone sequences using 12 different ISIs. The shortest ISI was 8 msec, the longest 4,062 msec.

The NL children performed significantly better than chance at all ISIs. According to Tallal and Piercy, this level of performance was not achieved by the SLI children at ISIs of less than 305 msec. Identical results were obtained when the task was altered so that the children pushed one panel when the two tones were the same and the other panel when the two tones were different. Because the same–different task required only discrimination of the tones, Tallal and Piercy suggested that the sequencing difficulties shown by the SLI children in the first task may have been secondary to their problem with discriminating the two tones when presented in rapid succession.

One aspect of the findings should be noted. Tallal and Piercy used the .001 level as indicating above-chance performance. My calculations of their data as they were presented indicate that, although the SLI children's accuracy was clearly lower than that of the NL children at the shorter ISIs, these children were above chance if less stringent levels were adopted (see Table 1, p. 469 in Tallal & Piercy, 1973a).

In a second experiment using the same children, Tallal and Piercy (1973b) examined the role of the duration of the tones as well as the modality of stimulus presentation in SLI children's perceptual performance. In this experiment, the children were asked to press the panels corresponding to the four two-tone patterns used in the earlier experiment. However, in this case, only seven different ISIs were used. The shortest was 8 msec; the longest was 428 msec. The procedure was carried out four times, a different tone duration being used on each occasion. The durations were 75, 125, 175, and 250 msec. When the tone duration was 75 or 125 msec, the SLI children performed below the level of the NL children for all ISIs of 150 msec or less. When tone duration was 175 msec, the NL children outperformed the SLI children only when ISIs were 15 msec or less. No differences were seen between the groups when the tone duration was 250 msec. Tallal and Piercy's statistical analyses of these data were confined to between-group comparisons. However, based on inspection of the data, conclusions can also be drawn concerning the SLI children's performance relative to chance. The 75-msec data reported in this study were the same as those discussed above for Tallal and Piercy (1973a). For each of the other tone durations, the SLI children met Tallal and Piercy's (1973a) criterion ($p < .001$) for above-chance-level performance for all ISIs employed.

Tallal and Piercy (1973b) made the interesting observation that the total duration of the stimulus pattern may have been a crucial factor in the SLI children's lower performance. That is, for each ISI, performance decreased with decreasing tone durations, and for each tone duration except 250 msec, performance tended to decrease with decreasing ISI. The correlation between total duration of the stimulus pattern and the SLI children's percentage of correct responses was .89.

The same procedures were used to test the children's performance with visual stimuli. The two stimuli in this case were light flashes of two different shades of green. Stimulus duration was not manipulated; all flashes were 75 msec in duration. Several ISIs were employed, the shortest being 30 msec in duration and the longest 428 msec. No differences between the two groups of children were seen for any of the ISIs. This finding led Tallal and Piercy to conclude that the SLI children's problems with discrimination and sequencing were probably specific to the auditory modality.

A serial memory task was also administered to the children in each modality. For the auditory modality, the ISI was constant at 428 msec, and tones were either 75 or 250 msec in duration. The two complex tones used in the previous experiments were used again here. The stimulus patterns involved random combinations of these two tones that were three, four, or five elements in length. The children were required to press the panels in a manner that corresponded to the order in which the tones were presented. Identical ISIs and procedures were followed for the visual modality, but stimulus duration was limited to 75 msec. For the auditory modality the SLI children's performance decreased with an increase in elements as well as with a decrease in the duration of the tone. Only on three-element patterns using the longer (250 msec) duration did the SLI children perform at the level of the NL children. No differences were seen between the two groups of children for the visual modality. Although the serial memory findings again implicated the auditory modality in particular, Tallal and Piercy suggested that the SLI children's poorer performance could have been due entirely to their requiring disproportionately more time to process additional auditory elements or to a deficit in auditory memory in addition to a slowness in processing auditory information.

Tallal and Piercy (1974) tested the same children using synthesized vowel and consonant stimuli. The two vowel stimuli corresponded to [ɛ] and [æ]. Each had a fundamental frequency falling linearly from 130 to 116 Hz and a duration of 250 msec. For [ɛ] the first three formants were 673, 1601, and 2539 Hz. For [æ] these values were 524, 1836, and 2662 Hz. The other two stimuli corresponded to [ba] and [da]. Both were 250 msec in duration. The first 13 msec simulated prevoicing with a low-amplitude first formant, followed by a 30-msec transition period in which the first three formant frequencies moved toward the steady-state portion of the vowel. The steady-state portion was identical for the two stimuli in terms of duration (207 msec), formant frequencies (700, 1102, and 2478 Hz), and fundamental frequency (falling linearly to 74 Hz). According to Tallal and Piercy (1975) the frequencies of the transitional components were incorrectly reported in the 1974 paper. These values were not provided in the later paper.

For both [ɛ] and [æ] as well as [ba] and [da], the children participated in the discrimination and two-element sequencing tasks with varying ISIs and on the serial memory task used in their earlier studies. The previously described same–different task was also used for [ba] and [da]. For vowel stimuli no differences were seen between the SLI and NL children on the discrimination and two-element sequencing tasks at any ISI. For the serial memory task the two groups differed only on the five-element patterns. The results were quite different for [ba] and [da]. Although the NL children had little difficulty with these stimuli, fewer than half of the SLI children could discriminate between these syllables, and only two of those who could were able to sequence them appropriately at the longest ISI used, 428 msec. The same subjects were also successful at shorter ISIs. Essentially identical results were obtained using the same–different task. On the serial memory task, too, the SLI children did relatively poorly; only two of these children reached criterion on three-element sequences, only one on longer sequences. Again, it is not clear whether on any of these tasks the SLI children performed above the level of chance if less stringent criteria (e.g., $p < .01$ or $.05$) were adopted. It is clear, however, that these children performed quite poorly relative to same-age peers on [ba] and [da].

It can be recalled that in Tallal and Piercy (1973b) the SLI and NL children performed at comparable levels on two-element sequencing at all ISIs when the stimuli were complex tones of 250 msec duration. Identical results were obtained by Tallal and Piercy (1974) when vowels of the same duration were used. This led Tallal and Piercy to conclude that merely changing from nonverbal to verbal stimuli does not adversely affect SLI children. They proposed, however, that when demands are placed on rate of auditory processing these children have difficulty with both verbal and nonverbal stimuli. The evidence supporting this view in the 1974 study was the fact that the children had great difficulty with [ba] and [da]. Although each syllable was 250 msec in duration, the only basis for distinguishing the two syllables, the formant transitions, occurred in the first 43 msec.

In a final collaboration of Tallal and Piercy (1975) these investigators attempted to demonstrate that the findings of their 1974 study were attributable to the short duration of the distinguishable information in [ba] and [da], not to the fact that this information took the form of a transitional character. Accordingly, they tested the same children on (1) synthesized vowel stimuli containing an initial 43-msec steady-state vowel followed immediately by a different steady-state vowel of 207 msec duration (these stimuli, [ɛɪ] and [æɪ], contained no formant transitions) and (2) synthesized [ba] and [da] with the same duration as those in the 1974 study, but with the formant transition period extended from 43 to 95 msec and the steady-state portion reduced to 155 msec. These two types of stimuli were presented in the previously described discrimination and two-element sequencing tasks with varying ISIs and in the same–different task using varying ISIs.

The SLI children had difficulty with the vowel stimuli on all tasks and ISIs, performing well below the level of the NL children (accuracy levels not reported). For the [ba] and [da] syllables with extended formant transitions, however, the two groups of children performed at comparable levels on all tasks and ISIs. Even at the shortest ISI, the SLI children showed high accuracy levels. These results seem to confirm Tallal and Piercy's contention that a major limiting factor in the SLI children's performance was the duration of the acoustically discriminable characteristics of the stimuli, independent of their transitional or steady-state character.

Aspects of the Tallal and Piercy paradigm were reexamined with a different sample of children by Tallal, Stark, Kallman, and Mellits (1981). The 36 SLI children who participated ranged in age from 5 to 9 years. Thirty-eight NL children of the same age constituted the comparison group. Tallal et al.'s principal question was whether the auditory-specific deficit seen in the Tallal and Piercy (1973b) work would be found with other SLI children and whether cross-modality (auditory and visual) processing proved more or less difficult than unimodality processing. The latter will not be discussed here, because both groups of children tended to perform better on cross-modality than on unimodality stimuli, contrary to expectations.

The auditory stimuli were the same 75-msec complex tones used by Tallal and

Piercy (1973a). The visual stimuli were not those used by Tallal and Piercy (1973b). Instead, slides of two nonsense letters were used, made visible through light flashes 75 msec in duration. For each modality, the discrimination and sequencing tasks with varying ISIs (in this study, 10, 70, and 500 msec) as well as the serial memory task were employed. The two groups performed at comparable, high levels on the discrimination task for each modality. On the sequencing task, the NL children outperformed the SLI children at all ISIs in both modalities. According to my calculations, the SLI children performed above the level of chance ($p < .001$) at the longest ISIs for each modality but not for the two shorter ISIs. The SLI children's performance was also lower than that of the NL children on the serial memory task for each modality. The finding that the SLI children showed limitations in the visual modality as well as the auditory modality did not accord with the findings of Tallal and Piercy (1973b). Tallal et al. reasoned that this discrepancy might be explained in part by age factors. When the children were divided into younger (5 and 6 years) and older (7 and 8 years) age groups, the older SLI and NL children differed only in performance in the auditory modality. These older children were approximately the same age as those in the Tallal and Piercy (1973b) study.

The same children's ability on a perceptual constancy task was examined by Tallal, Stark, Kallman, and Mellits (1980a). Six different synthetic syllables 250 msec in duration were used. These were [ba], [be], [bi], [dɛ], [dæ], and [di]. The durations of the formant transitions were not specified, but since these were "synthetic copies of natural utterances" the transitions were probably brief. Following a period of instruction, the children were presented the syllables one at a time. For all stimuli containing [d] one panel was to be depressed; for those containing [b] the other panel was to be used. The SLI children performed well below the level of the NL children on this task. Although the SLI children as a group seemed to perform above chance level if less stringent statistical levels were used, only 14 of the 34 SLI children met the $p < .001$ criterion set by Tallal et al. In contrast, this criterion was met by 24 of the 38 NL children.

To determine whether these findings were attributable solely to a problem the SLI children had in perceptual constancy or were influenced at least in part by these children's difficulties with rapid formant transitions, the same task was employed using only the [ba] and [da] stimuli of Tallal and Piercy (1974). Although overall accuracy levels were not reported, the SLI children performed well below the level of the NL children. Thus, difficulty with distinguishing information occurring in a brief time span probably contributed to the perceptual constancy findings.

A subgroup of the children in the preceding two studies participated in another investigation by Tallal, Stark, Kallman, and Mellits (1980b). These were the 14 SLI and 23 NL children meeting the $p < .001$ criterion on the perceptual constancy task. In one condition the same syllables used in the perceptual constancy task were used. Pairs of these syllables that when blended could form words ([be]–[bi], [ba–di], [dɛ–bi], [dæ]–[di]) were presented with a 500-msec ISI, and the children responded as in the two-element sequencing task previously described. In another condition, synthesized words involving the same syllable combinations were prepared ([bebi], [badi], [dɛbi], [dædi]). These words were approximately 350 msec in duration, with the two syllables (150 msec each) separated by a stop closure of approximately 50 msec. Thus, in this condition both the duration of the syllables and the duration of the interval between the syllables were reduced.

The two groups of children performed at comparable levels in the first condition. However, the SLI children had significantly more difficulty in the second condition than did the NL children. Because the stimuli in the second condition clearly resembled words, Tallal et al. suggested that added linguistic redundancy was not sufficient to eliminate the effects of auditory-processing deficits in the SLI children's performance. "Thus, the results of this study provide empirical evidence that allows us to extend our original findings of a rate specific deficit in processing auditory information to include the processing of linguistically meaningful stimuli" (p. 281). At the same time, Tallal et al. acknowledged that the SLI children may have had difficulty in segmenting words into their component syllables.

The ability of the same children to discriminate other types of verbal stimuli was explored by Tallal and Stark (1981). Along with [ba]–[da], the children were presented with the contrasts [ɛ]–[æ], [da]–[ta], [dab]–[dæb], [sa]–[sta], and [sa]–[ʃa]. The stimuli [ɛ] and [æ] were only 40 msec in duration; [da] had a voice-onset time (VOT) of 0, [ta] of 60 msec; [sta] contained a silent interval of 100 msec, [sa] no such interval; [sa] and [ʃa] differed primarily in fricative formant frequency, centered at approximately 4500 Hz for [sa] and 3000 Hz for [ʃa]; and [dab] and [dæb] differed in their formant frequencies across the approximately 200-msec steady-state portion. For each type of contrast the children heard lists of syllables, presented one at a time, that contained examples of the two syllables in random order. They pressed a response panel when one of the syllables was heard, and made no such response when the other was heard.

The SLI children performed below the level of the NL children on [ba]–[da], [da]–[ta], and [da]–[ʃa]. What is interesting about this finding is that brevity of acoustic cues did not have the same effect for all stimuli. The [ɛ] and [æ] stimuli were only 40 msec in duration, yet the SLI children were able to distinguish them. This was contrary to Tallal and Piercy's (1975) finding with the same vowels. In that study, however, these vowels were concatenated to [ɪ]. Tallal and Stark suggested that the SLI children's difficulty may rest with stimuli whose acoustic cues are brief and are followed in rapid succession by other acoustic cues.

Bernstein, Tallal, and Stark (1982) conducted a 4-year follow-up study of the children participating in the studies published in 1980 and 1981. Fourteen of the

NL and 29 of the SLI children were seen. These children now ranged from 8 to 12 years of age. Synthesized [ba] and [da] syllables similar to those used by Tallal and Piercy (1974) served as the stimuli. The tasks administered to the children were the previously described discrimination and two-element sequencing tasks with varying ISIs as well as the serial memory task. The two groups of children performed at high levels on the discrimination and sequencing task. A single SLI child failed to meet the $p < .001$ criterion for sequencing with the longest ISI and was therefore not presented pairs with ISIs of shorter duration. The NL and SLI children also showed comparable performance on the serial memory task. However, neither group performed at ceiling level.

Bernstein et al. noted that most of the SLI children still met the criterion of language impairment 4 years later. However, this criterion is based on a norm that itself changes with increasing age. In absolute terms most of the SLI children's language abilities were greater than before. Clearly, speech perceptual development, as measured by the tasks employed, also occurred. Bernstein et al. hastened to point out, however, that the SLI children may have performed below age level on more advanced perceptual tasks.

Henderson (1978) examined SLI children's ability to identify and discriminate [ba] and [da], as well as [da] and [ta]. Twelve SLI and 12 age-matched NL children participated. The children were 9 and 10 years of age. For the [da] and [ta] stimuli, seven synthetic syllables were created that represented 10-msec incremental steps in VOT and amount of cutback of the first formant transition. At one extreme, a clear [da] stimulus had a VOT of 0; at the other, a clear [ta] stimulus had a VOT of 60 msec. For [ba] and [da], synthesized syllables were created that represented degrees and direction of second-formant movement during the 40-msec transitional period. At one extreme, a clear [ba] showed a rising second-formant transition; at the other, a clear [da] showed a falling transition.

In one task the children heard each stimulus singly and judged which of two categories it belonged to ([da] or [ta], [ba] or [da]). In the other task the children heard pairs of syllables (the ISI was not specified) and judged whether they were the same or different. For [da] and [ta] the two groups performed in a similar manner on both tasks (in contrast to Tallal & Stark, 1981). They showed similar category assignments and were more sensitive to differences in pairs that were near presumed phoneme boundaries than those more distant. Neither group of subjects showed a sharp phonetic boundary when identifying [ba] and [da] syllables. The two groups were also similar in their discrimination of the [ba] and [da] syllable pairs. However, when they were compared in terms of their discrimination of the two syllables representing the boundaries for the [ba] and [da] categories, the NL children proved superior.

One interesting aspect of this study is that the [da]–[ta] contrast, which the SLI children could make, is based on cues of brief duration, like the [ba]–[da] contrast. Henderson proposed that the SLI children may have performed better with [da] and [ta] either because these children can perceive certain brief cues such as VOT or because these syllables contained more than one brief cue (VOT, first-formant cutback). In contrast, [ba] and [da] could be distinguished only according to second-formant transition.

One of the limiting factors in all of the preceding studies is that the SLI children were compared with age-matched NL children – children with language abilities much greater than those of the SLI children. Thus, although the findings of these studies have been taken as evidence for an auditory-rate-processing deficit independent of language in SLI children, the absence of language-matched control children has been a problem. This seems particularly so because children under age 4;6 seem unable to perform this task with much success (see Tallal, 1976), and many of the SLI children studied showed language abilities that approximated a 3- and 4-year level (see Stark & Tallal, 1981; Tallal & Piercy, 1973b).

Nevertheless, Tallal (1976) provided some data suggesting that SLI children may not perform exactly like younger NL children. Five groups of 12 NL children (ages 4;6, 5;6, 6;6, 7;6, and 8;6) were tested along with 12 adults on the discrimination and two-element sequencing tasks with varying ISIs previously described. The complex tones used in Tallal and Piercy (1973a) served as stimuli. Tallal found that, on pairs with long ISIs, NL children age 6;6 and older performed as well as adults. For ISIs of 428 msec and below, only the NL children age 8;6 performed at an adult level. At the short ISIs, there was a progressive decrease in performance with decreasing age. Tallal compared these data with those of Tallal and Piercy (1973a). The SLI children in that study performed as well as the oldest NL children for the long ISIs but performed below the level of the youngest NL children for the short ISIs. Thus, the profile of the SLI children did not match that of the NL children at any age.

Tomblin and Quinn (1983) tested the hypothesis that rapid auditory processing may not be the lower-level ability it appeared to be in these earlier studies. That is, they challenged the view that poor performance on these tasks reflected an inherent limitation in the temporal resolving capability of the children's auditory systems. Instead, poor performance may have reflected a lower level of perceptual learning on the children's part.

Tomblin and Quinn used two complex tones modeled after those of Tallal (1976). They also used Tallal's task, with minor modification. Six ISIs were employed ranging from 10 to 300 msec. The subjects were 10 NL children (ages 5;8 to 6;9). After the initial training period, the children were presented the two-tone pairs with varying ISIs. This procedure was repeated for four additional sessions (with no additional instruction) spanning 5 to 7 days. The results were enlightening. Along with the expected finding that performance increased with increasing ISI, the children's performance also increased across sessions. Tomblin and

Quinn took the position that children's responses on this type of task "do not necessarily reflect the status of a low-level perceptual mechanism; rather they may be
the products of the same learning capability that underlies language" (p. 372).

Relation to speech production and higher-order linguistic processing. If the
data from SLI children do reflect a deficit in rapid auditory processing, it is reasonable to ask how such a deficit influences the speech characteristics of these
children. Tallal, Stark, and Curtiss (1976) pursued this question by examining the
speech production of the children participating in the Tallal and Piercy (1973a,
1973b, 1974, 1975) studies. These children were asked to name pictures of objects
whose names contained stop consonants, stop consonant clusters, and nasals in
the initial and/or final position. The children also imitated nonsense syllables with
the same phonetic characteristics as well as isolated vowels. The SLI children
made many more errors than the NL children. Furthermore, they had more difficulty with the stop consonant cluster and stop consonant productions than with the
vowel and nasal consonant productions. Because the sounds giving the children
the most difficulty were those that involved rapid acoustic changes, Tallal et al.
concluded that the children's productions were probably related to their auditory-
processing limitations.

Stark and Tallal (1979) examined the nature of the children's stop consonant
production errors in greater detail. They found that the greatest number of errors
were errors in voicing (e.g., [b] for [p] in the initial position), followed by errors
in place of articulation. The majority of the latter were substitution of an apical
consonant for a velar consonant (e.g., [d] for [g] in the initial position). It is interesting that there were no cases of either [b] replacing [d] or [d] replacing [b] in the
initial position, a finding that may have been expected given the results on the
discrimination and sequencing tasks.

Frumkin and Rapin (1980) attempted to determine whether SLI children's perception of consonant–vowel (CV) and vowel stimuli would vary as a function of
their phonological abilities. Seven of the SLI children (ages 7;7 to 11;11) were
regarded as showing relatively "normal" phonology. That is, these children had
difficulties with only a few specific sounds. Nine other SLI children showed clear
phonological difficulties. Finally, nine NL children served as age controls. (Four
children diagnosed as having auditory agnosia also participated in this study.
Their performance will not be described here.)

Synthetic [ba] and [da] as well as [a] and [u] syllables were the stimuli. The
former were 250 msec in duration. Two versions of the [ba] and [da] syllables were
created, one with second- and third-formant transitions of 40 msec, the other with
transitions of 80 msec. Three versions of the vowel stimuli were created, with
durations of 40, 80, and 250 msec. An adaptation of Tallal and Piercy's (1973b)
method was used. The four [ba] and [da] syllables (two different syllables × two

different transition durations) were presented one at a time in random order, and the children indicated, with a pointing response, whether they heard [ba] or [da]. The same procedure was used for the six different vowel stimuli (two different vowels × three different durations).

All children showed high accuracy with the CV stimuli containing longer formant transitions. The SLI children with phonological deficits showed an increase in errors when the stimuli involved short transitions (mean accuracy dropped from approximately 99 to 93% correct). The results for the vowel stimuli were more surprising. Both the NL and phonologically deficient SLI children showed a small increase in errors with decreasing duration. The SLI children with relatively normal phonology, however, showed a larger increase in errors when duration decreased (dropping to 88% accuracy with 40-msec stimuli).

In a second experiment, the same children were administered a two-element sequencing task with three different ISIs (20, 75, 250 msec). The duration of the vowels (40, 80, 250 msec) or formant transitions (40, 80 msec) were the same for the stimuli in any given pair. The results of this experiment were quite perplexing. For the CV stimuli, the phonologically deficient SLI children performed below the level of the controls and showed lower performance levels when formant transition and/or ISI decreased. However, the SLI children with normal phonology performed at an even lower level than the phonologically deficient SLI children. They, too, showed a decrease in performance with a decrease in formant transition duration and/or ISI. The same pattern of performance was seen for the vowel stimuli. Decreases in duration as well as ISI led to decreases in performance, with lower performance by the phonologically deficient SLI children than the controls, and the lowest performance by the SLI children with normal phonology. It should be noted, however, that all three groups of children performed above the level of chance for CV as well as vowel stimuli for almost all durations and ISIs.

Finally, Thal and Barone (1983) explored the relation between SLI children's identification and sequencing of complex tones identical to those used by Tallal and Piercy (1973a) and their ability to perform the same tasks with naturally produced single words and meaningful word combinations. Eight SLI children (ages 4;2 to 8;1) participated in the first experiment, three (ages 4;0 to 5;4) in the second. (There was no NL comparison group.) In the first experiment, the children identified and sequenced the stimuli in two conditions: with the complex tones alone and with the complex tones preceded by the words *high* and *low* for the tones with the higher and lower fundamental frequency, respectively. For each, task performance was either the same or higher on the tone plus word condition.

In the second experiment, children identified and sequenced types of stimuli: the complex tones and utterances (without tones) one, two, three, and four words in length. For all three children identification performance was higher on each of the linguistic conditions than on the tone condition. The same pattern was seen for one child on the sequencing task. For the remaining children performance was below the level of chance across stimuli. Thal and Barone interpreted their findings as suggesting that SLI children's difficulty with presumably fundamental auditory distinctions does not prevent them from processing higher-order linguistic units. Of course, the multitude of auditory cues available in the linguistic stimuli of this study prevents us from ruling out the presence of a deficit in rapid auditory processing in these children.

Interpretation. The general methodology first used by Tallal and Piercy (1973a) and adapted by others seems largely successful in identifying below-age-level performance by SLI children on tasks requiring processing of rapid acoustic events. This seems to include nonverbal as well as verbal stimuli and rapid formant transitions as well as rapid changes in steady-state characteristics with transitions removed. A particularly intriguing aspect of this work is that SLI children can perform above the level of younger NL children in certain conditions yet below the level of these children in others (see Tallal, 1976). An elusive feature of these studies is that brevity of the ISI has the same effect as brevity of the stimulus itself and that the latter is a critical factor only if concatenated to other acoustic information that need not be brief (contrast [ɛɪ]–[æɪ] with [ɛ]–[æ] in Tallal & Piercy, 1975, and Tallal & Stark, 1981, respectively). A mechanism that accounts for this has yet to be proposed in the 12 years since this work first appeared.

Although this work has raised some interesting questions, a rapid auditory processing deficit account of specific language impairment does not seem to be correct. There are two reasons for this. The first is that no plausible relation between SLI children's difficulty with rapid auditory processing and their language problems has been established. It may be true that stop consonants and stop consonant clusters involve briefer acoustic cues than vowels and nasals and are more likely to be produced in error by SLI children (Tallal et al., 1976). However, this is only part of the story:

1. Most SLI children, like younger NL children, have the greatest difficulty producing continuant sounds (e.g., [s], [ʃ], [θ]) the acoustic properties of which include longer durations, making the perception of these sounds less dependent on vowel formant transitions (Leonard, 1982). They also frequently reduce clusters to single stop consonants, yet SLI children did not differ from NL children in the [sa]–[sta] discrimination in Tallal and Stark (1981).
2. The most common production errors for stop consonants for SLI as well as younger NL children are voicing errors. Although Tallal and Stark (1981) found that SLI children did not perceive the rapid changes involved in the voiced–voiceless distinction as well as age controls, Henderson (1978) found no difference between SLI children and same-age peers on the perception of this distinction.
3. The most common place of articulation error for stop consonants is the use of an apical for a velar (Stark & Tallal, 1979). This error is common as well in the speech of young NL children (Ingram, 1981). Productions of [b] for [d] or vice versa are very uncommon, leading to the unsettling conclusion that the children in these studies had difficulty perceiving a distinction that they could make in production with no difficulty (see Stark & Tallal, 1979).

4. The perceptual difficulties of SLI children with and without phonological deficits in the Frumkin and Rapin (1980) study seem to defy explanation. The SLI children who had the most difficulty identifying brief vowels and sequencing CV and vowel stimuli were the children with normal phonology.

The second reason for questioning deficits in rapid auditory processing as an explanatory factor in specific language impairment has to do with the construct of auditory processing itself. An assumption underlying the auditory-processing work is that there are fundamental perceptual and memory processes that are necessary for, but distinct from language learning (Tomblin, 1984). There are two types of descriptions of these processes. One treats them as mechanisms that may be intact or in disrepair. For example, Frumkin and Rapin (1980) noted that their findings for the phonologically deficient SLI children suggest "the possibility of specific left hemisphere damage for this group" (p. 453). The other description allows for the possibility of slow development of these processes. Tallal and Piercy (1974), for example, state that "the possibility exists that developmental dysphasia results, not from a permanent deficit, but from delayed development of rapid auditory processing" (p. 92).

The notion of such specific abilities has been challenged by a number of authors (Bloom & Lahey, 1978; Rees, 1973, 1981; Tomblin, 1984). The reason is that such abilities are not passive processes independent of the orientation and knowledge state of the listener (Tomblin, 1984). Perception of speechlike stimuli, for example, differs depending on whether or not the listeners can attach linguistic significance to what they hear. Auditory memory span increases only with the listeners' increasing ability to code the stimuli in useful ways, by relating them to one another or to events, words, and so on in the listeners' own experiences. And, of course, we cannot lose sight of the fact that, although normal children improve across time in their performance on auditory-processing tasks, there has been no serious attempt to explain normal language development on the basis of developing auditory skills.

It can also be argued that the tasks used require an ability to make judgments about auditory stimuli. That is, the children must decide whether they are the same or different or whether the stimulus was one associated with the panel on the left-hand or right-hand side. For sequencing the child must reflect on a perceived sequence to the point of translating it to a series of panel responses. To the extent that the stimuli were verbal, and many were, this is clearly a metalinguistic ability. Metalinguistic skill is typically not seen on formal tasks until about age 4 years. Examples of metalinguistic requirements in action can be seen, for example, when normal 3-year-olds seem unable to judge the suitability of utterances containing obvious grammatical errors (e.g., *Cake the eat*) that they themselves do not commit (e.g., deVilliers & deVilliers, 1972). The fact that children under the age of 4;6 cannot perform the rapid-auditory-processing tasks is consistent with this interpretation. Of course, because SLI children do not have the metalinguistic abilities of NL children and indeed are often more comparable to 3- and 4-year-olds in this regard, their poor performance is no surprise.

For stimuli in the form of complex tones the explanation is not as straightforward. The children are required to make judgments about auditory stimuli, and thus a "meta" skill is clearly involved. In addition, this task can become linguistic by virtue of verbal mediation (e.g., *low–high, left–right*). However, we do not know if such mediation was employed by the NL children, which would have enhanced their performance relative to the SLI children, who would not have been able to make as much use of this strategy. Nevertheless, the fact that children can show improvement with these stimuli simply through experience over a few days (Tomblin & Quinn, 1983) suggests that more than a fundamental temporal resolution capability is at work. In summary, the studies involving rapid auditory processing have provided interesting data that may be as much a product of the general language learning limitation of these children as an explanation for it.

Mental representation

The third major account of specific language impairment is that SLI children experience symbolic deficits in nonlinguistic as well as linguistic areas. The implication of such an account, of course, is that specific language impairment may not be specific at all. The bulk of the work in this area has operated in the general Piagetian framework that assumes that language is just one of several mental representational abilities. The abilities that have received the greatest attention in relation to SLI children are symbolic play and mental imagery.

Symbolic play. Investigators of normal language development have often noted the parallels between symbolic play and language. A child's use of one object (e.g., a pencil) to stand for another (e.g., a spoon) in play, for example, bears a certain resemblance to the use of a word to stand for its referent. Relating one pretend object to another (e.g., using a piece of paper as a dish towel to "dry" the pencil representing a spoon) can be likened to forming a semantic relationship by combining words. These possible parallels have not escaped the notice of investigators studying SLI children.

Lovell, Hoyle, and Siddall (1968) were possibly the first investigators to examine this issue. They studied 10 SLI children (ages 3;4 to 4;8) and 10 NL children matched according to age. The children were subdivided into younger and older groups. The play behavior of each child was observed in the children's nursery school. No differences in symbolic play were noted for the younger age group, although the younger NL children spent more time than the younger SLI children engaged in play representing a transitional level between mere practice play and symbolic play. The older NL children spent more time in symbolic play than the older SLI children. A relationship was also seen between the SLI children's MLU and the time they spent in symbolic play.

Brown, Redmond, Bass, Liebergott, and Swope (1975) presented children with specific toys and encouraged them to pretend they were performing particular activities. For example, the children were given such objects as an egg carton, a box, straws, a shell, popsicle sticks, and blocks and were asked to create a birthday party. Using this procedure, the investigators examined the symbolic play of 10 SLI children (ages 3;0 to 5;0) and 10 age-matched NL children. The SLI children showed less adaptiveness in their use of objects in a pretend manner and less integration of play behaviors around a theme than did the NL children.

Williams (1978) used a different measure of symbolic play: the number of discrete symbolic play acts performed in a play session. Fifteen SLI children (ages 2;6 to 5;6) and 15 NL age controls participated. The NL children engaged in a greater number of symbolic play acts than the SLI children.

Still another study comparing SLI children and NL children matched for age was conducted by Udwin and Yule (1983). Two types of measure were used. One was a rating given to the children's spontaneous play based on the degree to which they introduced elements of time, space, or character not immediately given in the perceptual environment. The other measure was a more formal symbolic play test in which the children were given four sets of miniature toys and were then scored on the basis of the number of toys meaningfully used and related to one another. A comparison of the 15 SLI (ages 3;8 to 5;0) and 15 NL children of the same age revealed higher levels of performance by the NL children on both measures.

Terrell, Schwartz, Prelock, and Messick (1984) used the same symbolic play test employed by Udwin and Yule (1983) but compared the performance of SLI children with that of language-matched rather than age-matched controls. The 15 SLI (ages 2;8 to 4;1) and 15 NL children showed comparable expressive vocabularies and utterances limited to one word in length. The SLI children performed at a higher level than their younger but normally developing counterparts.

In another study, Terrell and Schwartz (1983) studied the symbolic play abilities of SLI children operating at higher levels of expressive language ability. The 10 SLI children who participated ranged in age from 3;1 to 4;1 and in MLU from 1.50 to 2.38 morphemes. Ten age-matched and 10 MLU-matched NL children also served as subjects. The children were given sets of objects that could be readily substituted for other objects in pretend play. The children's object transformations in play were noted. The results of this study differed from the preceding one in that, although age controls showed greater use of object transformations than the SLI children, the latter did not differ from the MLU-matched controls.

The relation between symbolic play and expressive language ability in SLI children was examined by Folger and Leonard (1978). Eight SLI children (ages 2;8 to 3;10) served as subjects. Five of the children showed productive use of two-word utterances; the remaining children used speech limited to single-word utterances. Folger and Leonard presented each child with a set of objects and determined whether the children used these objects to stand for others. Although four of the children showed clear evidence of symbolic play, this ability seemed unrelated to expressive language ability. One of the three single-word-utterance users engaged in symbolic play, whereas two of the five multiword-utterance users provided no evidence of this ability.

Another investigation exploring the relation between SLI children's symbolic play and language ability was the longitudinal study of Skarakis (1982). Three SLI children (ages 1;10 to 2;7) were studied monthly over a 6-month period. During each period the children's symbolic play, spontaneous speech production, and language comprehension abilities were assessed. Skarakis concluded that these children progressed through the same sequence of symbolic play development described for normally developing children. However, they did so at a later age. Even at the end of the study the children rarely substituted one object for another in play. The children's language abilities also progressed slowly. Skarakis attempted to uncover parallel developments in symbolic play, language production, and language comprehension. However, specific parallels are not clear from an inspection of her data. All children comprehended multiword combinations before exhibiting true symbolic play, and two of the children showed MLUs above 2.35 morphemes before demonstrating such play behavior.

Another longitudinal study of SLI children's symbolic play was conducted by Shub, Simon, and Braccio (1982). Three SLI children (ages 2;0 to 3;0) and two NL children (ages 1;0 to 1;2) served as subjects. At the onset of the study, all children possessed fewer than five "nouns" (presumably object and person names) in their expressive vocabulary. Each child was seen every 4 months until the child achieved an expressive vocabulary of 50 words and showed evidence of multiword combinations. At this point the children were seen at 12-month intervals. In total each child was followed for 3 years. Measures of play and language were obtained at each session. This paper gives few details, but the authors report that for all children object substitutions in play appeared at the same time as productive naming of absent referential objects and comprehension of nonconventional use of verbs.

Panther and Steckol (1981) examined the relation between symbolic play and language ability through a training paradigm. Six SLI children (ages 2 to 5 years) were assigned to one of three conditions: training in word use, training in the nonconventional use of objects, and training in both word and nonconventional object use. The training was largely successful, but effects were specific to the focus of training. Children assigned to the first condition showed greater gains in symbolic play than children in the second condition. The latter children, however, showed greater increases in expressive vocabulary than the former. Only the children assigned to the third condition showed significant gains in both areas.

Mental imagery. Another form of mental representational ability studied in connection with language impairment is mental imagery. This link is somewhat surprising in that these two types of abilities seem quite different. Unlike language, imagery is largely depictive in character. That is, images are generated from stored information about the shape of the physical world. The possible relation between imagery and language ability in SLI children was first noted by Inhelder (1963). This investigator noted that one SLI child (age 9;6) had little difficulty with several cognitive tasks but experienced considerable difficulty with an imagery task. For example, when asked to describe the direction of the level of water in a tilted glass container, the child was unable to disassociate the horizontal direction of the water from the inclined position of the container. Similar findings were reported in a study of 17 SLI children (ages 4;3 to 10;10) by de Ajuriaguerra et al. (1965). These children had particular problems with imagery tasks, as when, for example, they were asked to analyze the movement of a projected shadow.

In a study first reported in 1977, Johnston and Ramstad (1983) examined the performance of seven SLI children (ages 10;4 to 12;1) on a variety of Piagetian tasks. The children performed at the lowest levels on those involving imagery. For example, they exhibited difficulty with a task in which they blindly felt geometric forms and then had to select the visual shapes that corresponded to them. They also performed poorly on a task in which they were required to draw a line on a figure to predict the orientation of water in a tipped jar. Johnston and Ramstad noted that the children's relative difficulty on the imagery tasks was not related to the customary age at which children pass the tasks employed.

Perhaps the first investigation to employ comparison groups was Kamhi's (1981) study of 10 SLI children (mean age 4;11, mean MLU 4.82 morphemes), 10 mental-age-matched (MA-matched) NL children, and 10 MLU-matched NL children. Six different Piagetian tasks were administered to the children. For each, the performance of the SLI children fell between that of the MA controls and the MLU controls. In only one, however, was there a significant difference. This was the only task that clearly involved imagery – blindly feeling geometric forms and then selecting the corresponding shapes from a visual array. It is noteworthy that, although the SLI children performed significantly more poorly than the MA controls on this imagery task, they performed significantly better than the younger, MLU-matched NL children.

One of the tasks employed in a study of SLI children by Siegel, Lees, Allan, and Bolton (1981) tapped imagery abilities. In this case, 26 SLI children (ages 3 to 5 years) and 26 age-matched NL children were required to select the drawing that correctly depicted the water level in a tilted glass. Apparently, this task was too difficult for children of the ages studied; both groups of children performed poorly.

Noting that it is difficult to ensure that imagery has been invoked even in tasks that seem to involve this process, Johnston and Ellis Weismer (1983) selected a task that had built-in controls to assess whether imagery was reflected in the subjects' performance. A mental rotation task was used in which drawings of pairs of linear arrays of geometric forms were presented and the children were to push one of two buttons corresponding to same versus different. The left-hand array was always vertical, whereas the right-hand array was either vertical or rotated about its center 45°, 90°, or 135°. Subjects were six first-grade and six third-grade SLI children (ages 6;5 to 7;5 9;3 to 10;3) and age-matched controls. Analysis of the children's reaction times on this task revealed that older children were faster than younger children, NL children were faster than SLI children, and reaction time increased linearly with degree of rotation. The last observation suggested that the children did make use of imagery when solving this task. An analysis of reaction time as a function of degree of rotation revealed a difference between the SLI and NL children in the intercept values (reflecting generally slower reaction times for the SLI children) but not those for slope. These findings led Johnston and Ellis Weismer to conclude that (1) SLI children invoke imagery while solving certain tasks, but they solve such tasks rather slowly, and (2) their limitations seem to involve image generation, maintenance, and/or interpretation rather than image transformation processes.

An imagery task was among the tasks used by Kamhi, Catts, Koenig, and Lewis (1984) in their investigation of 10 SLI (mean age 5;10) and 10 MA-matched NL children. The task was identical to the one used by Kamhi (1981), in which the appropriate shape was to be selected after the children had held a corresponding form in their hand without seeing it. The NL children performed at a higher level than the SLI children. For the SLI children, there was a relationship between performance on a test of vocabulary comprehension and performance on this imagery task. Similar correlations were not computed for the NL children because their generally high performance restricted the variability in their scores. Kamhi et al., like Kamhi (1981), interpreted the imagery findings as suggesting a limitation in SLI children's ability to generate, maintain, and interpret symbolic representations. Because the vocabulary test required the children to respond without the presence of contextual cues, these investigators reasoned that it may have placed considerable symbolic processing demands on the children.

Camarata, Newhoff, and Rugg (1981) employed a Piagetian perspective-taking task that required imagery ability in their study of 10 SLI children (ages 3;6 to 5;6 with MLUs ranging from 1.50 to 3.90 morphemes). Ten age-matched and 10 MLU-matched NL children served in the comparison groups. In this task, the children had to select objects that matched the form seen from the angle of the experimenter. Thus, the children's ability to imagine the objects in different orientations was assessed in this task. The age-matched NL children performed at a higher level than the SLI children, who in turn showed higher performance levels than the NL children with comparable MLUs.

Murphy (1978) studied SLI children's imagery abilities using both Piagetian and psychometric tasks. One Piagetian task required the children to draw a line representing the water level in containers tipped at various angles; the other required them to anticipate the movement of a moving object along paths of different shapes. For one of the psychometric tasks the children selected from among several alternatives the configuration that represented the assembly of seven smaller constituent shapes. The remaining psychometric task required the children to decide if two views of a flag represented the same or different sides. Participants were 11 SLI children ages 5;9 to 8;6 and 11 NL children who were matched according to both age and performance on a reasoning task.

The results were somewhat surprising given the previous findings. The NL children showed higher scores than the SLI children on only one of the four tasks, that involving the selection of a configuration representing the proper assembly of shapes. This discrepancy may have been due to a feature of the research design, however. The reasoning task on which the subject groups were initially matched seems itself to have involved imagery. Thus, only SLI children whose imagery abilities were approximately age appropriate and/or NL children whose abilities were somewhat depressed may have been included.

This interpretation of Murphy's (1978) findings seems especially plausible given the work of Savich (1983). In this study, 18 SLI children (ages 7;6 to 9;6) and 18 age-matched NL children were administered two Piagetian and three psychometric imagery tasks. One of the Piagetian tasks and one of the psychometric tasks were also used by Murphy. Others included observing the examiner fold a piece of paper and predicting its appearance when it was unfolded and choosing which of five blocks was a representation of an irregularly shaped target block as seen from another angle. Savich observed differences favoring the NL children on all five tasks.

Interpretation. Two conclusions can be drawn from studies of the symbolic play and imagery abilities of SLI children. First, it is clear that a number of language-impaired children who show age-appropriate performance on commonly used nonverbal intelligence tests are not free of limitations in nonverbal mental representational abilities. Johnston (1982) suggests why this may be so. She notes that these children may perform relatively well on tasks involving visual perception of static figures, shapes, and designs, as seen on many items of the Leiter International Performance Scale (LIPS) and Performance Scale of the Wechsler Intelligence Scale for Children – Revised (WISC-R), for example. In fact, Johnston performed an item analysis of the LIPS that revealed that the majority of items in the 2- to 8-year range were perceptual.

Should this be interpreted to mean that, instead of being selectively impaired in language, these children are selectively intact in visual matching ability? Before an affirmative answer is given to such a question, the following might be considered. Stark and Tallal (1981) asked speech-language pathologists to identify for them language-impaired children receiving treatment who on the basis of clinical impressions seemed to possess normal hearing, normal intelligence, and adequate social and emotional adjustment. Of the 132 children referred, 50 showed performance IQs on the WISC-R below 85 when actually tested. In contrast, only three failed a hearing examination and only one proved to experience serious emotional problems, as indicated by parent and teacher reports. Thus, although language-impaired children who meet the IQ criterion of specific language impairment may be those who possess relatively good visual matching skills, it is also clear that there are children with significant language limitations who are not so strong in visual matching and who, because of this fact, are not even included in studies of SLI children. I shall return to the issue of the somewhat artificial distinction between SLI children and other language-handicapped children in the final section of this chapter.

The second conclusion that can be drawn from the symbolic play and imagery studies is that neither of these abilities can account for the language problems of SLI children. That is, although SLI children clearly fall below the performance level of same-age peers on symbolic play and imagery tasks, they appear to perform above the level of younger normal children with comparable language abilities (see Camarata et al., 1981; Kamhi, 1981; Terrell et al., 1984). Studies involving language-matched controls have used expressive language ability as the basis for matching, so other findings may obtain if language comprehension abilities are considered. However, this has yet to be demonstrated.

Another reason for questioning the assumption that limitations in these mental representational abilities are integrally tied to SLI children's language problems is that clear structural parallels among these different skills have rarely been delineated. Shub et al. (1982) provided evidence for one such parallel, that of object substitutions in play and productive naming of absent referential objects. Such parallels are simply not obvious in most of the other studies, however. Furthermore, the varied patterns of temporal asynchronies among presumably related linguistic and nonlinguistic representational abilities raise doubts that specific but camouflaged parallels exist at all. For example, when Skarakis's (1982) three SLI subjects first exhibited true symbolic play, they showed three different levels of language production ability and somewhat different receptive vocabulary skills. All three performed at the highest level of word combination comprehension assessed, but differed in the time they required to achieve this level before demonstrating symbolic play. Additional examples of discrepant levels of symbolic play and language ability can be seen in the work of Folger and Leonard (1978) and Panther and Steckol (1981).

To summarize, some SLI children seem to have limitations in nonverbal representational ability. It is likely that the incidence of such limitations in SLI children is no coincidence. Many of these children may have weaknesses in a variety of symbolic skills. However, the relation between these nonlinguistic and linguistic skills is too gross to have much explanatory potential. These children seem to vary in the range of nonlinguistic representational skills that are deficient as well as the degree to which any of these skills is deficient.

Specific language impairment as a construct

In this section I argue that the above accounts of specific language impairment fall short not only because they fail to identify the proper cause of this condition, but also because they assume that the condition is one for which a tangible cause must exist. In considering this argument, we should return to the two points made at the beginning of this chapter:

1. SLI children's language profiles show a great deal of variation in terms of relative strengths and weaknesses. Furthermore, other types of skills (e.g., imagery ability, perceptual motor skill) can be below age level to various degrees in these children, although, as we have seen, they are not causally involved.

2. These children are given the label of SLI primarily because they do not clearly fall into other handicapped-child categories. However, the recent evidence for mental representational deficits in these children suggests that they are not as distinct from other types of children (e.g., "mildly retarded" children with language limitations) as originally believed.

Some writers have responded to these facts by speculating that specific language impairment may have a variety of causes or that several factors may operate in combination to create this impairment, but even in the latter cases a defect is assumed. That is, because SLI children's language abilities are well below those typical for their age, the assumption is made that these abilities are abnormal in more than the statistical sense.

There are a number of risks in assuming that a defect exists. Most basic of all is the possibility that, if we choose the wrong metrics, even our statistical criterion for identifying SLI children may be incorrect. Snyder (1982) has made the important point that in much of our research we have failed to demonstrate that our sample of SLI children represents a population that differs significantly from other children. She noted, for example, that, if SLI children are identified on the basis of verbal IQ–performance IQ discrepancies, a very large discrepancy must be required, because 28% of the population can be expected to show verbal IQs at least 15 points below performance IQ. In addition, measurement error in language age, grade equivalent scores, or mental ages when the latter serve as reference points can give the appearance of discrepancies that do not exist.

Snyder's point is well taken: There probably have been children included in SLI groups who did not truly deviate significantly from the norm in language ability. But even where such statistical deviations exist, an assumption of disorder can be suspect. Tomblin (1983) has offered two observations in this respect. First, he has noted an inconsistency in the manner in which we interpret statistical discrepancies as disorders. Only deviations on the lower end of the distribution are thought to constitute a disorder. A 7-year-old who functions at age level in most respects but shows the language abilities typical of an 11-year-old is not viewed as disordered. Second, only certain types of abilities are considered disordered when they deviate from the norm. This issue warrants elaboration.

Gardner (1983) has pointed out that there are a variety of abilities that can be elevated to the status of "intelligences." In our own culture, we typically consider only two – language and logical-mathematical ability – because of their importance in our education system. However, Gardner makes a strong case for considering other abilities, such as musical, spatial, bodily-kinesthetic, and introspective abilities. Within the general population there are those who excel in these abilities and those who are very limited. Yet the latter are not viewed as disordered. Unless their musical ineptness can be attributed to a hearing impairment or their gracelessness to a motor impairment, for example, these individuals are not counted among the handicapped.

It should be pointed out that the quality of life and perhaps the employment potential of these individuals can be improved through instruction that focuses on these skills, just as language intervention is a worthwhile enterprise for individuals with limited language abilities. But receiving instruction that focuses on improving, say, physical agility is not tantamount to overcoming a disorder. To date, the same has not been true for children with language limitations. However, it is my view that the "cause" of these children's language limitations is simply the product of the same types of variations in genetic and environmental factors that lead some children to be clumsy, others to be amusical, and still others to have little insight into their own feelings.

The argument presented here is not equivalent to a "language delay" versus "language deviance" distinction of the type described in earlier articles. Like the "language-delayed" children described in earlier works, the SLI children under discussion in this chapter show no evidence of frank neurological impairment. However, there are three assumptions about "language-delayed" children that are not being made here: (1) After the late emergence and initially slow development of language, "language-delayed" children eventually catch up to peers in language ability; (2) these children's language behavior mirrors that of younger NL children; and (3) with the exception of language ability, these children resemble same-age peers. Instead, the following assumptions are made:

1. SLI children are not simply late in reaching early language milestones but have limitations in their language abilities that are long standing, at least in the absence of intervention. Again, the analogy with other types of abilities can be helpful. It does not seem appropriate to regard children with limited musical abilities, for example, as "musically delayed." Such children may be late in acquiring certain fundamental musical abilities, but in the absence of specific instruction their musical talent may always fall below the level seen in the general population.

2. Taken singly, the characteristics of SLI children's language do not differ appreciably from those seen at early stages of normal language development. However, the overall language behavior of these children will often differ from that of young

NL children. There are two reasons for this. The first is strictly statistical. By definition, NL children do not differ significantly from the norm in their performance on any aspect of language. As a result the possible relations among these aspects are more restricted than in the case of SLI children, who are identified on the basis of discrepant performance on any aspect of language (e.g., the production of bound morphemes, the use of a range of speech acts).

We can best explain the second reason by borrowing some ideas presented by Kirchner and Skarakis-Doyle (1983).[1] Discrepant performance on certain aspects of language, which may vary from child to child, creates an initial imbalance. This imbalance may prompt movement toward equilibrium, whereby abilities constituting areas of relative strength, which also differ from child to child, are called on for compensatory purposes. Because language systems operate as a whole, alterations not only will provide compensation for areas of particular weakness, but will change the complexion of the child's language in general. Finally, children differ in the speed with which these adaptations occur and the degree to which they occur. The result is not only substantial heterogeneity among children with limitations in language ability, but also relationships among components of language that often differ from those seen in younger NL children. By analogy, suppose that an older child or adult lacks the skill to draw a picture that adequately represents three-dimensional space. This individual may make use of his or her knowledge of relations between size and distance and clarity of detail and distance to draw foreground and background details to improve the three-dimensional quality of the drawing. Although such a drawing is likely to remain an inadequate representation of three-dimensional space, it will not resemble a drawing attempted by a younger child.

3. SLI children often show limitations in nonlinguistic skills. Although limitations in such abilities as imagery and symbolic play cannot account for limitations in language ability, these abilities probably share a general connection by virtue of their symbolic character. Children who have a limitation in their ability to assign words to objects, for example, may also be limited to some degree in their ability to represent one object with another in play. Relationships such as these can probably be seen in other areas. For example, individuals with insufficient skill to coordinate physical movements required in particular athletic activities might well perform below the level of the general population on, say, perceptual–motor reaction time tasks requiring a single motor response.

Ironically, the view that specific language impairment in the absence of frank neurological damage is not really an impairment attributable to a particular cause requires no change in current assessment practices. Factors that can be bona fide causes of disruption in language development, such as hearing loss, are routinely examined during the evaluation process. Included in this process is a screening for gross signs of neurological dysfunction that can serve as a basis for referral. The factors that have been previously related to specific language impairment, such as auditory discrimination and symbolic play, are sometimes evaluated as well. This practice has dubious value if performed with the intent of uncovering a cause of the child's limitations. However, it is a reasonable undertaking if designed to determine other potentially weak areas that may be in need of intervention. In current practice, the major emphasis during the evaluation process is on activities that are in keeping with the general position of this chapter. These activities are a careful description of the characteristics of the child's language and determination of the degree to which each differs from age-level expectations.

The implications for treatment are somewhat greater. There are, for example, approaches designed to increase children's auditory perception and sequencing skills (e.g., Eisenson, 1972), presumably because gains in these skills will have a positive impact on language ability. As means of facilitating language abilities such approaches are questionable and must take a back seat to those that focus on language itself. Fortunately, most common treatment approaches deal directly with language skills.

Given the inadequacy of previous accounts of specific language impairment, it may seem paradoxical that assessment and treatment of these children can occur at all. Johnston (1983) has claimed that language intervention cannot proceed without theory, and she is right. However, the rejection of previous theories of the cause of language limitations does not mean an absence of theory. In fact, the position adopted here constitutes a theory of sorts. The claim is that many children given the label of SLI are not impaired in the sense of being damaged but rather are much less skilled than their peers in such acts as extracting regularities in the speech they hear, registering the conversational contexts in which these regularities occur, examining these regularities for word–referent associations and evidence of phonological and grammatical rules, and using these associations and rules to formulate utterances of their own. Some of these acts may be more difficult than others for a particular child, and they may even reflect an extraction or computation limitation that influences nonlinguistic as well as linguistic abilities. Assumptions such as these suggest that intervention might be designed to make these regularities and their contexts highly salient to the child and to provide the child with ample practice in formulating utterances reflecting these regularities. Even when details are added to this prescription to match a child's specific areas of weakness, they would not seem especially innovative; but neither are they random swipes at a problem that must await the discovery of a cause for direction. As Johnston stated so well, the notion of theory includes one's assumptions about the mechanisms of change and the dimensions that are relevant or possible to change.

The present account has the greatest implications for future research. The position that most children regarded as SLI do not suffer from an impairment attributable to a particular cause suggests that research efforts in search of such causes will not be high-yield enterprises. Because the cessation of such efforts would constitute a major shift in research direction, the present proposal should also undergo investigative scrutiny. The following hypotheses can be offered:

1. Children given the label SLI (excluding those with frank neurological impairment) will form a continuum with NL children with slightly below average language abilities. They will differ from these NL children in degree of language limitation and in degree of discrepancy among individual features of language, but not in the language characteristics themselves.
2. These children will also form a continuum with the same NL children in a variety of nonlinguistic skills that correlate with language, the SLI children showing a lower level of ability in these nonlinguistic areas. Again, no characteristic unique to the SLI children will emerge.
3. SLI children will show substantial discrepancies among individual language skills and between language and certain nonlanguage skills, owing in part to the fact that their identification as SLI was based on their very low placement on the distribution in particular areas of language. Accordingly, the degree of discrepancy among skills in these children should resemble that seen for children who have *very high* placement on the distribution in certain areas of language.
4. Children with very high scores in certain areas of language will form a continuum with NL children with slightly above average language abilities in a variety of nonlinguistic skills that correlate with language, the language-superior children showing a higher level of ability in these nonlinguistic areas. Furthermore, the language-superior children will show greater discrepancies among individual features of language than will the children with slightly above average language abilities.

The first three hypotheses deal with the present proposal itself. The fourth is necessary to establish that discrepancies among features of language and certain linguistic–nonlinguistic relations are not unique to the low end of the distribution and offer no special insight into the cause of SLI children's problems.

In summary, specific language impairment seems to be neither specific nor an impairment. Instead, children given this label simply demonstrate a low level of skill in language and, often, related areas. As with any subpar skill, special instruction may be appropriate but seems especially so here given the importance placed on verbal ability in our culture. One implication arising from the present view is that research focusing on specific language impairment should change its emphasis. In particular, continuing the search for the causes of this amorphous condition seems unjustified. Before such a departure from the current research trend is undertaken, however, the present proposal itself might be evaluated. To this end, four seemingly testable hypotheses have been offered.

Note

1. In one important respect the present description differs from the model of Kirchner and Skarakis-Doyle (1983). These authors propose that the initial imbalance is created by a

genetic or lesion-based disorder. I argue here that the same imbalance can be created by discrepancy among skills, without invoking the notion of defect.

References

Bernstein, L., Tallal, P., & Stark, R. (1982, November). *Speech perception development in language impaired children: A four-year follow-up study.* Paper presented at the American Speech-Language-Hearing Association Convention, Toronto.

Blank, M., Gessner, M., & Esposito, A. (1979). Language without communication. *Journal of Child Language, 6,* 329–52.

Bloom, L., & Lahey, M. (1978). *Language development and language disorders.* New York: Wiley.

Bondurant, J. L., Romeo, D., & Kretschmer, R. (1983). Language behaviors of mothers of children with normal and delayed language. *Language, Speech, and Hearing Services in Schools, 14,* 233–42.

Brown, J., Redmond, A., Bass, K., Liebergott, J., & Swope, S. (1975, November). *Symbolic play in normal and language-impaired children.* Paper presented at the American Speech-Language-Hearing Association Convention, Washington, DC.

Bruck, M., & Ruckenstein, S. (1978, October). *Teachers talk to language delayed children.* Paper presented at the Boston University Conference on Language Development, Boston.

Bzoch, F., & League, R. (1970). *Receptive–expressive emergent language scale for the measurement of language skills in infancy.* Gainesville, FL: Computer Management Corp.

Camarata, S., Newhoff, M., & Rugg, B. (1981). Perspective taking in normal and language disordered children. *Proceedings from the Symposium on Research in Child Language Disorders, 2,* 81–8.

Conti-Ramsden, G., & Friel-Patti, S. (1983). Mothers' discourse adjustments to language-impaired and non-language-impaired children. *Journal of Speech and Hearing Disorders, 48,* 360–7.

Conti-Ramsden, G., & Friel-Patti, S. (1984). Mother–child dialogues: A comparison of normal and language impaired children. *Journal of Communication Disorders, 17,* 19–35.

Cramblitt, N., & Siegel, G. (1977). The verbal environment of a language-impaired child. *Journal of Speech and Hearing Disorders, 42,* 474–82.

Cromer, R. (1978). The basis of childhood dysphasia: A linguistic approach. In M. Wyke (Ed.), *Developmental dysphasia* (pp. 85–134). London: Academic Press.

Cromer, R. (1983). Hierarchical planning disability in the drawings and constructions of a special group of severely aphasic children. *Brain and Cognition, 2,* 144–64.

Cunningham, C., Siegel, L., van der Spuy, H., & Bow, S. (1982). *Developments in the behavioral and linguistic interactions of specifically language delayed and normal children with their mothers.* Unpublished manuscript, Chedoke-McMaster Hospital, Hamilton, Ontario.

de Ajuriaguerra, J., Jaeggi, A., Guignard, F., Kocher, F., Maquard, M., Roth, S., & Schmid, E. (1965). Evolution et prognostic de la dysphasie chez l'enfant. *La Psychiatrie de l'Enfant, 8,* 291–352.

deVilliers, P., & deVilliers, J. (1972). Early judgments of semantic and syntactic acceptability by children. *Journal of Psycholinguistic Research, 1,* 299–310.

Eisenson, J. (1972). *Aphasia in children.* New York: Harper & Row.

Folger, M. K., & Leonard, L. (1978). Language and sensorimotor development during the early period of referential speech. *Journal of Speech and Hearing Research, 21,* 519–27.

Fried-Oken, M. (1981, June). *What's that? Teachers' interrogatives to language delayed and normal children.* Paper presented at the Symposium on Research in Child Language Disorders, Madison, WI.

Friel-Patti, S. (1976, November). *Good-looking: An analysis of verbal and nonverbal behaviors in a group of language disordered children.* Paper presented at the American Speech-Language-Hearing Association Convention, Houston, TX.

Friel-Patti, S. (1978). *The interface of selected verbal and nonverbal behaviors in mother–child dyadic interactions with normal and language disordered children.* Unpublished doctoral dissertation, Purdue University, West Lafayette, IN.

Frumkin, B., & Rapin, I. (1980). Perception of vowels and consonant–vowels of varying duration in language impaired children. *Neuropsychologia, 18,* 443–54.

Gardner, H. (1983). *Frames of mind: The theory of multiple intelligences.* New York: Basic Books.

Giattino, J., Pollack, E., & Silliman, E. (1978, November). *Adult input to language impaired children.* Paper presented at the American Speech-Language-Hearing Association Convention, Los Angeles.

Henderson, B. (1978, November). *Older language impaired children's processing of rapidly changing acoustic signals.* Paper presented at the American Speech-Language-Hearing Association Convention, San Francisco.

Ingram, D. (1981). *Procedures for the phonological analysis of children's language.* Baltimore, MD: University Park Press.

Inhelder, B. (1963). Observations sur les aspects opératifs et figuratifs de la pensée chez des enfants dysphasiques. *Problemes de Psycholinguistique, 6,* 143–53.

Johnston, J. (1982). Interpreting the Leiter IQ: Performance profiles of young normal and language-disordered children. *Journal of Speech and Hearing Research, 25,* 291–6.

Johnston, J. (1983). What is language intervention? The role of theory. In J. Miller, D. Yoder, & R. Schiefelbusch (Eds.), *Contemporary issues in language intervention* (ASHA Reports 12) (pp. 52–7). Rockville, MD: American Speech-Language-Hearing Association.

Johnston, J., & Ellis Weismer, S. (1983). Mental rotation abilities in language-disordered children. *Journal of Speech and Hearing Research, 26,* 397–403.

Johnston, J., & Ramstad, V. (1983). Cognitive development in preadolescent language impaired children. *British Journal of Disorders of Communication, 18,* 49–55.

Kamhi, A. (1981). Nonlinguistic symbolic and conceptual abilities of language-impaired and normally developing children. *Journal of Speech and Hearing Research, 24,* 446–53.

Kamhi, A., Catts, H., Koenig, L., & Lewis, B. (1984). Hypothesis-testing and nonlinguistic symbolic abilities in language-impaired children. *Journal of Speech and Hearing Disorders, 49,* 169–76.

Kirchner, D., & Skarakis-Doyle, E. (1983). Developmental language disorders: A theoretical perspective. In T. Gallagher & C. Prutting (Eds.), *Pragmatic assessment and intervention issues in language* (pp. 215–46). San Diego, CA: College-Hill Press.

Lamesch, B. (1982). Language acquisition by a child in an institutional environment. In F. Lowenthal, F. Vandamme, & J. Cordier (Eds.), *Language and language acquisition* (pp. 303–8). New York: Plenum.

Laskey, E., & Klopp, K. (1982). Parent–child interactions in normal and language-disordered children. *Journal of Speech and Hearing Disorders, 47,* 7–18.

Lederberg, A. (1980). The language environment of children with language delays. *Journal of Pediatric Psychology, 5*, 141–59.

Leonard, L. (1982). Phonological deficits in children with developmental language impairment. *Brain and Language, 16*, 73–86.

Lovell, K., Hoyle, H., & Siddall, H. (1968). A study of some aspects of the play and language of young children with delayed speech. *Journal of Child Psychology and Psychiatry, 9*, 41–50.

MacKenzie, J., Newhoff, M., & Marinkovich, G. (1981, November). *Normal children address language disordered peers: Dimensions of communicative competence.* Paper presented at the American Speech-Language-Hearing Association Convention, Los Angeles.

Macpherson, C., & Weber-Olsen, M. (1980, June). *Mother speech input to deficient and language normal children.* Paper presented at the Symposium on Research in Child Language Disorders, Madison, WI.

Marinkovich, G., Newhoff, M., & MacKenzie, J. (1980, November). *"Why can't you talk?": Peer input to language disordered children.* Paper presented at the American Speech-Language-Hearing Association Convention, Detroit.

Messick, C., & Prelock, P. (1981, November). *Successful communication: Mothers of language-impaired children vs. mothers of language-normal children.* Paper presented at the American Speech-Language-Hearing Association Convention, Los Angeles.

Millet, A., & Newhoff, M. (1978, November). *Language disordered children: Language disordered mothers.* Paper presented at the American Speech-Language-Hearing Association Convention, San Francisco.

Murphy, V. (1978). *A comparison of four measures of visual imagery in normal and language-disordered children.* Unpublished master's thesis, Northern Illinois University, DeKalb.

Nakamura, P., & Newhoff, M. (1982, November). *Clinician speech adjustments to normal and language disordered children.* Paper presented at the American Speech-Language-Hearing Association Convention, Toronto.

Newhoff, M. (1977). *Maternal linguistic behavior in relation to the linguistic and developmental ages of children.* Unpublished doctoral dissertation, Memphis State University, Memphis, TN.

Olswang, L., & Carpenter, R. (1978). Elicitor effects on the language obtained from young language-impaired children. *Journal of Speech and Hearing Disorders, 43*, 76–88.

Panther, K., & Steckol, K. (1981, November). *Training symbolic play skills in language impaired children.* Paper presented at the American Speech-Language-Hearing Association Convention, Los Angeles.

Rees, N. (1973). Auditory processing factors in language disorders: The view from Procrustes' bed. *Journal of Speech and Hearing Disorders, 38*, 304–15.

Rees, N. (1981). Saying more than we know: Is auditory processing disorder a meaningful concept? In R. Keith (Ed.), *Central auditory and language disorders in children* (pp. 94–120). San Diego, CA: College-Hill Press.

Robinson, M. (1977). *Mothers' questions to three year old children with different language abilities.* Unpublished master's thesis, Memphis State University, Memphis, TN.

Savich, P. (1983). *A comparison of the anticipatory imagery ability of normal and language disabled children.* Unpublished manuscript, California State University at Los Angeles.

Schodorf, J., & Edwards, H. (1981, November). *Analysis of parental discourse to linguistically disordered and normal children.* Paper presented at the American Speech-Language-Hearing Association Convention, Los Angeles.

Shub, J., Simon, J., & Braccio, M. (1982, October). *The development of symbolic play in language delayed children*. Paper presented at the Boston University Conference on Language Development, Boston.

Siegel, L., Cunningham, C., & van der Spuy, H. (1979, April). *Interactions of language delayed and normal preschool children with their mothers*. Paper presented to the Society for Research in Child Development, San Francisco.

Siegel, L., Lees, A., Allan, L., & Bolton, B. (1981). Nonverbal assessment of Piagetian concepts in preschool children with impaired language development. *Educational Psychology, 1*, 153–8.

Silverman, L., & Newhoff, M. (1979, November). *Fathers' speech to normal and language delayed children: A comparison*. Paper presented at the American Speech-Language-Hearing Association Convention, Atlanta, GA.

Skarakis, E. (1982). *The development of symbolic play and language in language disordered children*. Unpublished doctoral dissertation, University of California, Santa Barbara.

Snyder, L. (1982). Defining language disordered children: Disordered or just "low verbal" normal? *Proceedings from the Symposium on Research in Child Language Disorders, 3*, 197–209.

Stark, R., & Tallal, P. (1979). Analysis of stop consonant production errors in developmentally dysphasic children. *Journal of Acoustical Society of America, 66*, 1703–12.

Stark, R., & Tallal, P. (1981). Selection of children with specific language deficits. *Journal of Speech and Hearing Disorders, 46*, 114–22.

Stein, A. (1976, October). *A comparison of mothers' and fathers' speech to normal and language-deficient children*. Paper presented at the Boston University Conference on Language Development, Boston.

Tallal, P. (1976). Rapid auditory processing in normal and disordered language development. *Journal of Speech and Hearing Research, 19*, 561–71.

Tallal, P., & Piercy, M. (1973a). Defects of non-verbal auditory perception in children with developmental aphasia. *Nature, 241*, 468–9.

Tallal, P., & Piercy, M. (1973b). Developmental aphasia: Impaired rate of non-verbal processing as a function of sensory modality. *Neuropsychologia, 11*, 389–98.

Tallal, P., & Piercy, M. (1974). Developmental aphasia: Rate of auditory processing and selective impairment of consonant perception. *Neuropsychologia, 12*, 83–93.

Tallal, P., & Piercy, M. (1975). Developmental aphasia: The perception of brief vowels and extended stop consonants. *Neuropsychologia, 13*, 69–74.

Tallal, P., & Stark, P. (1981). Speech acoustic-cue discrimination abilities of normally developing and language-impaired children. *Journal of the Acoustical Society of America, 69*, 568–74.

Tallal, P., Stark, R., & Curtiss, B. (1976). Relation between speech perception and speech production impairment in children with developmental dysphasia. *Brain and Language, 3*, 305–17.

Tallal, P., Stark, R., Kallman, C., & Mellits, D. (1980a). Perceptual constancy for phonemic categories: A developmental study with normal and language impaired children. *Applied Psycholinguistics, 1*, 49–64.

Tallal, P., Stark, R., Kallman, C., & Mellits, D. (1980b). Developmental dysphasia: The relation between acoustic processing deficits and verbal processing. *Neuropsychologia, 18*, 273–84.

Tallal, P., Stark, R. Kallman, C., & Mellits, D. (1981). A reexamination of some nonverbal perceptual abilities of language-impaired and normal children as a function of age and sensory modality. *Journal of Speech and Hearing Research, 24*, 351–7.

Terrell, B., & Schwartz, R. (1983). Object transformation: The linguistic aspect of symbolic play? *Proceedings from the Symposium on Research in Child Language Disorders, 4*, 127–36.

Terrell, B., Schwartz, R., Prelock, P., & Messick, C. (1984). Symbolic play in normal and language-impaired children. *Journal of Speech and Hearing Research, 27*, 424–9.

Thal, D., & Barone, P. (1983). Auditory processing and language impairment in children: Stimulus considerations for intervention. *Journal of Speech and Hearing Disorders, 48*, 18–24.

Tomblin, J. B. (1983). An examination of the concept of disorder in the study of language variation. *Proceedings from the Symposium on Research in Child Language Disorders, 4*, 81–109.

Tomblin, J. B. (1984). Specific abilities approach: An evaluation and an alternative method. In W. Perkins (Ed.), *Language handicaps in children* (pp. 27–41). New York: Thieme-Stratton.

Tomblin, J. B., & Quinn, M. (1983). The contribution of perceptual learning to performance on the repetition task. *Journal of Speech and Hearing Research, 26*, 369–72.

Udwin, O., & Yule, W. (1983). Imaginative play in language disordered children. *British Journal of Disorders of Communication, 18*, 197–205.

VanKleeck, A., & Carpenter, R. (1978, November). *Effects of children's language comprehension level on language addressed to them*. Paper presented at the American Speech-Language-Hearing Association Convention, San Francisco.

Wellen, C., & Broen, P. (1982). The interruption of young children's responses by older siblings. *Journal of Speech and Hearing Disorders, 47*, 204–10.

Williams, R. (1978, November). *Play behavior of language-handicapped and normal-speaking preschool children*. Paper presented at the American Speech-Language-Hearing Association Convention, San Francisco.

Wulbert, M., Inglis, S., Kriegsmann, E., & Mills, B. (1975). Language delay and associated mother–child interactions. *Developmental Psychology, 11*, 61–70.

Wyatt, G. (1969). *Language learning and communication disorders in children*. New York: Free Press.

2 Teaching language form, meaning, and function to specific-language-impaired children

Phil J. Connell

The art and science of language teaching has a long and varied history that traverses several different teaching professions including the teaching of English as a second language, language-arts instruction, and speech and language pathology. Language is taught in different ways to different people for different reasons. Second-language teaching is one of the more visible forms of language teaching in that most people encounter some formal instruction in a foreign language sometime in their educational histories. Language-arts instruction, which is one of the more visible forms of first-language teaching, is an integral part of elementary education. The approach taken in these two types of language teaching is similar in many ways because, in both cases, teaching is provided to students who already know a language. In contrast, anyone who has observed language teaching in a clinical situation realizes that the approach taken with normal students is considerably different from that taken with children who experience difficulty acquiring their native language.

One difference is that the goal of teaching is different with normal children than with abnormal children. The goal of nonclinical language teaching is for the students to learn either how to express their implicit linguistic knowledge in educationally and culturally appropriate ways or how to express their intentions in another language. The goal of clinical language teaching is for children to learn how language is structured, how people use language, and, most critically, how they can use language to communicate their simplest and most complex meanings.

Another difference stems from the assumption that children who fail to learn a first language cannot be taught language metalinguistically. That is, it is assumed that teachers cannot rely on verbal explanation to give these children insights into language meaning and structure, and they cannot provide analogies within a language or between languages to illustrate a particular principle or rule. In other words, language cannot be the medium of teaching for these children as it can in second-language teaching and language-arts instruction. The teachers of language-disordered children have to teach language, in most cases, without explanation or analogy, usually to students who are unaware that they are learning any-

40

thing. In order to be successful, a teacher must create a teaching situation in which a student can learn to recognize consistencies in language input and to formulate rules that describe a relation between inferred meanings and perceived utterances. To do this, the teacher has to have some understanding of the nature of language rules, the order by which these rules can be acquired, and the type of language input and the type of instruction that are most conducive to rule learning. It is obvious to those who follow the developments in language-teaching fields that teachers at present cannot fully understand these things because research efforts have not provided universally accepted and comprehensive explanations of the language-learning process.

The purpose of this chapter is to present one perspective, based on observations, hypotheses, and some empirical data, on the issues most critical to the process of teaching language to children who are specific-language-impaired. In this discussion the term *language-disordered* refers to any child who either experiences difficulty in acquiring or fails to acquire a first language. The major portion of the discussion is limited to a subgroup of these children who are labeled *specific-language-impaired* (Rosenberg, 1984). These children have an apparently isolated language disorder in that there is no known intellectual, emotional, perceptual, or physical basis for their problem. The perspective developed in this chapter is presented as a series of premises, which constitute a model for teaching language to language-disordered children. The premises are tentative conclusions about certain basic aspects of the process of teaching and learning language. They are, in most cases, supported by theory and experimental evidence and, in some cases, only by logical conjecture. The premises are not meant to represent a resolution of the issues they address, but rather are to be viewed as hypotheses that can be experimentally examined.

The selection of these particular premises for this chapter is based on the decision that they have practical significance to language teachers. That is, they represent conclusions about issues that are critical to the practice of language teaching. These issues were selected because it is assumed that language teaching would not be possible if any one of them were not in some way resolved by a language teacher. That is, in order to teach, language teachers would have to construct a personal set of premises covering these issues or otherwise have no basis on which to decide what to teach, how to teach, or how to measure progress.

Currently, there are several approaches to the basic issues of language teaching. These approaches generally correspond to the several different theoretical orientations to language. The reason for this correspondence can be traced to the commonly accepted view that the goal of language teaching is to teach the learner to construct a mental representation of language that is qualitatively identical to that acquired by a normal learner. Thus, theories that have focused on phonological, syntactic, semantic, and pragmatic aspects of language have served as the basis for constructing premises on which teaching decisions have been made.

This seems to be a strange state of affairs, because one would assume that the strongest influence on the selection of teaching methods would be exerted by the outcome of particular methods. The results of language-teaching research, however, have had very little influence on teaching practice, which leads to the conclusion that clinicians do not place much value on outcome data (Johnston, 1983). One reason for their apparent skepticism might be that they are not convinced that the relevant studies have adequately controlled for spontaneous language learning. It is commonly accepted that most children with language disorders can and do learn language on their own. Usually, their problem is not that they cannot learn language at all but that they cannot learn language rapidly enough compared with their age peers (e.g., Chapman, 1983). Consequently, any experimental procedure based solely on measurements of pre- and postteaching performance will indicate that learning has occurred regardless of the methods being tested.

What is needed for this type of research is to differentiate language learning that results from teaching and language learning that results from natural environmental and innate sources. As Leonard (1981) points out in a review of the teaching literature, only a small percentage of these studies have applied the appropriate controls to make such a distinction possible.

But clinicians' reluctance to use outcome data runs much deeper than the methodological problems of many of the relevant studies (Johnston, 1983). Clinicians realize that, in order to do teaching research, a researcher has to decide what is to be taught, what type of teaching methods are to be tested, how the methods are to be implemented in terms of what the learner hears and does, and how success will be defined. Too little is known about the process of language learning and teaching to support an approach to each of these issues that is exclusively or even primarily data-based. This means that, regardless of how well controlled an outcome study is, its results are intrinsically tied to theory and the success or failure of a particular method tested must be interpreted in light of the validity of its theoretical orientation. Thus, the emphasis of clinicians on the theoretical assumptions underlying teaching and the relative deemphasis of outcome data are quite justifiable given the present state of clinical science.

With this analysis of the situation in mind, the position taken here is that we must examine two kinds of information when searching for resolutions for some of the basic issues of language teaching: the findings of experimentally controlled research, and the theoretical assumptions concerning language learning and teaching that underlie such research. It is with these two kinds of information in mind that the following premises are presented. Each of the premises is based on a set of theoretical assumptions, and each is falsifiable. That is, each derives from a theory of language knowledge and language acquisition that can be either accepted or rejected on principled grounds. Also, each makes a claim about the outcome of language teaching that can be tested through outcome research. As would be expected, outcome data are cited here in support of the premises, but the opportunity exists for others to test the premises and, in the process, to accept, reject, or modify them to better fit the evidence at hand.

Premises of a model of language teaching

1. *The goal of language teaching is for the student to learn language rules.*
This premise perhaps more than any of the others conforms to most theoretical orientations to language (e.g., Bates, 1976; Chomsky, 1965, 1980; Fillmore, 1968). The differences among theories concern such issues as the content and domain of rules and the way context is incorporated into rules, not whether the general construct of "linguistic rule" is an adequate descriptive device for language knowledge. The wide acceptance of the construct probably derives from its use as an explanation for the creativity of language users: their ability to produce and understand an infinite number of sentences with an admittedly finite set of linguistic resources.

Although the exact formulation of language rules varies from theory to theory, a common attribute of rules or their descriptions can be extracted and used as a definition. The attribute concerns their function: They are used to describe the relation between language meanings and language utterances (e.g., Slobin, 1970). This functional definition will be used here. It is sufficiently general not to contradict any theoretical conception of a rule, and as will be demonstrated, it is sufficiently specific to be useful for making language-teaching decisions.

The terms *language meaning* and *language utterance* will be used in the way they are used by theorists such as Jackendoff (1972) and Lakoff (1971). *Language meaning* is a general term that includes the lexical, attributional, propositional, and intentional meanings expressed by language. *Language utterance* is a general term that means the manner in which speech is used to express meanings. This includes a number of expressive devices or mechanisms available to a language user such as lexical selection, word order, morphology, prosody, ellipsis, and pronominalization.

Empirical support for the psychological reality of language rules can be found in the normal acquisition literature and in teaching outcome research. Berko's (1958) demonstration of the generalization of English morphemes to nonsense words and the commonly observed overregularization of irregular allomorphs are frequently cited to support the argument that children learn rules rather than forms (Slobin, 1970). In terms of language teaching, Leonard (1981) reviewed several studies designed to teach language to language-disordered children and found that the common outcome of teaching is the usage of a taught linguistic form in instances where the form was not taught. Thus, similar to Berko's (1958) findings, these results indicate that language-teaching methods can create generalizations about language forms and meanings and that these generalizations can be observed to operate in untrained contexts. Leonard (1981) notes, however, that extensive generalization has not been shown in these studies and that more evidence of such generalization must be forthcoming before claims of rule learning become totally convincing. This criticism is valid and is addressed in the next section, where the problems of generalization are treated. It is argued there that generalization is possible only if rules are taught in appropriate ways (Connell, 1982).

There are two well-known alternatives to teaching language rules (for a summary of approaches, see Aram & Nation, 1982). One approach is to teach auditory-processing tasks, which are thought to be basic processes involved in decoding language input and in learning language. The other approach is to teach cognitive tasks, which are thought to be related to cognitive achievements that are precursors to language learning. These two alternatives are rejected by the premise on both theoretical and empirical grounds and because they are counterintuitive.

The theoretical problem is similar in both cases. The theoretical foundations of both approaches have not been extended to language-learning disorders. The auditory-processing or speech-perception models that have been proposed are attempts to characterize the decoding of speech by normal speaker-hearers and have not been adequately related to children who have no obvious perceptual difficulty but who experience difficulty learning language (see Saunders, 1977, for a review of relevant theories). From an empirical perspective, Bloom and Lahey (1978) and Hammil and Larsen (1974) have surveyed and analyzed the information available about the relation between auditory-processing teaching and language learning and have found no convincing evidence that children with language disorders would accelerate their language learning by learning auditory-processing tasks.

In terms of cognition, the Piagetian theoretical framework of cognitive development characterizes language as symbolic activity that is a realization of general cognitive growth (see Leonard, 1978, for a review of the language–cognition relation). However, attempts to uncover the proposed causative relation between cognitive attainments and language development in normal children have been generally unsuccessful. The strongest statement that can be supported about the relation between the two domains is that both cognition and language are developmental phenomena (Bowerman, 1978; Miller, Chapman, Branston, & Reichle, 1980; Siegel, 1983). Moreover, there are no controlled studies that I am aware of that have shown that language learning results from teaching cognitive skills.

The lack of theoretical and empirical support for selecting auditory-processing and cognitive approaches does not mean that these two areas are not in some way related to language learning. It is obvious that they must be. The position being taken here is that the relation between these areas and language disorders is too tenuous, as presently conceived, to receive the full focus of a language-teaching approach. It is more conservative and intuitive to direct teaching efforts toward the problem that can be observed rather than toward suspected and unproved problems, at least until more evidence is gathered (see Kleffner, 1975, for similar arguments).

Applying the first premise to language learning, it is assumed in this discussion that language is learned by a process of hypothesizing rules to capture consistencies in language input between the meanings expressed by speakers and the utterances used to express them. It is also assumed that the learner is not passive in the process of language learning. On the contrary, the learner, either by innate predisposition or by earlier learning, approaches the language-learning task with the intent of forming such rules, and he or she actively searches for consistencies in the input (e.g., Bowerman, 1978; Slobin, 1970). No assumption is made, however, about whether the learner has some preconceived idea of the nature of the rules to be learned (Chomsky, 1980). The possibility that such notions exist has been discussed in relation to language-disordered children by others (e.g., Rosenberg, 1984) and is addressed under Premise 6.

In order to apply this framework to the details of language learning, the process of learning will be separated into four tasks that can be defined by example. The first task of learners is to perceive a difference in utterance, that is, to recognize the means by which a particular meaning is expressed. For example, they must recognize that *dogs* is pronounced differently than *dog*. Simultaneous with this, they must perform a second task. They must understand that a difference in meaning is intended by speakers who produce different utterances. For example, they must recognize that the speaker who uttered *dogs* meant to express a meaning in addition to the meaning "canine," namely, plurality. Third, they must recognize that the difference or contrast in meaning (e.g., between singular and plural) and the difference in utterance (e.g., between final /z/ and no final /z/) correspond to one another. Finally, they must understand that a rule can be formulated to capture this correspondence and all other instances in which the same meaning is intended.

The use of a morphological example here does not imply that the method is designed for teaching morphology exclusively. Rather, it will be shown that the method can be applied to other components of language knowledge.

This framework would also have a basis for explaining apparent errors in rule learning such as overregularization by the claim that rules are formulated to cover limited linguistic data and consequently do not initially match adult rules. The learning of rules is a dynamic process in that a rule is a generalization about currently available linguistic facts, and encountered facts that are not explainable by the rule will eventually change the rule to its adult counterpart.

2. Rules can be effectively taught to children by means of contrast teaching.

The process of simplification of the rule-learning tasks described above has been labeled "contrast teaching" (Connell, 1982). The application of contrast teaching represents a hypothesis on the part of the language teacher that the learner constructs rules in the manner described by the four tasks. The outcome of this teaching method would constitute evidence by which to evaluate the model and the method. It would perhaps be helpful to explain ways in which the procedure differs from other teaching methods before presenting evidence of its effectiveness.

The procedure described by Gray and Ryan (1973) can be used as a prototype of what might be called behavioral approaches to language teaching. An approach of this type can be used as an example because the procedures are presented in sufficient detail for specific methods to be compared. The basic procedure in such programs is to teach the learner to produce language forms in response to pictures or other eliciting contexts. The goal is to teach the learner to produce the target form in these contexts in much the same way that an adult would. This goal is met by first having the learner imitate the target form several times and, after fading the imitative stimulus, having the learner say the form in response to an illustrative picture with and eventually without imitative assistance. For example, if the target form were the auxiliary *be*, the progressive steps in training might follow this pattern: (1) *is,* (2) *is* walking, (3) the boy *is* walking (Gray & Ryan, 1973). Each of these steps would be presented in conjunction with a picture of a boy walking and each would have both imitative and nonimitative substeps. The purpose of segmenting the sentence into successively longer parts is to sequence the imitation tasks in terms of difficulty so that the entire sentence can eventually be imitated.

In terms of the previous discussion about rule learning, it is apparent that this procedure could not provide the learner with the type of language input necessary for rule learning. The procedure creates no link between the meaning of the target form and its utterance. The only rule a learner might formulate after this procedure is that the form *is* comes after the initial noun phrase or perhaps comes before the verb, assuming the learner has knowledge of these structural categories. It should be noted that such a rule would be quite useful if the learner were tested on similar pictures to determine if the form had generalized to other contexts. The learner might be able to say, "The dog is barking," and "The girl is skating," thus giving evidence of what appears to be rule generalization (Connell, 1982). Obviously, however, the rule is not a language rule, and there is no conceivable way a language rule could be learned on the basis of language input provided by the program.

It is more difficult to analyze language-teaching methods that are not behavioral in approach, because the procedural details are less specific and more is left to the reader to interpret in light of the theoretical approach. In one of the more detailed accounts of such an approach, Miller (1978) described a teaching method that is based on the theory that children can learn language through representational play in which a child directs a play interaction and an adult facilitates language learning by modeling target forms in contexts where the forms would serve a useful communicative purpose. Miller described the teaching of the conjunction *but* in terms of the following conversational interaction. A child said, "He sleeping," during a play activity and the teacher responded, "Last night we slept in our beds. And tonight I'll sleep in my bed. But now I'm not sleeping. I'm awake." The inclusion of *but* in the response to the learner's statement was intended to provide an example of the meaning and form of the conjunction.

Although this procedure provides some input on both the meaning and utterance characteristics of the target form, it appears to sacrifice teaching for naturalness. That is, there does not appear to be anything about the situation that differentiates it from the interaction a child would encounter in daily living. Certainly, the form was uttered in an appropriate context, and a normal language learner might be able to store the form and the context in memory to be used, when enough input had been stored, to formulate a rule. But the form would be uttered in an appropriate context whenever it was used by an adult talking to a child, and the child in question apparently had not learned the form in these interactions. Thus, the tutorial strategy here is no different from a typical interaction, and we can assume that this type of interaction has been ineffective by the fact that the child has a language problem in spite of interacting in this fashion on many occasions. This is not to say that naturalness has no value in the teaching process, but that its value should not be overemphasized. The balance between retaining naturalness in teaching methods and providing the learner with sufficient information for rule learning is addressed more fully under Premise 3.

As a final comment about the method, the claim that the modeled form was in some way related to the child's communication intent is difficult to justify. In the interaction described, the child's intent was apparently to describe or inform the listener about a particular state of affairs. The sentences in which the target form was used were not related to this topic but another topic of the teacher's choosing, and this topic was expanded to include reference to the target form. Consequently, the target form was a component of the teacher's communicative intention that was triggered by the child's comment, and whether or not the child followed or was interested in the shift in topic is a point of conjecture.

The final comparison between an alternative teaching method and contrast teaching will be made with reference to a teaching study performed by Courtright and Courtright (1976). These authors reported a procedure of presenting a target form in a group of sentences to a learner while presenting pictures that represented the state of affairs described by the sentences. They compared this "modeling" procedure with an "imitative" teaching method whereby the learner was required to imitate the same sentence containing the form as well as look at the picture. The target form was a non-English usage of *means to* preceding a verb phrase. For example, "The man *means to* walking." The authors reasoned that the non-English form had not been previously encountered by any of the language-disordered children who served as subjects; therefore, each of them would start learning the form at the same point. Thus, any differences in learning between those who received modeling teaching and those who received imitation teaching could be attributed to differences in the effectiveness of the two procedures.

The outcome of the study is not of importance here but will be discussed under Premise 5. What is important is the way the form was taught. In the modeling condition, the children listened to 20 sentences while viewing 20 associated pictures. The imitation condition differed only in that the children were required to repeat the sentences after the teacher. The sentences contained the *means to* form inserted into different noun and verb phrases. The stated purpose of this procedure was to teach the subjects a linguistic rule that described the use of the target form. As with the Gray and Ryan (1973) example, the major shortcoming of this procedure is that it could teach the production of a particular utterance but not a relationship between a meaning and an utterance (Connell, Gardner-Gletty, Dejewski, & Parks-Reinick, 1981). The only rule the children could have learned is to place the *means to* form after the initial noun phrase or before the verb phrase. This is obviously not a linguistic rule even though it proved to be generalizable to different contexts such as new but similar pictures. Thus, generalization is not conclusive evidence that a linguistic rule has been learned. It only indicates that the learner has learned a generalization about one situation and can apply it to another.

Now that some features of contrast teaching have been delineated with reference to other procedures, the outcome of using the procedure can now be addressed. The procedure has been used in three recently completed research projects of mine. Two of these are described briefly, and the other is discussed under Premise 3.

In the first study, a group of six 3-year-old language-disordered children who used one word at a time were taught the relation between word order (first, second, or third word) and semantic role (agent, action, and patient) through contrast teaching (Connell, 1986). The acquisition of this rule is one of the major accomplishments of children between the ages of 18 months and 2 years; therefore, the children demonstrated a significant delay in language learning (Crystal, Fletcher, & Garman, 1976; Dale, 1976). The rule is that agents occur before the action described by a sentence, or preverbally, and patients occur postverbally. Thus, the sentences "The cat chased the dog" and "The dog chased the cat" are reversible pairs in terms of who chased whom and in terms of which noun phrase precedes and follows the verb.

The procedure for teaching the rule was to create a contrast in meaning and a contrast in utterance using reversible pictures such as those described. The children were taught to say one sentence in response to a picture and a reversed sentence in response to a reversed picture. Thus, they performed the four tasks of the rule learning outlined earlier as a result of learning to describe the pairs of pictures. First, they learned that word order was the difference in utterance as a result of having to say sentences that differed only in the order of the first and last noun phrase. Second, they learned simultaneously that the difference in meaning was the semantic role associated with the respective noun phrases as a result of viewing pictures that differed only in the entity depicted as the agent and patient of an action. Third, they learned that the contrast in word order and the contrast in semantic role were related to one another. Fourth, they learned the domain across which the rule held as a result of viewing pictures containing varied objects and actions.

As indicated by the description of the tasks, the outcome of the procedure was that the subjects learned to produce sentences containing agent, action, and patient in response to pictures similar to those used in training. They also began to use word order to designate semantic roles in their newly acquired two- and three-word utterances in spontaneous speech. In order to ensure that the change was due to teaching, experimental control was exerted during the study by a multiple baseline across subjects designed in which one child was taught at a time while the others remained in a testing mode. The fact that none of the children learned the rule on their own during the preteaching period (which was as long as 5 months) together with the fact that all the children learned the rule during the teaching period supports the claim that the instructional method was responsible for their having learned the rule.

The second experiment (Connell, in press a) concerned teaching an invented morpheme by means of a contrast teaching procedure. The purpose of the study was similar to that of the Courtright and Courtright (1979) study described earlier. Two methods were tested for their effectiveness in teaching an invented form to specific-language-disordered children. The two procedures were similar to the imitation and modeling ones used by Courtright and Courtright, but they differed in that they were constructed to teach a rule. The rule being taught was *a*, which was expressed as a noun suffix to mean "part of." Thus, *booka* means "part of a book."

A group of 40 specific-language-disordered children who were from 3 to 6 years old and a group of 40 normal children matched for age were taught the rule for the morpheme by means of either the modeling or the imitation procedure. The modeling procedure involved presenting a list of 20 nouns with and without the suffix while displaying pictures of the nouns, in the one case, and pictures of parts of the nouns (e.g., part of a book), in the other. The imitation procedure differed only in that the children were required to imitate the noun or noun plus suffix as they looked at the pictures.

The comparison between the two procedures will be discussed under Premise 5. Of interest here is the finding that children from both groups learned the invented morpheme as indicated by their generalization to other nouns. Thus, the evidence from the two studies supports the hypothesis that children can use the information provided by contrast teaching to construct a linguistic rule. Obviously, it cannot be suggested that the only way to provide language-disordered children with the data necessary to construct rules is to use contrast teaching. Some children may be able to perform rule formulation tasks successfully given only minor intervention. These children probably would not need the intensity of support given by the procedure and might be better helped by intensifying more natural forms of input.

   3. *Rules can be learned in noncommunicative settings.*

It is perhaps by now obvious from the preceding discussion that the language-teaching model presented here does not require that language rules be learned during communicative interaction. The lack of such a requirement is counter to the general movement in language-teaching practice toward pragmatic approaches (e.g., Gallagher & Prutting, 1983). The emphasis of "pragmatic" approaches is to teach language as a communicative tool rather than as an abstract formula concerning the structure of sentences (e.g., Seibert & Oller, 1981). Anything that is taught out of a communicative context is viewed as being counterproductive to the process of language learning (Muma, 1978). Play activities are thought to be best suited for language teaching because they allow the learner and teacher to interact naturally (Craig, 1983).

   The movement toward pragmatic approaches to teaching language has emanated from the theoretical shift in linguistics toward functionalism (Wilber, 1983). As with other shifts in theory, this one has caused changes in the way children with language disorders are described. The tendency now is to describe these children in terms of pragmatic language problems as opposed to the syntactic or semantic problems that were holdovers from previous shifts. The evidence supporting the validity of describing such children in this way is meager. Fey and Leonard (1983) reviewed a series of studies indicating that, in general, language-disordered children have poorer or lower-level pragmatic performance than their age peers. This is to be expected, however, given that their structural linguistic knowledge is also less than would be expected for their age and that language is the primary means of communication. The finding that has importance for determining whether these children have a pragmatic language disorder is that their pragmatic performance is not lower than would be predicted given the stage of their structural language development (see the difference between Snyder's, 1978, findings and those of Rowan, Leonard, Chapman, & Weiss, 1983, as an illustration). In other words, the pragmatic skills of specific-language-impaired children appear to be at least on a par with those of language-matched, younger, normal children. In fact, Skarakis and Greenfield's (1982) results suggest that language-disordered children know more about some presuppositional devices than younger language-matched children, suggesting that their lack of age-appropriate pragmatic skills may be the result of their syntactic and semantic (structural) language deficit and not the result of problems specifically related to communication development.

   Thus, the rationale for teaching language-disordered children with methods that are designed to overcome a problem with learning the communicative functions of language is weak. Simply put, there is no convincing evidence that these children have had any more difficulty learning the functions of language than have language-matched normal language learners. The premise here is that such children can quickly recognize or will easily learn how to use rules that can express their communicative intentions even though they learn them in noncommunicative situations.

Thus, the teaching procedure embodied in the second premise is based on the presumption that the learner shares with the teacher an awareness of the purposes of communication. Until given convincing evidence to the contrary, the teacher should also assume that most learners are able to learn language rules in situations in which natural motives for communicating are missing if the rules are carefully selected in terms of a learner's language status and, once having learned the rules, will use them when the occasion arises in natural settings. Of course, some children will have difficulty learning to use these rules in communicatively appropriate ways, and these children will need instruction in use. Many, however, will have been previously identified as having difficulty in social interaction and will not be of the type defined as specific-language-disordered by Leonard (1979). This type is not the reluctant-to-talk type identified by Fey and Leonard (1983) but a type that has more severe problems in socialization. Others who may have difficulty are those who use the rules in careful monologue speech but not during unguarded conversation. These children will require the type of generalization activities that are generally used in such situations. The purpose of such procedures will not be to teach a rule but to extend the social situations in which a rule is used to express meanings.

It is obvious that the use of language in discourse is the most natural way to use language, and those who advocate teaching language in discourse have yielded to this intuitive logic. The problem with teaching language in discourse, however, is that the resulting naturalness detracts from teaching. Discourse creates a problem for teaching because maintaining the topic of conversation may eliminate the type of input necessary to teach rules to language-disordered children. Not only does discourse constrain the type of input that can be given; it constrains the number of times a particular type of input can be used. As Miller's (1978) description of modeling in discourse reveals, any attempts to arrange a conversation so that particular forms are included can create discourse that is unnatural and probably uninteresting to the child.

Given that the type of input presented to a child cannot be significantly modified without stripping it of its naturalness, the only type of input that can be presented to a student in true discourse teaching is not much different than that which is available in a student's everyday communication environment. Although natural input is sufficient for normal children to learn a rule, it is clear that language-disordered children do not learn rules efficiently from natural input. Undoubtedly, this overstates the case; there are probably many teachers who can manipulate conversational topics adroitly enough to keep the topic relevant while giving useful language input. But it is difficult to imagine how even the most skillful teacher could modify the character of the input to the extent that it is simplified by contrast teaching procedures. The basic question is whether discourse is important enough to make teaching conform to it and by doing so to remove all the teaching techniques that have proved successful in other areas of learning.

The answer from the viewpoint of the previous discussion is no – there is no convincing evidence to support such a radical departure from typical teaching methods. It seems more efficient to assume that most learners will be able to integrate newly learned rules into a usable format on their own. Of course, the validity of this assumption should be tested in each case, and those for whom the assumption proves to be inaccurate will have to be taught how to use their newly acquired rules. Rectifying the situation for a few learners is a much more plausible procedure than removing the teaching emphasis from children with a learning weakness in order to make the process more natural.

As a final note, it can be said that there is room for compromise on the issue of discourse in teaching. It is likely that the use of communicative situations as an aid to language teaching would be more helpful if placed at the end of the teaching process rather than during the beginning or middle stages of teaching a rule. In these two stages, the focus of teaching should be on the rule itself, and once the rule is learned, the focus can shift to the contexts in which the rule can be used. Thus, it is possible to combine the positive aspects of both approaches to make the teaching process more effective.

4. *Practice with a manageable set of examples of a rule will facilitate rule formulation.*
This premise is based on observations of the subjects in the semantic role and modeling–imitation studies referred to earlier. These children learned a rule without having been given a great number of examples. For example, the subjects who learned the semantic-role and word-order rule generalized the rule to 10 sets of pictures that they had not encountered in teaching sessions and to their spontaneous speech after learning only three reversible sentences. In the non-English suffix rule study, the subjects were trained on 20 examples, but some of them were anticipating the teacher's presentation of noun plus suffix after hearing only a few of the examples. This evidence indicates that these children learned a pattern from relatively few examples. The number of examples required, however, cannot be determined by these studies because they did not address that particular issue.

The fact that the children learned a rule from the procedures after being presented with only a few exemplars may be positive in terms of teaching time, but it may be negative in view of the overall goal of teaching. There is evidence that rules that are learned as a result of contrast teaching are not initially the same as adult rules. Connell (1982) reported a subject who learned auxiliary *is* and who generalized the form to inappropriate contexts such as *They is* and *I is*. It seems possible that the first rules taught with this system will be too general in their application and that subsequent teaching will have to be performed in order to reduce their domain. In this case, the domain of *is* could be limited by contrasting the use of *is* with *am* and *are*. The need to redefine rules is not unlike the process of learning irregular forms for overregularized rules in normal acquisition. Obviously the problem will be much more prevalent in a teaching system that provides a selected sample of language input to the learner.

The only reason for suggesting that a small number of examples be used is that fewer examples will allow for more practice on each one. The procedure has generally been used with production teaching methods, although it has also been attempted with comprehension methods. The outcome of these methods is discussed under Premise 5. The first step in the production procedure is to teach learners to imitate the contrasting utterances while they are viewing contrasting pictures. Using the semantic-role study as an example (Connell, 1986), the learner imitates "The cat chases the dog" while looking at a picture depicting the action and subsequently imitates "The dog chases the cat" while looking at a picture of the reversed action. Once learners have met the criterion for imitation on this and two other reversible sentences, they are required to say the sentences in full form while viewing only the pictures (i.e., without verbal models). Errors are corrected with an imitative prompt until the subjects are able to say the sentences without help. By the time both steps are completed to criterion, the learners have had as many as one hundred opportunities to say the utterances in association with their meanings. Thus, it is possible that the frequent repetition of the task may make the pattern across the examples more salient to the learners and the rule formulation task easier to perform.

As a final note, the procedure relies on reinforcement to keep the learner on task during the teaching process. The reinforcement is not used to teach the learner a rule but to keep the learner on task so that he or she can accumulate the information necessary to formulate a rule. As indicated previously, it is assumed that children are rule learners, that they normally need no incentive to learn a rule, and that the problem with language-disordered children is that they cannot perform the tasks necessary to learn a rule given only natural language input. Consequently, the purpose of reinforcement as it is used in contrast teaching is to motivate the learner to attend to a noncommunicative task during which he or she can experience saying the contrasting forms in association with contrasting meanings so as to recognize a pattern and formulate a rule. Thus, reinforcers increase the likelihood of capturing the learner's attention and thereby, indirectly, the likelihood of the learner's formulating a rule. The main determiner of rule formulation is the learner's intention to find patterns and form rules.

Comparing the teaching process with normal acquisition, the function of reinforcers in the teaching process is to fill a motivational void created by the use of noncommunicative contexts. When normal children learn language, they are motivated to interact, and the products of this interaction provide the language input they need to learn rules. The noncommunicative aspect of contrast teaching removes this motivation from the learning situation, and an artificial motivator has to be used so that children can obtain the information they require. The practice of artificial motivation, either explicitly or implicitly structured, is in operation in most teaching situations regardless of the subject matter being taught, and its use in language teaching is no more than an extension of a successful practice to a specific area of learning (but see Courtright and Courtright, 1979, for an opposing position).

> 5. *Production teaching procedures have a stronger effect on rule learning than do comprehension and comprehension-related teaching procedures for specific-language-impaired children.*

This premise should probably be limited to instances in which language is taught in a nondiscourse, noncommunicative setting, but because there are no controlled-outcome studies that have taught language in the context of natural discourse, the premise will stand as is. The premise is limited to specific-language-impaired children because of evidence of a difference in the way normal and specific-language-impaired children react to comprehension and production procedures. This evidence will be presented after a discussion of the research on the relative effects of comprehension and production teaching.

Several studies support the use of production training procedures for language-disordered children. Leonard (1981) has reviewed the majority of the controlled-outcome studies and has concluded that they were more or less successful. Most of these studies used production procedures that had imitative and spontaneous teaching steps similar to those outlined earlier.

Some of the studies reported by Leonard used the modeling approach described earlier, which can be considered one of the comprehension-related methods alluded to in the premise. A comprehension or comprehension-related procedure can be distinguished from a production procedure by the method used to give the learner appropriate input and by the way the learner is expected to process the input in order to form a rule. In comprehension procedures, the learner listens to structured input and is expected to recognize a pattern and formulate a rule without having to repeat or otherwise say components of the input. As outlined earlier, modeling is one such procedure; the learner listens to examples spoken by the teacher, or possibly a third person, and then is asked to perform as the model does (Bandura & Harris, 1966). It is proposed by those who practice modeling procedures that learners become less concerned with the irrelevant detail of the language input, as they might if they had to imitate a sentence, making them more apt to identify a pattern in the input and form a rule (Courtright & Courtright, 1979). The possible differences between modeling and a comprehension procedure in which a learner responds by pointing to an object or a picture is an important issue, as will be discussed later under this premise.

The outcome of modeling procedures has been positive in three cases but has been questionable in one other case. Leonard (1975) and Wilcox and Leonard (1978) found that language-disordered children could learn rules governing auxiliary and *wh*-question inversion after hearing lists of sentences containing the forms. Similarly, Courtright and Courtright (1976) presented evidence that such children can learn to produce the pronoun *they* after hearing it used in the context of 20 sentences.

A second study by Courtright and Courtright (1979), already discussed in terms of rules, is rather difficult to interpret because there is conflicting evidence in the literature regarding its results. As indicated before, these authors found that 12 language-disordered children learned to produce sentences of the noun phrase + *means to* + verb phrase form after hearing the form used in 20 sentences. In an attempt to replicate this result, Connell et al. (1981) found that normal children of about the same age could not learn the form using the same procedures.

Before comparing comprehension and production procedures in terms of their effectiveness, it is necessary to define what counts as evidence of successful teaching. Earlier it was argued that evidence of an acceleration of language learning accompanied by evidence that the acceleration would not have been expected by normal development alone are basic to a determination of effectiveness. In addition, two other requirements were discussed briefly. The first was that there be evidence that the learner has acquired a language rule, and the second was that there be evidence that the teaching procedure provided sufficient language data for the learner to have learned a rule.

The rationale for the first of these two requirements is that children can learn strategies for correctly solving language problems presented to them in testing sessions without actually having learned a language rule. The Courtright and Courtright (1979) study was discussed earlier as an example of a teaching study that did not appear to teach a language rule even though the subjects appeared to generalize to novel contexts. The Courtright and Courtright (1976) modeling study is an example of another such study, and it will be used to illustrate the kind of data that are necessary to support the conclusion that a rule has been learned. These authors claimed that the subjects in their study learned a rule that controlled the use of *they* as a result of their teaching procedures. However, the evidence they provided to support their claim is not convincing, because there is no way to decide whether the children learned a rule or a strategy.

The teaching procedure was to have language-disordered children listen to a set of sentences describing pictures. The sentences were first spoken with a plural noun serving as the subject and subsequently spoken with the pronoun *they* replacing the plural noun. The evidence for rule learning consisted of the results of a generalization test in which the subjects were tested on whether they used *they* to replace the first noun phrase of sentences describing novel pictures. The problem with this evidence is that the subjects could have used *they* on the test for reasons other than that they had learned a rule. Because the generalization test was so similar to the teaching situation, it is entirely possible and probable that the subjects could have learned something as simple as "Say all sentences with *they* in place of the first noun phrase" and this would have resulted in correct responses on the generalization test.

There are two types of data the authors could have offered as evidence of rule learning. By presenting other pictures, they could have tested the use of other persons of nominative pronouns (*I, he, she, it, we, you*) and shown that *they* was restricted to instances of third-person-plural referents. By showing where a form is used as well as where it is not used, it is possible to rule out simple strategies like the one proposed above as alternative explanations and indirectly provide evidence that a rule was learned (Connell, 1982). This procedure would also rule out the use of inappropriate language rules or inappropriate modifications to existing language rules as the source of generalization. For example, another explanation of the results could be that the subjects learned that *them* should be pronounced *they*. This is perhaps more probable than the strategy referred to above, because the subjects apparently had used *them* as the first word in sentences like those presented in the study before teaching began and because language-disordered children would probably not find it unusual to be taught to pronounce a word differently given the prevalence of misarticulations in this population (Aram & Nation, 1982). In order to rule out this explanation, the authors could have provided data on the form of the children's pronouns that functioned as syntactic objects in sentences such as *"The man gave *they* a ball."

The authors could have also provided language sample data as evidence of rule learning. From a comprehensive sample that contained obligations for all the forms described above, the privileges of occurrence of a particular form could have been examined and evidence of rule learning could have been ascertained. The usefulness of this procedure is reduced in cases in which the form does not readily generalize to different communication contexts, such as when a learner has not extended a rule to conversational speech. In such a case, it would be impossible on the basis of sample data alone to determine whether failure to use a form meant that a rule was not learned or learned but not used. Also, the procedure could not be used to test the learning of a non-English (or invented) rule.

The second type of evidence necessary to claim that a teaching procedure is successful is the conclusion that it provides the kind of language data that would be necessary for one to formulate a rule. That is, there should be some reason to believe that the subjects could have learned an appropriate rule from the procedures. For example, there is no reason to believe that a child would learn the meaning and form of a nominative-case pronoun in the Courtright and Courtright study simply by hearing it used in sentences that describe pictures. There is nothing in the sentences or the pictures that tells the learner how *they* differs in function from *them*, only that they sound different. Certainly, the complexities of the pronoun case system of English as it relates to syntactic function are not represented in the reading of lists of sentences containing *they*.

My criticisms of the Courtright and Courtright study are not meant to single it out as a particularly deficient study, because the same criticisms can be made of most if not all of the studies reported here. What I am claiming is that these authors do not provide convincing evidence that a rule was learned or, if it was learned, that the teaching procedures were instrumental in the learning. That is, I am not claiming that the subjects did not actually learn a rule, only that the evidence of such knowledge is missing. Moreover even if they knew a rule just like the one their teachers wanted them to learn, they could not have learned it from the teaching procedures because the procedures did not provide the linguistic facts that rule learning requires. Thus, the rule knowledge of these children must be both proved and explained.

The failure of Connell et al. (1981) to replicate the results of the Courtright and Courtright (1979) teaching procedure suggests one explanation. The procedure employed by Connell et al. involved teaching a non-English form to normal children. Because the rule was arbitrarily constructed by the teacher, the subjects knew nothing about the rule before the study. As was indicated, normal children failed to learn the form through modeling procedures very similar to those that were successful for teaching *they* (Courtright & Courtright, 1976). The fact that the procedure failed in one case and was successful in another suggests that familiarity with a rule is a critical factor. On the one hand, it may be that rules that are novel to the learner cannot be taught without providing the necessary linguistic facts. On the other hand, rules that are familiar may be taught with deficient input. In other words, it seems possible that language input can be reduced to information about pronunciation and still be effective if and only if the learner has had sufficient previous input about the rule to be learned. Thus, it may be possible to teach a rule successfully using any procedure within reason as long as the learner has sufficient prerequisite knowledge about the rule before teaching begins. How one would identify this type of learner before the initiation of teaching is an important clinical question that will be addressed under Premise 7. It is assumed, however, that there are learners who have no knowledge of a rule before they encounter it in a teaching situation. These children will need structured language input that will allow them to form a rule.

Returning to the premise, there are two reasons the studies discussed thus far cannot be used to compare the effectiveness of comprehension and production training procedures. First, as indicated in the discussion, they do not provide convincing evidence that the subjects were taught a rule or that they learned a rule from the teaching. Second, most of the studies did not compare the two procedures so that their results could be assessed within the same study.

Even though this group of studies cannot be taken as support for the premise, there are studies of language teaching and language acquisition that can be. One of these concerns teaching language to normal children. One of the recurring issues in normal language development research concerns the relative contribution of hearing versus speaking to language learning. It has been a traditional position that children acquire language primarily from hearing it used by others and that their speech is merely a reflection of what they have learned through comprehension (e.g., Ingram, 1974). On one level, this position makes intuitive sense in that children must learn from the language spoken around them since they end up speaking the language of their caregivers. On another level, however, this position appears to oversimplify the process of language learning because children have been found to perform at different developmental levels on comprehension and production tests given at the same time. Bloom (1974) was the first to disagree seriously with the position that comprehension has a dominating role in language acquisition. She held that language production plays an important role in that different aspects of language knowledge are acquired through talking as opposed to only listening. More recently, Clark and Hecht (1983) concluded after a review of the literature that differences found in children's comprehension and production performances suggest that the mental representation of the language underlying comprehension may be substantially different from that underlying production.

The failure to understand the relation between the two performances has had consequences for many aspects of language acquisition research and theory and for language teaching. For example, Brown's (1973) landmark description of five stages of language development was based on the talking or language samples of three children and was not influenced by the way in which the children's understanding of language developed. Also, descriptions of the relation between parental language input and children's language-learning achievements have typically been based on language sample data (Gleitman, Newport, & Gleitman, 1984). As is always the case, areas that present descriptive and explanatory problems for theories of language acquisition also present problems for language teaching.

In order to study the relation between comprehension and production during language learning, Connell and McReynolds (1981) examined the lexical learning of twelve 5½-year-old children who were taught a nonsense lexicon of three words to refer to three nondescript geometric figures. Several studies have examined lexical learning in natural situations (Benedict, 1979; Golden-Meadow, Seligman, & Gelman, 1976; Huttenlocher, 1974), and the results indicate that children's comprehension lexicon is larger than their production lexicon throughout the developmental period. However, because of the observational nature of these studies, there is no way to tell from the results what role production practice plays in the acquisition of lexical items or how directed production practice influences comprehension. The specific purpose of the Connell and McReynolds study was to examine the role of production practice in comparison with comprehension practice in learning a lexicon.

The subjects of the study were introduced to two sets of figures: one for which they were taught names and another for which they were expected to generalize the names given to the first set. So that the children would not be biased toward comprehension or production learning from the beginning, they were taught names to the first set of pictures by means of both comprehension and production teaching procedures. That is, the children were taught to name each of the figures and to identify each figure as it was named by the teacher. After they had learned these names, they were taught that the second set of figures was similar to the first set by indirect means. That is, they were not told that members of the first set shared names with the second set but were left to hypothesize this on their own. The children were led to this hypothesis by being taught to select each figure from the second set as a match for one of the figures of the first set. After they gave evidence of having used the same names for the two sets of figures, they were subsequently taught different names for the first set of figures, and the effect of this change was measured on the generalized names of the second set.

Because the names for the second set of figures were not directly taught, it was reasoned that they would not be as greatly affected by the manner in which they were learned as were other words. That is, since the names for the figures were learned indirectly, they could not be said to have been learned through comprehension or production but rather by a deductive process that was unrelated to language performance modality. This special characteristic of these names was used in the study to examine the respective roles of comprehension teaching procedures and production teaching procedures in lexical learning and lexical change. We examined these roles by comparing the results of three methods of teaching the subjects to change the names they gave the first set of figures. The three name-changing teaching methods were (1) teaching different names through comprehension procedures, (2) teaching different names through production procedures, and (3) teaching different names through a combined procedure in which one name was taught by production methods and another was taught simultaneously by comprehension methods. The effect of these three kinds of changes was reflected by the names given to the second set.

The results of the three procedures indicate a difference in learning efficiency and generalization in favor of production teaching. The children took longer to learn to change names and they generalized the names to the second set less extensively during comprehension teaching. Thus, production teaching appears to be the superior teaching method. Also, the superiority appears to be specific to young children, because a group of 12 adults who performed the same task indicated no preference for either procedure.

Two studies of specific-language-disordered children discussed earlier support the superiority of production procedures found in this study of normal children, although in one of the studies the support is conditional. These two studies concerned teaching morphological and word-order rules to specific-language-impaired children. The first of these was the previously mentioned modeling and imitation study (Connell, in press a). In this study forty 3- to 6-year-old specific-language-disordered children and forty age-matched normal children were taught an invented noun suffix *a* to denote "part of" either through imitation or modeling procedures. For example, they were taught that *cata* was "part of a cat" and *booka* was "part of a book."

The results of the study indicate that imitation is the superior procedure for language-disordered children, whereas modeling is superior for normal children. The learning preference shown by the language-disordered children seems to support the results of Connell and McReynolds' study, whereas the results for the normal children seem to be contradictory. They are contradictory, however, only if comprehension procedures such as that used by Connell and McReynolds are seen as functionally equivalent to modeling procedures. They are not contradictory if one views modeling procedures as being essentially different from comprehension procedures on the grounds that modeling procedures require no active participation in the teaching task as do comprehension or production procedures. In modeling, the successful learner must selectively process the input and induce rules, but no overt action is required (Courtright & Courtright, 1976, 1979). The absence of overt action is seen by some as being the important attribute of modeling teaching in that the learner can concentrate on the mental operations that must be performed (Bandura & Harris, 1966).

Thus, the study may not have been comparing production and comprehension procedures but rather production and a nonproduction procedure. Viewed in this way, the results indicate that production procedures are more effective than nonproduction procedures for some learners and not others. The superiority of the modeling procedure to the production procedure for the normal children merits further experimental work.

The difference in the effectiveness of the two procedures with the two groups of children can be viewed as an indication of a difference in the learning preferences of the two groups. This difference suggests that specific-language-impaired children cannot use language input to induce rules as well as normal children unless they are given assistance. The inefficiency with which the language-disordered children induced the rule during modeling teaching further suggests that they are not as well equipped to select information from language input that would lead them to induce a rule. The reason for the effectiveness of production teaching may be that it assisted the children in the selection process. Through the imitation of nouns and suffixes, the children's attention may have been drawn to the difference in form between a noun such as *cat* and the noun plus a suffix such as *cata*, which led them more directly to the correct induction. Thus, what may have been distracting to the inductive process of normal children may have been facilitative for the language-disordered children. The differential effect of modeling and imitation (production) found in this study may indicate a basic characteristic of the rule acquisition of language-disordered children.

The second study is the semantic-role study referred to previously (Connell, 1986). The purpose of the study was to compare the effects of teaching specific-language-impaired children the relation between semantic role and word order through comprehension procedures as opposed to production procedures. The reason for comparing the two procedures with respect to the semantic role rule is that there is an unusual finding in the normal-development literature concerning this rule. Several researchers have found that children appear to use the rule in their speech considerably earlier than they use it to comprehend the speech of others (see Bridges, 1980, and Chapman & Miller, 1975, for a review of the issue). Such an unusual finding in normal acquisition suggests that there is something different about learning this rule.

The procedure was to teach a group of six 3-year-old language-disordered children who were pre-Stage 1 (Brown, 1973) to comprehend or produce word order in relation to semantic role. Before the teaching, their language consisted entirely of one-word utterances. The children were taught the rule with a set of three reversible-action pairs of pictures in a multiple-baseline design described earlier. Three of the subjects were initially taught to comprehend word order, and three were initially taught to produce three-word sentences containing agent, action, and patient. The children were regularly tested on their ability to comprehend and produce sentences describing a set of 10 similar pairs of reversible-action pictures and to use semantic-role distinctions in their conversational speech.

The results indicate that there was a considerable difference between the two procedures in terms of the children's performance. The three children taught to produce word-order distinctions learned to do so in fewer than 10 sessions ($M = 6.3$), but the three taught to comprehend word-order distinctions failed to progress at all after 11 sessions and were subsequently given production teaching (each session contained approximately 40 examples or trials). They then reached criterion in fewer than 8 sessions ($M = 5$). The children's responses to the set of 10 pairs of test pictures were similar for both groups during and after production teaching. During production teaching, their ability to say three-word sentences containing correct semantic distinctions gradually increased to the point that they generalized to the majority of pictures ($M = 95\%$) and they used the structure in conversational speech. In contrast, they never performed better than chance on the same pictures tested by means of comprehension procedures during the production teaching period. As would be expected from the other results, there was no generalization resulting from the comprehension teaching.

The results of the study are difficult to interpret because, on the surface, they are contradictory. The finding that the children were unable to learn to point to pictures in response to word-order cues is not especially surprising in itself. There are undoubtedly many language rules that are beyond the language-learning abilities of young language-disordered children. But the finding that the children could learn the same rule through production teaching is unusual. It has been claimed previously that production teaching has a stronger effect than comprehension teaching, but it was assumed that, if a rule could be learned through production teaching, it could also be learned to some extent through comprehension teaching. Even though this finding does not support this assumption, its oddity from a language-learning perspective is surpassed by the finding that the children could not use the rule to comprehend sentences even though they could use it to describe pictures and in their conversational speech. On further analysis, however, the finding is no more odd than the finding referred to earlier concerning comprehension and production of the rule in normal acquisition; that is, that normal children appear to use word order to represent meaning in their own sentences before they use it to decode the sentences of others (see Bridges, 1980, for a review). The results of the study indicate that the language-disordered children learned the rule by the same pattern as normal children.

One explanation for the dilemma found here and in normal language development is provided by Lempert and Kinsbourne (1983). They claim that normal children actually learn the semantic-role rule from language input, but they have difficulty using the rule in their interactions with others and especially on tests that attempt to determine their knowledge of the rule. Their problem in these situations is that their performance is strongly influenced by world-knowledge cues. These cues lead them to make decisions about a state of affairs described in a sentence without reference to word-order information. For example, they would interpret "The cat chases the dog" as the dog having the agent role because they have learned from experience that dogs are cat chasers and cats are not dog chasers. This knowledge of the way the world works compels them to interpret sentences in one way and overwhelms any tendency to use a word-order rule.

The problem with applying this interpretation to these data is that it would apply to only some of the reversible pictures used to test the children, and even the data from these pictures do not support the interpretation. These pictures illustrated an event that was clearly more probable when depicted one way than when depicted another. For example, the picture of a woman feeding a baby depicted a more common event than its matched picture depicting a baby feeding a woman. Rather than selecting the more probable picture (i.e., the woman feeding the baby) in response to the sentences "The mommy is feeding the baby" and "The baby is feeding the mommy," the children selected both pictures apparently at random. Thus, there was no evidence that they were biased to select the more probable picture as the Lempert and Kinsbourne (1983) explanation suggests. In addition to this evidence, there is no support for the explanation in the children's selection of pictures that contained no apparent world-knowledge bias. The children did not select the correct picture in response to sentence pairs such as "The worm is kissing the frog" and "The frog is kissing the worm," indicating that there must have been some factor other than response bias that inhibited them from displaying their semantic-role knowledge on the comprehension task. Thus, the findings of this study indicate that children can learn to express semantic roles in their sentences through production training but that this learning cannot be obtained through comprehension training and cannot be measured through comprehension testing. The reason the ineffectiveness of comprehension training and testing methods was not uncovered in this study will be the focus of future research. The findings do suggest, however, that comprehension procedures must be applied with caution.

This interpretation provides further support for the strength of production teaching methods found in the other studies that have been discussed. Thus, it appears again that production teaching is more compelling than other influences on the learning and use of lexical and word-order rules. Production teaching is also more successful than nonproduction influences (modeling) on language-disordered children's learning of morphological and word-order rules, although it is possible that some nonproduction teaching procedures are more influential in normal children's learning of at least morphological rules.

   6. *The sequence of teaching rules should be only tentatively patterned after current descriptions of developmental sequence.*

Many authors suggest that normal acquisition data should guide both the content and the sequence of teaching (e.g., Bloom & Lahey, 1978; Crystal et al., 1976; Miller & Yoder, 1974). In order to follow this suggestion, it is necessary to define what the sequence of normal development is. Winitz (1983) addresses two problems associated with current attempts to define this sequence, problems that have a direct bearing on the usefulness of sequences in teaching.

The first has already been mentioned in the discussion about the role of comprehension and production in language learning. Winitz's criticism is that developmental sequences in current use are descriptions of children's production of forms and structures, not their comprehension of them. Since it is possible that children acquire comprehension of different rules in sequences that are quite different from what their production data suggest (Bloom, 1974; Clark & Hecht, 1983), it is impossible to describe the development of linguistic knowledge from the perspective of information obtained from production testing alone. Given that only production-based sequences are presently available to teachers, it is probably best not to rely on them as the sole authority for determining the direction of teaching.

The second problem Winitz discusses concerns the usefulness of the sequences for determining where to begin teaching. He points out that developmental sequences are based on the order in which certain forms are mastered by children (e.g., Brown, 1973). That is, developmental order is defined as the order of mastery of a form without regard to the process of mastery. However, the sequence in which language elements are mastered is not necessarily the sequence in which they were originally encountered by the learner. What would be more applicable to teaching are descriptions of initial learning patterns, because a teacher needs to know when to begin teaching, not when to end it.

Given that the developmental sequences as presently conceived are questionable sources of information for creating a teaching sequence, it is possible that useful information can be obtained from more theoretical sources. Functionalism provides one framework for describing and explaining the process of language learning (Bates & McWhinney, 1979), and consequently it can offer information to a language teacher who is constructing a teaching plan. One of the claims the theory makes is that syntax derives from pragmatic functions. In other words, pragmatic functions such as topic and comment have been hypothesized to form the basis for later-developing syntactic functions such as subject and predicate (Givon, 1979; Wilber, 1983). The theory predicts that children's first sentences will express intentions that are structured within topic–comment relations, and their later sentences will express intentions that will be structured by subject–predicate ones. This prediction receives some support from observations of children's sentence development. As Bates (1976) claims, children's first words appear to comment on a topic in the context of their immediate environment, and their first attempts at sentences are organized around the same topic and comment lines. Later sentences take on some of the syntactic qualities that are usually associated with the subject–predicate relation (Brown, 1973). Thus, as Givon (1979) claims, children appear to develop from a pragmatic knowledge of language to a syntactic knowledge by learning subject–predicate structure and related grammatical elements.

It should be noted that the relation between pragmatic development and syntactic development may not be as straightforward as the theory suggests. There is some evidence that certain language-disordered children, particularly those who are diagnosed as autistic, may develop a syntactic competence that would not be expected given their level of pragmatic development (Blank, Gesser, & Esposito, 1979). Whether the syntactic competence of these children should be viewed as counterevidence for the claim that pragmatic functions precede and participate in the development of syntactic functions depends on how nonfunctional their language usage can be shown to be. That is, in order for these cases to be viewed as strong evidence, it would have to be shown the children's sentences were not organized in terms of topics and comments and that the selection and expression of their utterances were not and never had been constrained by the real or imagined context in which they were spoken. The available observations cannot provide this evidence (e.g., Blank et al., 1979). What they do provide is the suggestion that caution should be taken in hypothesizing pragmatic precursors to syntactic development (Rosenberg, 1984).

Some of the implications of this theory for language teachers have already been discussed under Premise 3. The pragmatic stage is the earlier stage of language development and has its roots in preverbal communication. It is the more prominent stage until children begin making sentences and pass into the syntactic stage (Wilber, 1983). Children who have specific language disorders appear to have difficulty not at this primitive stage but rather at the transition to the syntactic stage, when the structure of their utterances should become governed more by syntactic relations than by context. As mentioned earlier, the communicative functions of specific-language-impaired children do not appear to be a part of their language problem (Skarakis & Greenfield, 1982); thus, the need for teaching such functions is minimal. What would appear to be more important for a teacher is the other half of the learning process – teaching syntactic relations.

Of course, there are children with language disorders who have problems at the pragmatic stage of language development, and the functional theory might guide the approach to teaching these children (see Rosenberg, 1984, for a review of the language problems of such children). Functionalism would suggest that children should be taught pragmatic relations first and syntactic relations later. These pragmatic relations could be taught by contrasting differences in utterances with differences in communicative functions.

The theory has some usefulness for teachers of specific-language-impaired children in that it differentiates on principled grounds between those aspects of language that are not a problem for such children and those that present a considerable problem. By conceptualizing certain properties of language as pragmatic properties and others as syntactic properties, it is possible to characterize the most consistently identified problem of specific-language-impaired children as one of acquiring certain syntactic properties of English. Although syntax has lost its prominence in clinical research, a considerable amount of evidence indicates that the basic nature of these children's language problem is syntactic (Eisenson & Ingram, 1972; Johnston & Schery, 1976; Lee, 1966, 1974; Leonard, 1972; Menyuk 1964a, 1964b; Menyuk & Looney, 1972; Morehead & Ingram, 1973). This is not to deny that these children could have semantic and pragmatic problems that may not be related to syntax, such as lexical problems and conversational difficulties, but rather that they have a well-established syntactic problem that has been easily overlooked as the focus of research has changed (Wilber, 1983).

In regard to how syntactic structure should be taught to language-disordered children, the functional theory provides little direction. Although the functional theory describes the change that occurs in the structure of children's sentences, it does not provide a mechanism for explaining how children learn syntactic structure from the language input available to them (Lightfoot, 1982). For example, Bates and McWhinney (1979) claim that the syntactic role of subject is learned to solve the problems caused by the communicative need to talk occasionally about elements of a state of affairs besides the agent – for example, the experiencer, patient, or instrument. However, this claim provides only a motivation for learning. How a child goes about learning the particulars of syntactic systems such as subject–predicate agreement, a system that has very little to do with communicative function, is left unexplained. In more general terms, the functional theory does not provide an explanation for the way children in the later stages of language development (that is, in Brown's Stages III, IV, and V) make the proper generalizations about language rules given that these rules are not dependent on context.

There are two competing theories of the acquisition of syntactic relations that could offer a language teacher some direction for selecting the content and sequence of teaching. They can be labeled the social interactionalist and innatist theories. The social interactionalist theory holds that the caregiver provides linguistic input that is perfectly tailored to the needs of a child who is trying to induce rules and that the input is sufficient for such learning to occur (see Wanner & Gleitman, 1982, for a review of this position). The innatist position holds that children do not appear to have access to the linguistic facts required to induce syntactic rules, which implies that they must be genetically endowed with linguistic principles to guide their acquisition of such rules (Chomsky, 1980; Lightfoot, 1982).

One way to determine which of these two positions best describes children's syntactic learning is to examine the relation between the nature of the language input provided by the environment and the pattern of syntactic acquisition of children in these environments. Gleitman et al. (1984) interpret the literature concerning this relationship as indicating that children selectively use linguistic input; that is, they select what to use, when to use it, and how to use it to formulate rules. A similar conclusion was reached by Rosenberg (1984) and Sachs, Bard, and Johnson (1981). Thus, the research supports the innatist position that rule learning is guided by factors that are not represented in language input.

The syntactic difficulties of language-disordered children provide the opportunity to compare the two positions in another way. Each position would predict a different pattern of generalization following syntactic rule teaching. The social interactionalist position would predict that language-disordered children will learn only as much as they are taught because they can only induce rules about the linguistic evidence that is available to them. The innatist position would predict that such children can learn more than they are taught because they have knowledge of principles that allow them to acquire rules that are not represented by the input.

The acquisition of syntax by language-disordered children was the focus of a study I have recently completed (Connell, in press b), and the results of the study provide interesting insights into the nature of syntactic acquisition. There is evidence that the acquisition of the syntactic functions of subject and predicate is one of the syntactic areas that are particularly difficult for these children (Rosenberg, 1984). This function includes those properties of sentences that have been called subject properties (Cole, Harbert, Herman, & Sridhar, 1980). Subject properties are morphosyntactic and transformational elements that are associated with the subject of sentences and have little semantic purpose. The morphosyntactic subject properties of English are the auxiliary *be*, the copula *be*, the nominative case of pronouns, and the third person singular. The transformational subject properties are question inversion and other syntactic operations on phrase structures.

Four specific-language-impaired children between the ages of 3½ and 4½ were selected as subjects because their sentences did not contain any of the subject properties listed above. These children were taught to use subject properties in a multiple-baseline design like the one described earlier. The teaching procedure was based on a sentence form that was found in all of the children's language samples taken before teaching was implemented. The form contained an accusative-case pronoun as the first constituent – for example, such sentences as "Him walking," "Her big," and "Him hit." These sentences were lacking the obligatory auxiliary *be,* copula *be,* and third-person-singular morphemes. From a pragmatic perspective, these sentences can be viewed as instances of the topic–comment relation. The pronoun identifies a topic, and the remainder of the sentence makes a comment about the entity referred to by the pronoun. The goal of teaching was to create a subject–predicate structure within these topic–comment sentences. Rather than attempt to replace the old structure with the new, the plan was to use the old structure as a framework into which syntactic relations were placed. Also, as Givon (1979) points out, pragmatic functions are not lost in development; they are merely made less prominent.

The method of reducing the prominence of topics and introducing subjects was to teach the children to say their own topic-prominent sentence form that had been modified by adding a subject. An example of these sentences is "Him, he is walking," in which the *him* performs the topic function and the *he* performs the subject function. These sentences were spoken in response to a question such as "Which one is walking?" about a picture depicting a man walking and several other people performing different actions. The children originally responded by pointing to the man or by pointing and saying "Him." They were taught through imitation methods to respond to the question by adding a subject and predicate to the topic *Him.* Simultaneously, and by way of contrast, they were taught to describe action pictures using only the subject–predicate forms such as "He is walking."

The result of learning a series of sentences like the preceding was that the children acquired subject properties on their own. That is, with no direct teaching on auxiliary *be* (with the exception of the form *is* used to teach two of the subjects), copula *be,* third person singular, nominative-case pronouns (with the exception of the gender forms used in teaching), and question inversion, the subjects acquired some level of mastery of each of these subject properties after the teaching process and showed no change in their use of them during the pretraining period. The results indicate that the children generally learned the properties as a class but that certain properties were mastered sooner and to a higher level. In particular, the nominative case was learned to a high level of mastery before any of the others showed any positive change. The others were learned more or less simultaneously afterward. Thus, it appears that there is something necessary and sufficient about pronoun learning in relation to learning the other subject properties.

The results of this study support the notion that the children could learn more than they were taught, which suggests that they knew something about syntax before teaching began. This result supports the contention of Rosenberg (1984) that the language learning of children with language disorders is governed by the same *specifically linguistic biological constraints* that govern the language learning of normal children.

Of course, the obvious question these results raise concerns why these children did not utilize their linguistic dispositions on their own. This failure may be another instance of the phenomenon suggested by the results of the modeling–imitation study on language-disordered children referred to earlier. It may be that such children do not make efficient use of linguistic input to induce basic categories such as subjects of sentences, and without such inductions they cannot use their knowledge of syntactic principles to acquire other aspects of syntax.

> 7. *Language sampling measurement procedures are not necessarily the most accurate means of estimating knowledge of language.*

As indicated previously, determining what a person knows about language is central to the process of clinical work. Also, in order to perform developmental and teaching research, we must make certain assumptions about the nature of a child's knowledge of language. In spite of Chomsky's (1965) warnings, the most common way to do this is to use performance data, in particular the language sample. Although language sample data have been shown to be more useful than data taken from some other sources such as standardized tests (Lund & Duchan, 1983), they have two rather major shortcomings that affect their validity as an estimate of language knowledge. The first is that, as samples of naturally occurring speech, language samples have the potential of not adequately representing the child's productive capacities. This problem arises because of the well-known influence of context on children's speech (Bates, 1976). The form of children's utterances is a reflection not only of what they know about language but also of their conception of the communicative context in which their utterances fit. Thus, variations in communicative context will affect the form of children's utterances, and these effects must be separated from other influences on performance if we are to estimate language knowledge from performance data. Consequently, a language sample taken in a single or even a few contexts will probably not provide the basis for separating the effects of the different influences.

The second drawback of using language samples was mentioned before in the context of language teaching. The problem is that language samples provide no information about a child's understanding of language. Language comprehension is a component of language performance that must be included in any estimate of what a person knows about language (Clark & Hecht, 1983). One of the few points of agreement among language theorists is the idea that the language knowledge used in speaking language is the same as that used in understanding it (Chomsky, 1965; Lakoff & Thompson, 1975). However, there is considerable evidence that children's performances in these two areas can be considerably different, which calls into question the value of language samples for estimating the actual language knowledge of children (e.g., Bloom, 1974; Clark & Hecht, 1983).

Given that these problems exist in language sampling, it is probably best to try to develop procedures that more closely approximate the level of children's knowledge of language. Slobin and Welsh (1973) propose that one way to assess children's level of language performance that removes the problem of contextual influence and involves language comprehension is imitation testing. Although some criticize imitation procedures for being devoid of communicative intent and thereby unnatural (e.g., Lund & Duchan, 1983), Smith (1973) suggests that the lack of intention neutralizes the influence of context, thus requiring the child to rely on the form and meaning of a structure rather than its function.

In order to determine whether contextual cues affect imitation performance or whether imitation performance is impervious to context, Connell and Myles-Zitzer (1982) provided four types of contextual cues to seven 3½- to 4½-year-old children while they were asked to imitate sentences. The context cues ranged from a video-taped presentation, which enacted a sentence presented to a child for imitation, to line drawings of the same event. The accuracy of the children's imitation of certain morphemes when given these cues was compared with their accuracy when no cues were given at all. It was found that there was no contextual effect, which supports the claim that imitation testing provides a measure of language performance that is not influenced by context.

Consequently, if the results of imitation testing were combined with those of language sample analysis and comprehension testing, it would be possible to separate more accurately the influences of context from knowledge on language performance. Those forms that were found to be missing in obligatory contexts in a sample could be presented as imitative models and as comprehension test items to determine whether there were any knowledge of the form and its meaning. In the imitative test, it would be best to present the form used correctly and incorrectly. For example, if the form found missing in a sample were auxiliary *be*, a correct model would be "The boy is swimming" and an incorrect one would be "The boy swimming." Only if the child did not correct the incorrect model or correctly imitate the correct model would there be reason to conclude a lack of knowledge about the *be* form. If, however, a child imitated the correct model and corrected the incorrect model, there would be reason to believe that the child knew more about the rule than was indicated in his or her speech. The distinction between these two types of children is important in terms of the structuring of their teaching programs. In the case of the child who had knowledge of a rule, teaching could focus on the implementation of the rule by procedures similar to those described above as not being sufficient to teach a novel rule. In the case of the child who apparently did not know the rule, the focus would be on teaching the rule by means of procedures that provided sufficient linguistic input.

Even though imitation testing could be valuable in most situations in which an assessment of what a child knows about language were needed, there are certain circumstances under which the results would not be useful (Connell & Myles-Zitzer, 1982). The process of imitation appears to be one in which imitators attempt to say an utterance that *means* the same thing as the utterance that they heard (Smith, 1973). Thus, it is assumed that the imitators decode the meaning of the utterance by means of their knowledge of language and encode the meaning using the same knowledge. The forms the imitators select to respond to the model represent the meaning they decoded and not necessarily the forms they heard. In other words, imitation responses are assumed to be processed through meaning. This assumed process of imitation might not be the way imitation is performed by some children. For example, some children may not have the memory ability to decode a long utterance or to remember the meaning of an utterance long enough for a sentence to be created. Other children may decode no meaning at all and remember only the forms used and then mimic the sounds they heard. Both types of children are claimed to exist in the population of language-disordered children, and their linguistic knowledge could not be estimated by the results of imitation tests (Aram & Nation, 1982).

Discussion

The discussion of rules presented in support of the teaching premises has been limited in most cases to teaching on a rule-by-rule basis and has not been expanded to teaching a system of language rules. Obviously, the ultimate goal of language teaching is for the student to acquire the entire language system. Depending on the extent of a child's language problem, the number of rules a child has to learn in order to have acquired even an approximation of the system can be large. In normal acquisition, progress toward the attainment of the system does not result from learning individual rules in sequential order. Rather, rules appear to be learned in groups, and several rules can be emerging and show mastery during the same period. The concept of developmental stages is an attempt to describe the interrelatedness of rule learning within and across certain periods (Crystal et al. 1976).

If the goal of teaching is to teach a system of rules, the process described here appears to be too narrow in scope. There has been no mention thus far of a means of teaching a student that a particular rule is to be grouped with certain rules and not with others. Each rule has been treated independently and there has been no process described to teach interdependence.

There is good reason for the failure to rectify this apparent problem in the approach described here. It is that the only theory that both explains how individual rules are related and explains the outcome of the subject properties study is an innatist theory. The linguistic principles that such a theory postulates as part of a child's endowment are only beginning to be described (see Lightfoot, 1982, for a description of some initial attempts). Therefore, there are no substantive theoretical claims that are sufficiently detailed to guide the construction of a teaching program that reflects the interrelatedness of rules.

Although the theory does not provide details, the results of the subject properties study suggest that teaching an individual rule can result in learning a system of rules. If a rule can be identified through observational research on normal children as a rule that is basic to other rules the student must learn, it is possible to test the interrelatedness of the rule and the other rules by teaching the rule and observing the generalization that results. The enterprise of searching for such rules and teaching them would be based on the assumption that children are endowed with the knowledge of certain principles of language learning and that input to these rules serves as a trigger that makes the principles available to the learner.

This type of approach to teaching is more realistic than an individual-rule approach because the time that would be required to teach a severely language disordered child a system of rules one by one would be excessive. In addition to the time expenditure, there would be no guarantee at the outset that the resulting rule system would be qualitatively similar to a system acquired by normal means. It is likely that a system of rules learned individually would be different in some very important ways from one learned as a system.

Of course, the current problem with implementing this approach is identifying the seminal rules related to each of the stages of language development. The seminal rule of the subject properties study was identified as a subject function rule because it was logical that subject properties are controlled by the subject of sentences and it was reasoned that the children would require knowledge of subjects before the properties could be learned. Even though this assumption was supported by the results of the study, it cannot be stated positively that the single or best seminal rule was taught, only that a group of rules were learned after the children learned something about the function of subjects. Further research would have to determine whether any other rule would generate the same results. Finding the seminal rule for other groups of rules is not as logically straightforward as subject properties. For example, the possible seminal rules for the verbal morpheme system of English are not quite as obvious and may require a considerable amount of searching.

In summary, if the process of language teaching is to be effective in the long run, the goal must be to teach students to acquire language on their own. Thus, teaching individual rules is viewed as having a facilitative effect on language learning. Proposing that teaching should be facilitative is not the same as claiming that teachers should facilitate language and not teach it. As has been shown, rules can be taught directly, and in the process, children may learn how to acquire language on their own. Teaching of this sort would prepare children for the task of acquiring linguistic knowledge from their own language environments by allowing them the opportunity to use their inherent language-learning skills.

References

Aram, D., & Nation, J. (1982). *Child language disorders.* St. Louis, MO: Mosby.

Bandura, A., & Harris, M. (1966). Modifications of syntactic style. *Journal of Experimental Child Psychology, 4,* 341–53.

Bates, E. (1976). *Language in context.* New York: Academic Press.

Bates, E., & McWhinney, B. (1979). A functionalist's approach to the acquisition of grammar. In E. Ochs & B. Schieffelin (Eds.), *Developmental pragmatics* (pp. 167–209). New York: Academic Press.

Benedict, H. (1979). Early lexical development: Comprehension and production. *Journal of Child Language, 6,* 183–200.

Berko, (1958). The child's learning of English morphology. *Word, 14,* 150–177.

Blank, M., Gesser, M., & Esposito, A. (1979). Language without communication: A case study. *Journal of Child Language, 6,* 329–52.

Bloom, L. (1974). Talking, understanding and thinking. In R. Schiefelbusch & L. Lloyd (Eds.), *Language perspectives: Acquisition, retardation and intervention.* Baltimore, MD: University Park Press.

Bloom, L., & Lahey, M. (1978). *Language development and language disorders.* New York: Wiley.

Bowerman, M. (1978). Semantic and syntactic development: A review of what, when and how in language acquisition. In R. Schiefelbusch (Ed.), *Bases of language intervention* (pp. 97–189). Baltimore, MD: University Park Press.

Bridges, A. (1980). SVO comprehension strategies reconsidered: The evidence of individual patterns of response. *Journal of Child Language, 7,* 89–104.

Brown, R. (1973). *A first language.* Cambridge, MA: Harvard University Press.

Chapman, R. (1983). Deciding when to intervene. In J. Miller, D. Yoder, & R. Schiefelbusch (Eds.), *Contemporary issues in language intervention* (pp. 221–5). Rockville, MD: American Speech-Language-Hearing Association.

Chapman, R., & Miller, J. (1975). Word order in early two- and three-word utterances: Does production precede comprehension? *Journal of Speech and Hearing Research, 18,* 355–71.

Chomsky, N. (1965). *Aspects of the theory of syntax.* Cambridge, MA: MIT Press.

Chomsky, N. (1980). *Rules and representations.* New York: Columbia University Press.

Clark, E., & Hecht, T. (1983). Comprehension and production and language acquisition. *Annual Review of Psychology, 34,* 325–50.

Cole, P., Harbert, W., Herman, G., & Sridhar, S. (1980). The acquisition of subjecthood. *Language, 56,* 719–43.

Connell, P. (1982). On training language rules. *Language, Speech, and Hearing Services in Schools, 13,* 231–40.

Connell, P. (1986). The acquisition of semantic role by language-disordered children: Differences between production and comprehension. *Journal of Speech and Hearing Research, 29,* 366–74.

Connell, P. (in press a). The effect of modelling and imitation teaching procedures on children with and without specific language impairment. *Journal of Speech and Hearing Research*.

Connell, P. (in press b). Teaching subjecthood to language-disordered children. *Journal of Speech and Hearing Research*.

Connell, P., Gardner-Gletty, D., Dejewski, J., & Parks-Reinick, L. (1981). Response to Courtright and Courtright. *Journal of Speech and Hearing Research, 46,* 145–8.

Connell, P., & McReynolds, L. (1981). An experimental analysis of children's generalization during lexical learning: Comprehension or production. *Applied Psycholinguistics, 2,* 309–32.

Connell, P., & Myles-Zitzer, C. (1982). An analysis of elicited imitation as a language evaluation procedure. *Journal of Speech and Hearing Disorders, 47,* 390–6.

Courtright, J., & Courtright, I. (1976). Imitative modelling as a theoretical base for instructing language disordered children. *Journal of Speech and Hearing Research, 9,* 655–63.

Courtright, J., & Courtright, I. (1979). Imitative modelling as a language intervention strategy: The effects of two mediating variables. *Journal of Speech and Hearing Research, 22,* 389–402.

Craig, H. (1983). Applications of pragmatic language models for intervention. In T. Gallagher & C. Prutting (Eds.), *Pragmatic assessment and language intervention issues in language* (pp. 101–27). San Diego, CA: College-Hill Press.

Crystal, D., Fletcher, P., & Garman, M. (1976). *The grammatical analyses of language disability: A procedure for assessment and remediation*. New York: American Elsevier.

Dale, P. (1976). *Language development: Form and function*. New York: Holt, Rinehart & Winston.

Eisenson, J., & Ingram, D. (1972). Childhood aphasia: An updated concept based on recent research. *Acta Symbolica, 3,* 108–16.

Fillmore, C. (1968). The case for case. In E. Bach & R. Harms (Eds.), *Universals in linguistic theory* (pp. 123–56). New York: Holt, Rinehart & Winston.

Fey, M., & Leonard, L. (1983). Pragmatic skills of children with specific language impairment (pp. 143–93). In T. Gallagher & C. Prutting (Eds.), *Pragmatic assessment and intervention issues in language* (pp. 143–93). San Diego, CA: College-Hill Press.

Gallagher, T., & Prutting, C. (Eds.). (1983). *Pragmatic assessment and intervention issues in language*. San Diego, CA: College-Hill Press.

Givon, T. (1979). From discourse to syntax: Grammar as a processing strategy. In T. Givon (Ed.), *Discourse and syntax*, Vol. 12 (pp. 213–56). New York: Academic Press.

Gleitman, L., Newport, E., & Gleitman, H. (1984). *Journal of Child Language, 11,* 43–80.

Golden-Meadow, S., Seligman, M., & Gelman, R. (1976). Language in a two year old. *Cognition, 4,* 189–202.

Gray, B., & Ryan, B. (1973). *A language program for the nonlanguage child*. Champaign, IL: Research Press.

Hammil, D., & Larsen, S. (1974). Effectiveness of psycholinguistic training. *Exceptional Children, 40,* 5–13.

Huttenlocher, J. (1974). Origins of comprehension. In R. Solso (Ed.), *Theories of cognitive psychology* (pp. 314–46). New York: Wiley.

Ingram, D. (1974). The relationship between comprehension and production. In R. Schiefelbusch & L. Lloyd (Eds.), *Language perspectives: Acquisition, retardation and intervention*. Baltimore, MD: University Park Press.

Jackendoff, R. (1972). *Semantic interpretation in generative grammar*. Cambridge, MA: MIT Press.

Johnston, J. (1983). What is language intervention? The role of theory. In J. Miller, D. Yoder, & R. Schiefelbusch (Eds.), *Contemporary issues in language intervention* (pp. 234–49). Rockville, MD: American Speech-Language-Hearing Association.

Johnston, J., & Schery, T. (1976). The use of grammatical morphemes by children with communication disorders. In D. Morehead & A. Morehead (Eds.), *Normal and deficient child language*. Baltimore, MD: University Park Press.

Kleffner, F. (1975). The direct teaching approach for children with auditory processing and learning disabilities. *Acta Symbolica, 6*, 65–93.

Lakoff, G. (1971). On generative semantics. In D. Steinberg & L. Jakobovits (Eds.), *Semantics* (pp. 123–43). Cambridge University Press.

Lakoff, G., & Thompson, H. (1975). Introducing cognitive grammar. In C. Cosen (Ed.), *Proceedings of the first annual meeting* (pp. 65–98). Berkeley, CA: Berkeley Linguistic Society.

Lee, L. (1966). Developmental sentence types: A method for comparing normal and deviant syntactic development. *Journal of Speech and Hearing Disorders, 31*, 311–30.

Lee, L. (1974). *Developmental sentence analysis*. Evanston, IL: Northwestern University Press.

Lempert, H., & Kinsbourne, M. (1983). Perceptual constraints on the use of language by young children. In K. Nelson (Ed.), *Children's Language (Vol. 4*, pp. 125–55). Hillsdale, NJ: Erlbaum.

Leonard, L. (1972). What is deviant language? *Journal of Speech and Hearing Disorders, 37*, 427–46.

Leonard, L. (1975). Developmental considerations in the management of language disordered children. *Journal of Learning Disabilities, 8*, 232–7.

Leonard, L. (1978). Cognitive factors in early linguistic development. In R. Schiefelbusch (Ed.), *Bases of language intervention*. Baltimore, MD: University Park Press.

Leonard, L. (1979). Linguistic impairment in children. *Merrill-Palmer Quarterly, 25*, 205–32.

Leonard, L. (1981). Facilitating linguistic skills in children with specific language impairment. *Applied Psycholinguistics, 2*, 89–118.

Lightfoot, D. (1982). *The language lottery: Toward a biology of grammars*. Cambridge, MA: MIT Press.

Lund, N., & Duchan, J. (1983). *Assessing children's language in naturalistic contexts*. Englewood Cliffs, NJ: Prentice-Hall.

Menyuk, P. (1964a). Comparison of grammar of children with functionally deviant and normal speech. *Journal of Speech and Hearing Research, 7*, 109–21.

Menyuk, P. (1964b). Syntactic rules used by children from preschool through first grade. *Journal of Child Development, 35*, 533–46.

Menyuk, P., & Looney, P. (1972). A problem of language disorders: Length versus structure. *Journal of Speech and Hearing Research, 15*, 264–79.

Miller, J., Chapman, R., Branston, M., & Reichle, J. (1980). Language comprehension in sensorimotor stages V and VI. *Journal of Speech and Hearing Research, 23*, 284–311.

Miller, J., & Yoder, D. (1974). An ontogenetic language teaching strategy for retarded children. In R. Schiefelbusch & L. Lloyd (Eds.), *Language perspectives: Acquisition, retardation and intervention* (pp. 505–27). Baltimore, MD: University Park Press.

Miller, L. (1978). Pragmatics and early childhood language disorders: Communicative interactions in a half-hour sample. *Journal of Speech and Hearing Disorders, 43*, 419–36.

Morehead, D., & Ingram, D. (1973). The development of base syntax in normal and linguistically deviant children. *Journal of Speech and Hearing Research, 16*, 330–52.

Muma, J. (1978). *Language handbook: Concepts, assessment, intervention.* Englewood Cliffs, NJ: Prentice Hall.

Rosenberg, S. (1984). Disorders of first-language development: Trends in research and theory. In E. S. Gollin (Ed.), *Malformations of development: Biological and psychological sources and consequences* (pp. 195–237). New York: Academic Press.

Rowan, L., Leonard, L., Chapman, K., & Weiss, A. (1983). Performative and presuppositional skills in language disordered and normal children. *Journal of Speech and Hearing Research, 26*, 97–106.

Sachs, J., Bard, B., & Johnson, M. (1981). Language learning with restricted input: Case studies of two hearing children of deaf parents. *Applied Psycholinguistics, 2*, 33–54.

Saunders, D. (1977). *Auditory processing of speech: An introduction to principles and problems.* Englewood Cliffs, NJ: Prentice-Hall.

Seibert, J., & Oller, D. (1981). Linguistic pragmatics and language intervention strategies. *Journal of Autism and Developmental Disorders, 11*, 75–88.

Siegel, G. (1983). Intervention context and setting: Where? In J. Miller, D. Yoder, & R. Schiefelbusch (Eds.), *Contemporary issues in language intervention* (pp. 253–8). Rockville, MD: American Speech-Language-Hearing Association.

Skarakis, E., & Greenfield, P. (1982). The role of new and old information in the verbal expression of language-disordered children. *Journal of Speech and Hearing Research, 25*, 462–7.

Slobin, D. (1970). *Psycholinguistics.* Glenview, IL: Scott, Foresman.

Slobin, D., & Welsh, C. (1973). Elicited imitation as a research tool in developmental psycholinguistics. In C. Ferguson & D. Slobin (Eds.), *Studies of child language development* (pp. 105–26). New York: Holt, Rinehart & Winston.

Smith, C. (1973). An experimental approach to children's linguistic competence. In C. Ferguson & D. Slobin (Eds.), *Studies of child language development* (pp. 75–103). New York: Holt, Rinehart & Winston.

Snyder, L. (1978). Communicative and cognitive abilities in the sensori-motor period. *Merrill-Palmer Quarterly, 24*, 161–80.

Wanner, E., & Gleitman, L. (Eds.). (1982). *Language acquisition: The state of the art.* Cambridge University Press.

Wilber, R. (1983). Where do we go from here? In J. Miller, D. Yoder, & R. Schiefelbusch (Eds.), *Contemporary issues in language intervention* (pp. 103–15). Rockville, MD: American Speech-Language-Hearing Association.

Wilcox, M., & Leonard, L. (1978). Experimental acquisition of wh-questions in language-disordered children. *Journal of Speech and Hearing Research, 21*, 220–39.

Winitz, H. (1983). Use and abuse of the developmental approach. In H. Winitz (Ed.), *Treating language disorders: For clinicians by clinicians* (pp. 25–42). Baltimore, MD: University Park Press.

3   Linguistic communication and mental retardation

Leonard Abbeduto and Sheldon Rosenberg

The concept of mental retardation has been subject to periodic definitional up-heavals, and even today there is no consensus as to its meaning (Krishef, 1983; Robinson & Robinson, 1976). The most popular current definition is that of the American Association on Mental Deficiency (Grossman, 1973). The AAMD def-inition requires deficits in age-appropriate adaptive behavior and lower-than-av-erage general intellectual functioning for a classification of mentally retarded. In practice, however, below-average performance on psychometric measures of in-telligence continues to be the main reason for labeling people mentally retarded (Smith & Polloway, 1979). Despite these definitional problems, those concerned with the care and treatment of people classified as mentally retarded have consist-ently indicated that these individuals experience language and communication problems (Krishef, 1983; Robinson & Robinson, 1976; Webb & Kinde, 1967). This is, perhaps, not surprising given that most of the instruments used to measure adaptive behavior or intelligence require linguistic communication (i.e., the use of language to communicate). It is surprising, however, that so little is known about the nature and extent of retarded people's problems in linguistic communi-cation. It is true that a good deal is known about their acquisition of linguistic competence (i.e., knowledge of phonology, syntax, morphology, and semantics), but little systematic research has been conducted into their linguistic *communica-tive* competence (i.e., their ability to use language for communication; Rosen-berg, 1982). This chapter examines recent efforts to understand linguistic com-munication in mentally retarded children and adults.

There are two reasons for studying the linguistic communication of mentally retarded people. One is to develop a technology for ameliorating their communi-cation problems. In order to develop effective remediation, however, we must first conduct basic research aimed at describing the nature, extent, and causes of the

The authors are indebted to Laurie Furman and Betty Davies for their comments on an earlier version of this chapter. Thanks are due also to Sherrie White, who typed the many versions of this chapter. Some of the research reported herein was supported by Grant HD18716 to Leonard Ab-beduto from the National Institute of Child Health and Human Development.

communication difficulties experienced by retarded people. This chapter is concerned with such basic research. The second reason for studying the linguistic communication of retarded individuals is to help construct a general theory of the acquisition of linguistic communicative competence. Many questions about the nature of normal development can be addressed by the study of disordered populations (Rosenberg, 1984). In this chapter, therefore, we also consider certain theoretical implications of research on the communication of mentally retarded people.

The plan of this chapter is as follows. We first define more formally the term *linguistic communicative competence* and present a partial list of the tasks that are managed by competent communicators. Next, we outline the knowledge bases and skills that are necessary for successful linguistic communication. We then use this outline to specify the questions that are important for basic research on communication in retarded individuals, present a methodology for addressing these questions, and indicate how this methodology can provide data relevant to theories of communicative development. Finally, we critically review existing studies on linguistic communication in mentally retarded individuals in terms of their relevance to the basic research questions identified and the adequacy of their methods and point out their theoretical implications. The reader should note that we have limited our review to studies of communication through spoken language.

The nature of linguistic communicative competence

The term *linguistic communicative competence,* in the most general sense, refers to the ability to use language for the purpose of communication. In this section, the term is defined more precisely, and some of the tasks that must be managed during the process of communication are described. The aim is to give the reader a sense of what it means to be a competent communicator.

Our use of the term *linguistic communicative competence* is based on the fact that there are many choices to be made during communication. One choice arises because a participant does not normally talk continuously throughout a communicative interaction. Rather, one person speaks while the other participant(s) listens, then a different person speaks, and so on. Each participant, therefore, is faced with the choice of whether to be the speaker or the listener. A second choice concerns the message to be communicated. In particular, there are choices to be made as to both the content and the function of the utterance. As to content, there are an infinite number of topics for conversation and an unlimited number of things that could be said on any topic. As to function, there are a variety of things that language can be used to do in a conversation; one can assert, request, promise, warn, permit, and so on (Rees, 1978). Consequently, a speaker must somehow choose the message to be conveyed by his or her utterance. Another choice results from the fact that language provides alternative forms for conveying the same message and allows the same form to convey different messages. For example, *That's mine, Give me that,* and *I want that back* could all be used to request the return of an object, whereas *What are you doing with that?* could be either a request for an object's return or a request for information about the listener's current action. Therefore, a speaker must choose a linguistic form for the intended message, and a listener must choose the message intended from among those that a form could convey.

These choices require more than linguistic competence (i.e., knowledge of phonology, syntax, morphology, and semantics; Abbeduto, 1983; Bach & Harnish, 1979; Levinson, 1983; Rice, 1984; Searle, 1975). To make these choices, language users must also follow pragmatic rules. Pragmatic rules specify the relations among the speaker's intended message (i.e., the content and function of the utterance), the linguistic code, and the context of communication. For example, although language provides several forms for expressing a request for action, the speaker's choice is constrained by various aspects of the communicative context, including the status of the addressee (Ervin-Tripp, 1977; Gordon & Ervin-Tripp, 1984; Olson & Hildyard, 1981; Rice, 1984). In the work place, *Sign this order for me* would be an appropriate request form if the listener were a subordinate, but not if the listener were a supervisor. *Would you mind signing this order?* would be more appropriate in the latter case. As another example, although a speaker has considerable latitude regarding the timing and content of his or her conversational contributions, the utterances of the other conversational participants can limit these options. If asked *What time is it?* a cooperative addressee has no option but to respond, and the content of the contribution is more or less fixed (i.e., the addressee can either provide the queried information or indicate an inability to do so). For their part, listeners also follow pragmatic rules. According to Clark, Schreuder, and Butterick (1983), for instance, a pragmatic rule governing the use of demonstrative noun phrases specifies that the referent be uniquely identifiable in the (linguistic or nonlinguistic) context. Listeners assume that speakers adhere to this rule and search the context accordingly. Thus, given two 6-foot-tall men and one 7-foot-tall man as potential referents, a listener will interpret *Look at that man* as though it referred to the unique member of the trio, namely, the 7-footer.

The foregoing discussion suggests that a competent communicator can be defined as a person who follows pragmatic rules so as to make choices about the use of language in a contextually appropriate manner. A competent speaker uses context in a manner dictated by pragmatic rules to decide when to talk, what the content and function of his or her utterance will be, and what linguistic forms to select. A competent listener relies on pragmatic rules and the communicative context to decide which message, of the many messages that an utterance could convey, is actually intended by the speaker.

A comment about what information can constitute "context" for language users is in order. The preceding examples of context included the socially defined category of status, the prior discourse, and visible properties of the world that co-occur with the utterance. As these examples suggest, many different types of information can serve as appropriate context for language use. It appears, in fact, that there are no limits on what can constitute relevant context (Bach & Harnish, 1979; Levinson, 1983). However, certain dimensions of context are more consistently related to language use than are others (Abbeduto, 1983; Levinson, 1983). Characteristics of the participants such as sex, role, relative age and status, their previous social interactions, and the knowledge and experiences they assume to be common to all people are often important determinants of language use (Abbeduto, 1983; Bach & Harnish, 1979; Levinson, 1983; Olson & Hildyard, 1981; Rice, 1984). Aspects of the physical setting such as visual salience (Clark et al., 1983) and features of the social setting such as formality (e.g., home vs. school; Rice, 1984) frequently have communicative relevance. In addition to these static dimensions, more dynamic aspects of context are also relevant to language users – dimensions such as the mood of the interaction (e.g., hostile vs. friendly; Ervin-Tripp, 1978; Rice, 1984), knowledge and experiences that are found to be shared by participants during the course of the communicative interaction (Bach & Harnish, 1979; Clark, 1979), and, of course, the content of the discourse the participants have constructed.

The communicative process involves several component tasks. Although all of these tasks require making choices in a contextually sensitive and pragmatic-rule-governed fashion, each involves somewhat different choices, pragmatic rules, dimensions of context, and so on. Descriptions of some of the tasks that comprise the communicative process follow.

Taking turns

In the communicative interactions of normal adults, generally only one person speaks at a time and, moreover, the switch from one speaker to the next occurs without overlap or noticeable hesitation (Duncan & Fiske, 1977; Sacks, Schegloff, & Jefferson, 1974). The success of adults' turn taking appears to be the result of their adherence to rules that dictate who can speak and when (Duncan & Fiske, 1977; Sacks et al., 1974). In particular, a competent speaker adheres to the rules and thus is able to signal that he or she does or does not wish to give up the speaker's role, whereas a competent listener adheres to the rules and thus can recognize the points at which a speaking turn may be claimed. Although turn taking in all communicative interactions appears to be rule-governed, the rules may change with the nature of the interaction (e.g., formal vs. informal; Sacks et al., 1974) and with characteristics of the participants (e.g., relative status; Schieffelin & Eisenberg, 1984). Thus, a competent communicator must also evaluate the context to determine the operative turn-taking rules.

Producing and understanding illocutionary acts

An illocutionary act is basically the function an utterance is intended to perform in the communicative interaction (Austin, 1962; Bach & Harnish, 1979; Levinson, 1983; Searle, 1969). In the appropriate circumstances, for example, *I promise that I'll return* could function as a promise, *Move over* as a request for action, *This is a dog* as an assertion, and *What time is it?* as a request for information. At the level of the utterance, the ultimate goal of the speaker is to ensure that the intended illocutionary act is recognizable, whereas that of the listener is to determine which of the range of possible illocutionary acts is actually intended. However, a major problem for both the speaker and the listener is that an illocutionary act is not inherent in either the form or the content of an utterance. For instance, *Could you help?* can function as a request for action or for information. Thus, expressing and understanding illocutionary acts require more than knowledge of language (Abbeduto, 1983; Bach & Harnish, 1979; Searle, 1975). A listener must also make inferences from the speaker's utterance and the context according to relevant pragmatic rules, whereas the speaker must also ensure that the intended illocutionary act is, in fact, inferable from the information available and the pragmatic rules.

Conversational obligations

A participant in a communicative interaction often has the option to speak or not to speak, and if he or she chooses to speak, there are options concerning what to say (Abbeduto & Rosenberg, 1980). Sometimes, however, a participant is obligated to respond if he or she is to be cooperative (Abbeduto & Rosenberg, 1980; Levinson, 1983; Schegloff, 1968). One may, for example, choose to say nothing after a coconversationalist has uttered the assertion *I agree with the president's action*. However, the question *What do you think of the president's action?* obligates the addressee to speak. Moreover, this question severely constrains the addressee's options regarding the content of his or her forthcoming utterance – the addressee must supply the queried information or signal an inability to do so. A listener, therefore, must recognize conversational obligations and possess the means of fulfilling them, whereas a speaker must recognize the obligations his or her utterance establishes, impose only reasonable obligations on the listener (i.e., it must be possible for the listener to meet the obligation the utterance establishes, and fulfilling the obligation should serve a purpose within the conversation), and allow the listener adequate time to respond to the obligation.

Topic generation

The preceding discussion of conversational obligations indicates that a communicative exchange is more than a series of unrelated speaking turns in that some utterances are responses to prior utterances. There is another level at which even longer sequences of utterances are related, however – namely, the level of topic. That is, multiutterance segments of a conversation are usually about the same person, object, or event. Moreover, there is a rule-governed, hierarchical organization to a sequence of topic-related utterances (Keenan, 1974; Ochs & Schieffelin, 1979; Snyder, 1984; Weiner & Goodenough, 1977). A competent speaker, therefore, selects the content of his or her utterance so that it concerns the current topic and is appropriate for that point in the development of the topic (e.g., it represents a logical progression), and a competent listener keeps track of the topic in order to make an appropriate contribution when he or she eventually claims a speaking turn.

Establishing referents

An integral part of understanding what a speaker means by a particular linguistic expression is the identification of his or her intended referents. That is, the listener must determine to which objects, persons, events, and places an expression refers. The speaker, in contrast, must ensure that referent identification is possible. Much of this referential communication can be managed linguistically. The definiteness of the article in a referential expression, for example, indicates whether the referent is being introduced for the first time or whether it has been previously identified. Lexical modifiers can also be used to specify a referent more precisely (e.g., *the small, red, rubber ball* vs. *the ball*). Establishing referents involves more than language, however. It also requires consideration of the context of communication. In particular, there are typically many objects, and thus many potential referents, present in any communicative situation. Thus, a competent speaker must formulate an utterance so that the referent can be discriminated from the nonreferents, whereas a competent listener must evaluate the potential referents and decide which best fits the utterance (Glucksberg, Krauss, & Higgins, 1975; Rosenberg & Cohen, 1966). Notice that the referent need not be specified entirely by linguistic means. For example, when a mature speaker's intended referent is an object that is more visually salient than the potential nonreferents, he or she will frequently produce an utterance that does not, by itself, distinguish the referent from the nonreferents (Clark et al., 1983). In such cases, the speaker will expect the listener to infer that the salient object is the referent, and competent listeners will in fact make such contextually based inferences (Clark et al., 1983).

Using discourse ties

The utterances of a communicative interaction are linked not only by conversational obligations and commonalities of topic but by linguistic devices such as conjunctive adverbs (e.g., *nevertheless, on the other hand*), anaphoric pronouns (e.g., *his, hers, this*), and the definite article *the*. These devices refer to linguistic constituents in sentences other than those in which they occur and create cohesion between utterances (Halliday & Hasan, 1976; Johnston, 1982). To illustrate, *The man tried to help the dog. The dog died* conveys the same content as *The man tried to help the dog. Nevertheless, it later died,* but the latter, which includes linguistic devices for cohesion, sounds more natural. A competent speaker, then, uses discourse ties to facilitate the listeners' search for the intended logical, temporal, and referential relations among the sentences composing the conversation, and a competent listener interprets the speaker's sentences in a way that is consistent with the discourse ties they contain.

Conversational repairs

Communication does not always succeed, not even when the communicators are normal adults. For example, a listener may, because of inattention, fail to perceive a portion of an utterance, or a speaker may evaluate the contextual information incorrectly so that the referents of his or her utterance cannot possibly be identified. When the communicative process breaks down, there are devices available for repairing the breakdown (Abbeduto & Rosenberg, 1980; Gallagher, 1981; Garvey & BenDebba, 1978). For instance, if one fails to hear part of an utterance, *What did you say?* can be used to elicit a repetition of the utterance. A competent listener, then, must identify breakdowns in the communicative process, request a repair, and indicate the nature of the problem as precisely as possible, whereas a competent speaker must recognize and respond to the requests for repair.

Comprehension and production: a methodological note

Each participant in a conversation must function in the roles of speaker and listener and, moreover, must manage each of the component tasks of communication in both roles. The point to be made here is that speaking and listening are not empirically separable processes in many types of communicative interactions. In a conversation, what one says is certainly influenced by how one has understood the preceding utterances of the exchange. For instance, a participant who interprets *I wonder what time it is* as an assertion might see acknowledgment (e.g., *Mm-hmm*) or silence as the only response options, whereas a participant who interprets the same sentence as a request for information will consider the only option to be to say what time it is. Similarly, a conversational participant's understanding of an utterance is frequently made explicit only by the utterances he or she produces. Consider, for example, a case in which a speaker intends *He's tall* to refer to Bob, but the listener thinks Tom is the referent of the sentence. The listener's misinterpretation may be apparent only if the listener subsequently says something like *Yeah, Tom sure is tall*.

The fact that speaking and listening are frequently not empirically separable has an important methodological implication. Specifically, it is often impossible to ascribe "blame" for a participant's poor communicative performance to deficient speaker or listener processes. For instance, a conversational participant who fails to respond to a question may have done so because he or she incorrectly interpreted the question as an assertion or because he or she interpreted the question appropriately but lacked the skills necessary to formulate the response. The former would be a problem in comprehension, the latter a problem in production. Notice that distinguishing between speaking and listening failures can be difficult in experimental situations as well as in more natural communicative situations. For example, experimental procedures that focus on productive aspects of communication often elicit speech in response to linguistic input, with the input requiring the subject's comprehension. The studies reviewed in subsequent sections should be interpreted with this problem in mind.

The bases of linguistic communication

In the preceding section, we briefly described some of the component tasks a person must manage to be considered a competent communicator. One of those tasks is the comprehension of illocutionary acts. Here we consider the knowledge bases and skills that enable a person to comprehend illocutionary acts. This task illustrates the varied and complex nature of the skills and knowledge bases underlying communication. The reader should note that, although our analysis of illocutionary act comprehension is intuitively plausible and consistent with the work of other theorists, parts of it are somewhat speculative. Moreover, our analysis should be taken as an idealized version of the process of illocutionary act comprehension. Specifically, it is unlikely that each of the skills and knowledge bases we discuss is involved in every instance of illocutionary act comprehension. For example, we suggest below that listeners consider several alternative illocutionary acts before arriving at the one intended. This is not always true. In familiar communicative situations or given highly familiar utterances, the intended illocutionary act may be arrived at without consideration of alternatives. Nevertheless, we believe that a listener must possess the knowledge bases and skills outlined in order to understand illocutionary acts in all situations and for all utterances.[1]

As indicated previously, an illocutionary act is basically the function an utterance performs in the communicative exchange. The illocutionary act a speaker can express via a given form is constrained by the propositional content assigned to the form by the grammar. Nevertheless, the same expression can be used to perform several different illocutionary acts. *I'll close the door,* for example, may be intended as an assertion, a promise, or a warning.

To illustrate how a listener might identify an illocutionary act, consider the following situation. Mary has been working in her garden for several hours on an extremely hot day. Joe comes out of the house and into the garden drinking a glass of lemonade. Mary wants Joe to get her some lemonade and to this end says, *It sure is hot*. Although Mary is making a request, her sentence is a declarative, a form conventionally used to make an assertion. Joe first considers an assertion interpretation. He decides, however, that Mary is not merely asserting something but intends to perform some other illocutionary act. Joe makes this decision because it is obvious to both him and Mary that it is hot, and therefore Mary would be unlikely to intend her utterance as an assertion of this fact. That is, Mary, being a cooperative conversational partner, would not produce an utterance that conveys no new information. Because Joe knows that heat plus physical labor leads to thirst, he reasons that Mary is probably thirsty. He further reasons that his drink has signaled the availability of something to drink and that, while Mary is busy, his standing there indicates his availability for action. Joe, therefore, opts for a request interpretation since such an interpretation is consistent with the fact that Mary is a cooperative conversationalist (i.e., Joe did not know that Mary wanted him to do something before the utterance, and thus the utterance does provide new information).

The identification of Mary's requestive intent in the preceding example, and the comprehension of illocutionary acts in general, require a number of abilities and knowledge bases. A listener must have internalized the grammar of the language and be able to use that knowledge to determine propositional contents for linguistic expressions. This is clearly demonstrated in the garden scenario. The listener's first step is to consider and reject the possibility that the speaker intends to assert the obviously true proposition assigned to the utterance by the grammar. Moreover, the propositional content indicates that the illocutionary act actually intended has some connection to the hot weather. The grammar, then, allows the listener to determine the propositional content of the utterance and thereby eliminate some illocutionary acts from consideration.

Illocutionary act comprehension also requires several general information-processing skills. One is the ability to draw inferences. That is, the listener must be capable of arriving at a conclusion about the speaker's intent by reasoning from evidence. In the preceding example, the speaker's requestive intent is not inherent in the message *It sure is hot* since there are many contexts in which this sentence would not function as a request for a drink. Nor is the requestive intent directly available in any aspect of the context. Simply observing that Mary was working, for example, would not tell Joe that she wanted him to bring her a drink; she might want some sunglasses, she might want him to replace her as the gardener, and so on. The utterance and the context are certainly clues to speaker intent, but the listener must go beyond the information given and reason deductively from these clues to the intent.

Despite its apparent ease and automaticity, the inferential process frequently requires the derivation and evaluation of several hypotheses about the speaker's intent. In particular, a listener may sometimes have to deduce several potential il-locutionary acts and test each against the utterance and relevant context. In the garden scenario, for instance, the listener arrives at the request interpretation only after considering the contextual plausibility of an assertion interpretation. Fur-thermore, a listener may have to test several hypotheses about what information constitutes the "relevant" context, since it is clear that not every conceivable as-pect of a situation is useful for identifying the speaker's illocutionary act. In the garden scenario, for example, how does the listener know that the fact that he is wearing bermuda shorts is not relevant context? The answer is that he may not – at least not initially. The listener might have thought at first that his attire was relevant context. However, because he could find no interpretation that would fit both this fact and other aspects of the context such as the heat and his possession of lem-onade, he concluded that his attire was irrelevant. A listener, then, must be flexible enough to reject unsatisfactory solutions and persistent enough to continue the in-ferential process until an illocutionary act that "fits" the utterance and the dimen-sions of the context determined to be relevant is identified.

Another cognitive ability involved in the comprehension of illocutionary acts is the ability to integrate multiple sources of information. For instance, in order to identify the requestive intent of *It sure is hot* the listener had to coordinate four types of information: auditory-linguistic (i.e., the acoustic signal corresponding to the speaker's utterance and the associated propositional content), visual (i.e., the visible indications of the speaker's manual labor), tactile (i.e., the perceptible consequences of air temperature), and knowledge of the world (i.e., knowledge of the physiological consequences of heat plus physical exertion).

Other cognitive abilities that may be involved in illocutionary act comprehen-sion include those typically referred to as "metacognitive." Metacognition con-cerns the ability to reflect on and purposefully control one's cognitive processes (Campione, Brown, & Ferrara, 1982). These abilities may be involved in the com-prehension of illocutionary acts in three ways. First, listeners must be strategic in the sense of analyzing the task the speaker presents them and determining its re-quirements. For example, the listener in the garden scenario had to recognize that he was confronted with a task whose goal was the identification of illocutionary acts (as opposed to, say, memorization of the surface form of the speaker's utter-ance) and that this goal required inference making. Second, the identification of illocutionary acts requires that listeners engage in comprehension monitoring; that is, they must determine when they have understood the speaker and when they have not. The listener in the garden scenario, for example, could have stopped "working" with the assertion interpretation of the utterance – after all, he had identified an illocutionary act. However, he evaluated this interpretation, found it to be lacking, and then continued the inferential process until the request interpre-tation was reached. Third, illocutionary act comprehension would appear to de-pend on the metacognitive abilities involved in executive control. Executive control refers to the selection and use of cognitive processes and the accessing of various knowledge bases in a goal-directed fashion (Campione et al., 1982). For instance, a listener must be capable of retrieving both linguistic knowledge and knowledge about the world (e.g., that thirst results from heat plus physical exertion) when needed.

A social-cognitive skill necessary for the comprehension of illocutionary acts is the ability to take another person's perspective (i.e., to determine what another knows, feels, or sees). In particular, only contextual information that is shared by speaker and listener can be relevant to the listener's task. To illustrate, assume that in the garden scenario there was no lemonade left and that the listener, but not the speaker, was aware of this fact. In this case it would be inappropriate for the listener to conclude that, because there was no lemonade, the speaker could not have intended *It sure is hot* as a request for lemonade. Information the speaker is not privy to is not a useful clue to his or her intent. A listener, then, must be able to take the speaker's perspective so as to determine what contextual information is shared and thus potentially relevant for identifying illocutionary acts.

Mature illocutionary act comprehension also requires adequate knowledge of the world (Rice, 1984). More precisely, listeners frequently must draw on what they have learned about the world in order to determine a speaker's intent. The listener in the garden scenario, for example, would not have attributed the correct requestive intent to *It sure is hot* if he had not known that thirst is the likely result of physical exertion plus heat.

The comprehension of illocutionary acts also requires knowledge of pragmatic rules (Abbeduto, 1983; Abbeduto, Davies, & Furman, 1986; Bach & Harnish, 1979; Clark, 1979; Levinson, 1983; Searle, 1975). A listener assumes that the speaker is cooperative and adheres to the pragmatic rules and interprets the speaker's utterance accordingly. In particular, the listener searches for the most plausible interpretation of the utterance, where the most plausible interpretation is the one for which the speaker violates no pragmatic rule in the current context. The rule operating in the garden scenario is the "presumption of relevance" (Bach & Harnish, 1979), which requires, among other things, that the speaker's illocutionary act provide an adequate amount of information. If interpreted as an assertion, Mary's utterance would violate this presumption in this context. Because Joe assumes that Mary would not violate this presumption, he decides against this interpretation. He therefore generates a request interpretation and evaluates its plausibility in context. Joe accepts the request interpretation since such an interpretation does not violate the presumption of relevance (i.e., Joe did not know before the utterance that Mary wanted him to do something, and thus an adequate amount of information is provided as required by this rule).

In conclusion, it should be noted that knowledge of pragmatic rules is the only knowledge base or skill we have considered that is strictly communicative. That is, the domain of application for the other skills and knowledge bases we have discussed extends beyond communicative tasks.

Studying the linguistic communicative competence of mentally retarded people

As illustrated in the preceding section, "noncommunicative" skills and knowledge bases (i.e., those that have noncommunicative uses, such as inference-making ability and knowledge of the world) are recruited for communication. Here we consider the implications of this fact for the conceptualization and investigation of the linguistic communicative competence of mentally retarded individuals. To this end, we begin with a brief discussion of the factors that affect children's acquisition of communicative competence.

Factors affecting the development of communicative competence

We can identify two broad classes of factors that affect communicative development. The first includes environmental influences on a child's acquisition of pragmatic rules. One such influence consists of the communicative interchanges in which a child is a direct participant (Rice, 1984; Snow, 1984). Nonparticipant interactions, in which children are observers rather than participants (e.g., as is the case when children watch television), are a second environmental influence on the learning of pragmatic rules. If a child has access to less than optimal direct and/ or nonparticipant interactions, the task of becoming communicatively competent becomes more difficult.

The second class of factors that contribute to the development of mature linguistic communication is composed of what can be called "supporting" competencies. Supporting competencies are those linguistic, cognitive, and social abilities and knowledge bases that are utilized in communication as well as in other, noncommunicative tasks. The ability to draw inferences, for instance, is a supporting competence for communication inasmuch as it is involved in the comprehension of illocutionary acts and in such noncommunicative problem-solving tasks as determining the spatial locations of people and objects (see, e.g., Somerville, Hadkinson, & Greenberg, 1979). Impairments of supporting competencies, whether due to experiential or organismic factors, will have a negative impact on communication. For example, a failure to learn about social concepts such as status will preclude the selection of contextually appropriate linguistic forms for illocutionary acts in many communicative situations; underdeveloped inference-making skills will impair a listener's ability to determine illocutionary acts; deficient perspective-taking skills will prevent a person from accurately identifying shared contextual information, which will, in turn, hinder the comprehension of illocutionary acts; and a failure to acquire certain basic features of the linguistic code can have pervasive effects on many component communicative tasks and may even force the adoption of an alternative method of communication (e.g., a gestural system).

Research questions and methods

It is probable that mental retardation is associated with impaired development of most of the competencies that support communication. Acquisition of the phonological, syntactic, morphological, and semantic components of language begins later and proceeds more slowly in retarded than in nonretarded children (Rosenberg, 1982, 1984), although at least some high-functioning retarded individuals eventually master even some of the most complex features of language (Rosenberg & Abbeduto, in press). Mentally retarded individuals have also been found to be deficient in a variety of cognitive abilities and in their knowledge of the world. In particular, relative to nonretarded chronological age (CA) matches, retarded people are slower at executing basic mental operations such as scanning the contents of working memory (Maisto & Baumeister, 1984), encoding visually presented stimuli (Merrill et al., 1985), and making semantic category decisions (Davies, Sperber, & McCauley, 1981; Merrill, 1985; Sperber & McCauley, 1984); fail to employ task-appropriate strategies such as rehearsal consistently and spontaneously (Brown, 1974); are poor in metacognitive activities and executive control processes (Campione et al., 1982); and are deficient in most of the domains of world knowledge measured by psychometric tests (Krishef, 1983; Robinson & Robinson, 1976). As for competence in the domain of social cognition, Simeonsson, Monson, and Blacher (1984) suggest that, compared with nonretarded CA matches, retarded children and adults are deficient at spatial, conceptual, and affective perspective taking (i.e., knowing what the other person sees, thinks, and feels, respectively).

The fact that mentally retarded people are characterized by slowed and/or incomplete development in most, if not all, of the cognitive, social, and linguistic competencies that support communication has important implications for the conceptualization and investigation of their communicative development. In particular, if interest is in describing the extent and nature of retarded people's communication problems, as is the case in the studies reviewed in this chapter, the most appropriate question for mental retardation researchers is *not* whether the development of communication is impaired in this population. This question is problematic for two reasons. First, the impairments that mark retarded people's acquisition of the competencies that support communication ensure that their communicative development will occur more slowly than that of nonretarded people. Thus, the answer to this question is certain to be yes. Second, this question entails an exclusive focus on communicative performance with no concern for a retarded person's concurrent level of functioning in any of the competencies that support communication. However, without examining the relation between the subjects' communicative performance and their supporting competencies, it is impossible to determine whether poor communicative performance is indicative of a true communicative problem or is merely another reflection of some linguistic, cognitive, and/or social deficit. A true communication problem would be indicated if the poor communicative performance of retarded individuals could not be accounted for solely by deficits in their supporting competencies. Thus, a better question for mental retardation researchers to address is, instead, whether the extent and nature of the impairment in communicative development are completely predictable from impairments in the development of supporting competencies. By "predictable" we refer only to cases in which there is a positive relation between communicative performance and maturity in a supporting competency such that developmental improvements in the latter are invariably associated with improvements in the former. An inverse relation between the two domains would not be predictable in the way we intend.

The question we have formulated has both theoretical and practical importance. Regarding theory, investigating the association between impairments in communicative development and impairments in the acquisition of another, noncommunicative competence can help us to decide whether the organismic and experiential factors responsible for development are different across the two domains. Assume, for example, that the development of illocutionary act comprehension is found to be more impaired than some aspect of nonverbal cognitive development in retarded people. This would suggest, among other things, that the set of organismic and environmental conditions necessary for the normal development of illocutionary act comprehension is partly different from that underlying normal nonverbal cognitive development. That is, a lack of predictability between the impairment in some facet of communicative development and the impairment in the acquisition of relevant supporting competencies suggests that the conditions necessary for normal development differ in important ways across the two domains. Notice, however, that predictability across the domains does not imply that the factors responsible for development in each are identical.

As for practical matters, examination of the relation between communicative development and development in other areas of psychological functioning can aid in the selection of an approach to remediation. For example, finding that communicative development is more impaired than cognitive development in retarded persons would suggest that they have not acquired the pragmatic rules possessed by nonretarded children with the same cognitive abilities and/or that they fail to utilize their supporting cognitive competencies for communicative tasks. In this case, remediation of communication deficiencies would have to focus on teaching pragmatic rules and/or encouraging the use of supporting cognitive abilities for communication. Training in new cognitive skills would not be needed to improve communicative performance. A different intervention would be necessary if communicative development and cognitive development were found to be equally impaired in retarded individuals. In this case, remediation of communicative deficiencies might require an equal emphasis on improving cognitive functioning and on teaching pragmatic rules.

Investigating the relation between impairments in communicative development and those in other domains of psychological functioning requires a methodological approach that has, unfortunately, seldom been employed. One feature of this approach is the necessity of obtaining information about the subjects' developmental status in selected areas of linguistic, social, and/or cognitive functioning in addition to assessing their communicative performance. Ideally, the area(s) of psychological functioning selected as the standard(s) against which to evaluate communicative performance should be those that have the greatest potential to illuminate the nature and causes of retarded people's communication difficulties, namely, the competencies that support the aspect of communicative performance in which the researcher is interested. If it is found, for example, that retarded individuals are poorer at inferring illocutionary acts than would be predicted from their inference-making performance in other noncommunicative (e.g., spatial reasoning) tasks, we could conclude that the former is especially problematic for them and that deficient inferential ability was not the cause of this problem. In contrast, finding that retarded people are developmentally less advanced at inferring illocutionary acts than at making moral judgments would be somewhat less informative. It would indeed show that this aspect of communication is especially problematic for them, but no explanations of their communicative problem would be ruled out, because there is no reason to believe that the ability to make moral judgments is involved in the comprehension of illocutionary acts. From a practical standpoint, however, researchers may not know precisely what linguistic, social, and/or cognitive abilities are engaged by the communicative task of interest, or the supporting competencies may be known but may be too numerous or difficult to assess. One solution to this problem is to employ global measures of linguistic, cognitive, or social maturity, such as mental age (MA) or mean length of utterance (MLU), which are likely to be highly positively correlated with the supporting competencies of interest.

A second feature of this approach is that it requires evaluating the communicative performance of the retarded subjects against comparable data from normally developing individuals. That is, one must know what communicative performance is typical for nonretarded individuals who have achieved the same developmental status as the retarded people selected for study on the linguistic, social, and/or cognitive supporting competencies of interest. Without such normative data, it is impossible to determine whether communicative acquisitions are predictable from developments in supporting competencies.

A third feature of this approach concerns the developmental period for which communicative performance is to be investigated. In particular, questions about the relation of impairments in communicative development to impairments in other areas of psychological development require that the retarded individuals selected for study be in the developmental period during which the communicative skills in question emerge *in nonretarded people,* where developmental period is defined in terms of maturity in supporting competencies. That is, studying only people who have moved beyond this period can lead to the conclusion that the development of a particular skill was not impaired in retarded individuals when, in fact, it was. To illustrate, consider how one would select subjects for a study of the attainment of Stage VI sensorimotor functioning by retarded people. Intellectually normal children exhibit Stage VI performance near 1½ to 2 years of age (Brainerd, 1978). If the sensorimotor task performance of retarded adults with MAs of 10 years is compared with that of MA- or even CA-matched nonretarded subjects, one would likely find that the groups performed similarly. Such a study would force the erroneous conclusion that sensorimotor *development* is not impaired in mentally retarded people when, in fact, it is (see Klein & Safford, 1977). Questions about the development of Stage VI abilities require studying individuals with MAs closer to 1½ to 2 years.

In the approach we are advocating, then, a researcher must first identify, on the basis of previous research, the developmental period during which significant progress toward mastery of the communicative skill(s) of interest occurs in the nonretarded population and then select individuals within that period for study. Notice that there are large differences among normally developing individuals in age of acquisition for most communicative skills and, moreover, acquisition is often set at vastly different ages across studies due to task differences (Shatz, 1983). Consequently, the approach outlined will typically entail selecting a sample of subjects that spans a fairly wide developmental period, the period being defined as the time during which the majority of normally developing people move from a lack of the communicative skill of interest to mastery of it.

To summarize, the approach we have outlined involves studying retarded and nonretarded people matched on one or more measures of social, linguistic, and/or cognitive functioning at each of several developmental levels, the levels spanning the period during which the communicative skill of interest is thought to emerge in intellectually normal individuals. An example of this approach is a study of illocutionary act comprehension by Abbeduto et al. (1986). Because the literature on the development of illocutionary act comprehension in intellectually normal children suggests that important advances occur between the ages of 5 and 9 years, Abbeduto et al. selected groups spanning this period. In particular, developmental level was a factor in the design, retarded and nonretarded subjects at each of the levels of 5, 7, and 9 years being included. The retarded and nonretarded groups were matched on nonverbal MA. IQ was held constant across MAs within the retarded and nonretarded groups. The subjects' receptive linguistic competence was also assessed. This design allowed Abbeduto et al. to examine, cross sectionally, achievements in illocutionary act comprehension in relation to advances in non-verbal cognitive maturity and receptive linguistic competence. (This study is described in greater detail in the section on context and the comprehension of illo-cutionary acts.)

It should be noted that the Abbeduto et al. study represents only one way in which the approach outlined can be implemented. There are alternatives. The developmental pattern characteristic of a group can be determined by cross-sectional or longitudinal study. The design can be factorial, with developmental level and/ or intelligence as the factors, or correlational. One may directly assess and compare the communicative performance of both retarded and nonretarded subjects or, instead, assess only mentally retarded subjects but compare the pattern of development observed for them with that reported in the literature for nonretarded people at the same developmental level(s). Other instantiations of the approach we have outlined are also possible.

There are several other basic questions that researchers interested in mental retardation must address and that can be successfully investigated by the approach we have outlined. For example, are some aspects of communicative competence more impaired than others in mentally retarded individuals? Variation in the extent or nature of the impairment across communicative skills would be of theoretical interest in that it would suggest that communicative competence actually consists of several separable competencies, with at least partly different sets of factors responsible for the development of each. The answer to this question is of practical importance in that one may wish to direct the greatest effort toward remediating more severely impaired skills. Questions about differential impairment across communication skills can be investigated by employing a variation of the methodology already proposed. In this case, the necessary comparison is between the patterns of development for different aspects of communicative competence rather than, or in addition to, the comparison between development in communicative competence and development in another domain of psychological functioning.

A question closely related to the previous one asks whether there are distinct profiles of communicative deficits in the retarded population. That is, assuming that linguistic communication is actually the product of several separate sets of communicative skills, we can ask whether there are certain profiles, or patterns, of strengths and weaknesses across communicative skills (of all those possible) that tend to be associated with mental retardation. For example, as will be discussed in greater detail in the section on basic communication skills, it appears that turn-taking proficiency, success in fulfilling conversational obligations (e.g., by answering questions), and the extent of active participation in a conversation (e.g., as evidenced by the frequent production of questions) are all correlated. In particular, some retarded adults are poorer than their peers at turn taking and ful-filling obligations and are passive conversational participants, whereas others are more active participants who are highly skilled at turn taking and fulfilling obligations. The answer to this question will allow the greatest proportion of our resources to be directed toward designing programs of remediation for those profiles most frequently associated with mental retardation. The design of effective remediation, however, will require identification of the determinants of the profiles that occur. Whatever their source, the identification of profile differences requires the assessment of more than a single communicative skill and also demands the assessment of other, noncommunicative domains of functioning. Thus, the methodology already outlined is well suited to addressing this question.

Ultimately, the most important question to be investigated concerns the nature of the organismic and environmental variables that are responsible for the course of communicative development characteristic of mentally retarded persons. As we have indicated, the approach that we have presented in this section, although it is basically a methodology for describing communicative development, can be helpful in this regard. In particular, it can indicate whether the environmental and organismic factors underlying the development of a particular communicative skill are different from those responsible for a given cognitive, linguistic, or social development, and/or whether the factors underlying development vary across communicative skills. However, additional research, employing a variety of methodologies, will be needed to identify the specific factors involved. In fact, little is known about the causes of communicative development in retarded persons, in large part because the course of development has been adequately described for so few aspects of linguistic communicative competence.

Research on linguistic communication in the mentally retarded

In this section, we critically review recent, representative studies of linguistic communication in mentally retarded children and adults and evaluate the extent to which they address appropriate research questions and the adequacy of their methods.

Referential communication

Until recently, the bulk of research on the linguistic communicative competence of mentally retarded people has been concerned with the referential component of communication, that is, with how speakers indicate, and listeners select, the person, place, or thing to which an utterance refers. Most such studies have employed a variation of the laboratory procedure developed by Glucksberg and Krauss (Glucksberg et al., 1975; Glucksberg & Krauss, 1967) to study the development of referential communication skills in nonretarded children. The procedure is as follows. One member of a dyad, the speaker, is given an array of objects or pictures, one of which is arbitrarily designated as the referent. The listener receives the same array. The communicative situation is a non-face-to-face one; that is, the speaker and listener are separated by an opaque partition so that the speaker can see neither the listener nor the listener's array and vice versa. The speaker's task is to formulate a verbal message that enables the listener to pick out the referent from the nonreferents. The listener has to select an object or picture on the basis of the speaker's utterance or indicate when an utterance is inadequate for that purpose (e.g., by saying *I can't tell which one you mean*).

Longhurst (1974) used this procedure to study non-face-to-face referential communication in institutionalized retarded adolescents who were divided into three groups on the basis of severity of retardation (IQs 40–55, 56–69, and 70–90). The groups were matched on CA and thus differed in MA as well as IQ. Dyads were formed with the members matched on sex and IQ. Sets of unfamiliar nonsense designs served as the object arrays. Pretesting and pretraining ensured that the subjects were able to discriminate the stimuli perceptually and understood the requirements of the task.

Performance on Longhurst's measures of communicative skill (i.e., number of correct design choices by the listener, length of the speaker's verbal description, and diversity of the speaker's vocabulary) improved with increased IQ, although the pattern of significant group differences varied somewhat across measures. Even for the highest-functioning dyads, however, the listener's choices were correct on only half of the trials on the average. Longhurst claimed that the performance of nonretarded adult dyads, in contrast, could be expected to be nearly perfect. Moreover, normally developing children reach nearly adult competence on this type of referential task by 8 or 9 years of age (Glucksberg et al., 1975). The fact that many of Longhurst's highest-level subjects probably had MAs of 8 years or above suggests that the skills involved in referential communication may be especially impaired in mentally retarded persons; that is, their performance in this domain of communication may be poorer than would be predicted from their level of cognitive functioning.

The results of several additional studies led Longhurst to conclude that the poor performance of the dyads in the original study was due principally to impaired speaker, not listener, skills. Moreover, Longhurst (1972, 1974) has suggested that the failures of retarded speakers in referential tasks are due to the fact that they are egocentric and thus produce idiosyncratic messages (i.e., messages that are meaningful to them but not to their listeners).

Several problems limit the conclusions that can be drawn from Longhurst's work. One is that the retarded subjects may simply have lacked the linguistic knowledge (e.g., vocabulary) required to formulate accurate descriptions; that is, their poor performance may have reflected deficient linguistic competence rather than deficient communicative competence. The use of familiar referents and nonreferents describable by words and phrases known to be within the linguistic competence of retarded speakers would eliminate this problem. Another problem concerns the overall level of difficulty of the task. In particular, it has been suggested (e.g., Sperber & McCauley, 1984) that retarded individuals have less processing capacity to devote to any task than do nonretarded people. It is possible that processing capacity limitations exist even when the retarded are compared with MA-matched nonretarded people. If this is true, retarded–nonretarded differences are likely to increase as the difficulty of the task increases and the processing capacity of the retarded, but not the nonretarded, subjects is exceeded. The use of especially difficult to discriminate and describe nonsense designs in the Longhurst study, then, might have produced a "cognitive overload." Thus, the poor performance of Longhurst's subjects might have reflected, not a communicative deficit, but a more general cognitive deficiency. Rueda and Chan (1980) have offered a similar criticism of the Longhurst study.

Beveridge and Tatham (1976) avoided some of the problems that plagued the Longhurst (1972, 1974) studies by using trios of pictures of simple scenes (e.g., a girl cutting a cake) as the stimulus arrays in their study of non-face-to-face referential communication. The speakers were six male adolescents similar in IQ to Longhurst's lowest-level subjects. Each subject served with every other subject as both speaker and listener. A pretest demonstrated that all subjects could produce and comprehend verbal descriptions of the pictures. The informativeness of the speaker's utterance (from the listener's perspective) and the correctness of the listener's picture selection were the dependent measures.

Beveridge and Tatham found that the subjects were often unsuccessful in referential communication, even though, according to the pretest, they had the linguistic ability to produce and understand the verbal descriptions involved. Note, however, that it cannot be concluded from these results that referential communication is more impaired in the retarded than is strictly linguistic ability. An adequate test of this hypothesis requires comparison of the retarded subjects' referential performance with that of nonretarded children matched to them on linguistic ability. However, such normative data are not available in the literature and are not provided by Beveridge and Tatham. Consequently, it is impossible to determine whether the referential task performance of the retarded subjects is predictable from their level of linguistic ability. Moreover, Beveridge and Tatham found that subjects whose performance was initially poor showed substantial improvement over trials in both speaker and listener roles. This suggests that their difficulties may have stemmed, not from deficient communicative competence, but from a failure to understand the requirements of the task. A final result of this study was that good speakers tended to be good listeners and vice versa.

Rueda and Chan (1980) conducted a series of studies to determine the reasons for the poor referential communication performance of retarded people in the studies discussed. The subjects were adolescents with IQs that ranged from 35 to 50. Dyads matched on sex, CA, and IQ were constituted. In order to limit the cognitive and linguistic demands of the task, pairs of pictures of familiar objects served as the stimulus arrays. Moreover, a pretest indicated that the subjects could produce the appropriate object labels.

The dyads performed well (i.e., the listener nearly always chose the correct member of the stimulus pair) when the referent and nonreferent were from different categories (e.g., a bear and a bell). Their performance was poor, however, when the referent and nonreferent were from the same category but differed in their physical attributes (e.g., a clown with a hat and one without). According to Rueda and Chan, more careful perceptual comparison of referent and nonreferent is required in the latter condition than in the former, and therefore the results indicate that such comparison is problematic for retarded individuals. In a subsequent study, these researchers found that the comparison problems were the speakers', not the listeners'. In contrast to the claims of Longhurst (1972, 1974), however, there was no evidence that the speakers produced egocentric messages.

A problem with the Rueda and Chan study is that we do not know how nonretarded children matched to the retarded subjects on measures of supporting competencies would perform on this task; such data are not provided by Rueda and Chan or by the literature on normal development. Because a comparison of the retarded subjects with developmentally matched nonretarded children is not possible, the issue of whether referent–nonreferent comparison processes are especially problematic for the retarded is not resolved. Moreover, it is not possible to determine from Rueda and Chan's studies whether the comparison deficit is limited to communicative tasks. If the deficit is evident in a broader range of tasks, it is not, strictly speaking, a communicative problem.

In summary, the studies reviewed in this section indicate that retarded individuals perform poorly for their CAs as speakers in the standard, non-face-to-face, referential communication task. There is also some evidence that this aspect of communication is especially problematic for retarded people in that their referential performance is sometimes poorer than would be predicted on the basis of MA. Some evidence also suggests that speaker and listener referential abilities covary. However, the relation between the severity of retardation and referential performance has not been made clear. Nor has the developmental course of referential communication in the mentally retarded been adequately investigated. Moreover, it is not clear whether the referential problems of retarded individuals are strictly communicative. Listener performance seems to have been adequate in the tasks employed, but this is not surprising, given that these tasks have really placed the burden of successful communication on the speaker. There has been little concern with the ability of retarded listeners to help speakers ensure that referent identification is successful by, for example, indicating not only when but how the speaker's utterance is referentially ambiguous.

As the preceding review makes clear, different researchers interested in mental retardation have conceptualized referential communication in much the same way. However, in naturally occurring conversations the task of referential communication can vary dramatically from one situation to another. One obvious variation depends on whether the communicative interaction is a face-to-face one. In a face-to-face interaction, referential communication involves the coordination of linguistic expressions with nonverbal signals such as direction of eye gaze and gestures. Even though face-to-face interactions occur more frequently in retarded people's lives than non-face-to-face interactions, mental retardation researchers have studied only the latter. There is no guarantee that results in non-face-to-face referential tasks are generalizable to face-to-face interactions. Another variation in natural referential communication tasks that researchers have failed to appreciate concerns the specificity of the speaker's message. Normal adult speakers do not always explicitly indicate their referents either linguistically or nonverbally and yet this causes no problems for mature listeners (Clark et al., 1983). For example, given as possible referents two men of average height and one abnormally tall man, a listener will infer that *Look at that guy* refers to the tallest of the trio. Whether mentally retarded listeners draw inferences of this type is not known, although one of the present authors (Abbeduto) has begun investigating this issue. Finally, it is important to note that, in the studies reviewed, referent identification is usually the ultimate goal of the communicative interaction. This is seldom the case in everyday communication. We normally identify referents in order to assert something about them, ask a question about them, and so on. Thus, it is not clear what performance on the referential tasks employed in the studies discussed in this section tells us about performance in this other, more typical situation.

Researchers have become interested in aspects of linguistic communicative competence other than referential communication only in the past six or seven years. This research is reviewed in the following sections.

Basic communication skills

The bulk of recent studies on linguistic communication in mentally retarded people has consisted of descriptive analyses of naturally occurring face-to-face conversation. The aim of these studies has been to determine whether the subjects are in sufficient command of rudimentary communication skills (e.g., those involved in turn taking) to be adequate communicators. The level of mental retardation of the subjects in these studies has ranged from borderline to severe, and primarily only adolescents and adults have been studied. The constraints imposed on the subjects' conversational behavior by the investigators have been minimal. Subjects have been free to determine, for example, the conversational topics, when and how much to participate, the content and illocutionary force of their contributions, and the linguistic forms and vocabulary by which to express their intentions. The conversationalists have been, in general, familiar with each other and have typically functioned at a similar intellectual level.

This naturalistic approach to the study of retarded people's communicative competence has both strengths and weaknesses. One strength is that the subjects themselves decide on the timing, content, and form of their contributions to the conversation, and thus the cognitive demands are minimal. A topic such as nuclear physics will certainly not elicit optimal communicative performance from retarded individuals. Although this is an extreme example, there is currently no a priori method for deciding whether an experimenter-selected topic is too complex for retarded subjects. If, however, subjects select their own topic, as in the naturalistic studies to be reviewed, it is reasonable to assume that they will usually select a topic they can talk about as effectively as their communication skills will permit.

A weakness of the naturalistic approach to studying conversation is, as indicated previously, that it may not allow the locus of inadequate communicative performance to be identified. A subject who fails to respond to a question, for example, may not know that a question obligates a response or may be unable to determine what information the questioner seeks. These would be "listener problems." Alternatively, the subject may recognize the obligation established by the question and realize what information the questioner seeks, but be unable to formulate a response that fulfills these obligations and, moreover, lack the means for indicating this inability. This would be a "speaker problem." Naturalistic, descriptive studies, then, can identify component communicative tasks that are problematic for the retarded, but experimental studies will likely be needed to uncover the locus of the problems.

Abbeduto and Rosenberg (1980) took this naturalistic approach to studying linguistic communication. The subjects were seven mentally retarded adult males with CAs between 20 and 31. Their full-scale IQs ranged from 52 to 81, and performance and verbal IQs, which were available for only four of the subjects, ranged from 72 to 85 and 55 to 89, respectively. One subject was classifiable as moderately retarded, the remaining subjects as mildly or borderline mentally retarded. Estimated MAs ranged from 8 to 13 years and were perfectly correlated with IQs. Etiologies were unknown, except that no subject displayed Down syndrome. Three triads were formed from various combinations of the subjects. The data for the study consisted of three 15- to 45-min audiotaped mealtime conversations for each triad.

A nonretarded comparison group was not included in this study. Instead, the conversations of the retarded subjects were examined for evidence of behaviors that had been shown by previous work in the field to be characteristic of successful conversations between normal adults. Moreover, many of the behaviors selected for study indexed whether the participants were engaged in true conversation or were merely producing collective monologues (Piaget, 1926), and thus this study provided a test of Longhurst's (1972, 1974) claim that retarded people, even mildly retarded ones, are highly egocentric communicators.

Turn taking. Instances of overlap between the turns of different speakers and of one speaker interrupting another are infrequent in normal adult conversation (Duncan & Fiske, 1977; Sacks et al., 1974). Abbeduto and Rosenberg found that the retarded subjects also managed the vast majority of speaker changes appropriately. Overlaps or interruptions occurred in only about 10% of the speaker changes of each triad. Moreover, as in nonretarded adult conversation (Sacks et al., 1974), most overlaps were short (usually less than three words) because one or both participants "stopped short."

The nearly flawless nature of nonretarded adult turn taking is attributable to the fact that speaker change is highly rule governed (Sacks et al., 1974). Two findings suggested that the retarded subjects in the Abbeduto and Rosenberg study followed rules similar to those characteristic of normal adult conversation. One was the occurrence of a "third-party exclusion bias." That is, one person in each triad had far fewer speaking turns than the other members. A similar inequality in the distribution of speaking turns has been observed in the triadic conversations of nonretarded adults (Sacks et al., 1974). Sacks et al. have suggested that this inequality is a by-product of the fact that the availability of "current speaker selects next speaker" techniques (e.g., use of a participant's name) leads to the dominance of *speaker 1–speaker 2–speaker 1* sequences over *speaker 1–speaker 2– speaker 3* sequences. The same inequity in retarded adults' conversations is most likely the result of the same rule system.

The second finding suggesting that retarded and nonretarded adults follow similar rules for turn taking concerns the types of errors that occurred. In particular, Sacks et al. noted that a frequent type of nonretarded adult error is one in which a speaker adds an optional element after what could be the end of his or her turn just as another participant starts to speak. Many of the retarded subjects' errors were also of this type. The following is an example from Abbeduto and Rosenberg (1980) (the arrow indicates the starting point of the overlap):

A: ... where's that new bowling alley of yours ... by the way?
B: ↑ What are you?

Sacks et al. suggest that such errors occur in the conversations of nonretarded adults because the participants are under pressure, if they wish to speak, to claim a turn as soon as it is appropriate to do so. As a result, they sometimes claim the role of speaker at a point that could be, but is not, the end of the current speaker's turn. Apparently, Abbeduto and Rosenberg's subjects operated under similar pressures and were aware of the rules defining the potential ends of turns.

The results of Abbeduto and Rosenberg's analyses indicate that retarded adults in the IQ range studied do not find turn taking to be especially problematic and that they adhere to the same turn-taking rules as do normal adults. Price-Williams and Sabsay (1979) derived similar impressions from their observations of the conversations of severely retarded adults, although they presented no supporting data.

Expressing and responding to illocutionary acts. Normal adults use the linguistic code to perform many different functions, or illocutionary acts. A competent communicator can rely on language to seek or offer information, to indicate future plans, to get another person to believe or do something, to describe his or her own psychological states, to signal a willingness to engage in conversation, and to achieve a host of other communicative ends (Rees, 1978). Abbeduto and Rosenberg examined the conversations of the retarded subjects for evidence of their use of the major types of illocutionary acts found in nonretarded adult conversation. In particular, intelligible speaking turns were scored as *assertions,* if the speaker indicated a belief in a proposition and the intention that the listener take the proposition to be true (e.g., *But you made it*); *commissives,* if the speaker indicated commitment to a future course of action (e.g., *So we're extra late, I'm gonna buy some beer and drink . . .*); *expressives,* if the speaker indicated his feelings about, or evaluated, a proposition (e.g., *She's more important than this lousy meeting*); *questions,* if the speaker sought information (e.g., *Who's invited them?*); and *directives,* if the speaker sought nonverbal behavior from another participant (e.g., *Pass your applesauce*).[2]

Each triad produced all the major types of illocutionary acts. Assertions and questions occurred most frequently, however. These retarded adults, then, were largely concerned with getting their listeners to believe certain propositions and with obtaining information from other participants. Moreover, although relatively infrequent, the occurrence of expressives and commissives indicates that adults with moderate to borderline retardation encode fairly abstract content in their utterances; that is, they can express how they feel about certain propositions and indicate their future plans.

Other investigators (Owings, McManus, & Scherer, 1981; Price-Williams & Sabsay, 1979; Zetlin & Sabsay, 1980) have also found that retarded adolescents and adults across a wide range of intellectual levels express the same types of illocutionary acts as do normal speakers. However, Zetlin and Sabsay found that moderately retarded adults, in contrast to Abbeduto and Rosenberg's subjects, seldom asked questions. It may be, therefore, that the frequency of questioning is lower at lower levels of intellectual functioning. However, the one moderately retarded individual included in the Abbeduto and Rosenberg study did frequently ask questions (approximately one-fourth of his conversational turns contained questions). The discrepancy between studies may be due partly to variations in the settings in which the conversations took place. Zetlin and Sabsay's subjects were involved in unstructured cleanup activities, and questions might have been inappropriate in the context of those activities.

Abbeduto and Rosenberg's analysis of illocutionary acts also considered the relations among the turns of different speakers. In the conversations of normal adults, the illocutionary act conveyed by one conversational participant typically determines the illocutionary act the next speaker chooses to perform. If, for example, one speaker asks a question, the person addressed is obligated to respond and, moreover, the nature of the question specifies the range of permissible responses. Conversational turns that are related in this way are called *adjacency pairs* (Sacks et al., 1974; Schegloff, 1968; Schegloff & Sacks, 1973). Note that adjacency pairs do not consist exclusively of an obligating illocutionary act and the response to it (Abbeduto & Rosenberg, 1980). For example, if one participant makes an assertion, the next speaker is under no obligation to respond, but his or her turn is, nevertheless, typically a reaction to the assertion. The reaction may be to agree with the assertion, to disagree with it, to acknowledge it (e.g., *mm-hmm, oh*), and so on. Abbeduto and Rosenberg determined the extent to which the turns of different speakers formed adjacency pairs. They reasoned that a high proportion of turns in adjacency pairs would be indicative of mature conversational performance: Participants would be exchanging information, and the interaction would be transactional (i.e., each turn would be based on, but add to, a prior turn). A low proportion of adjacency pairs, however, would suggest that the retarded subjects were egocentric and that their "conversation" was akin to a collective monologue. Abbeduto and Rosenberg also examined the types of relations that existed between the turns of the adjacency pairs that did occur.

The findings of the adjacency pair analysis indicated that the retarded adults expressed and responded to illocutionary acts in a nonegocentric, mature fashion. The vast majority of each triad's intelligible speaking turns (between 72 and 92% for the triads summed over sessions) functioned as members of adjacency pairs. Each participant, then, considered what the previous speaker had said when formulating his conversational turn. Moreover, obligating illocutionary acts were nearly always responded to appropriately. Specifically, turns performing the obligating illocutionary acts of questioning, directing, greeting (e.g., *hello*), and summoning (e.g., *hey, Jim*) received appropriate responses between 93 and 97% of the time across the triads (summed over sessions). Thus, the mentally retarded adults in this study recognized the obligations established by a variety of illocutionary acts and possessed the means of correctly fulfilling these obligations. Abbeduto and Rosenberg's subjects were also active conversational participants. Slightly more than half of the adjacency pairs for each triad were initiated by nonobligating turns (i.e., assertions, expressives, and commissives). This means that the majority of their contributions to the conversation were volunteered rather than elicited by conversational obligations. The conversations of the retarded subjects, then, appeared to be nonegocentric and transactional.

Getting better and more information. Two types of conversational turn that occurred quite frequently were the *request for clarification* and the *request for more information*. Both are a type of question and served as responses to several types of illocutionary act. In a request for clarification, one participant, because he or she has not fully understood an utterance, asks the speaker to repeat, rephrase, or confirm his or her interpretation of the speaker's utterance (Gallagher, 1981; Paul

& Cohen, 1984). One retarded subject in the Abbeduto and Rosenberg study, for example, said *We need a good empazation with the phone* in the course of discussing the type of telephone he and his roommate should purchase. The roommate, confused by the nonword *empazation,* requested clarification by asking *What's a . . . ?* The fact that retarded adults in the IQ range studied use this type of request indicates that they are active conversational participants who are concerned with accurately identifying the other participants' messages. Zetlin and Sabsay (1980) have also reported that moderately retarded adults produce requests for clarification. Requesting clarification of problematic utterances is not consistent with a characterization of the retarded adult as egocentric.

In a request for more information, a participant asks a speaker to elaborate in some way on the proposition conveyed by the speaker's utterance. Often the request is for background facts that the original speaker apparently either did not think were relevant or assumed the other participants knew. For instance, one of the subjects, while discussing an upcoming dance and the fact that people from several residential facilities were to attend, said, *They're invited,* to which a second participant replied, *Who's invited them?* The use of requests for more information by retarded adults indicates that they are not egocentric and that they are attempting to build a coherent representation of the events that are the topic of conversation.

Abbeduto and Rosenberg also found that requests for clarification and for more information were as likely to receive appropriate responses as were other types of questions. Similarly, Longhurst and Berry (1975) found that mildly retarded adults were able to respond to requests for clarification that signaled that the referents of their utterances could not be identified. Zetlin and Sabsay's (1980) moderately retarded adult subjects responded appropriately to requests for clarification within the context of naturalistic conversational interactions. Paul and Cohen (1984) found that moderately and mildly retarded adults responded appropriately to different types of request for clarification and, furthermore, their performance was superior to that of autistic adults who were matched to them on IQ. Thus, like normal adults (Garvey & BenDebba, 1978), retarded adults across a wide range of IQs recognize the obligation to respond established by requests for clarification and requests for more information and possess the linguistic means to do so appropriately.

An interesting feature of requests for clarification and requests for more information is that they take priority when they occur in response to another obligating illocutionary act; that is, the request for clarification or for more information must be responded to before the temporally prior obligation is fulfilled (Garvey, 1975). Some of Abbeduto and Rosenberg's subjects used one or both types of request in response to prior obligating turns. This caused no problems for the original speaker; an appropriate reply to a request for clarification or for more information was as likely for those following obligating turns as for those following nonobligating turns. Moreover, the initial obligating turn was typically responded to after the request for clarification or request for more information had been satisfied. Thus, adults with moderate to borderline retardation recognize that conversational obligations can be temporarily suspended under certain conditions.

Maintaining the conversational topic. Intellectually normal adults are capable of engaging in extensive, uninterrupted discussion of a conversational topic (although, in practice, many topics introduced into conversation are short-lived). The participants in a conversation must work together to maintain a topic over an extended number of speaking turns: Each participant must use his or her knowledge of the other participants to introduce topics likely to be of interest to them, be willing to allow other participants to contribute to the conversation, and formulate his or her speaking turns so that the topic will progress (i.e., each turn must add information that is likely to be new for the other participants and appropriate for that point in the development of the topic).

Abbeduto and Rosenberg found that, although some of the topics introduced were discussed only briefly by the retarded subjects, many occupied a good deal of uninterrupted conversational time. The mean number of consecutive turns on the same topic ranged from 7 to 21 across the conversational triads. More important, the longest uninterrupted discussion of a topic by each triad ranged from 36 to 157 turns. Thus, retarded adults can sustain a topic over a significant number of speaking turns. However, this does not tell us about the adequacy of their topic development, in terms of its logical and temporal progression over the course of a conversation, whether they establish necessary background information, and so on. Research on this issue has yet to be conducted.

The results from the studies presented in this section indicate that adults with moderate to borderline retardation are not, in general, egocentric in their communicative behavior. Subjects took turns at speaking; quickly terminated instances of overlap; responded appropriately to the utterances of other participants, even when a response was not obligatory; spoke to get and to give information; sought clarification of problematic utterances; requested more information when it was necessary to understand the events being discussed; and cooperated to maintain conversational topics. This suggests that, contrary to Longhurst's claims, the failures of retarded adults in non-face-to-face referential communication are not due to an unwillingness or inability to consider their listener's needs. The results discussed also indicate that many aspects of mature communicative competence are eventually acquired by many retarded individuals despite cognitive and other limitations. Such communicative skills, therefore, need not be incorporated as objectives in curricula designed to improve communication in the retarded adult with moderate to borderline retardation.

Abbeduto and Rosenberg also examined individual differences in their measures of communicative competence, the extent to which these differences were associated with variations in cognitive maturity (i.e., IQ and MA), and the relations among the communicative measures. Furthermore, Rosenberg and Abbeduto (in press) have investigated the relation between individual differences in communicative performance and linguistic maturity for these subjects. These analyses speak most directly to the basic research questions outlined previously.

Individual differences in communicative competence. Although Abbeduto and Rosenberg's subjects, as a group, proved to be competent communicators, there were individual differences. That is, the subjects had reached different levels of maturity on the various aspects of communicative competence measured. Before we discuss these data, however, a potential objection to analyzing individual differences in conversational performance must be considered. In particular, one might argue that the behavior of each participant in a conversation is affected by the behavior of the others, and thus individual differences are meaningless. If asked a question, for instance, one is obligated to respond, and as mentioned previously, retarded adults consistently respond to such conversational obligations. Actually, however, the behavior of one participant only partially constrains the behavior of the remaining participants. Each participant has several options following any utterance, even an obligating utterance. For instance, confronted with the question *Did you know John went to the store?* one can answer (e.g., *Yes*), combine an answer with an obligating illocutionary act such as a question in the same converstional turn (e.g., *Yes, but do you know why?*), or answer and perform an additional nonobligating illocutionary act such as an assertion in the same turn (e.g., *Yes, I went with him*). Similarly, one can follow an nonobligating turn with no response, an obligating illocutionary act, or another nonobligating illocutionary act. Thus, there can be differences among individuals in the options selected, and these selections are to some extent independent of the behavior of the other participants. An analysis of individual differences in conversational behavior, therefore, can be meaningful.

Abbeduto and Rosenberg found that their subjects could be contrasted in terms of their conversational style, the dimension of difference being defined by the "active" conversationalist at one end and the less mature, "passive" conversationalist at the other. An active conversationalist was one whose turns were frequently responsible for the creation of adjacency pairs. For example, asking a question creates the opportunity for an adjacency pair because it obligates a response, whereas an acknowledgment creates an adjacency pair with a preceding turn, which would not otherwise have been a member of an adjacency pair at all. An active turn, then, was one that performed an obligating illocutionary act or that functioned as a response to a nonobligating turn. A passive turn, in contrast, was one that served as a response to an obligating illocutionary act, was a nonobligating turn that functioned as the first part of an adjacency pair, or was a nonobligating turn that was not a member of an adjacency pair. There were clear differences among the subjects in terms of the proportion of active turns they produced.

Conversational style was related to certain aspects of communicative competence. In particular, subjects who produced the greatest proportion of active turns also made the fewest errors in turn taking and in fulfilling conversational obligations. Thus, the Abbeduto and Rosenberg study indicates that the answer to the question of whether there are distinct profiles of communicative deficits in the retarded population is yes. One possible explanation of these results is that the facets of communication that define the profiles depend directly on one or more of the others for their development. It might be, for example, that a passive conversational style develops as the result of deficits (relative to one's peers) in basic communicative skills. Perhaps problems in reading the signals concerning the times at which speaker change is permissible force the retarded individual to limit conversational participation to responding to obligating illocutionary acts and the occasional production of assertions, expressives and commissives. The direction of causation might be the reverse, however. A longitudinal study that follows retarded individuals over a considerable period of time will likely be required to answer the question, What variables are responsible for the development of these aspects of communicative competence and style in mentally retarded individuals?

No correlation was observed between IQ (or MA) and turn-taking ability, competence in fulfilling conversational obligations, or conversational style. Thus, at least some of the development that occurs in these three aspects of communication is due to factors other than increased cognitive ability and the organismic and experiential variables that underlie cognitive development. Note, however, that the subjects in this study were, for the most part, very high functioning and that the ranges of IQs and MAs were relatively narrow. A wider range of cognitive abilities would almost certainly have produced significant positive correlations between the communicative measures and both IQ and MA.

On the basis of findings such as the above and the results of existing research on linguistic competence in mentally retarded people (see Rosenberg, 1982, for a review), Abbeduto and Rosenberg (1980) concluded that retarded individuals' achievements in the domain of conversational communicative competence tend to outdistance their achievements in the area of linguistic competence. However, data on the linguistic competence of high-level mentally retarded adults are scarce. Moreover, investigators may have underestimated the linguistic achievements of retarded children and adolescents because of the cognitive demands of the controlled observation procedures that most of them have employed (Rosenberg & Abbeduto, in press). Rosenberg and Abbeduto (in press), therefore, have reevaluated this conclusion by examining linguistic characteristics of the conversational turns previously identified by Abbeduto and Rosenberg (1980). In particular, they assessed the subjects' level of mastery of two important aspects of mature linguistic competence: grammatical morpheme (e.g., verb tense and pluralization markers) and complex (i.e., embedded, compound, and conjoined) sentence usage.

The grammatical morphemes that were studied consisted of the 14 items that had been the subject of research by Brown (1973) and others on the development of grammatical morphemes in normal children. Contrary to the findings of previous research using controlled observation procedures (e.g., Lovell & Bradbury, 1967), which had strongly suggested that retarded individuals are especially delayed in grammatical morpheme development, errors in grammatical morpheme usage were infrequent for Rosenberg and Abbeduto's subjects. Thus, high-functioning retarded individuals do eventually master these grammatical morphemes, in spite of the fact that they get off to a very slow start in this domain of linguistic competence (Rosenberg, 1982). What is more, Rosenberg and Abbeduto's results suggest that even moderately retarded individuals may possess the capacity to achieve, eventually, a relatively high level of mastery of grammatical morphemes given that the one moderately retarded subject in the sample used the 14 grammatical morphemes correctly in 94% of the linguistic contexts that required their use.

One of the most striking findings of Brown's (1973) study was that, developmentally, the order of mastery of the 14 grammatical morphemes generalized across subjects. Thus, it is of interest that Rosenberg and Abbeduto (in press) found a significant correlation between Brown's rank order of acquisition and mean percent correct usage in obligatory contexts of the 14 grammatical morphemes, such that the earlier a morpheme developed in young intellectually normal children, the higher was its level of mastery in the retarded subjects. This finding suggests that the process of acquisition for the 14 grammatical morphemes is similar in normally developing children and higher-level and (possibly) moderately mentally retarded individuals.

The more than 1,400 speaking turns that constituted the basic data for the analysis of conversational competence in Abbeduto and Rosenberg (1980) were examined by Rosenberg and Abbeduto (in press) to determine the presence of complex sentences. The percentages of utterances containing such sentences varied from 16 to 40 across subjects. The percentage of speaking turns containing one or more complex sentences varied from 19 to 48. The percentages in question for the moderately retarded subject mentioned above were, respectively, 28 and 32. Overall, 28% of the speaking turns contained one or more complex sentences. The corpus of complex sentences, moreover, contained instances of the majority of the complex sentence structures that are found in adult English grammar (Jacobs & Rosenbaum, 1968).

On the basis of the limited amount of information available in the literature on the development of complex sentences in nonretarded children, Rosenberg and Abbeduto constructed a preliminary seven-level order-of-development scale for complex sentences and applied it to their corpus. At the earliest-to-develop end of this scale are embedded infinitival complements whose subject is identical to that of the matrix clause (e.g., *Try to brush her hair*). Levels 6 and 7 of this scale contain, respectively, instances of two simple sentences joined by a subordinating conjunction, as in *John will be late for school if he misses the 8:30 train,* and instances of the use of more than one sentence combining operation in a single complex sentence, as in *The landlord decided to take a club and try to knock him down.*

With the exception of level 5 structures (subject noun phrase relative clauses, subject noun phrase complements, nominalizations), Rosenberg and Abbeduto's corpus of complex sentences contained tokens of all of the levels in their scale of complex sentences. However, the relative frequency of occurrence of sentences at the various developmental levels did not correlate with the assumed order of development, although the rank order of the various levels in frequency of use was highly similar across subjects. Moreover, the level of complexity most frequently used was level 7, the most complex level of the scale. Thus, complex sentence use in this study very likely depended on situational factors that were similar across subjects rather than on the developmental difficulty of the sentences.

Complexity, however, as defined by order of acquisition, may have played a role in determining what complex sentences were combined into the structures of level 7. At this level, Rosenberg and Abbeduto did observe a significant correlation between developmental level and complex sentence use. Specifically, the early-acquired complex sentences were used more frequently than the late-acquired complex sentences as constituents of the most complex sentence type of the scale. The patterns of use, moreover, were significantly similar across subjects. In sum, then, it appears that the present subjects were constrained to some extent in combining complex sentences by the developmental difficulty of those sentences.

Mean percent correct usage of the 14 grammatical morphemes and relative frequency of complex sentence use did not correlate significantly in the Rosenberg and Abbeduto study. Nor did morpheme use correlate significantly with a measure of overall communicative competence based on the relative frequencies of turn-taking errors, failures to fulfill obligations, and active turns reported by Abbeduto and Rosenberg. However, a significant negative correlation was found between relative frequency of complex sentence use and overall communicative competence such that the higher a subject's ranking on overall communicative competence, the lower was the percentage of use of complex sentences. But the subjects produced few turn-taking errors and communication failures on turns containing complex sentences. Moreover, although all but one of the subjects produced relatively more dysfluent complex sentences than dysfluent simple utterances, neither of these variables correlated significantly with overall communicative competence. And although relatively more dysfluent than simple utterances, complex sentences were not difficult to comprehend; that is, only a small percentage of the 441 complex sentences identified by Rosenberg and Abbeduto were followed by requests for clarification.

IQ was not significantly correlated with morpheme or complex sentence use, a finding that can be most readily attributed to the relatively limited range of scores in the present study on this estimate of cognitive competence, coupled with the relatively high level of mastery of grammatical morphemes and complex sentences that was observed.

Clearly, Rosenberg and Abbeduto's (in press) findings are not consistent with Abbeduto and Rosenberg's (1980) earlier claim that retarded individuals' achievements in the domain of conversational communicative competence outdistance their achievements in the area of linguistic competence. It appears now that high-functioning retarded (and possibly moderately retarded) adults have overcome most of their earlier lag in linguistic development, as estimated from an examination of grammatical morpheme and complex sentence use in an unconstrained, cognitively undemanding, familiar situation involving conversational participants who know each other and who possess similar intellectual abilities. Moreover, their findings offer additional support for the observation that communicative competence involves factors other than linguistic knowledge, inasmuch as neither morpheme nor complex sentence use predicted (in the sense of being positively related to) overall communicative competence. Indeed, complex sentence use was inversely related to overall communicative competence. It remains to be determined, however, why those who had low scores on overall communicative competence tended to produce relatively more complex sentences than the high scorers did.

Rosenberg and Abbeduto's correlational findings across subjects must be considered tentative, given the small number of subjects in their sample and the narrow range of scores for some of the variables. The findings in question are interesting, however, and certainly worthy of further investigation.

Context and the expression of illocutionary acts

Language provides a variety of forms for conveying any given illocutionary act. The forms differ on such dimensions as how explicitly or politely they convey the act. For example, a directive (i.e., the intention that the person addressed engage in a particular nonverbal behavior) can be expressed by an imperative (e.g., *Open the window*) or by an interrogative (e.g., *Could you open the window? Would you open the window?*), but the former is less polite than the latter. Competent speakers choose linguistic forms for their illocutionary acts according to relevant dimensions of the communicative context. For instance, a polite form is typically used to express a directive when the addressee is of higher status than the speaker (Ervin-Tripp, 1977; Gordon & Ervin-Tripp, 1984; James, 1978; Rice, 1984) or when the directive imposes on the addressee (Gordon & Ervin-Tripp, 1984; James, 1978).

The selection of contextually appropriate linguistic forms requires several sets of pragmatic knowledge and ability. First, the speaker must know that the relation between illocutionary acts and linguistic forms is flexible (i.e., there exists a one-to-many mapping of illocutionary acts onto linguistic forms) and recognize the illocutionary acts that each form can express. Second, the speaker must be able to distinguish among the linguistic forms in his or her repertoire in terms of the explicitness, politeness, and so on, with which they perform particular illocutionary acts. Third, the speaker must know which contextual dimensions are relevant to linguistic form selection.

Abbeduto (1984) examined the contextual appropriateness of the linguistic forms retarded and nonretarded children select for their illocutionary acts by eliciting directives from them in role-playing situations that depicted different types of communicative context. Because context-sensitive form selection requires, in addition to pragmatic knowledge, a certain level of linguistic competence (i.e., a speaker must have command of the linguistic forms that have the potential to convey a particular illocutionary act) and cognitive competence (i.e., a speaker must be able to analyze communicative contexts correctly so as to determine, for example, addressee status), the retarded and nonretarded groups were matched on measures of these competencies. In particular, the retarded children, who ranged in CA from 6.7 to 9.9 years, were compared with normally developing kindergarten children, with the groups matched on measures of nonverbal MA and the linguistic maturity of their spontaneous speech (i.e., MLU, mean independent clause length, and the ratio of syntactically different utterance types to tokens). In addition, all subjects participated in a prompted production task to ensure that the retarded and nonretarded groups could produce an equal number of the yes–no interrogatives commonly used to convey directives (e.g., *Would you play cars with me? Could you play cars with me? Won't you play cars with me?*). Both groups, then, had similar repertoires of linguistic forms available for coding directive intents and possessed similar cognitive and linguistic skills, and thus the question addressed by this study was whether the level of context-sensitive form selection evidenced by the retarded children was predictable from their level of cognitive and/or linguistic functioning.

In the role-playing situations, the subjects, who were tested individually, heard a series of four-sentence paragraphs about two people. Each paragraph depicted events that served as the context for the production of a directive by one story character, the speaker, to the other story character, the addressee. The subject was to pretend to be the speaker for each situation. The following is an example of the paragraphs:

> The man is hitting your new doll. He is breaking it. He shouldn't do that. You want the man to stop hitting your doll.

A directive was elicited by asking the subject what he or she would say to the addressee (e.g., *What would you say to the man?*). Two dolls were presented, one representing the subject and the other the addressee.

The contexts depicted in the paragraphs varied on three dimensions thought to be important determinants of mature communicative performance. One dimension was the age of the addressee; the addressee was identified as either an adult or a 2-year-old child. In the former case, the doll representing the addressee was larger than the speaker doll, whereas in the latter case, it was smaller than the speaker doll. Competent communicators, on the average, select more polite directive forms for addressees who are older than they are than for addressees who are younger (Ervin-Tripp, 1977; Gordon & Ervin-Tripp, 1984; James, 1978; Rees, 1978). The second contextual dimension on which the paragraphs varied was the cause of the directive. Specifically, the directive was either caused by the prior behavior of the addressee (e.g., the addressee had imposed on the speaker) or caused solely by desires of the speaker that were independent of the addressee's behavior (e.g., the speaker sought a favor). Directives that seek to end an imposition tend to be expressed via less polite forms by competent speakers than are directives that seek an imposition (Gordon & Ervin-Tripp, 1984; James, 1978). The third dimension of context that varied was the goal of the directive. In particular, the directive sought either social interaction with the addressee (e.g., the speaker wanted the addressee to draw with him or her), the performance of an action by the addressee (e.g., the speaker wanted the addressee to put some books away), or termination of the addressee's current action (e.g., the speaker wanted the addressee to stop singing). Speaker goals have been shown to be relevant to the comprehension processes of communicatively competent individuals (Clark, 1979) and thus were expected to influence language production as well. Addressee age, directive cause, and directive goal were included in a factorial design and varied within subjects so that the interactive effects of these factors on choice of directive form could be determined.

It was found that the retarded and normally developing groups employed an equally wide range of linguistic forms for their directives. In particular, the retarded group used a mean of 4.7 different forms, which was not significantly different from the mean of 5.1 for the nonretarded group. The relation between illocutionary acts and linguistic forms, therefore, is as flexible for retarded children as for nonretarded individuals with comparable cognitive and linguistic abilities, at least at the developmental levels studied. This finding is in sharp contrast to that of Abbeduto and Rosenberg (1980), who found that the mapping between illocutionary acts and linguistic forms was essentially one-to-one in the naturally occurring conversations of their retarded adult subjects. For example, most of their retarded adults expressed directive intentions via the imperative exclusively. One explanation for the discrepancy between the studies is that appropriate opportunities for the variable expression of directives or other illocutionary acts did not occur in the Abbeduto and Rosenberg study. This is the explanation that Abbeduto and Rosenberg offered for their subjects' apparent lack of flexibility. A second possibility, however, is that the variety of forms used for directives actually decreases with CA for mentally retarded individuals. This could result if parents and teachers failed to support retarded children's use of forms other than the imperative, the prototypical form for directives. An analysis of the communicative environment of the retarded child and its effects on directive production, examined longitudinally, will be needed to evaluate this explanation.

In order to examine the influence of the three contextual variables on the selection of linguistic forms, politeness scores were assigned to the directives the children produced on the basis of their form using adult norms of the politeness of 24 commonly used directive forms (see Abbeduto, 1984, for the norms). The results indicated that the three contextual variables interacted in a complex fashion to determine the choice of linguistic form and, moreover, had similar effects on the choices of the retarded and normally developing children. In particular, directives seeking an addressee action and those attempting to initiate social interaction were more polite when caused by speaker desires than when caused by addressee behavior. Directives seeking an action were also more polite when the addressee was an adult rather than a child. Directives attempting to halt an addressee action were more polite when caused by speaker desires than when caused by addressee behavior, but only if the addressee was a child.

Retarded and intellectually normal children at the developmental levels studied, then, appropriately consider dimensions of the context that are important determinants of mature communicative performance when selecting linguistic forms for their directives. Moreover, they distinguish among the linguistic forms in their repertoires on the basis of adult-defined politeness and categorize communicative interactions as to the level of politeness they merit.

On the basis of the results discussed, Abbeduto concluded that the development of the pragmatic abilities and knowledge involved in the selection of contextually appropriate forms is no more impaired in mentally retarded persons than is their cognitive and linguistic development. Thus, according to Abbeduto, the question of whether the impairment in the development of communication is predictable from impairments in other aspects of psychological functioning can be answered affirmatively for this facet of pragmatic competence.

Such a conclusion is tentative, however, given that Abbeduto's subjects may not have spanned the period during which the pragmatic skills and knowledge in question emerge in nonretarded children. More precisely, one could argue that the individuals studied might have been beyond the developmental period in which the pragmatic competencies in question emerge in nonretarded children. As an illustration, assume that normally developing children attain the degree of context-sensitive form selection Abbeduto observed at age 3 years but that retarded children do not reach the same point until the MA of 4 years. If this were true, the difference in relative rate of development between retarded and nonretarded children would not have been detectable in Abbeduto's study because his subjects had MAs between 5 and 6 years. Nevertheless, there is evidence that Abbeduto's conclusions may be correct. In particular, his subjects may not actually have been beyond the developmental period during which advances in context-sensitive form selection normally take place. For example, research by Axia and Baroni (1985) and Gordon and Ervin-Tripp (1984) indicates that the use of several dimensions of context, including directive goal, begins only at age 5 or 6 in nonretarded children. Abbeduto's nonretarded subjects, then, may have only recently learned, or been in the process of learning, to use the contextual dimensions studied, and thus major retarded–nonretarded differences in relative rate of communicative development, if they existed, would probably have been detectable.

An analysis of individual differences indicated that choice of directive form was determined not only by relevant dimensions of the communicative context but also by certain biases of the speaker. More precisely, many children, both retarded and nonretarded, had a single preferred linguistic form for their directives that they produced frequently, although seldom exclusively, and in several different types of context. Which form was preferred appeared to depend partly on the cognitive and linguistic maturity of the speaker, since within both the retarded and nonretarded groups, those children who preferred a polite form (e.g., *Would you please draw with me?*) were more cognitively and linguistically advanced than children who preferred impolite forms (e.g., *Draw with me*).

Two findings indicated that cognitive and linguistic maturity far from perfectly predicted form preferences, however. The first was that more normally developing children exhibited a form preference than did retarded children. The second was that the retarded and nonretarded children differed as to what forms they preferred. Specifically, approximately half of the normally developing children who demonstrated a preference preferred an interrogative-plus-*please* form (e.g., *Would you please stop singing? Could you stop singing, please?*), whereas the remainder preferred one of several imperative forms that did not include *please* (e.g., *You stop singing, Stop singing*). According to the adult norms collected by Abbeduto, these two classes of forms define the polite and impolite end points of the adult politeness scale. The form preferences of the retarded subjects, in contrast, were not restricted to the end points of the adult politeness scale, but ranged over the entire scale. These retarded–nonretarded differences in choice of form occurred despite the fact that the groups were matched in terms of cognitive and linguistic competence.

Although both retarded and nonretarded children were sensitive to relevant dimensions of the communicative context, then, they frequently relied on different linguistic forms for their directives despite possessing similar repertoires of forms from which to choose. Moreover, this difference in form use cannot be attributed to variations in cognitive and/or linguistic competence. However, the different social histories inherent in any comparison of retarded and nonretarded individuals may be responsible for the group differences. In particular, adults may address different forms or the same forms but at different rates to retarded and nonretarded children functioning at the same developmental level. There is some evidence that this is true between the MAs of 2 and 4 years (Cardoso-Martins & Mervis, 1981; Jones, 1977; Maurer & Sherrod, 1985).

The results of the Abbeduto study also suggest that communicative competence is not a unitary ability but a set of abilities, the variables responsible for development differing somewhat across abilities. In particular, the consideration of relevant contextual information, the use of a variety of linguistic forms to express the same illocutionary act, and the evaluation of the social properties of the forms (e.g., politeness) were highly positively related to cognitive and linguistic maturity. The development of form preferences, in contrast, depends in important ways on factors other than cognitive or linguistic competence and the set of organismic and experiential factors that determine cognitive and linguistic development.

Several other studies have examined the use of context by mentally retarded speakers. These studies, however, have been concerned with global effects of context on speaking behavior. Thus, contextual influences on the propositional contents conveyed, the illocutionary acts intended, and the forms used to express messages have typically not been distinguished in these investigations.

The ability of retarded speakers to consider the characteristics of their listener was investigated by Hoy and McKnight (1977). The subjects were mentally retarded individuals who ranged from 6 to 18 years in CA and from 2 to 8 years in MA. Each subject explained a board game he or she had been taught to a naive listener. The dependent measures included verbal productivity, vocabulary diversity, the occurrence of attention-getting devices, and the use of gestures. Hoy and McKnight found, among other things, that both high- and low-functioning speakers adjusted their communications according to the intellectual level of their listener. Without a normal comparison group, however, we do not know whether the adjustments made by Hoy and McKnight's subjects were appropriate given their developmental level, and thus we cannot address the issue of the predictability of communicative development from the level of linguistic, social, and/or cognitive competence achieved.

Bedrosian and Prutting (1978) found that their four severely retarded adult subjects exhibited different communicative styles (primarily in terms of their questioning behavior) with different conversational partners (e.g., a child, a speech pathologist). It cannot be concluded from these results, however, that the subjects actively adjusted their style of communicating according to partner characteristics. Their behavior may have been nothing more than a passive response to the communicative behavior of their partners (Abbeduto, 1984). For example, a speech pathologist, in contrast to a child, would be likely to demand highly specific communicative behaviors from retarded adults. Moreover, it is not clear whether the contextually based adjustments made by Bedrosian and Prutting's subjects were appropriate for their developmental level given the lack of comparable nonretarded data. Thus, this study did not address the question of whether the impairment in communicative development is predictable from impairments in other domains of functioning.

Finally, Price-Williams and Sabsay (1979) reported that the speaking behavior of severely and profoundly retarded Down syndrome adults was appropriately constrained by the communicative context. This claim, however, is based only on these researchers' impressions, not on objective data.

Context and the comprehension of illocutionary acts

The same linguistic expression can perform different illocutionary acts in different contexts. Consequently, linguistic competence (i.e., knowledge of the phonological, syntactic, morphological, and semantic components of language) is not sufficient to enable a listener to determine which illocutionary act is actually intended by the speaker. A listener must also draw inferences from the propositional content of the expression and features of the communicative context according to relevant pragmatic rules. Abbeduto et al. (1986) investigated the development of this listener behavior in nonretarded children and mentally retarded children and adolescents.

Abbeduto et al. (1986) examined the retarded and nonretarded listeners' understanding of *yes–no* interrogatives (e.g., *Could you open the telephone book? Would you make the pencil roll?*). The interrogatives employed can be used as questions (i.e., requests for information) or as directives (i.e., requests for action). Normal adult listeners infer that one interpretation or the other (or both) is intended according to whether the answer to the question is obvious or nonobvious (Clark, 1979). That is, normal adults assume that speakers are cooperative and thus ask questions only to gain information they lack. Consequently, they are more likely to reach a directive interpretation (and less likely to arrive at a question interpretation) for the interrogative when the answer to the question it poses is obvious than when it is nonobvious. Abbeduto et al. manipulated answer obviousness by varying both the contextual information available to the listener and the type of propositional content the speaker's interrogative conveyed in ways known to influence normal adult comprehension. The interpretations of the retarded and nonretarded listeners were then examined as a function of the variations in context and propositional content so as to determine whether they had appropriately inferred the illocutionary act intended from these two sources of information.

In the experimental task, an adult speaker addressed the interrogatives one at a time to the subjects, who were tested individually. Each interrogative concerned the performance of an action on a three-dimensional object placed before the subject and within his or her reach. For example, a telephone directory was presented and the speaker said, *Could you open the telephone book?* The subject was instructed to respond by simply doing or saying what the speaker wanted. The seating arrangement prevented the subject from seeing the speaker and thus from responding on the basis of inadvertent nonverbal cues from the speaker.

How a subject interpreted an interrogative was indicated by the type of response made. A response such as *yes, no,* or a nod of the head was scored as an answer and taken to indicate that the listener had interpreted the interrogative as a question, whereas the (successful or unsuccessful) performance of the action mentioned in the interrogative or a verbal indication of noncompliance, such as *I can't* or *The telephone book won't open,* was seen as reflecting the fact that the listener had arrived at a directive interpretation.[3] Responses that included both an answer and either an action or a verbal indication of noncompliance were seen to reflect the fact that the listener understood the interrogative to convey both a question and a directive. Several dependent measures, each an estimate of the likelihood of a directive or a question interpretation, were derived.

To ensure that the subjects' responses accurately reflected how they had interpreted the speaker's sentence, filler sentences were administered along with the experimental interrogatives. Half of the filler sentences were interpretable only as directives (e.g., *Turn the glass upside down*), and half were interpretable only as questions that had nonobvious answers (e.g., *Did you ever play this game with your mother?*). Abbeduto et al. reasoned that if subjects were unable or unwilling to respond in a manner consistent with their interpretation of a sentence (e.g., by saying *yes* to a question or by performing an action in response to a directive), such problems would be reflected in responses to the unambiguous filler sentences as well as in responses to the experimental interrogatives. However, all subjects consistently responded with appropriate actions or verbal statements of noncompliance to filler items intended as directives and with verbal or nonverbal indications of affirmation or negation to filler sentences intended as questions. Thus, the subjects' overt responses provided an accurate measure of their comprehension.

Answer obviousness in the Abbeduto et al. (1986) study was jointly determined by the context and the propositional content of the speaker's interrogative. The contextual determinant of answer obviousness was the degree of compatibility between the action mentioned in the interrogative and the physical properties of the referent. Specifically, the referent was either well suited (the *compatible object* condition) or poorly suited (the *incompatible object* condition) to the successful performance of the action. If, for example, the action in the interrogative was *roll*, a baseball would have been a compatible object and a shoebox an incompatible object. A pilot study with subjects comparable to those included in the actual experiment was conducted to ensure that the latter judged object–action compatibility as intended. Propositional content was varied by including three types of interrogative: the *Could you?* (e.g., *Could you roll the shoebox?*), the *Would you?* (e.g., *Would you open the telephone book?*), and the *Do you think?* (e.g., *Do you think you could turn the flashlight on?*). A factorial design was employed with the two factors varied within subjects.

On the basis of a pilot study with nonretarded adult listeners, Abbeduto et al. developed a model of the effects of compatibility and interrogative type on answer obviousness. In particular, they reasoned that, as a question, *Could you?* asks about the listener's ability to perform an action. The answer to this question is obvious for compatible objects but nonobvious for incompatible objects. For example, anyone who recognizes that roundness permits rolling knows the answer to *Could you roll the baseball?* However, the answer to *Could you roll the shoebox?* is not obvious. Rolling a shoebox might be possible, but more effort would be required and success less certain than would be the case for rolling a baseball.[4] Consistent with this account, normal adult listeners treat *Could you?* as a question in the incompatible condition but as a directive in the compatible condition.

As a question, *Would you?* asks about the listener's willingness to perform the action named. Abbeduto et al. hypothesized that, as a listener's ability to act becomes less certain, his or her willingness to act becomes less obvious as well. Therefore, as in the case of *Could you?* mature listeners interpret the *Would you?* interrogative as a question more often, and as a directive less often, in the incompatible condition than in the compatible condition. However, in contrast to *Could you?* answer obviousness is not determined solely by compatibility for *Would you?* In particular, listeners are cooperative and thus may be willing to attempt most actions, even some they are not certain they can perform successfully. Consequently, the answer to a question about a listener's willingness to perform an action may be fairly obvious even for incompatible objects. Competent listeners, therefore, interpret *Would you?* as a question less often, and as a directive more often, than *Could you?* and, moreover, the effect of compatibility on their comprehension is less pronounced for the former interrogative than for the latter.

As a question, *Do you think?* concerns the listener's thoughts about his or her ability to perform the action named in the interrogative. A listener's thoughts on this matter are, presumably, least obvious when his or her ability to perform the action is most unclear. Therefore, *Do you think?* is interpreted as a question more often, and as a directive less often, for incompatible objects than for compatible objects by normal adult listeners. In contrast to the *Could you?* interrogative, however, compatibility is not the only determinant of answer obviousness for *Do you think?* Specifically, another person's thoughts are, strictly speaking, never completely obvious because they are not directly observable. Consequently, the answer to a question about a listener's thoughts may be less than obvious even for a compatible action. As a result, competent listeners are less influenced by compatibility for *Do you think?* than for *Could you?* interrogatives and, moreover, reach a question interpretation more often, and a directive interpretation less often, for the former interrogative than for the latter.

Twelve individuals with moderate to borderline mental retardation and 12 non-retarded children were included at each of the nonverbal MAs of 5, 7, and 9 years. The mean CAs of the MA 5, 7, and 9 retarded subjects were 10.2, 13.0, and 15.3 years, respectively. Nonverbal IQ was held constant, through subject selection, across the MA levels within the retarded and the nonretarded groups. Mental age was correlated with CA, therefore, for the retarded subjects as well as for the non-retarded subjects. The Test for the Reception of Grammar (Bishop, 1982), or TROG, which is a standardized test of receptive linguistic competence, was also administered. Abbeduto et al. had originally intended to include groups of re-tarded and nonretarded subjects who were matched on mean TROG score at each level of nonverbal MA. This turned out to be impossible because most of the re-tarded subjects tested had TROG scores that were significantly lower than pre-dicted on the basis of their nonverbal MAs. However, differences in the subjects' TROG scores were not associated with variations in performance on the experi-mental task. This study is a clear example of the design advocated earlier: The developmental course of illocutionary act comprehension, examined cross sec-tionally, was compared in retarded and nonretarded individuals who were matched on measures of the competencies that support communication.

Analyses of the subjects' responses to the experimental interrogatives uncov-ered differences between the retarded and nonretarded groups as well as differ-ences associated with MA. Regarding the retarded–nonretarded difference, com-patibility type and interrogative type were found to affect listeners' interpretations of the experimental interrogatives at all levels of MA and for both the retarded and nonretarded groups. More specifically, directive interpretations were, overall, most frequent for *Would you?* sentences and least frequent for *Do you think?* sen-tences and more frequent in compatible contexts than in incompatible contexts, whereas question interpretations exhibited the converse pattern across conditions. However, interrogative type and compatibility type were found to have an inter-active effect on normally developing children's sentence interpretations. In partic-ular, the effect of compatibility on the frequency of their directive interpretations varied in magnitude across interrogative types in much the same way as seen for nonretarded adults, the contextual manipulation having the largest, most consist-ent effect on the interpretation of *Could you?* sentences. In contrast, no interaction of context type and interrogative type was seen for the retarded subjects.

By the age of 5, then, nonretarded children, like normal adults, inferred illo-cutionary acts from communicative contexts and the propositional contents of sen-tences according to pragmatic rules and, moreover, they coordinated these sources of information appropriately. That is, the inferences they drew from a particular piece of contextual information depended on co-occurring properties of the speak-er's sentence such as the particular modal auxiliary it contained. In contrast, al-though the mentally retarded listeners inferred illocutionary acts from relevant properties of contexts and propositional contents, they did not coordinate these sources of information: The same inferences were drawn in a given context regardless of the type of interrogative the speaker produced.

The fact that the retarded and nonretarded subjects were matched on nonverbal cognitive maturity indicates that the coordination of propositional content information and contextual information is especially problematic for mentally retarded people; that is, their performance in this area of communication is not predictable from the maturity of their supporting competencies. This conclusion is supported by the observation that level of receptive linguistic competence was not correlated with performance on the experimental task. Similarly, Leifer and Lewis (1984) found that 3- and 4-year-old retarded children with Down syndrome responded differently to the illocutionary intent of maternal interrogatives than did nonretarded children matched to them on MLU. Apparently, then, the set of organismic and environmental conditions necessary for the normal development of some facets of illocutionary act comprehension is, to a significant extent, different from that required for the normal acquisition of linguistic and cognitive competence.

As to the MA difference, Abbeduto et al. (1986) found that, although all children used the communicative context to help decide between the question and directive readings of the interrogatives, the effect of compatibility on the frequency of directive interpretations was greater at higher MAs. This suggests that the children made more consistent use of context as they aged and their cognitive and linguistic abilities improved. Despite the relatively mature pragmatic skills and knowledge evidenced by even the youngest nonretarded children, then, there is developmental change during the early school years. That the retarded listeners made progress in the consistency of their use of context without concomitant improvements in their coordination of contextual and propositional content information suggests that these two aspects of illocutionary act comprehension are somewhat independent; that is, each involves partly different knowledge and skills and, moreover, somewhat different sets of organismic and environmental factors may be responsible for the normal development of each.

Discussion

On the basis of an analysis of the tasks that competent communicators normally manage, we identified the questions that researchers interested in linguistic communication and mental retardation should be asking and how they should be addressed. We also tried to show how answers to these questions will contribute to our understanding of communicative development in the normal population as well as in disordered populations. Finally, we reviewed research on linguistic communication in mentally retarded individuals and evaluated it in relation to the questions outlined. Although research on this topic has been limited and there are many gaps in our knowledge, it is possible to draw several tentative conclusions

about the development of linguistic communicative competence by mentally retarded persons.

Several of the studies reviewed concerned the relation between the extent of impairment in communicative development and maturity in other areas of psychological competence. Turn-taking proficiency, the ability to recognize and fulfill the
obligations established by illocutionary acts, the ability to be an active participant
in conversation, the existence and nature of preferred linguistic form–illocutionary act pairings, and proficiency in the coordination of propositional content and
contextual information when inferring illocutionary acts are not completely predictable from one's level of linguistic competence or nonverbal cognitive maturity.
This reaffirms our previous analysis of communication as involving not only linguistic and cognitive abilities, but social and strictly communicative abilities
(i.e., knowledge and use of pragmatic rules). Moreover, these findings suggest
that the acquisition of these communicative competencies depends on a set of
oganismic and experiential factors that is at least partially different from those underlying the development of linguistic competence and nonverbal cognition. In
contrast, the development of the ability to select contextually appropriate linguistic forms for illocutionary acts and to use, although not in a coordinated fashion,
linguistic (i.e., type of propositional content) and contextual information to infer
illocutionary acts appears to be highly related to nonverbal cognitive maturity, at
least during the developmental periods studied. That is, retarded and nonretarded
individuals matched on global measures of nonverbal cognitive ability exhibit
equivalent performance on tasks assessing these aspects of communicative competence. The ability to select linguistic forms in a contextually sensitive manner
is also correlated with level of (productive) linguistic competence during the early
school years. In contrast, although improvements in the consistent use of context
to infer illocutionary acts during the developmental period studied keep apace with
cognitive advances, these improvements are unrelated to the acquisition of (receptive) linguistic competence. The latter proceeds more slowly, although high-functioning and, perhaps, moderately retarded individuals eventually master even the
most complex facets of language. This suggests that at least partly different sets
of organismic and/or experiential factors underly developments in linguistic competence, on the one hand, and developments in cognitive ability and the use of
context in illocutionary act comprehension, on the other, for the developmental
period examined.

The results of the studies reviewed tell us not only about the developmental relation between communication and other domains of functioning, but also about
the relation among different aspects of communicative competence. In particular,
the ability to respond to conversational obligations, the ability to take turns appropriately, and the extent of active conversational participation are highly related and
may even depend on one another for their development. In contrast, the use of
context in linguistic form selection, on the one hand, and the existence and nature

of preferred linguistic form–illocutionary act pairings, on the other, develop at least partly independently of one another. Similarly, developments in the consistent use of context to infer illocutionary acts during the school years are independent of those underlying the coordination of contextual and linguistic information to infer illocutionary acts. Because communicative competence is not a unitary ability, mental retardation and other disorders can be associated with distinct profiles of communicative deficit.

There is much that is not known about the development of linguistic communicative competence in mentally retarded persons. As we have pointed out, only tentative conclusions can be drawn from many of the studies reviewed owing to methodological limitations. The most common limitations are the unavailability of comparable normative data and a failure to sample developmental levels that span the period during which the communicative acquisition of interest is known to occur in people without intellectual impairments.

Other gaps in our knowledge exist as well, however, First, the communicative performance of retarded subjects has been assessed in only a few of the many types of situations in which communication can occur. Shatz (1983) has pointed out that normally developing children are extremely variable in their use of communicative knowledge and skills across situations. Such variation can be due to differences in the noncommunicative demands of the situations (i.e., some situations pose noncommunicative difficulties that prevent the child from exhibiting a certain feature of his or her communicative competence) or to the fact that children have to learn the range of situations in which a particular pragmatic rule or skill is applicable. Such variation across communicative situations is also likely to be characteristic of retarded people. Therefore, the communicative performance of retarded individuals must be assessed in more situations than have been sampled to date before a complete picture of their communicative competence will emerge. Second, for the most part, only mildly and moderately retarded individuals have been studied. Thus, we know little about more severely impaired individuals. We do not know, for example, whether their communicative development is merely more delayed than that of mildly or moderately retarded people or whether there are qualitative differences as well. Third, primarily older children and adults functioning at fairly advanced developmental levels have been studied. As a result, we know little about the transition from prelinguistic to linguistic communication or other early communicative developments (but see Coggins, Carpenter, & Owings, 1983, and Greenwald & Leonard, 1979, for exceptions). Fourth, there are still component communicative tasks for which the performance of mentally retarded people has not been thoroughly investigated. The production and comprehension of discourse ties are but one example. In this regard, a preliminary study by Abbeduto (1981) suggests that retarded adults may make greater use of syntactic marking of given and new information during listening than do nonretarded adults. Thus, further research on this aspect of communication is certainly warranted and may uncover important retarded–nonretarded differences. We have indicated elsewhere in the chapter questions that remain concerning several other component tasks. Finally, the mental retardation literature has had little to say about the causes of impaired communicative development. The research reviewed here has indicated potential similarities and differences in the organismic and experiential determinants of development among communicative skills and between particular communicative skills and cognitive and linguistic competencies. However, specific linguistic, social, or cognitive advances or particular environmental and organismic conditions have not been linked to the development of particular communicative abilities. In all fairness, however, it must be added that such causal connections have yet to be identified in work on normally developing children (see, e.g., Shatz, 1983). These gaps must be filled if we are to plan adequate programs to improve the communicative performance of retarded people and at the same time construct an adequate theory of communicative development, since such a theory must be applicable to all persons, retarded and nonretarded alike.

Notes

1. More technical discussions of illocutionary acts and their comprehension can be found in Abbeduto (1983), Bach and Harnish (1979), Gibbs (1983, 1984), Levinson (1983), and Searle (1979).
2. The categories employed by Abbeduto and Rosenberg differed somewhat from those of Searle (1969, 1975). In particular, Searle's expressive category included only social routines, such as *Thank you, I'm sorry,* that convey the speaker's feelings. Searle included nonroutine expressions of the speaker's feelings, such as *She's more important,* in the category of assertion. However, the conclusions of Abbeduto and Rosenberg hold even if Searle's categories are employed.
3. Verbal responses such as *I can't* or *It won't work* are seen as reflecting a directive interpretation because a pilot study demonstrated that listeners make these same responses to imperatives that are interpretable only as directives (e.g., *Roll the shoe box*). The listeners in the pilot study included a representative sample of the subjects from the actual experiment as well as other individuals who were similar to them on such variables as CA, IQ, and MA.
4. Only reasonable incompatible actions were included. By a reasonable action, we mean one that is not obviously impossible, such as throwing an object through a solid wall, or one that would embarrass the listener, such as putting on ridiculous clothing.

References

Abbeduto, L. (1981, April). *Retarded and nonretarded adults' use of given and new information in discourse production and comprehension.* Paper presented at the 14th Annual Gatlinburg Conference on Mental Retardation and Developmental Disabilities, Gatlinburg, TN.
Abbeduto, L. (1983). Review of *Linguistic communication and speech acts* by K. Bach & R. M. Harnish. *Applied Psycholinguistics, 4,* 397–407.
Abbeduto, L. (1984). Situational influences on mentally retarded and nonretarded children's production of directives. *Applied Psycholinguistics, 5,* 147–66.

Abbeduto, L., Davies, B., & Furman, L. (1986, April). *Inferring illocutionary acts from contextual and linguistic information: Age and intellectual differences*. Paper presented at the Conference on Human Development, Nashville, TN.

Abbeduto, L., & Rosenberg, S. (1980). The communicative competence of mildly retarded adults. *Applied Psycholinguistics, 1*, 405–26.

Austin, J. L. (1962). *How to do things with words*. New York: Oxford University Press.

Axia, G., & Baroni, M. R. (1985). Linguistic politeness at different age levels. *Child Development, 56*, 918–27.

Bach, K., & Harnish, R. M. (1979). *Linguistic communication and speech acts*. Cambridge, MA: MIT Press.

Bedrosian, J. L., & Prutting, C. A. (1978). Communicative performance of mentally retarded adults in four conversational settings. *Journal of Speech and Hearing Research, 21*, 79–95.

Beveridge, M. C., & Tatham, A. (1976). Communication in retarded adolescents: Utilization of known language skills. *American Journal of Mental Deficiency, 81*, 96–9.

Bishop, D. (1982). *Test for reception of grammar*. Available from author, University of Manchester, England.

Brainerd, C. J. (1978). *Piaget's theory of intelligence*. Englewood Cliffs, NJ: Prentice-Hall.

Brown, A. L. (1974). The role of strategic behavior in retardate memory. In N. R. Ellis (Ed.), *International review of research in mental retardation* (Vol. 7, pp. 55–111). New York: Academic Press.

Brown, R. (1973). *A first language: The early stages*. Cambridge, MA: Harvard University Press.

Campione, J. C., Brown, A. L., & Ferrara, R. A. (1982). Mental retardation and intelligence. In R. J. Sternberg (Ed.), *Handbook of human intelligence* (pp. 392–490). Cambridge University Press.

Cardoso-Martins, C., & Mervis, C. B. (1981, April). *Maternal speech to prelinguistic Down's syndrome children*. Paper presented at the 14th Annual Gatlinburg Conference on Mental Retardation and Developmental Disabilities, Gatlinburg, TN.

Clark, H. H. (1979). Responding to indirect speech acts. *Cognitive Psychology, 11*, 430–77.

Clark, H. H. Schreuder, R., & Butterick, S. (1983). Common ground and the understanding of demonstrative reference. *Journal of Verbal Learning and Verbal Behavior, 22*, 245–58.

Coggins, T. E., Carpenter, R. L., & Owings, N. O. (1983). Examining early intentional communication in Down's syndrome and nonretarded children. *British Journal of Disorders of Communication, 18*, 99–107.

Davies, D., Sperber, R. D., & McCauley, C. (1981). Intelligence-related differences in semantic processing speed. *Journal of Experimental Child Psychology, 31*, 387–402.

Duncan, S., Jr., & Fiske, D. W. (1977). *Face-to-face interaction: Research methods and theory*. Hillsdale, NJ: Erlbaum.

Ervin-Tripp, S. (1977). Wait for me, roller skate! In S. Ervin-Tripp & C. Mitchell-Kernan (Eds.), *Child discourse* (pp. 165–88). New York: Academic Press.

Ervin-Tripp, S. (1978, September). Whatever happened to communicative competence? In *Proceedings of the Linguistic Forum*, Champaign–Urbana: University of Illinois.

Gallagher, T. (1981). Contingent query sequences within adult–child discourse. *Journal of Child Language, 8*, 51–62.

Garvey, C. (1975). Requests and responses in children's speech. *Journal of Child Language, 2*, 41–64.

Garvey, C., & BenDebba, M. (1978). An experimental investigation of contingent query sequences. *Discourse Processes, 1,* 36–50.

Gibbs, R. (1983). Do people always process the literal meanings of indirect requests? *Journal of Experimental Psychology: Learning, Memory, and Cognition, 9,* 524–33.

Gibbs, R. (1984). Literal meaning and psychological theory. *Cognitive Science, 8,* 275–304.

Glucksberg, S., & Krauss, R. M. (1967). What do people say after they have learned how to talk? Studies of the development of referential communication. *Merrill-Palmer Quarterly, 13,* 309–16.

Glucksberg, S., & Krauss, R., & Higgins, E. T. (1975). The development of referential communication skills. In F. D. Horowitz (Ed.), *Review of child development research* (Vol. 4, pp. 305–45). University of Chicago Press.

Gordon, D., & Ervin-Tripp, S. (1984). The structure of children's requests. In R. L. Schiefelbusch & J. Pickar (Eds.), *The acquisition of communicative competence* (pp. 295–321). Baltimore, MD: University Park Press.

Greenwald, C. A., & Leonard, L. A. (1979). Communicative and sensorimotor development Down's syndrome children. *American Journal of Mental Deficiency, 84,* 296–303.

Grossman, H. (Ed.). (1973). *Manual on terminology and classification in mental retardation, 1973 revision.* Washington, DC: American Association on Mental Deficiency.

Halliday, M. A. K., & Hasan, R. (1976). *Cohesion in English.* New York: Longman.

Hoy, E. A., & McKnight, J. R. (1977). Communication style and effectiveness in homogeneous and heterogeneous dyads of retarded children. *American Journal of Mental Deficiency, 81,* 587–98.

Jacobs, R. A., & Rosenbaum, P. S. (1968). *English transformational grammar.* Waltham, MA: Blaisdell.

James, S. L. (1978). Effects of listener age and situation on the politeness of children's directives. *Journal of Psycholinguistic Research, 7,* 307–17.

Johnston, J. R. (1982). Narratives: A new look at communication problems in older language-disoriented children. *Language, Speech, and Hearing Services in the Schools, 13,* 144–55.

Jones, O. H. M. (1977). Mother–child communications with prelinguistic Down's syndrome and normal infants. In H. R. Schaffer (Ed.), *Studies in mother–child interaction* (pp. 379–401). New York: Academic Press.

Keenan, E. O. (1974). Conversational competence in children. *Journal of Child Language, 1,* 163–83.

Klein, N. K., & Safford, P. L. (1977). Application of Piaget's theory to the study of thinking in the mentally retarded: A review of research. *Journal of Special Education, 11,* 201–16.

Krishef, C. H. (1983). *An introduction to mental retardation.* Springfield, IL: Thomas.

Leifer, J. S., & Lewis, M. (1984). Acquisition of conversational response skills by young Down syndrome and nonretarded young children. *American Journal of Mental Deficiency, 88,* 610–18.

Levinson, S. C. (1983). *Pragmatics.* Cambridge University Press.

Longhurst, T. M. (1972). Assessing and increasing descriptive communication skills in retarded children. *Mental Retardation, 10,* 42–5.

Longhurst, T. M. (1974). Communication in retarded adolescents: Sex and intelligence level. *American Journal of Mental Deficiency, 78,* 607–18.

Longhurst, T. M., & Berry, G. W. (1975). Communication in retarded adolescents: Response to listener feedback. *American Journal of Mental Deficiency, 80,* 158–64.

Lovell, K., & Bradbury, R. (1967). The learning of English morphology in educationally subnormal special school children. *American Journal of Mental Deficiency, 72,* 609–15.

Maisto, A. A., & Baumeister, A. A. (1984). Dissection of component processes in rapid information processing tasks: Comparison of retarded and nonretarded people. In P. Brooks, R. Sperber, & C. McCauley (Eds.), *Learning and cognition in the mentally retarded.* Hillsdale, NJ: Erlbaum.

Maurer, H., & Sherrod, K. B. (1985, March). *Context of directives given to young normally developing and Down syndrome children: Mental age vs. chronological age.* Paper presented at the 18th Annual Gatlinburg Conference on Mental Retardation and Developmental Disabilities, Gatlinburg, TN.

Merrill, E. C. (1985). Differences in semantic processing speed of mentally retarded and nonretarded persons: Comparison of short- and long-term memory processing. *American Journal of Mental Deficiency, 90,* 71–80.

Merrill, E. C., McCauley, C., Sperber, R. D., Littlefield, J., Rider, E. A., & Shapiro, D. (1985). *Age- and intelligence-related differences in semantic processing speed.* Paper presented at the convention of the Society for Research in Child Development, Toronto.

Ochs, E., & Schieffelin, B. B. (Eds.) (1979). *Developmental pragmatics.* New York: Academic Press.

Olson, D., & Hildyard, A. (1981). Assent and compliance in children's language. In W. P. Dickson (Ed.), *Children's oral communication skills* (pp. 313–35). New York: Academic Press.

Owings, N. O., McManus, M. D., & Scherer, N. (1981). A deinstitutionalized retarded adult's use of communication functions in a natural setting. *British Journal of Disorders of Communication, 16,* 119–28.

Paul, R., & Cohen, D. J. (1984). Responses to contingent queries in adults with mental retardation and pervasive developmental disorders. *Applied Psycholinguistics, 5,* 349–57.

Piaget, J. (1926). *The language and thought of the child.* New York: Harcourt Brace & World.

Price-Williams, D. P., & Sabsay, S. (1979). Communicative competence among severely retarded persons. *Semiotica, 26,* 35–63.

Rees, N. S. (1978). Pragmatics of language: Applications to normal and disordered language development. In R. L. Schiefelbusch (Ed.), *Bases of language intervention.* Baltimore, MD: University Park Press.

Rice, M. (1984). Cognitive aspects of communicative development. In R. L. Schiefelbusch & J. Pickar (Eds.), *The acquisition of communicative competence* (pp. 141–89). Baltimore, MD: University Park Press.

Robinson, N., & Robinson, H. B. (1976). *The mentally retarded child.* New York: McGraw-Hill.

Rosenberg, S. (1982). The language of the mentally retarded: Development, processes and intervention. In S. Rosenberg (Ed.), *Handbook of applied psycholinguistics: Major thrusts of research and theory* (pp. 329–92). Hillsdale, NJ: Erlbaum.

Rosenberg, S. (1984). Disorders of first-language development: Trends in research and theory. In E. S. Gollin (Ed.), *Malformations of development: Biological and psychological sources and consequences.* New York: Academic Press.

Rosenberg, S., & Abbeduto, L. (in press). Indicators of linguistic competence in the peer group conversational behavior of mildly retarded adults. *Applied Psycholinguistics.*

Rosenberg, S. D., & Cohen, B. D. (1966). Referential processes of speakers and listeners. *Psychological Review, 73,* 208–31.

Rueda, R., & Chan, K. S. (1980). Referential communication skill levels of moderately mentally retarded adolescents. *American Journal of Mental Deficiency, 85,* 45–52.

Sacks, H., Schegloff, E. A., & Jefferson, G. (1974). A simplest systematics for the organization of turn-taking for conversation. *Language, 50,* 696–735.

Schegloff, E. A. (1968). Sequencing in conversational openings. *American Anthropologist, 70,* 1075–95.

Schegloff, E. A., & Sacks, H. (1973). Opening up closings. *Semiotica, 8,* 289–327.

Schieffelin, B. B., & Eisenberg, A. R. (1984). Cultural variations in children's conversations. In R. L. Schiefelbusch & J. Pickar (Eds.), *The acquisition of communicative competence.* Baltimore, MD: University Park Press.

Searle, J. R. (1969). *Speech acts.* Cambridge University Press.

Searle, J. R. (1975). Indirect speech acts. In P. Cole & J. L. Morgan (Eds.), *Syntax and semantics* (Vol. 3, pp. 59–82). New York: Academic Press.

Shatz, M. (1983). Communication. In P. H. Mussen (Ed.), *Handbook of child psychology: Cognitive development* (Vol. 3, pp. 841–89). J. H. Flavell & E. M. Markman, Vol. Eds. New York: Wiley.

Simeonsson, R. J., Monson, L. B., & Blacher, J. (1984). In P. Brooks, R. Sperber, & C. McCauley (Eds.), *Social understanding and mental retardation* (pp. 389–417). Hillsdale, NJ: Erlbaum.

Smith, J. D., & Polloway, E. (1979). The dimension of adaptive behavior in mental retardation research: An analysis of recent practices. *American Journal of Mental Deficiency, 84,* 203–6.

Snow, C. E. (1984). Parent–child interaction and the development of communicative ability. In R. L. Schiefelbusch & J. Pickar (Eds.), *The acquisition of communicative competence* (pp. 69–107). Baltimore, MD: University Park Press.

Snyder, L. S. (1984). Communicative competence in children with delayed language development. In R. L. Schiefelbusch & J. Pickar (Eds.), *The acquisition of communicative competence* (pp. 423–78). Baltimore, MD: University Park Press.

Somerville, S. C., Hadkinson, B. A., & Greenberg, C. (1979). Two levels of inferential behavior in young children. *Child Development, 50,* 119–31.

Sperber, R., & McCauley, C. (1984). Semantic processing efficiency in the mentally retarded. In P. Brooks, R. Sperber, & C. McCauley (Eds.), *Learning and cognition in the mentally retarded* (pp. 141–63). Hillsdale, NJ: Erlbaum.

Webb, C. E., & Kinde, S. (1967). Speech, language, and hearing of the mentally retarded. In A. A. Baumeister (Ed.), *Mental retardation: Appraisal, education, and rehabilitation* (pp. 86–119). Chicago: Aldine.

Weiner, S. L., & Goodenough, D. R. (1977). A move toward a psychology of conversation. In R. Freedle (Ed.), *Discourse relations: Comprehension and production* (pp. 213–25). Hillsdale, NJ: Erlbaum.

Zetlin, A. G., & Sabsay, S. (1980, April). *Characteristics of verbal interaction among moderately retarded peers.* Paper presented at the 13th Annual Gatlinburg Conference on Research in Mental Retardation, Gatlinburg, TN.

4 Interactions between linguistic and pragmatic development in learning-disabled children: three views of the state of the union

Mavis Donahue

Early pioneers in the field of learning disabilities were convinced of the important role that immaturity in oral language played in reading failure (Johnson & Myklebust, 1967; Orton, 1937); however, this direction in research was in large part sidetracked when theories of reading as a primarily "visual" act became prominent. For a number of years the dominant characterization of learning disabilities was that they reflected "visual–perceptual" deficits (see Vellutino, 1979). However, one reemerging conclusion that comes as no surprise to psycholinguists is that reading disabilities and oral language deficits are intricately interrelated. A sizable body of research indicates that children identified on the basis of underachievement in reading are less skilled than normally achieving readers on a wide variety of phonological, semantic, and syntactic tasks (see Donahue, 1986a, for a review of this literature).

The emergence of this body of literature coincided with a major conceptual shift in the study of language development, that is, from a dominant focus on children's syntactic and semantic growth to a broader consideration of how children learn to communicate with others. Researchers began to turn their attention to the major role that context – social, physical, and linguistic – plays in determining how and what language structures are acquired and used.

These two trends – the characterization of reading-disabled children as a subgroup of the language-handicapped population and a shift to the study of communicative development – converged on a third new area also forecast by early researchers in the learning disabilities field. Namely, accumulating evidence indicates that learning-disabled (LD) children's difficulty in information processing extends to the processing of social information. Studies have found that these individuals are deficient in the perception and interpretation of social cues and in the skills needed to achieve social acceptance from others (see Pearl, Donahue, & Bryan, 1986, for a review). The intersection of these three research trends obviously presents LD children as a group likely to develop communicative skills inferior to, or at least different from, those of normally achieving (NA) children. Consequently, a number of studies examining various aspects of LD children's

126

pragmatic competence have recently been completed (e.g., language variation, providing referential information, conversational turn taking). In general, these studies verify that LD children's pragmatic development differs from that of NA children in significant ways, although not in every domain.

As with any new direction in research, however, these studies have raised almost as many questions as they have answered. One unresolved issue that is primary to both the study of language acquisition and the field of learning disabilities concerns the relations among syntactic-semantic knowledge, social cognition, and pragmatic development. Although the basic assumption that social and language deficits contribute to pragmatic deficiencies seems defensible in general terms, the ways in which these skills interact in various domains and at various developmental stages remain unspecified.

The purpose of this chapter is to use the new data base on pragmatic knowledge in LD children to explore possible relations among developing syntactic-semantic and pragmatic systems. This data base is a particularly appropriate site for generating hypotheses about these interactions for several reasons. First, as is the case for most research on atypical populations, an analysis of LD children's communicative development can contribute much to the study of normal acquisition processes in that the wider variability in underlying skills allows for the examination of individual differences and strategies.

Second, as indicated earlier, there is independent evidence that LD children as a group have problems with the presumed social and linguistic underpinnings of pragmatic competence. Yet relative to other handicapped populations, LD children's deficits in each area are subtle, and therefore their effects on pragmatic development are more intriguing. For example, some autistic and schizophrenic individuals show extreme separation between their knowledge of syntax and their communicative effectiveness (Curtiss, 1981). However, although this pattern is useful for making the point that the two domains are indeed separable, it is not particularly helpful for drawing inferences about normal development. Similarly, unlike the language abilities of many young mentally retarded or language-impaired children, LD children's language skills are sophisticated enough to make it possible to examine a wide range of pragmatic abilities, including some fairly advanced skills (e.g., narrative production, referential communication). Furthermore, even a cursory review of these studies shows that not all skills or tasks pose problems for LD children; that is, there is neither a simple nor a direct relation between learning disability and pragmatic deficits.

A final reason that the study of LD children's communicative skills is a fertile site for unraveling syntactic-semantic and pragmatic relations lies in the notion that language performance reflects speaker-listeners' perceptions of themselves as communicators. To the extent that LD children are aware of their social and language difficulties, they may select compensating communicative styles, which may in turn constrain further social and linguistic growth. This "metapragmatic" explanation may be extremely productive in accounting for individual differences in syntactic-semantic and pragmatic interactions.

It could be argued that raising questions at this time about the syntactic-semantic and pragmatic interdependencies in LD children's language is premature. The number of relevant studies is small and, although they are increasing, there have been few attempts to replicate the results. Furthermore, the purpose of this first wave of studies was primarily to establish whether LD children do, in fact, have pragmatic deficits, rather than to examine interactions among language domains. Thus, relations among skills are not directly tested; in fact, the typical pragmatics study does not provide descriptive information on LD subjects' syntactic or vocabulary knowledge. Thus, possible interdependencies can only be interpolated from these data.

Another important reason for the possibility that associations between syntactic-semantic and pragmatic knowledge cannot be delineated at this point is related to the definition of pragmatics. Using Bates's (1976) widely accepted definition, knowledge underlying the rules governing the use of language in context, *pragmatics* is an umbrella term for a vast range of abilities. Skills as diverse as producing polite requests and terms of address, understanding presupposition, making cohesive ties across utterances in conversation, participating appropriately in turn taking, and correctly using definite versus indefinite articles are all construed as aspects of pragmatic competence. Furthermore, a number of skills formerly considered semantic have been recast as pragmatic, for example, the use of deictic terms. Clearly, the question asked here should not be How does syntactic-semantic development in LD children relate to pragmatic development? but rather What aspects of syntactic-semantic development relate to which aspects of pragmatic development? (i.e., what Bates, Bretherton, Beeghly-Smith, & McNew, refer to as "local homologies"). At this point, there is no data-driven or theoretical taxonomy of pragmatic abilities that would allow us to make predictions about which skills are most constrained by syntax and vocabulary knowledge. In fact, some recent work by Snow and Cancino (1985) suggests that, even within the pragmatic domain, skill in one task is not correlated with skill in another (e.g., maintaining a conversation versus producing a narrative).

Obviously, then, definitive solutions to the syntax–semantics–pragmatics puzzle must await further theoretical and empirical work in each of these research strands. However, as Shatz (1978) pointed out, "If the field of language acquisition is to go beyond the level of phenomenal description of behavior, the theoretical question of relations among kinds of knowledge must be addressed more explicitly." For the field of language disorders, this claim is even more compelling. Therefore, the goal of this chapter is merely to raise the questions and examine the existing data base for some possible answers.

Three views of the interactions between syntactic-semantic and pragmatic development will be put forth, and evidence for each position will be presented. For rhetorical purposes, each view is couched in strong terms; of course, the answer lies somewhere in the intersection of the weak forms of these positions:

> View 1: Learning-disabled children's syntactic-semantic knowledge is unrelated to their pragmatic competence.
>
> View 2: Learning-disabled children's syntactic-semantic knowledge constrains their pragmatic competence.
>
> View 3: Learning-disabled children's pragmatic competence constrains their syntactic-semantic knowledge.

View 1: Syntactic-semantic knowledge is unrelated to pragmatic competence

The null hypothesis is that LD children's knowledge of language structure is unrelated to their pragmatic knowledge; that is, the two domains function independently. At best, this position seems counterintuitive. Lexical and syntactic development cannot take place in the absence of some (as yet unspecified) kind of social interaction and seems to be fueled at least in part by the desire or need to communicate. Conversely, conveying and processing appropriate social intentions seem circumscribed to some degree by a speaker-listener's available repertoire for formulating and comprehending propositions. Therefore, it seems obvious that the two emerging domains interact in important ways.

However, the possibility of this relation has historically not been obvious to either linguists or psycholinguists. Traditional transformational-generative grammar thrived for more than a decade before linguists gave serious consideration to the role that context – social, linguistic, and nonverbal – may play in accounting for speakers' comprehension and production of sentences. Even current linguistic theory has difficulty explaining the increasing evidence of pragmatic constraints on phonological, lexical, and syntactic production (Gazdar, 1980). It is interesting that the theme of the 1986 Chicago Linguistics Society's parasession, typically focused on a topic on the "cutting edge" of linguistic theory, was the relation of pragmatics to grammatical theory. The call for papers suggested such topics as "To what extent can pragmatic aspects of language be incorporated in theories of grammar?" "How are grammatical factors exploited by speakers for pragmatic purposes?" This choice of topics indicates that research on interactions between the linguistic code and its use is just emerging.

A similar time lag occurred between the Chomsky-inspired explosion of research on children's syntactic and semantic development and the onset of interest in emerging sociolinguistic knowledge. Even now, theories that assign a primary role to functional systems (i.e., topicalization) to account for the ways in which grammatical devices are used and acquired (Bates & MacWhinney, 1982) are still perceived as novel and somewhat out of the mainstream (Gleitman & Wanner, 1982). Although most researchers would argue against the claim that the two systems of language structure and language use bear little relevance to one another, the precise nature of any relation between the two domains remains to be specified.

This gap stems in part from the theoretical thrust of early work on pragmatic development. First, much of the research published during the early 1970s was motivated by the desire to refute Piaget's well-known claim that young children's communication was largely egocentric and insensitive to listener or situational features (Ervin-Tripp & Mitchell-Kernan, 1977; Garvey, 1975; Keenan, 1974; Shatz & Gelman, 1973). These studies effectively demonstrated that preschool children are remarkably skilled conversational partners with peers as well as adults. In fact, rudimentary conversational skills have been documented in children with very limited linguistic ability, that is, from the very onset of single-word use (Greenfield & Smith, 1976), and even in prelinguistic stages (Bates, Benigni, Bretherton, Camaioni, & Volterra, 1979; Snow, 1977). Therefore, the implication typically drawn was that children's apparently sophisticated pragmatic skills were due not to linguistic development but to social-cognitive abilities that were more advanced than Piaget had perceived.

Armed with these studies, a number of researchers then took on the task of broadening the focus of research from syntactic to communicative development. Of course, the burden of proof fell to these investigators to show that pragmatic skills are not simply reducible to or predictable from syntactic-semantic maturity. In their efforts to demonstrate that pragmatic knowledge is a domain worthy of investigation in its own right, these researchers may have inadvertently reinforced the notion that syntactic-semantic development and pragmatic development are separate but equal domains.

For example, *Child discourse* (Ervin-Tripp & Mitchell-Kernan, 1977), one of the first and most influential books on pragmatic development, included chapters discussing children's skills on a wide range of communicative behaviors, for example, contextual variation in speech acts, conversational turn taking, narratives, and dispute episodes. None of these chapters, however, made more than a token allusion to the role that syntactic or lexical constraints might play in children's evolution of strategies for fulfilling the social uses of language. The implicit assumption seemed to be that children's pragmatic knowledge and syntactic-semantic skills were asymmetric enough that they could be studied as separate domains.

The apparent lack of interest of these early studies in the relations among syntactic, semantic, and pragmatic performance seemed to serve as a model for later research; studies of communicative development typically do not include measures of vocabulary or syntax. The few exceptions generally support the "separate-but-equal" assumption. Dale (1980) attempted to correlate a measure of syntactic ability (i.e., mean length of utterance) with toddlers' ability to express a variety of communicative intentions. His results supported "the claim that pragmatic function is not perfectly correlated with lexical and syntactic form" (p. 3); when age effects were partialed out, the range of pragmatic functions that the children produced was not predictable from utterance length.

Similarly, 3-year-olds who outscored other 3-year-olds on the ability to judge and produce polite requests did not differ in syntactic ability but were more advanced in perspective taking (Nippold, Leonard, & Anastopoulos, 1982). Studies of the developing ability to respond appropriately to a listener's request for clarification of their messages compared groups of preschool children differing in language skills (e.g., Gallagher, 1977; Wilcox & Webster, 1980). Neither vocabulary size nor syntactic maturity seemed to influence whether children responded with another utterance; even children at the one-word stage who had fewer than 70 words in their productive vocabulary had mastered the appropriate conversational rules for dealing with a listener who had not understood (Wilcox & Webster, 1980). However, as might be expected, language level *did* predict what kinds of strategies were used to reformulate the original message (e.g., repetition vs. lexical substitution vs. elaboration).

At the other end of the developmental continuum, Paul (1985) examined third- and fifth-grade children's ability to identify given versus new information in active, passive, and cleft sentences. All children demonstrated full comprehension of the vocabulary and syntactic structures used in the pragmatic task. The results indicated that syntactic comprehension of these marked sentence types clearly preceded the understanding of the given–new distinction that these complex structures signal. In fact, 25% of the children performed at chance level on the pragmatic comprehension task. The author interpreted these findings as evidence for the autonomy of some aspects of syntactic acquisition relative to pragmatic development, at least for comprehension. In contrast, Lempert (1984) demonstrated that the ease with which children comprehended one marked sentence form (i.e., the passive) *was* significantly affected by such pragmatic factors as the perceptual salience and animacy of the nouns in the sentence.

Evidence from language-handicapped populations

One body of research that provides further support for the hypothesis that linguistic skills develop independently of the acquisition of pragmatic knowledge is the literature on communicative competence in language-disordered populations (e.g., mentally retarded, specific-language-impaired, and autistic children). Perhaps because this research has a tradition of concern with delineating individual differences in language abilities and disabilities across domains, these investigators have shown much more interest in examining the intersection between deficits in language structure and language use than have researchers of normal language development.

Rees (1978) and Bloom and Lahey (1978) were among the first to suggest that the separation between language structure and language use may be even more pronounced in language-disordered children's language profiles than in those of normally developing children. The clearest statement was made by Bloom and Lahey (1978), who suggested that asymmetry among the three components of language form, content, and use is actually a defining feature of language disorder: "Normal language development has been described as the successful interaction among the three. . . . Disordered language development can be described as any disruption within a component *or* in the interaction among the components" (p. 291). They went on to provide examples of children with disorders specifically in language form, content, or use. Bloom and Lahey admitted that the intersection of these three domains in some language-handicapped children may be intact but developing more slowly than is age appropriate. However, they implied that a more appropriate term for this condition is *language delay* or *maturational lag* rather than *language disorder.*

This was a curious, although provocative, position to set forth, especially in 1978. First, there were virtually no published data on the pragmatic abilities of language-handicapped individuals at that point; the only evidence that pragmatic skills could be discrepant from other language skills came from clinical reports. Furthermore, most of the research on semantic and syntactic ability in specific-language-impaired, mentally retarded, and even hearing-impaired populations has not uncovered patterns of deviant development, at least in terms of sequence. With some exceptions (e.g., see Cromer, 1974), language-handicapped individuals seem to be similar to normally developing children matched on relevant variables, for example, mean length of utterance (MLU) or mental age (MA) (Leonard, 1982; Rosenberg, 1982), although delayed relative to age-matched groups. Although typical studies do not include both syntactic and semantic measures, the findings that language-handicapped and nonhandicapped children progress through similar sequences and stages suggest that the domains of syntax and semantics are not autonomous.

However, recent research on pragmatic competence in language-handicapped individuals suggests that the Bloom and Lahey model was, in some ways, "before its time." Pragmatic performance in these populations does not appear to be necessarily commensurate with syntactic-semantic maturity. For example, Blank, Gessner, and Esposito (1979) reported a case study of a preschool-aged child with apparently normally developing syntactic-semantic skills whose discourse exhibited virtually no sensitivity to listener or contextual variables. Similarly, high-functioning autistic adults with quite sophisticated language skills have been described as having persistent deficits in conversational interaction, particularly in the use of prosody to convey emotional meanings (Caparulo & Cohen, 1983).

More compelling evidence of a discrepancy between pragmatic and linguistic development can be drawn from group-design studies comparing language-handicapped children with normal children at similar stages of syntactic development.

Although a number of studies have found the pragmatic skills of language-handi-capped subjects to be equivalent to those of younger, MLU-matched children, re-search that *has* uncovered differences suggests that language-handicapped chil-dren are even more deficient in their language use than would be predicted from their syntactic-semantic ability. Compared with younger normal children with similar linguistic skills, language-impaired children have been found to produce a more restricted repertoire of communicative intentions on both structured and unstructured tasks (Fey, Leonard, & Wilcox, 1981; Shatz, Bernstein, & Shulman, 1980; Snyder, 1978). Similarly, Watson, Martin, & Schaffer (in press) indicated that autistic children's spontaneous utterances were more limited in semantic and communicative functions than the speech of normal children at the same levels of syntactic skill.

Many language-handicapped children also seem to have difficulty playing an active role in conversation. For example, young language-impaired children ask very few questions, even when question-formation rules are part of their syntactic repertoire (Morehead & Ingram, 1976). Similarly, in a comparison of a wide va-riety of syntactic and semantic skills in normally developing, language-impaired, and mentally retarded children matched on MA (5 years), mentally retarded chil-dren were found to be essentially equivalent to the normal children and more ad-vanced than the language-impaired subjects. The mentally retarded children, however, were much less likely than the other two groups to produce questions, a finding that the authors attributed to possible differences in social and motiva-tional factors (Kamhi & Johnston, 1982). Leifer and Lewis (1984) also cited so-cial-experiential factors to explain the *opposite* findings in their comparison of the conversational skills of retarded and nonretarded children at the one-word stage of development. Retarded children were found to be *more* advanced than normal sub-jects matched on syntactic and vocabulary level in their ability to respond appro-priately to mothers' questions and directives. In either case, whether language-handicapped children's language structure lags behind their pragmatic skill or vice versa, these findings of asymmetry between the two domains provide some evidence that the order of acquisition of syntactic and semantic forms is not nec-essarily disrupted even when pragmatic development is following a different time-table.

Asymmetry across domains in learning-disabled children

Whether or not asymmetry among language abilities (phonology, syntax, seman-tics, and pragmatics) is a defining feature of language disorders, uneven patterns of development across domains have historically been an important diagnostic characteristic of learning disabilities. The most widely accepted definition of learning disabilities describes them as "a disorder in one or more of the basic psy-chological processes involved in understanding or using language, spoken or written," despite normal sensory, cognitive, and emotional development and adequate environmental support (U.S. Office of Education, 1977, p. 65083). The federal operational guidelines specify further that a significant discrepancy between the child's academic potential and achievement be demonstrated. By definition, then, an LD child is a student whose development in some areas significantly outstrips development in other (typically academic) areas.

Thus, the language development of LD children may also be likely to show disparities among domains. Of course, the evidence that LD children as a group exhibit deficits in most aspects of language form and function suggests that the development of these domains is intertwined. However, it is possible that, for individual children, the acquisition of the linguistic code and the rules for using it effectively are separable dimensions.

The overwhelming majority of LD children are referred and identified on the basis of reading failure. However, for many children, the label "reading problem" signals a constellation of other problems that are not so salient and/or quantifiable for teachers. As any introductory textbook in the learning disabilities field will point out, LD children as a group exhibit a large inventory of attentional, memory, social, and emotional disorders, ranging from subtle to severe. It is possible that, rather than language problems leading to pragmatic difficulties, other cognitive and affective deficits affect the development of both language form and language use, although in different ways.

For example, one possibility is that memory deficits particularly impair lexical acquisition and retrieval, a commonly reported disability of LD children (e.g., Denckla & Rudel, 1976a, 1976b). In contrast, Bates and MacWhinney (1979) suggest that selective attention underlies children's development of pragmatic structures, that is, the awareness of given versus new information that is at the root of topic–comment relations in discourse. Thus, an LD child's attentional problems may lead directly to pragmatic deficits, which in turn may lead to deficits in those grammatical devices that encode topic–comment relations. In fact, hyperactive boys with attentional deficits have been found not only to be ineffective communicative partners with normal peers, but also to be insensitive to opportunities for social learning (Whalen et al., 1979).

More globally, impaired social development or low self-esteem may lead LD children to assume a passive or inappropriate stance in social interaction, such that opportunities for learning or practicing new language forms and/or conversational strategies are reduced. In any case, the point is that deficits in language form or language use could occur separately, or even co-occur in the absence of direct causal relations between them.

More evidence for the "separate-but-equal" position on LD children's language and pragmatic skills comes from the body of literature on the communicative correlates of peer social acceptance in NA children. Generally, children who have difficulty making friends have been found to be less adept than popular children at producing clear, listener-adapted messages and requests and resolving social conflict through persuasive arguments (e.g., Asher & Renshaw, 1981; Gottman, 1983; Gottman, Gonso, & Rasmussen, 1975). Thus, these children have pragmatic deficits in spite of apparently age-appropriate language ability. (Of course, no information on these subjects' syntactic-semantic maturity is provided, so it is possible that some may have deficient linguistic systems relative to children high in peer acceptance. At least, however, it can be assumed that none of these subjects had been referred or identified on the basis of a need for special education services.) One well-documented finding is that LD children are rejected or isolated by their classmates (e.g., Bryan, 1974; Scranton & Ryckman, 1979). Thus, regardless of their oral language abilities, LD children's pragmatic problems may simply reflect those of other samples of children low in peer acceptance.

The possibility of this combination of effects obviously points to the presence of distinct language subgroups within the LD population, and some new evidence for LD subtypes is emerging. First, of course, not all LD children exhibit obvious oral language problems; even investigators who find group main effects in language ability usually caution that there was considerable within-group variability. However, some estimates suggest that more than 50% can be categorized as language disabled (Feagans & Appelbaum, 1986; Wiig & Semel, 1984). Furthermore, investigators that have attempted to delineate LD subtypes generally find that the largest clusters are children with poor syntactic-semantic skills (see McKinney, 1984, for a review of this literature).

The only study to date that has included pragmatic skills as well as measures of syntax and semantics in order to subgroup children is part of an extensive longitudinal study of LD children's language and academic development carried out at Frank Porter Graham Child Development Center in North Carolina (Feagans & Appelbaum, 1986). Syntactic-semantic measures were a test of the comprehension of late-acquired syntactic structures (e.g., "ask" versus "tell") and the Vocabulary subtest of the WISC-R. Pragmatic (narrative) variables were the number of trials a child needed in order to enact correctly a story that had been read to the child (comprehension) and the communicative quality of the child's retelling of the same story (paraphrase). The child's narratives were coded for the number of words and subordinate clauses produced.

These measures for 55 LD children were used in a cluster analysis, resulting in six clusters representing diverse patterns of narrative and syntactic-semantic abilities and disabilities. In brief:

Cluster 1 was a group of LD children who appeared to have more normal skills in the building blocks of language, vocabulary and syntax, relative to their narrative skills (comprehension and paraphrase). Cluster 2 showed a rather depressed pattern of language skills except in vocabulary. This cluster was more globally language-impaired. Cluster 3 appeared to be a group who talked a lot using a high proportion of complex structures, but their basic language skills and narrative discourse skills were much lower. This cluster was characterized as hyperverbal. Cluster 4 showed the opposite pattern from Cluster 1. That is, their narrative skills exceeded their skills in word meaning and grammatical structures. Cluster 5 had the same shape as Cluster 4 but was at a higher level. Cluster 5 was really a normal looking group with means which were comparable to or exceeding our normally achieving children. Cluster 6 was again a more high functioning cluster but whose pattern was opposite to Cluster 5 and most like Cluster 1 – poor narrative skills, relative to their good vocabulary and syntax skills (Feagans & Appelbaum, 1986).

A forecasting technique was then used to try to fit NA controls into these six clusters. Only 10.6% of the normal subjects fell into the two most impaired groups (Clusters 1 and 2), which included one-third of the LD sample, whereas 71% of the normal sample was included in the less impaired Clusters 4 and 5. These two clusters showed narrative skills that were more advanced than vocabulary or syntax. Thus, subgrouping of the LD sample did produce distinctive clusters of skills that the NA children did not typically exhibit. However, NA children were as likely as LD subjects to show discrepancies between syntactic-semantic and narrative development. The only group whose skills in language form seemed commensurate with their narrative abilities was Cluster 2, which was most impaired in both domains.

Evidence from studies of learning-disabled children's pragmatic competence

Several studies of pragmatic skills in LD students provide some evidence that the domains of language form and language use function independently, in that LD children's performance has been found to be equivalent to that of NA controls in one domain but deficient in the other. Of course, our ability to sort out interdependencies among skills is circumscribed by the quality and quantity of information available on subjects' vocabulary and syntactic growth. Studies vary greatly in the extent to which relations can be logically inferred. First, some studies (e.g., Donahue, 1981; Feagans & Short, 1984) directly assessed syntactic or semantic performance on the pragmatic task itself. Second, other studies provided background information on language skills (e.g., standardized test scores) in the description of subjects. Finally, most studies provided neither kind of information; relations among syntactic-semantic and pragmatic abilities can only be interpolated from the ways in which communicative behaviors were coded.

Two studies present the traditional pattern of skills that might be expected from children with specific deficits in language structure but compensatory communicative abilities. Pearl, Donahue, and Bryan (1981) used a referential communication task to examine LD children's ability to interpret and respond to requests for clarification that varied in explicitness. Children in grades 1 through 8 were assigned the encoder's role of describing abstract shapes so that an adult confederate could identify them. All children were pretested on the ability to generate two descriptions of a subset of the referents. After each description the adult either selected the correct referent or requested more information explicitly ("Tell me something else about it"), implicitly ("I don't understand"), or nonverbally (with a puzzled facial expression).

Although this descriptive task did not demand the use of precise vocabulary or the elaborate sequencing or embedding of information, LD children's descriptions were still less syntactically complex than those of NA children (Donahue, Pearl, & Bryan, 1982). However, LD subjects in grades 3 through 8 were as adept as NA children at recognizing and complying with the verbal and nonverbal requests. Although responses to the puzzled look increased with age in both groups, the only group effect revealed that the youngest group of LD girls failed to respond to the puzzled look more often than NA girls, whereas the youngest LD boys were *more* likely than NA boys to recognize this nonverbal feedback.

This study, then, is an example of skilled pragmatic performance in spite of syntactic deficiency on the same task. Of course, it could be argued that this actually provides evidence for the developmental interaction of syntactic and pragmatic skills. Because of their history of language disorder, LD children might have had greater experience with adults' requests for clarification, as well as a greater need for skills in repairing communicative breakdown. Furthermore, those variables on which syntactic resources might be more likely to have an impact, that is, the communicative quality of the initial descriptions and their revisions, were not examined.

A second study with a similar pattern of results (Donahue, 1984a) assessed LD children's performance on a task in which syntactic and pragmatic knowledge more clearly intersected. Hornby's (1971) paradigm was used to examine children's ability to understand and use grammatical devices for distinguishing given or already mentioned ideas in discourse from propositions that are new and therefore informative. This depends not only on the pragmatic ability of speakers and listeners to differentiate what knowledge they share and what information must be made explicit, but also on a repertoire of syntactic strategies for producing and interpreting this distinction. Children in grades 1 through 6 were tested on the comprehension and production of five sentence types for marking new propositions, that is, active, passive, cleft, pseudocleft, and sentences with contrastively stressed elements. Pairs of simple, actor–action–object drawings were presented; one element was held constant and two elements differed in each pair. Stimulus sentences matched neither picture perfectly; the child's task was to select the picture that best fit the sentence (signaling which element of the sentence the child considered to be presupposed or given information) and then *correct* the sentence (thereby producing some grammatical device for marking the mismatched element as new information).

Generally, LD children were equivalent to NA subjects on the comprehension phase of the task. Similarly, LD students had no difficulty correctly marking the new information on the production task, although this skill increased with age in both groups. However, they clearly relied on strategies for signaling the given–new distinction that required less complex grammatical structures; they were less likely than NA subjects to produce passive, cleft, and pseudocleft sentences. In other words, LD children made effective use of their more limited syntactic repertoire.

The results of both studies corroborate previous findings that LD children sustain delays in the production of complex grammatical structures (e.g., Idol-Maestas, 1980; Vogel, 1975; Wiig & Semel, 1984). It is important to note that these findings held even on tasks in which communicative rather than linguistic goals were emphasized; most previous studies used the traditional language assessment techniques of sentence completion and repetition and the elicitation of oral speech samples. Even so, however, the relation between performance on these single-message, contrived tasks and the ability to participate effectively in a conversational context is not known. MacWhinney and Price (1980) suggest that these experimental tasks may tap metalinguistic awareness that is acquired later and through very different routes than the ability to identify new information in natural discourse. Thus, the findings that LD children are generally equivalent to NA peers in the comprehension and production of isolated sentences or requests does not necessarily indicate that their ability to mark new information or repair breakdowns in natural communicative contexts is unimpaired.

Other studies add to the findings that LD children show discrepancies between syntactic-semantic and pragmatic maturity, but in the opposite direction; that is, their pragmatic performance is deficient even on tasks in which their syntactic-semantic repertoire seems to be adequate. Two studies assessed children's ability to formulate communicative intentions whose form and content reflect an awareness of the needs and feelings of listeners. The ability to vary the linguistic form of propositions appropriately obviously depends on the social-cognitive ability to perceive socially significant listener characteristics and understand their implications for appropriate speech, as well as a linguistic repertoire of surface forms for conveying the same message in different contexts.

One skill that particularly taps a speaker's ability to adjust message content in order to take into account a listener's feelings is the ability to deliver bad news tactfully. Pearl, Donahue, and Bryan (1985) used a role-playing paradigm requiring children (grades 1 through 4) to give negative feedback to classmates by telling them, for example, that they had been rejected for a role in the class play or had not been invited to go to the movies. Messages were scored according to a three-point scale that represented the degree to which speakers attempted to make the bad news less hurtful or insulting to listeners. The least tactful responses were blunt statements of the news ("You can't go"), more skilled responses reflected an awareness of the listener's feelings ("I'm sorry, but the other kid got the part"), and the most tactful statements couched the news in terms that allowed the listener to save face or to feel better ("The other kid was just a little better than you" or "You can go with me next time").

Developmental and group differences indicated that LD and younger children produced less tactful messages than their comparison groups. These findings seemed to reflect LD children's social deficits in predicting or accommodating others' feelings (e.g., Bachara, 1976) more than limitations in linguistic proficiency. First, although no independent measures of syntactic-semantic ability were available, sociometric data collected on this sample demonstrated that the LD subjects were less socially accepted than NA controls. Furthermore, tactfulness in this task did not demand much linguistic sophistication. Possible differences in language productivity were controlled for by the coding procedure. Each response was scored according to the highest-level strategy the child used. For example, a child who responded, "You can go next time," earned the same score as a child who said, "I'm sorry, you can't go with me today, but I promise to take you next time." Finally, both groups of children not only were able to produce the most tactful strategy, but in fact used it more often than the other response types. This suggests that LD subjects were less consistent than NA children in their use of the tactful responses available in their repertoire.

A second study of language variation (Donahue, 1981) used the role-playing paradigm popularized by Bates (1976) that requires children to make requests of listeners differing in age or social status. Children in grades 2, 4, and 6 made requests and persuasive appeals to imaginary listeners varying on the dimensions of power (adults vs. classmates) and intimacy (father and best friend vs. priest and newcomer to the classroom). The expectation that LD children's linguistic and social problems would limit their ability to adjust the politeness and persuasiveness of their requests to listener differences was not borne out. Learning-disabled girls differed from NA girls only in the finding that LD girls were more polite to all listeners and actually produced somewhat more persuasive appeals.

Learning-disabled and NA boys had an equivalent range of linguistic forms with which to express politeness, and both groups were able to manipulate the forms of their requests to reflect listener features. However, NA boys' requests attended to intimacy, whereas those of the LD boys attended to power. Normally achieving boys were more polite to low-intimate than to high-intimate listeners. Surprisingly, LD boys produced more polite requests to low-power (i.e., peers) than to high-power targets. This pattern points to differences in the understanding of social relationships rather than to deficits in linguistic repertoire.

Furthermore, compared with NA boys, LD boys produced fewer, and a smaller variety of, persuasive appeals as well as fewer appeals requiring advanced levels of listener perspective taking. In spite of this deficient repertoire, LD boys' appeals were sensitive to listener characteristics. Again, variations in appeal levels of the LD and NA boys did not reflect the same dimensions in that the intimacy dimension was salient for LD boys, whereas the power factor influenced normal boys. More sophisticated appeals were addressed to nonintimate listeners by LD boys and to peers by NA boys.

Thus, LD boys were able to vary the politeness of their requests and the elaboration of persuasive appeals as a function of listener features, although in a different manner than nondisabled boys. This suggests that these boys (1) had an adequate linguistic repertoire and (2) were able to perceive the distinctive features of listeners but (3) differed from control boys in their understanding of the implications of these differences for socially appropriate speech. It is possible, then, that LD children are aware of the general social rules for polite requests but believe that a different set of rules may be more appropriate for their own communicative behavior. This "metapragmatic" explanation of LD children's communicative styles receives additional support from studies (discussed below) whose results support View 3.

Most likely, then, the findings of neither study can be explained by vocabulary and syntax factors. This does not mean, of course, that LD children as a group do not exhibit general language delay; it is more likely that there was a ceiling effect on the syntactic-semantic skills needed to produce polite requests and tactful messages in these tasks. For example, by the age of 5 years, most children have mastered a variety of surface forms needed to produce polite requests; in fact, there were no age differences in the children's range of linguistic forms used in the requesting task (Donahue, 1981).

Two investigations examined LD children's performance on a more challenging task that seemed to place greater demands on syntactic and semantic proficiency, that is, a referential communication task requiring the description of an abstract figure so that a listener could identify or reconstruct the same referent. Noel (1980) measured both the descriptive characteristics and the communicative effectiveness of messages by asking 9-year-old boys to describe ambiguous figures to an adult experimenter. A subset of these descriptions was analyzed for number of words and number and type of attributes mentioned (e.g., shape, size, label). Although the LD boys did not differ from the nondisabled children in the number of words or categories used, the LD boys were more likely to refer to the shapes of the figures (e.g., "It's pointed"), whereas their nondisabled peers were more likely to provide general labels (e.g., "It looks like a tree"). In the second phase of the study, the latter strategy was more useful to listeners. The tape-recorded descriptions were played to another sample of LD and nondisabled boys between 9 and 11 years of age, whose task was to select the correct picture on the basis of the clues. The listeners' accuracy in referent selection was used as a measure of the speaker's effectiveness in providing descriptive information. The messages of the nondisabled students elicited more correct picture selections from both groups of listeners than did the clues from the LD boys.

Spekman (1981) also found LD boys to be less proficient than nondisabled boys on measures of the ability to produce informative messages, even in a less controlled communicative task involving peer dyads. Learning-disabled pupils between the ages of 9 and 11 were paired with NA classmates. These dyads were compared with dyads composed of two nondisabled boys. A pretest of the lexical items needed to describe and identify the referents was included to ensure that the children had the prerequisite vocabulary skills. Each peer in the dyads played both the roles of speaker and listener. The speaker described patterns of geometric shapes varying in attributes of color, size, shape, and thickness. The listener constructed the pattern with blocks.

Performance was analyzed by means of measures of dyadic interaction, as well as of specific speaker and listener behaviors. Although no differences were found between the NA dyads and the dyads including an LD partner in the amount of time or number of conversational turns exchanged, the block arrangements of the NA dyads were more accurate than those of the LD dyads. Thus, dyads including an LD child were less efficient in their exchange of information. The LD children in the speaker role produced less informative descriptions, suggesting that they had difficulty identifying the essential or new information and presenting it in an effective way. On a measure similar to Noel's "label" category, LD children were somewhat less likely than NA speakers to describe the overall pattern or gestalt of the design.

Thus, the results of both studies suggest that LD boys are less proficient than nondisabled boys in formulating descriptions that are useful to their partners. Neither study provides a direct means of determining the degree to which these less adequate messages result from LD children's deficits in productive language or from social difficulties in assuming the perspective of their listener. However, several considerations provide support for the latter explanation. First, none of the LD boys in either study had been identified as having expressive or receptive language problems, and in the Spekman study the children were explicitly screened for the prerequisite vocabulary knowledge. Similarly, measures of language comprehension obtained when the same subjects played the listener role indicated that the LD and NA groups were equivalent in both studies. Second, neither study revealed group differences in the amount of time used or in the amount of talk exchanged between dyads (Spekman, 1981), or in the mean length of descriptions or the mean number of categories used (Noel, 1980). Thus, in spite of engaging in the same amount of talk and interaction, LD boys were not as capable of communicating the stimulus descriptions as nondisabled boys. Note that this result was obtained across both studies even though the stimulus sets placed different demands on the message encoder's linguistic skills. The Spekman task required the specification of several discrete dimensions in order to formulate an informative message. The novel shapes used in the Noel study allowed for less precise, and a wider range of, strategies for message encoding. Finally, the finding that LD boys were comparatively less likely to describe the overall pattern of the referent than to describe its isolated parts seems more reflective of difficulty in using the listener's perspective to realize the effectiveness of the gestalt approach than of linguistic problems in formulating the descriptions.

Another referential communication paradigm (Donahue, Pearl, & Bryan, 1980) was used to assess the contribution made by linguistic knowledge in children's ability to request clarification of ambiguous messages when playing the listener role. This pragmatic skill encompasses three fairly independent subskills:

1. The linguistic ability to appraise the adequacy of a message by monitoring its informational value and to formulate a request for more information when a message is inadequate
2. The understanding of the conversational rule that cooperative listeners are obligated to take responsibility for the success of a communicative exchange by indicating to their partners when a message is unclear
3. The language comprehension skills to use the information conveyed to select the correct referent

Following a procedure similar to those used by Cosgrove and Patterson (1977) and Ironsmith and Whitehurst (1978), LD and nondisabled children in grades 1 through 8 played the role of listeners in a referential communication task requiring them to choose the correct picture from among four drawings that differed in terms of binary features. Messages provided by the experimenter systematically differed in the amount of information they presented. In one-third of the 12 trials, the messages were fully informative, providing enough details to identify the correct referent. In the other trials, the message sender *created* a communication breakdown by giving descriptions that applied to more than one picture. In another third of the trials, the messages were partially informative in that they eliminated two of the pictures as potential referents but failed to differentiate the other two. The remaining messages were completely uninformative in that they did not differentiate any of the four pictures.

The results indicated that, although all children were able to choose the correct picture after hearing the informative clues, developmental and group differences emerged on the two types of inadequate messages. Younger children and LD children were less likely than their comparison groups to request clarification of the partially informative and uninformative messages, and consequently they were less able to choose the correct referent in those trials.

Although several possible explanations were explored, none seemed to account adequately for LD children's failure to initiate the repair of the communicative breakdowns. Their conversational unassertiveness in this task did not seem due to language problems that would interfere with their ability to recognize inadequate messages. A second task immediately following the referential communication task required that the children appraise the adequacy of the messages by predicting whether an imaginary listener who heard them would be able to select the correct referent. Learning-disabled children in grades 3 through 8 did not differ from their normal age-mates in the ability to identify inadequate clues.

Although LD children produced fewer requests than normal children, an examination of the types of requests that *were* produced indicated that the linguistic skills required to produce appropriate requests for more information were within these children's productive language abilities. Fewer general requests were produced by LD children than by normal children; however, this request type did not depend on syntactically complex speech. Any utterance indicating that the child did not understand functioned to elicit more information from the experimenter (e.g., "I don't get it"). Those requests that specified the features of the stimuli that needed to be made more explicit required a wider syntactic and semantic repertoire ("Is the seal holding a ball on its nose?"). Surprisingly, although the use of these specific requests increased with age, LD children did not differ from normal children in the mean number of specific requests produced.

These findings, then, seem to indicate difficulty in the second component underlying message clarification skills, that is, the understanding of the conversational rule that the obligation for initiating the repair of communicative breakdown falls to the listener. Even though most LD children had the linguistic ability to recognize ambiguous messages and formulate questions about them, they failed to perceive the situation as one in which these skills were relevant.

A similar pattern of findings in studies of younger normal children's communicative skills has been characterized as a "strategy deficit," termed by Whitehurst and Sonnenschein (1981) as "knowing how versus knowing when." Donahue (1984b) assessed this strategy-deficit explanation of LD children's inactive listening by testing the effects of an intervention designed to emphasize and provide practice in question asking, that is, by having children play Twenty Questions with an experimenter. Although grade and group differences replicated the findings of Donahue et al. (1980), the intervention did not increase the inactive listeners' use of requests for clarification.

The finding that LD children's performance was resistant to brief training seems to rule out a strategy-deficit hypothesis. However, a second hypothesis may clarify the failure of these children to be active listeners by pointing out a more basic difference in the understanding of conversational rules. The children's history of communicative and social difficulties may have led them to doubt their own comprehension skill and overestimate their partner's ability to provide adequate messages. If these children found it unlikely that an adult would violate the Gricean (Grice, 1975) principles of informativeness, honesty, relevance, and clarity, they could only conclude that their inability to select just one referent must be due to their own misunderstanding of the task.

An analysis of children's picture selection strategies provided support for the latter hypothesis: Children who failed to request clarification of inadequate messages almost invariably selected the picture with the fewest features, apparently under the assumption that the adult would have specified the additional details if she had intended the other referents. This response reflects an overreliance on the

Gricean principles that cooperative speakers provide informative messages but do not include more details than are necessary (i.e., the maxim of quantity). The consequence is that LD listeners appear to be shirking their responsibility to indicate that they have not understood something, thereby shifting the burden of responsibility for a successful exchange of information to the adult.

The studies described above have examined pragmatic skills that require single utterances or short descriptions of unrelated referents. However, other studies suggest that LD children's difficulty in formulating and conveying information extends to the production and comprehension of discourse units beyond the sentence level (i.e., narratives). One investigation (Roth & Spekman, 1985) reported the narrative abilities of a carefully described sample of LD children between the ages of 8 and 14 years. None of these children demonstrated problems in language structure; all had WISC-R Verbal IQs of 90 or above and performed within the normal range on a battery of receptive and expressive oral language measures. These subjects, who attended a private school for LD students, were not receiving any remediation for phonological, syntactic, or semantic skills. Both LD and control subjects were required to achieve average or above-average scaled scores on the Vocabulary subtest of the WISC-R; the two groups performed similarly on this subtest.

Children were asked to "make up a story about something that is make-believe or something that is not real." Thus, unlike studies of children's ability to recall narratives that were read to them, this paradigm did not require verbal memory resources. Narratives were analyzed according to Stein and Glenn's (1979) story grammar schema. In general, LD children's stories presented the essential elements (i.e., the description of a protagonist, an initiating event, and an outcome), but were less mature than those of NA peers in that they contained fewer propositions and a smaller proportion of complete episodes. The LD children were less likely than controls to "set the scene" of the story and to describe the main character's attitude about initiating events and his or her plans and actions dealing with those events. Episodes in LD children's stories were also infrequently linked by temporal relations involving causality or simultaneity of events.

The authors interpreted this pattern of findings as the effects of impaired social-role-taking skills in LD children. The failure to describe the motivations, intentions, and actions of the protagonist may reflect these youngsters' lack of understanding of others' psychological states and social relationships (e.g., Bachara, 1976). For example, in a social-perception study by Pearl and Cosden (1983), LD children who were shown brief emotion-laden vignettes had difficulty identifying the relationships among the actors and gauging their emotional reactions to what was said. Another explanation is that LD storytellers may be aware of the importance of this information but may not recognize that these details are not obvious to the listener and must be explicitly reported. This assumption that adult listeners are omniscient is similar to the interpretation offered by Donahue (1984b) to account for children's failure to request clarification when adults give ambiguous messages.

A third possibility, of course, is that the LD children in the Roth and Spekman study lacked sufficient vocabulary to describe characters' feelings and intentions or the grammatical skill to embed this tangential information into the story's skeleton of events. The fact that this LD sample demonstrated age-appropriate oral language ability according to standardized tests does not preclude the possibility that the control group might still have outstripped the LD subjects in the semantic-syntactic formulation skills needed for this task. It is not unusual for middle-class and upper-middle-class LD children to score within or even above the normal range according to the norms provided by standardized achievement tests; their disabilities emerge only in comparison with social-class peers. Since the NA children in this study were not administered the same battery of oral language tests, it is not possible to determine whether group differences in syntactic-semantic ability existed. However, LD and NA samples were matched in at least one aspect of vocabulary knowledge, namely, the Vocabulary subtest of the WISC-R.

Whatever the explanation, the net effect of LD children's impoverished stories is more communication "work" for their audience; in order to make sense of the story, listeners must make inferences about the protagonist's behavior that may or may not be correct. This increased burden of responsibility, as well as the likelihood of communicative breakdown, probably contributes to others' perception of many LD children as unsatisfying or uncooperative conversational partners, a reaction that in turn may set into motion a long cycle of communicative difficulty for these children.

Summary

These data provide some evidence of asymmetry in LD children's linguistic and pragmatic skills in a variety of communicative tasks, namely, language variation, requesting clarification, and conveying referential information. The apparently asynchronous developmental courses of the two domains point to the possibility of different cognitive roots; for example, grammatical knowledge may be driven by some form of innate language acquisition device, whereas pragmatic knowledge may depend primarily on social-cognitive development. However, as with any null hypothesis, the failure to find relationships does not allow us to conclude that no relationships exist.

Instead, these findings seem to highlight the methodological difficulties of identifying the specific linguistic skills that may be related to specific pragmatic tasks. Compared with the sophisticated methods available for examining grammatical and semantic knowledge, techniques for assessing pragmatic skills are still fairly limited and unrefined. Therefore, even less attention has been given to identifying ways of uncovering interactions between syntactic-semantic and pragmatic knowledge. Another methodological issue involves researchers' ability to predict *when* possible interactions may occur. In other words, some aspects of pragmatic and linguistic knowledge may interact at some stages of development and "disengage" at other stages. For example, the use of listener-adapted requests may be related to the acquisition of linguistic forms up to the age at which a basic repertoire is established, at which point further sophistication may depend on continuing so-cial-cognitive growth. Thus, "ceiling" or "floor" effects on one set of measures may obscure earlier or future interdependencies. This possibility highlights the need for a developmental perspective in identifying linguistic–pragmatic interactions.

View 2: Syntactic-semantic knowledge constrains pragmatic competence

The most intuitively obvious position on the interplay among syntactic, semantic, and pragmatic deficits follows the same historical sequence as research in language disorders; that is, delay in acquiring the linguistic code is primary but then leads to communicative difficulties. Clearly, pragmatic tasks require the child to mobilize vocabulary and grammatical structures rapidly and flexibly for a variety of purposes and contexts. Difficulties with any aspect of the comprehension and production of language form (e.g., articulation, word finding, syntactic structures) would seem to inhibit most aspects of the ability to be an effective communicative partner. Furthermore, one could predict that pragmatic tasks that depend on a large repertoire of surface forms for the same communicative intentions would especially be disrupted.

Evidence confirming this hypothesis is provided by work on the ability of children with specific language impairments to produce and interpret intentions, adjust speech style to listener needs, and revise their own utterances. In general, expressive syntactic skills seem to be a rather good measure of these pragmatic abilities; several studies indicate that the performance of language-impaired children is similar to that of younger, normal children matched on MLU but less advanced than that of normal children matched on age (e.g., Fey et al., 1981; Leonard, Camarata, Rowan, & Chapman, 1982; Messick & Newhoff, 1979; Skarakis & Greenfield, 1982). For example, language-impaired children seem to be sensitive to listener differences and alter aspects of their speech accordingly (Leonard, 1983). However, their choice and range of linguistic features that accommodate listener characteristics seem to be constrained by grammatical maturity. For example, in a comparison of children's speech styles during interactions with adults, age peers, and babies, Fey (1981, cited by Leonard, 1983) found that language-impaired children made several speech style adjustments similar to those of age-matched subjects. However, the expected changes in utterance length and complexity seemed to be beyond the language-impaired children's grammatical capacity; in fact, their longest utterances (addressed to adults) were less complex than the age-matched children's shortest utterances (addressed to babies).

Prinz and Ferrier (1983) also argue that pragmatic skills are greatly circumscribed by grammatical development. Scores on a sentence repetition task (the CELI) were correlated with the range of request surface forms produced and perception of politeness within a group of 30 language-impaired children (ages 3 through 9). (However, because all skills increased with age, the failure to partial out age effects is likely to have inflated these correlations.) Twenty-one of the 30 children could be classified into three severity categories representing isomorphic grammatical and pragmatic levels, indicating that "pragmatic and grammatical abilities are closely linked to one another in comprehension, production and judgment of requests in language-impaired children" (p. 49). In an earlier requesting study, Prinz (1977) found that, even compared with MLU-matched subjects, language-impaired children used fewer grammatical devices to achieve politeness, relying on "please," interrogatives, and intonation changes. Because many advanced politeness forms require mastery of the auxiliary verb system (e.g., "Could I have some candy?" "Will you give me some candy?"), an aspect known to be problematic for many language-impaired children, it is not surprising that these devices are not often used.

Of course, some language-impaired children are able to compensate for their restricted vocabulary and grammatical capabilities by drawing on social knowledge and experience. Findings of a study by Meline (1978, cited in Leonard, 1983) suggest what might be expected from a comparison of the communicative effectiveness of language-impaired children, MLU-matched younger children, and age-matched children on a referential communication task allowing for a wide selection of communicative strategies. Language-impaired children's descriptive adequacy (as measured by listeners' accuracy in identifying the referents) was midway between the performance of the age-matched and the language-matched groups; this pattern suggests that language-impaired children's communicative experience helped them to use their grammatical skills more effectively than the younger normal subjects but was not sufficient to overcome their language disabilities relative to their age-mates.

Clearly, then, a case can be made for the major role that syntactic-semantic deficits play in language-impaired children's pragmatic development. The question that arises, of course, is why these studies are relevant in explaining pragmatic skills of children typically identified on the basis of failure in academic achievement rather than by oral language deficits. However, because of the rapid expansion of research on oral language development in LD children in the past 15 years, it is not difficult to argue that many LD youngsters should be considered a subset of the language-handicapped population. In fact, it has been suggested that the terms *language-impaired* and *learning-disabled* refer to the same group of children at different ages; that is, children are labeled language-impaired if identified on the preschool level and learning-disabled if identified in elementary school (Carrow-Woolfolk & Lynch, 1982; Snyder, 1984b). In fact, Snyder (1984b) describes "the great disappearing act" of many language-impaired children as they enter school, encounter academic difficulties, and are recategorized as LD. Owen, Adams, Forrest, Stolz, and Fisher (1971) reported that almost half of their large sample ($N = 71$) of LD children had been identified during routine kindergarten screening as having speech and language problems severe enough to warrant speech therapy. Prospectively, follow-up studies indicate that children diagnosed as language-delayed on the preschool level typically experience problems in learning to read and write (Aram & Nation, 1980; Hall & Tomblin, 1978; Strominger & Bashir, 1977).

In any case, there is abundant evidence that LD children sustain underlying deficits in lexical, morphological, semantic, and syntactic knowledge (Donahue, 1986a; Snyder, 1984b). These problems emerge in both comprehension and production, on standardized language tests (e.g., MaGee & Newcomer, 1978), in structured research paradigms (e.g., Denckla & Rudel, 1976a; Fletcher, Satz, & Scholes, 1981; Vogel, 1975), and in spontaneous speech samples collected under various conditions (Donahue et al., 1982; Fry, Johnson, & Muehl, 1970; Idol-Maestas, 1980). Although many LD children's problems have been characterized as subtle, the fact remains that differences between LD and NA subjects have been demonstrated in the early elementary years and seem to persist into adolescence (Fletcher et al., 1981; Whitehouse, 1983; Wiig & Semel, 1974, 1975) and adulthood (Blalock, 1982). The consistency of these findings is particularly compelling in light of the well-known heterogeneity of the LD population and the wide variability across research studies in subject selection criteria and subject characteristics (e.g., age, IQ, sex, socioeconomic status). In fact, these important marker variables are often not reported (Keogh, Major-Kingsley, Omori-Gordon, & Reid, 1982; Torgesen & Dice, 1980).

A few studies have attempted to specify more clearly the nature of LD children's oral language disabilities by comparing them with language-impaired children or with other relevant subgroups. For example, Wong and Roadhouse (1978) found reading-disabled children without a history of language deficits to be indistinguishable from language-impaired children on several subtests of the Test of Language Development, although both groups were deficient relative to NA subjects. Similarly, Lieberman, Moore, and Hutchinson (1984) matched 14 children diagnosed as LD with 14 language-impaired subjects on the variables of age, IQ, and reading achievement and compared their performance on the Clinical Evaluation of Language Functions, a test of syntactic and semantic processing and production. Overall skills in the two groups were remarkably similar; 12 of the language-impaired and 11 of the LD children were considered to have "failed" the CELF (i.e., scored below the 20th percentile on either the processing or production dimensions). Syntactic tasks (particularly sentence repetition) were more difficult for the language-impaired children, but a qualitative analysis of all errors revealed no differences between the two groups.

In a series of studies comparing word retrieval skills in two groups of LD children, that is, those with reading disabilities versus those with learning disabilities in areas other than reading, LD children with age-appropriate reading ability still evidenced word retrieval errors (although qualitatively different from those of reading-disabled subjects) and oral vocabulary deficits equivalent to those of reading-disabled subjects (Denckla & Rudel, 1976a, 1976b; Denckla, Rudel, & Broman, 1981; Rudel, Denckla, & Broman, 1981). Finally, nondisabled children with good and poor auditory memory still achieved higher scores on a sentence repetition task than two groups of LD children with similar auditory memory abilities (Hresko, 1979).

These findings strengthen the argument that some type of oral language disorder may be an even more pervasive characteristic of LD children than has been realized. At this point, research studies do not provide a direct (or even correlational) means of determining the impact of these various language deficits on communicative development. However, it is likely that syntactic-semantic proficiency influences pragmatic performance both directly and indirectly. Direct, causal links might be observed when limitations in vocabulary and/or grammatical resources also limit the range and quality of pragmatic devices available. Indirect relations may appear when a speaker-hearer's selection of linguistic and pragmatic behaviors is mediated by his or her self-perceptions as a communicator, shaped by a history of syntactic-semantic deficits and communicative difficulties. Obviously, direct and indirect influences of syntactic-semantic skills on pragmatic development are likely to co-occur, despite the following attempt to discuss them separately.

Possible direct influence of syntactic-semantic deficits on pragmatic performance

Several referential communication studies provide some evidence that linguistic deficits are implicated in the well-documented finding that LD children are relatively unsuccessful in conveying referential information to listeners (e.g., Feagans & Short, 1984; Noel, 1980; Spekman, 1981). In two studies (Caro & Schneider, 1982; Schneider, 1982), subjects were LD adolescents rated by their teachers as having expressive language problems but adequate comprehension ability. They were compared with NA adolescents on noninteractive tasks requiring them to describe a formal operations problem and a film to a listener who had no prior or contextual information. The investigators assessed the ability to produce cohesive texts, that is, narratives whose sentences are tied together in logical ways. This entails the skill of creating referents by using a linguistic device signaling whether a topic is new information for the listener or has already been mentioned in the dialogue (e.g., "a lady," "some friends" vs. "the lady," "she," "they"). Another aspect of text cohesion is the use of connective devices that link a sentence to a previous sentence or episode (e.g., "also," "another thing is," "so this shows that"). Compared with NA students, the LD subjects used fewer appropriate referent-creating features and connective devices on both tasks; that is, their narratives and explanations were less adapted to their listener's need for explicit and cohesive information.

In other studies, information on LD subjects' oral language ability was not provided, but measures of syntactic maturity were included in the referential task itself. Tasks requiring children to retell stories or instructions just presented to them by an experimenter assess not only narrative production skills, but also verbal memory. Knight-Arrest (1984) attempted to eliminate this confusion by enlisting LD and NA boys (ages 10 to 13 years) to teach an adult how to play checkers. (Unfortunately, no effort was made to ensure that the children had a thorough understanding of the game.) Measures of syntactic-semantic skill (i.e., number and length of t units, disfluencies, vocabulary diversity and maturity) as well as communicative effectiveness (i.e., amount of information, adequacy of responses to requests for clarification) were included. The WISC-R Vocabulary scores not only seemed to be correlated with most of the variables, but also accounted for more of the variance in group differences than any other variable. Only two communication measures added a significant proportion of unique variance: LD boys were more likely to produce indefinite references (i.e., to use a pronoun or deictic form that had no prior referent or context) and gave less helpful responses to the adult's verbal requests for clarification. When responding to both verbal and nonverbal clarification requests, NA boys produced significantly longer t units, more multisyllabic words, and fewer disfluencies than did LD boys. These data suggest that the LD boys' ability to provide explicit instructions and reformulations to listeners was constrained by both syntactic formulation skills and vocabulary flexibility and knowledge.

Two studies using a "training" paradigm to separate the skills of narrative comprehension and production provide additional evidence that LD children have difficulty reproducing listener-adapted narratives in spite of adequate comprehension of the ideas to be conveyed. Subjects were drawn from the extensive longitudinal project carried out at Frank Porter Graham Child Development Center in North Carolina (McKinney & Feagans, 1984), that is, newly identified LD children (6 or 7 years old at first testing) who were assessed on the same communicative and achievement tasks over a 3-year period. Young and newly identified subjects were chosen so that the sample would be relatively free of the social and emotional problems often accompanying a long history of school failure. The LD subjects were well matched with NA controls on classroom, sex, race, and socioeconomic status; although all children scored within the normal range on the WISC-R, LD children performed more poorly than controls.

Feagans and Short (1984) used both cross-sectional and longitudinal designs to assess a subset of the LD sample described above, that is, children with reading disabilities. The subjects were read and reread a scriptlike narrative about a trip to the grocery store until they demonstrated full comprehension by nonverbally enacting all important "action units" with props. Then the children were asked to retell the story to the experimenter in their own words, in the absence of the props. Both the communicative content and the linguistic complexity of the paraphrased narratives were examined. In general, there were no consistent group differences in narrative comprehension (number of trials needed for the child to act out the story correctly); however, there were reliable cross-sectional and longitudinal group differences on several measures of narrative production. Compared with those of NA peers, LD children's narratives included fewer words, fewer idea units, a smaller proportion of syntactically complex sentences, and a greater proportion of pronouns whose noun referents had not been previously specified. The longitudinal study indicated that, although the performance of both groups improved from the first through the third grades, the disparity between reading-disabled and NA children remained the same. The only variable consistently related to reading achievement was the total number of words produced in the production task; this relation was found across all three years for the reading-disabled group but only for the first year for the NA group. For the reading-disabled group, WISC-R IQ was correlated with the narrative measures, but not with reading achievement. Thus, in contrast to the normal group, where IQ was related to achievement, a measure of linguistic output was a better predictor of reading skills than was IQ for reading-disabled children.

A second referential communication task (Feagans & Short, 1985) seemed more difficult in that the ideas to be comprehended and reproduced were not related to one another, and script knowledge could not be recruited to organize the information. Children drawn from the Frank Porter Graham sample were taught to retrieve candy from a trick box by manipulating a series of knobs in six steps (e.g., "Take the taller knob on the top of the box and push it away from the short knob on the top"). All subjects exhibited knowledge of the vocabulary for the requisite movements and placements on a pretest. As in the grocery store narrative, instructions were repeated until the children successfully opened the box; then they were asked to teach the trick to a naive listener, that is, a puppet. After the child's initial instructions, the puppet said, "I'm sorry, but I can't remember all that. Can you tell me just the first (next) thing I have to do?" thereby eliciting step-by-step rephrases of the instructions. After each rephrase, the puppet signaled noncomprehension either verbally ("I don't understand") or nonverbally (by touching the wrong knob).

Comprehension measures for this task, unlike those for the story task, revealed group differences favoring the NA subjects. The LD children not only required more repetitions of the instructions to master the trick, but also remembered fewer steps in their first attempt to retrieve the candy. In particular, LD children had difficulty recalling the directions in which to move the knobs.

The production aspect of the task also revealed reliable group differences that persisted across the 3-year period. In both their initial descriptions and their step-by-step rephrasings, LD children in the teaching role produced fewer words and information units. When responding to requests for clarification, LD and NA children were equally likely to elaborate by providing new information, and both groups improved over the 3 years. Paraphrased responses (adding no new information but using synonyms or syntactic revisions) also increased with age in both groups, but NA children showed a dramatic growth in paraphrase ability in the third year that was not matched by the LD group. The LD children also produced more nonreferential units (e.g., "here," "there," "thing" when the explicit reference was not available in the immediately preceding discourse) in both their initial descriptions and their responses to requests for clarification, but, inexplicably, only in the second year of testing.

Finally, communicative skill in the speaker role of this task also seems to predict reading achievement in LD children. The ability to produce informative messages (but not IQ) was strongly related to reading comprehension both concurrently and 3 years later. For normal children, however, the reverse was true; IQ was a much better predictor of reading skill than were the communicative measures.

Thus, the results of five studies confirm that oral language deficits co-occur with difficulties in producing narratives. Obviously, no causal links can be drawn; however, the consistency of these findings is compelling in light of the wide age range of the subjects and the differences in narrative type and coding procedures used across the studies.

Lack of syntactic and vocabulary flexibility seems to be implicated in the performance of each task. Because cohesive devices of the type examined by Caro and Schneider (1982) and Schneider (1982) are likely to add grammatical complexity on the phrase and clause level, they are likely to be avoided by adolescents with expressive language deficits. The adequacy of responses to clarification requests analyzed by Knight-Arrest (1984) and Feagans and Short (1985) shows a pattern characteristic of language-impaired subjects; LD children interpreted these signals appropriately, but the need to reformulate the messages seemed to tax their syntactic-semantic resources. The revisions of Knight-Arrest's LD subjects were not only less helpful, but also less complex, less semantically sophisticated, and more disfluent. That this pattern reflects a syntactic-semantic paraphrase problem is also supported by the fact that group differences in the Feagans and Short (1985) revision analyses emerged, *not* in the ability to elaborate by adding new details, but rather in the likelihood of reformulating the initial message by using synonyms or syntactic paraphrases. Similarly, deficient syntactic paraphrase skills seem to account for the Feagans and Short (1984) findings that LD children who demonstrated the necessary vocabulary and comprehension skills still produced shorter and less complex stories when asked to retell them in their own words.

Another striking similarity across these studies is the finding that LD subjects were less likely than NA peers to introduce new referents explicitly to their listeners. Attempting to account for this overuse of nonreferential pronouns and deictic words provides an excellent example of the complex intertwining of linguistic and pragmatic factors. For example, one social-cognitive explanation is that LD children have difficulty recognizing and/or acting on the fact that their own background knowledge is not shared by their listeners (e.g., Wong & Wong, 1980). This leads to an overestimation of their listeners' ability to identify new versus given information and to comprehend the essential elements of the narrative. This social egocentrism may be a reasonable explanation for younger LD children's performance; however, it is less convincing as a source of the communicative problems exhibited by older LD subjects (i.e., in early adolescence and beyond).

One linguistic explanation of the failure to signal new referents appropriately points to limitations in expressive vocabulary knowledge or, more likely, the ability to access known words rapidly. The pervasive nature of word retricval problems of LD children has been well documented; these difficulties emerge in a variety of naming tasks (e.g., rapidly naming pictures, letters, numbers, as well as completing a sentence and responding to a description) (German, 1979; Rudel et al., 1981; Wolf, 1981) and seem to persist into adolescence (Wiig & Semel, 1975) and adulthood (Blalock, 1982). Although the relation between word retrieval difficulties in naming tasks and during narrative production has not been specifically explored, it seems reasonable to hypothesize that slow word retrieval would be manifested by an increased use of pronouns and deictic words (e.g., "he" instead of a character's name, "over there" instead of "in the upper left-hand corner"). Liles (1985a, 1985b) also found that, relative to the narratives of age-mates, the narratives of language-impaired children contained more cohesive devices whose referents could not be found in the preceding text (termed incomplete or erroneous ties), even when the language-impaired subjects had good narrative comprehension abilities.

Word retrieval deficits would also seem to lead to disfluency and disorganization during narrative production. Wiig and Semel (1984) cite clinical reports of LD children's attempts to compensate for word retrieval problems by using frequent circumlocutions, imprecise words, and "fillers" (e.g., "and then," "ummmm," "let's see"). When interviewed about their favorite television shows, LD subjects produced somewhat more filled pauses (e.g., "umm") than NA boys (Bryan, Sherman, & Fisher, 1980), indicating that the former group may have needed more time to formulate words and sentences. Blalock (1982) reported that many LD adults had significant word retrieval delays, evidenced during spontaneous speech as well as in naming tasks. These adults were well aware of their difficulties and reported experiencing considerable frustration due to word-finding problems during conversation. These disfluencies are a possible explanation for the difficulty many LD individuals experience in social interaction in that these hesitancies have been found to be salient to teachers as well as to other children. Frequent disfluencies have been shown to be negatively related to teachers' evaluations of children's language ability and willingness to engage in talk (Williams, 1976). Similarly, Silliman (1984) found that classmates' interest in attending to language-disabled children's narratives was affected more by disfluencies than by the level of narrative complexity.

Possible indirect influences of syntactic-semantic deficits on pragmatic performance

The most convincing evidence of the role of linguistic deficits in directly constraining pragmatic effectiveness seems to have come from contrived and structured referential communication tasks in which the child is squarely in the spotlight. It might be expected that the effects of linguistic deficits would be mitigated during more spontaneous conversations that allow participants to evade topics or speech events that they believe might tax their vocabulary or grammatical resources. According to this hypothesis, communicative performance is greatly influenced by the ways in which a speaker-hearer views his or her abilities as a communicator. In the same way that bilingual speakers may choose to use their stronger language when it is necessary to maximize their communicative impact, individuals may select particular linguistic and conversational strategies to compensate for their language disabilities.

Of course, the usefulness of this "metapragmatic" hypothesis depends on the degree to which LD children are aware of their language and communicative problems. Although no studies have directly assessed self-perceptions of communicative ability, LD children readily recognize their academic and social shortcomings (e.g., Chapman & Boersma, 1979; Garrett & Crump, 1980). Dunn, Pearl, and Bryan (1981) found that LD children rated themselves lower than classmates on such classroom survival skills as the ability to "pay attention in class" and "follow teacher's directions," but perceived themselves as similar to peers on "verbally expressing yourself in class" (possibly a rare event for many children). It is likely, then, that LD children are aware, at some level, of their difficulty in comprehending and/or formulating discourse.

If this ability to evaluate one's communicative performance can be shown to lead to the selective use of certain communicative behaviors, a powerful explanation for some LD children's pragmatic behavior could be put forth. It may even be possible that the choice of *linguistic* devices is governed by the on-line scanning for structures that may be beyond one's grammatical repertoire. For example, on a sentence completion task assessing knowledge of past-tense suffixes, Moran and Byrne (1977) found not only that LD subjects were less proficient than controls, but also that some LD children attempted to hide their difficulties by offering a past-tense marker that did not involve inflecting the main verb (e.g., saying "Yesterday she did *climb*" or "She finished *climbing,*" instead of the target verb "Yesterday she *climbed*"). Similarly, language-impaired children of school age were less likely to exploit pronouns as cohesive ties in retelling a narrative (Liles, 1985a, 1985b). Because the pronominal system is a late-acquired structure for many language-impaired children, they may have devised an early strategy of using lexical and demonstrative items instead of pronouns. Liles suggests that this pronoun-avoiding tactic persisted even after the pronominal system was mastered, in that no pronominal errors on the sentence level occurred in the narratives.

This suggestive bit of data provides an excellent example of two important aspects of the metapragmatic hypothesis. First, it shows how awareness of grammatical or lexical limitations may influence a speaker's evolution of pragmatic strategies. Second, it focuses on the usefulness of a developmental perspective in accounting for linguistic–pragmatic interactions. Obviously, the latter aspect can go a long way in accounting for many of the findings presented to support View 1; that is, LD children who seem to have the necessary language abilities still differ from NA peers on some pragmatic tasks. For example, it sheds light on the puzzling finding that LD children fail to request clarification of unclear messages, even though they recognize the ambiguity and have the language skills to indicate their uncertainty. As discussed previously, repeated experiences of failure to understand oral directions may have shaken these children's confidence in their ability to recognize when requests for clarification are necessary. Unpublished data revealed that, for both LD and NA subjects, the use of requests for more information was correlated with children's beliefs about the causes of their successes (i.e., locus of control). Children who believed that their own actions were responsible for successful outcomes were more likely to request clarification than those who tended to attribute success to factors outside their control. Similarly, with the same locus-of-control measure, children's belief in internal responsibility for failure outcomes was related to their willingness to respond to an implicit request for clarification "I don't understand" (Pearl et al., 1981).

It has been proposed that LD children may fail to produce questions spontaneously because they lack the ability to monitor their comprehension of incoming messages. Kotsonis and Patterson (1980) taught LD and NA boys the rules of a novel board game. After each rule was given, the experimenter asked, "Do you know how to play yet, or do you need another rule?" LD boys claimed to have mastered the game after fewer rules were presented than did NA boys. Although interpreted by the authors as a deficit in the metacognitive skill of appraising one's understanding of how to perform a task, these results can also be explained in a way that supports the metapragmatic hypothesis. Given their history of failure in learning tasks like this one, LD boys may have simply interpreted the experimenter's repeated questions to mean that they *should* have already learned the game. Thus, one obvious face-saving technique was simply to pretend to have learned enough rules and to go on with the game.

Rumelhart (1983) makes a similar case for the important role of speaker beliefs about his or her competence in explaining conversational behavior. In an ethnographic study of developmentally disabled adults, she described a set of strategies that they used when unsure of their understanding of topics under discussion or the context:

Upon finding oneself unsure about the definition of the situation, it would ordinarily be easier either to admit one's confusion and ask for clarification or else to walk out (literally or figuratively) on the interaction. The motivation to avoid these obvious alternatives arises from a conviction that one probably *ought to know* what is happening and, furthermore, that acknowledging one's doubt entails significant jeopardy. (p. 378)

These face-saving techniques were categorized as either offensive or defensive. Offensive strategies were attempts to manipulate the situation or topic so that the speaker could both mask his or her lack of knowledge and feel competent to participate, for example, by changing the subject to one that was comfortable and then controlling it by elaboration. More insecure participants used defensive strategies that allowed them to say as little as possible while still fulfilling their social obligations, for example, by producing yes or no answers, vague agreements, or stock phrases and failing to volunteer relevant comments or to request clarification when necessary.

These strategies, particularly the defensive ones, are remarkably similar to the conversational behaviors that characterize conversational interactions of LD children. In fact, LD adults with residual deficits in language comprehension or production reported using these techniques when engaged in fast-paced conversation and bantering in groups (Blalock, 1982). Because they often failed to follow the dialogues, they were reluctant to contribute their own remarks. Furthermore, they reported trying to hide their uncertainty by simply nodding and smiling or by laughing when other members of the group laughed.

Two studies examined LD children's conversational performance in a context in which they were compelled to take the offensive position; that is, they were given the role of a television talk show host, interviewing another child about favorite television shows and movies. Learning-disabled children in grades 2 and 4 (Bryan, Donahue, Pearl, & Sturm, 1981) had difficulty maintaining the flow of dialogue. Although they contributed the same proportion of talk as NA hosts, LD children asked fewer questions in general, and a smaller proportion of their questions obligated their interviewees ("guests") to produce explanations or narratives (i.e., open-ended or "process" questions). Some LD children (particularly LD girls and LD second graders) were more likely to smooth the transition between turns with content-free conversational devices (e.g., "oh," "okay," "uh-huh"), possibly as a means of compensating for difficulty in formulating propositions that were tied to their partners' turn.

The performance of the talk show guests (NA classmates) provided corroborating evidence of the LD children's tendency to lose conversational control. The LD subjects' guests were less likely to go beyond the minimal demands of the questions addressed to them. Furthermore, the guests' questions directed to LD hosts were more likely to solicit a yes–no answer (i.e., choice question), suggesting that guests were not confident of the LD hosts' ability to respond to a less constraining question. Finally, of 40 dyads, nine spontaneously reversed roles in that the designated guest also interviewed the host; eight of these dyads included LD subjects as hosts.

More subtle evidence that partners assigned to an LD host were at a social disadvantage comes from research on strangers' immediate impressions of children's nonverbal behavior during conversation. A number of studies by J. Bryan and his associates indicate that LD children (presented on videotape with no audio information available) elicit rapid negative impressions from naive judges (e.g., Bryan & Sherman, 1980). Using a subset of the videotapes collected from the talk show task, Bryan, Bryan, and Sonnefeld (1982) not only replicated the finding that LD children are viewed less positively than NA children, but also found a "contagion" effect; children who interacted with LD hosts were perceived less favorably than guests of NA hosts, even though judges were able to view only the child being rated. (This finding applied to the fourth-grade but not the second-grade subjects.) This evidence of discomfort or hostility on the part of the guests cannot be attributed solely to LD children's history of low social status; sociometric scores indicated that this particular sample of LD subjects was not rejected by classmates. Furthermore, in a posttask interview, guests of LD children were just as likely as guests of NA hosts to indicate a desire to enact the talk show again with the same rather than a new host.

Obviously, the different roles played by direct versus indirect effects of language deficits cannot be unraveled by this study; no syntax or vocabulary measures on the subjects or during the task itself were available. However, the finding that LD children asked fewer questions could be interpreted as a reflection of problems in formulating question transformations. Furthermore, although process questions (e.g., "Why . . . ?" "How . . . ?") do not necessarily require more grammatical knowledge than product questions (e.g., "Who . . . ?" "What . . . ?" "When . . . ?") or choice questions, they do tend to elicit longer and less predictable responses. Perhaps LD children avoid posing open-ended questions in order to reduce their comprehension load and/or inhibit their partners from meandering into uncharted topics, to which the host must then respond. Whether these self-doubts are warranted, the finding that guests produced fewer elaborated responses suggests that the content or structure of LD children's questions was difficult to process or expand.

A second study (Donahue & Bryan, 1983) attempted to sort out these hypotheses by testing the effects of a brief model on children's interviewing strategies and on their perceptions of conversational skills. It was hypothesized that LD children may have the necessary conversational skills in their repertoire but do not activate them because (1) they do not recognize what social contexts call for their use and/or (2) they believe that excessive demands will be placed on their linguistic resources. Two subtests from the Clinical Evaluation of Language Functions (Semel & Wiig, 1980) were administered; LD boys were found to be equivalent to NA boys in comprehension (Processing Word and Sentence Structure) but deficient in the production subtest (Formulated Sentence Scores). Before each 4-minute talk show, LD and NA boys in grades 2 through 8 listened to either (1) a dialogue of a child interviewer modeling process questions, conversational devices, and contingent comments and responses, or (2) a monologue presenting only the guest's responses (i.e., the control condition). The LD children in the monologue condition produced a smaller proportion of process questions and comments (i.e., spontaneously offered opinions or expansions of the guest's remarks), and they contributed less talk to the interaction. However, the dialogue condition was sufficient to increase their use of these behaviors and their talkativeness to the level of their NA counterparts.

Surprisingly, although modeling facilitated the use of certain conversational skills by LD hosts, these changes did not enhance the performance of their guests. For older subjects (grades 5 through 8), the dialogue condition increased the likelihood that guests would elaborate in response to the process questions of NA hosts, but the reverse was true for LD hosts. Relative to the monologue condition, the dialogue condition actually depressed the use of elaborated responses to process questions by guests of LD hosts. These results suggest that, as LD children changed the *form* of their questions to match the process questions of the model, they may have also made the content more difficult to comprehend or to elaborate. Another explanation is that, in their efforts to produce process questions that encourage their listeners to give lengthy responses, the older LD children may have instead generated questions that were too vague or unconstrained to answer in an extended way. Further evidence that problems in linguistic structure may have interfered with these children's formulation of coherent questions and comments is provided by the results that LD children elicited more requests for clarification from their guests than did NA children, and this difference was especially apparent in the dialogue condition. Taken together, these data point to the subtle but significant deficits in productive language ability found in this sample of LD youngsters as one source of the guests' behavior.

It seems likely, then, that LD children's communicative experiences have convinced them that the conversation flows more smoothly if they avoid spontaneous comments and restrict themselves to asking questions that are easy to answer. Analyses of children's perceptions of conversational skills support this metapragmatic hypothesis by demonstrating that LD children were remarkably sensitive evaluators of their own performance and the behavior of their listeners. After the talk show task, children were asked, "Now that you've been a host on a talk show, suppose you were going to give advice to another kid to help him be a good talk show host [and guest, in a second question]. What things would you tell him?" Analyses of these responses indicated that the LD children recognized their difficulties in conversational interaction. The LD children were more likely than the NA subjects to be concerned about the hosts' emotional states (e.g., "Don't be nervous"), suggesting that they perceived the conversational task as a stressful one. Furthermore, the dialogue condition increased the LD hosts' recognition of their need to prepare themselves for the role of talk show host, suggesting that this condition magnified the differences between their conversational style and that of the model.

Even more striking is the evidence that the LD children were sensitive to the effects of the modeling condition on their guests' performance. The LD subjects in the dialogue condition were less likely than their monologue controls to mention the quality and quantity of their guests' responses as relevant to a successful interaction, perhaps because the model provided the LD hosts with techniques to take control of these aspects of the conversation. Instead, the dialogue condition heightened their awareness of their guests' responsibility to maintain the surface form of the conversation, that is, of their affective states, fluency, and nonverbal appropriateness. These findings parallel the behavioral data that guests of LD children in the dialogue condition produced fewer elaborated responses and more requests for clarification.

In general, it appears that, after exposure to the dialogue model, some linguistic or possibly paralinguistic features of the LD children's conversational style caused their guests to feel less comfortable in their role. This interpretation is consistent with the previous study, in which the nonverbal behavior of children interacting with an LD classmate was viewed as more hostile and less relaxed than that of children interacting with an NA child (Bryan et al., 1982; Bryan, Donahue, Pearl, & Sturm, 1981).

This pattern of conversational style and perceptions indicates that LD children are aware that their attempts to gain conversational control are met by subtle resistance from peers, probably because of difficulty in processing and expanding LD partners' remarks. In this instance, LD children's perceptions that their linguistic limitations may prohibit the use of certain conversational strategies seem warranted.

In the next set of conversational interaction studies, the case for the metapragmatic hypothesis was not so clear in that measures of syntactic-semantic ability or conversational perceptions were not available. However, the LD subjects seemed to be operating under the same defensive principles evident during the talk show task: When uncertain about one's language proficiency, one should exploit those conversational behaviors that do not demand sophisticated syntactic skills and avoid those that do. Three studies used a group problem-solving task to examine LD children's conversational assertiveness and persuasive skills.

The subjects for all three studies were drawn from a large sample of experimenter-identified LD and NA children from parochial schools that did not identify or provide special education services for students with learning problems. Although no oral language measures were available from this subsample, other subsamples identified with the same criteria showed differences between LD and NA subjects in MLU (Donahue et al., 1982) and the comprehension of various kinds of relative clauses (Haber, 1981). Also, sociometric data from the large sample indicated that LD children were not as well accepted by their peers as were NA controls (Bryan, Donahue, & Pearl, 1981).

Bryan, Donahue, and Pearl (1981) matched LD and NA children in grades 3 through 8 with two same-sex classmates; the triads were asked to reach a consensus on the ranking of 15 potential gifts for their classmates. Although LD children contributed as many conversational turns as NA subjects, their style of participating in the discussions was clearly less assertive. When a response that was accessible from the linguistic context was required or salient, the LD children appeared eager to participate. Compared with NA subjects, LD children were more likely to agree with their classmates' opinions and to respond to their requests for opinion or clarification. They were as likely as controls to nominate a particular gift as a topic for discussion. Given the nature of the task, all three strategies seemed to provide an easy opening into the conversation. However, those communicative intentions that may demand more sophisticated syntactic-semantic skills were avoided, in that LD children were less likely than NA subjects to disagree or to attempt to negate their partners' arguments. They also seemed unwilling to assume the group leader's role, providing fewer "conversational housekeeping" utterances, that is, whose purpose was to keep the group on task. Finally, LD children rarely made bids to claim the conversational floor.

Although this style of interaction seemed to provide an easy and even adaptive means for LD children to participate in the task, the consequence was that they had little impact on their group's decisions. Not surprisingly, LD children's initial gift preferences (made independently before the group task began) were less likely to be included among their group's final favorites. A pretask "pep talk" given to half the children emphasized that they had made good choices and promised a "special reward" if they could convince their partners to make the same choices. Even this inducement had no effect on the LD children's persuasiveness. In fact, naive judges rated LD children in the pep talk condition *less* cooperative with peers than LD children who had not received these instructions.

Donahue and Prescott (1983) replicated this finding of deficient persuasive skills with a group decision-making task adapted for children in grades 1 and 2; the ability to resolve spontaneously occurring disputes was examined. No group differences were apparent in the frequency of conversational turns, topic initiations, agreements, or disagreements. Nevertheless, LD youngsters were less capable than the other children of winning the final moves in the disputes. Thus, young LD children's opinions were less likely to be accepted by their classmates, even though they seemed to be playing an active role in the dispute episodes. These findings suggest that the passive conversational style of older LD children may have evolved from their history of communicative ineffectiveness in earlier years; by middle childhood, these children seem to have given up attempting to influence their classmates' ideas.

Finally, this unassertive style does not seem to be limited to talk with familiar peers, but extends even to interactions with mothers (Bryan, Donahue, Pearl, & Herzog, 1984). In a variation of the group decision-making task, LD subjects were found to be more likely to agree and less likely to disagree with their mothers than were NA controls.

Summary

Obviously, direct versus indirect influences cannot easily be isolated in explaining pragmatic performance. That LD children are more likely to agree and less likely to disagree or debate with their partner's opinions illustrates this point clearly. Even young children recognize that, relative to agreements, the opposing of another's intentions is much more likely to call for justification of one's position (Eisenberg & Garvey, 1981). This requires not only more talk, but probably more sentence embedding and the use of more subordinate clauses; in fact, Campos, de Castro, and de Lemos (1979, cited in Ervin-Tripp and Gordon, 1986) showed that young children's production of reasons to justify their requests is related to the growth of "because" clauses. Children with less proficient grammatical skills might not be able to mobilize these structures rapidly, which provides support for direct influences on pragmatic behavior. On the other hand, for a speaker who feels out of his or her linguistic or communicative depths, agreements are an effective defensive strategy for getting by; disagreements place a speaker at risk for revealing a (perceived) lack of understanding or persuasive skills.

Of course, these need not be competing hypotheses; direct and indirect influences may occur concurrently or may apply differentially to each pragmatic task. For example, as suggested earlier, tasks that allow for a wider range of conversational strategies may show fewer direct effects of syntactic-semantic disability. More important, these two kinds of linguistic constraints on pragmatic skill may represent a developmental continuum for some children.

As Fletcher et al. (1981) suggested, the observable manifestations of language disability may change over time, in that deficits in particular language domains that are salient at younger ages may be replaced by problems in other language skills at a later point. Some LD children who show early signs of deficient grammatical and lexical knowledge may actually "catch up" to NA peers; however, their self-perceptions as poor communicators, as well as the interactional style that evolved to compensate for early language problems, may linger. To test these hypotheses, we should seek evidence that metapragmatic beliefs are better predictors of communicative styles than are linguistic abilities.

In sum, these hypotheses of linguistic constraints on pragmatic performance have some face validity, but obviously more data are needed to identify which language structure deficits are most detrimental to pragmatic development. However, rather than randomly correlating aspects of syntactic-semantic knowledge with pragmatic development and then trying to come up with post hoc explanations, we must formulate a theory-driven model to derive hypotheses about the local effects of specific linguistic skills on specific pragmatic behaviors.

View 3: Pragmatic knowledge constrains syntactic-semantic development

This view holds that pragmatics, rather than being a mere taxonomy of language uses mapped onto syntactic-semantic devices, is actually the primary motivation for language growth. The most compelling and detailed model is the Bates and MacWhinney (1979, 1982) functionalism approach; their characterization of the relations between form and function is that "the point-making function (i.e., topicalization) plays a strong causal role in the way particular forms have evolved and in the way those forms are used by adults and acquired by children" (1982, p. 175). They review a number of studies showing a developmental relation between syntax and pragmatic functions. For example, the use of such diverse grammatical structures as ellipsis, fronting, clefting, contrastive stress, pronominalization, and definite or indefinite articles is governed by the intent to distinguish for one's listener new information from given or shared information. In fact, Bates et al. (1982) suggest that "even the earliest rules of child grammar respect a division between 'proposed' and 'presupposed' information. To make that division properly, the child will have to be able to make a vast set of rapid calculations of listener knowledge. *This is inherently social knowledge, not derivable from any other aspects of cognition*" (p. 68).

In reaction to the prevalent innateness explanation of language acquisition, other theorists made similar claims for the central role of social interaction in fueling linguistic development. One strong antinativist position holds that "both the strategies for acquiring syntactic knowledge, and the child's development of semantic categories, depend upon an awareness of social relationships, and these strategies continue to structure social reality for the child" (Cook-Gumperz, 1977, p. 103; see also Bruner, 1975; Nelson, 1973). This interactionist position emphasizes the importance of reciprocal and harmonious caregiver–child interaction in the early months of life. These prelinguistic dialogues then provide the scaffolding within which the child can see relations between interactional knowledge and language forms. For example, Bruner (1975) proposed that the child could derive semantic relations and even word-order rules by drawing an analogy from experiences of joint actions on objects. Furthermore, the research literature on maternal language input is often cited to support the claim that the social and linguistic context is "fine-tuned" to the child's language level, in that motherese purportedly provides an ordered set of data that can account for the order of acquisition of language features (but see Shatz, 1982b).

Whether or not characteristics of mother–child interaction can be shown to facilitate specific aspects of language acquisition in *normal* children, the importance of mutually satisfying communication for later language learning seems obvious when one is examining interactions that are nonoptimal or dysfunctional. However, it must be pointed out that there is very little specific evidence of a causal role played by social-communicative factors on language growth. In a comprehensive review of studies attempting to find a social base for language acquisition, Bates et al. (1982) point out that nonsignificant effects of even correlational data far outweigh the significant effects. However, before dismissing the role of social-communicative input, these authors suggest a possible conceptual confound that seems directly relevant to speculations about the nature of LD children's early interactions with caregivers and the consequences of these interactions.

Namely, the important role of the child's motivation has been neglected in the search for links between early interaction and language development. Bates and her colleagues (1982) suggest that the child's temperament and sociability could directly or indirectly facilitate language development on several levels. First, a warm relationship between parent and child will lead to the child's increased willingness to observe, imitate, and interact with adults, thereby allowing the mother to guide her infant's attention to joint activities and the verbal and gestural input that accompanies them. The child is then able to use the resemblance between preverbal dialogues and shared activity to derive primitive semantic, pragmatic, and even syntactic rules. Meanwhile, changes in mothers' linguistic input are timed to be just one step ahead of the child's language abilities.

Bates et al. (1982) provide two examples of how the consideration of emotional and motivational factors can cast a new perspective on correlational data. Tulkin and Covitz (1975) found a negative correlation between mothers' "prohibition ratio" at 10 months of age and the child's vocabulary comprehension at 6 years. As these researchers point out:

Do we really want to argue that saying "no" to children decreases their vocabulary? It is likely that the link is much more indirect: a relationship characterized by high rates of saying "no" may be one in which (because of the child's character, the mother's, or both) very little decent conversation ever gets underway. . . . Because the relationship was so bad, the child's progress in language has suffered across the board. (p. 51)

Similarly, one finding from the motherese literature is often cited as an example of the specific effects of mothers' use of one syntactic structure on children's language learning; that is, the frequency of auxiliary fronted questions (e.g., "Are you making a tower?") was related to the child's later use of auxiliary verbs (Newport, Gleitman, & Gleitman, 1977). However, as Bates et al. point out, even this is subject to a motivational interpretation in that mothers and children in mutually satisfying interaction are simply more likely to attend to and talk about the other partner's actions, leading to a high proportion of progressive verb forms. These examples are intriguing because they illustrate how pervasive the role of harmonious caregiver–child relationships may be.

The dyad's motivation to participate in early interaction seems to be necessary to "bootstrap" themselves into the language-facilitating cycle described above; therefore, infants who may be temperamentally "difficult" to establish warm relationships with or to engage in shared activity may be at risk of experiencing later language delay. Thus, if there were evidence of differences in LD children's pragmatic or interactional style from the onset of language acquisition, it could be argued that their linguistic progress is actually disrupted, or at least may be governed by different (perhaps less efficient) social mechanisms.

At this point, View 3 is the least defensible, yet most provocative position. It could be a powerful explanation for the findings of pervasive and persistent language and communicative deficits in many LD students. Despite the enormous heterogeneity of the LD population, these individuals share one defining characteristic: an inefficient style of processing information. Since learning disabilities are presumed to be intrinsic to the child and not the primary result of environmental factors, it is possible that, however subtle, these cognitive deficits are apparent in infancy and significantly influence the nature of the caregiver–child relationship from the very beginning.

Obviously, there are no studies of communicative interaction in LD children and their mothers during infancy or early childhood, because children are rarely identified as learning-disabled before they start school. However, two bodies of research help build the case that many LD children's language problems may be traceable to atypical social interactions during early childhood, that is, research on mothers' interactions with high-risk children and with language-impaired children.

Perinatal factors (e.g., gestational age, birthweight, respiratory distress) are related not only to later language disabilities (e.g., Field, Goldberg, Demsey, & Shuman, 1979; Lassman, Fish, Vetter, & La Benz, 1980; Siegel, 1982) but also to social and personality differences in later childhood (e.g., Davies & Stewart, 1975; Werner, Bierman, & French, 1971). However, as the interactionist position would predict, the quality of mother–child interaction is a powerful mediator of the effects of birth-related complications. In fact, there is increasing evidence that assessments of mother–child interactions during the first year are better predictors of preschool and school-age developmental outcomes than are perinatal variables (e.g., Beckwith & Cohen, 1980; Bee et al., 1982; Cohen, Parmelee, Sigman, & Beckwith, 1982).

The sizable literature on mothers' interactions with high-risk infants generally portrays these mothers as more directive and controlling than mothers of normal-birth infants (see Field, Goldberg, Stern, & Sostek, 1980, for reviews). Not surprisingly, the less organized and less adapted responses of the preterm infant cause the mother to work harder to keep her child engaged in the dialogue. Thus, the risk of interactive difficulty is relatively high. In fact, that these special adaptations are stressful and beyond the capabilities of a small proportion of parents is shown by the disturbing findings that preterm infants are overrepresented in the incidence of child abuse and failure to thrive (e.g., Elmer & Gregg, 1967, cited by Goldberg, Brachfeld, & DiVitto, 1980).

At the least, these data suggest that the mother–preterm infant communicative relationship may follow a different developmental course from that of full-term dyads. Donahue and Pearl (1984) showed that a more directive communicative style persisted even in mothers' interactions with 4-year-old children who had been preterm but whose language and cognitive skills were developing normally.

Studies of communicative interactions of mothers with their language-impaired children raise similar issues about whether differences in mothers' styles reflect or interfere with their children's language development. In general, there seems to be a consensus that the conversational style of most mothers represents natural and appropriate adaptations to their language-impaired children's comprehension and production abilities. However, there is some evidence that the discrepancy between their child's language disability and his or her normal development in (non-verbal) cognitive and other domains is difficult for mothers to understand and deal with. Two studies compared mothers of language-impaired children with two groups of mothers of children with language skills commensurate with their mental age, that is, mentally retarded Down syndrome children and normally developing children.

In an evaluation of the quality of maternal support and home environment of these three groups (Wulbert, Inglis, Kriegsmann, & Mills, 1975), no differences were found between the normal and retarded groups; however, mothers of language-impaired children were observed to be less emotionally and verbally responsive and less involved with their children, as well as more likely to criticize and punish them, than were other mothers. These observations were significantly correlated with the degree of discrepancy between children's nonverbal IQ and verbal ability. Petersen and Sherrod (1982) confirmed the findings that mothers were less responsive to their language-impaired children than were mothers of retarded or normal subjects, even though all children were matched on MLU. A larger proportion of mothers' utterances were unrelated to their language-impaired children's play activities (i.e., asynchronous), and this trend became exaggerated as the children aged. Amazingly, for language-impaired 2-year-olds, almost one-third of the mothers' utterances were asynchronous, and this proportion increased to almost one-half for the language-impaired 3-year-olds. Mothers of language-impaired children also made fewer approving comments on their children's conversational contributions than did either of the other two groups of mothers.

Similarly, in a study of five domains emerging from a large data archive of 718 language-impaired children (i.e., IQ, language history, socioeconomic status, physical history, and social and emotional background), Schery (1985) found that social-emotional and personality factors assessed through parent questionnaires were not related to severity of language disorder at initial testing. However, this cluster (along with a weak contribution of nonverbal IQ) was the *only* significant predictor of relative growth in language ability over 2 to 3 years. The strongest of the social-emotional variables, negatively related to language gain, were the child's preference for isolated versus social play, behavior problems, enrollment in counseling, low incidence of positive comments volunteered by the parent about the child, and parents' use of physical methods of discipline.

Taken together, these findings indicate that the role of early social-emotional relationships in communicative development should not be underestimated. Both preterm and language-impaired children have been found to be at risk for later emotional problems. Language-impaired children in particular are characterized by both teachers and parents as having attentional deficits and poor social relationships (e.g., Baker, Cantwell, & Mattison, 1980). Although it has been claimed that these emotional problems are caused by the speech and language disorders (Cantwell & Baker, 1977), it is more likely that, from infancy, communicative problems, social-emotional status, and caregiver–child interactions are intertwined in complex ways.

The negative attitudes of parents toward their high-risk or language-impaired infants or children are virtually mirrored by the research on parent perceptions of their school-aged LD children, as well as their memories of their children's behavior as infants. For example, parental attitudes were included in a landmark study of a large sample of LD children ($N = 71$) and their same-sex nondisabled siblings, as well as comparison groups of NA subjects (Owen et al., 1971). Compared with both NA controls and siblings, LD subjects were perceived by their parents as having less verbal ability, less impulse control, less ability to structure their environment, and more anxiety. These characteristics were related to decreased affection expressed by parents. Furthermore, LD youngsters were described as having more serious problems and as causing their parents more worry. Parents' awareness of their children's communicative problems was indicated by the findings that mothers of LD children were more likely to report that their children had difficulty attending to stories read to them and to describe their LD children as "more difficult to talk to" than siblings.

Medical history information portrayed the LD children during infancy as more irritable, more colicky, and less likely to babble; poor listening skills after age 2, difficult mother–child communication, and temper tantrums were also more frequently reported by parents of LD children than by parents of NA subjects. Similarly, mothers of severely LD sons reported that, as infants, their children had been less active, slower to respond, less sociable, less predictable, and more irritable than normal boys, as perceived by their mothers (Scholom & Schiff, 1980). Of course, these retrospective data are likely to be contaminated by parents' knowledge of their children's current personalities and learning problems. However, the similarity of their reports to the findings of prospective studies of high-risk infants gives the results some face validity.

In any case, this constellation of negative attitudes and social interactions of parents of high-risk, language-impaired, and LD children is not consistent with the finely calibrated and supportive communication network that interactionists believe is necessary for optimal language growth. Of course, it is probable that these disjointed relationships reflect the atypical temperaments and responsiveness of some infants. Almost immediately, these effects are likely to become bidirectional; the difficult personality of the infant leads to a less harmonious relationship with the mother, which in turn limits the mother's opportunities to provide optimal social and language input, which further shapes the child's communicative style.

Of course, the possibility exists that neither the caregiver's nor the child's contribution to the dyad is atypical or pathological; rather, the "goodness of fit" between the two partners' expectations and interactive style may be the critical issue. Nelson (1973) proposed that a mismatch between mother and child communicative strategies can have serious consequences for the child's syntactic and vocabulary growth.

Allocation of resources model

Another version of the interactionist hypothesis that seems particularly useful is the "allocation-of-resources" model sketched by Shatz (1982a):

> This alternative takes as a given that in any conversational situation young children have essentially two tasks, one to create a productive grammar on the basis of the language to which they are exposed, and the other to function as active participants in their social worlds. To the extent that the interactive task can be accomplished with relative ease, more resources can be allocated to the analytic task. (p. 14)

Thus, this position assigns a larger role to the child in the determination of how and what linguistic structures are acquired. Presumably, young children evolve efficient interactive strategies that enable them not only to get by in conversation, but also to manipulate the linguistic input to highlight those grammatical and lexical structures that may be just beyond their current language knowledge.

Snyder-McLean and McLean (1978) describe some conversational "gimmicks" that they believe serve children's language learning needs by means of "verbal information gathering." For example, selective imitation is a productive strategy for maintaining dialogue, yet also seems to give children the opportunity to rehearse newly acquired forms and elicit more data from the adult. Similarly, metalinguistic speech acts function as a means by which the child acquires further linguistic knowledge; these range from direct questions to utterances whose purpose seems to be hypothesis testing, that is, by eliciting an adult's confirmation or correction. In turn, increases in linguistic skill that flow from the use of these strategies then enable the child to engage in more sophisticated and more wideranging social exchanges, creating bidirectional effects between pragmatic and linguistic development.

This allocation-of-resources model seems particularly useful for explaining how LD children's pragmatic knowledge may constrain linguistic growth. The notion of limited resources and the failure to use efficient strategic behaviors has been widely invoked to characterize LD children's attentional and memory deficits (e.g., Torgesen, 1977). Snyder (1984a) recruits a similar "multiple-resources" framework for examining the variability across communicative domains in language-disordered children (Snyder & Downey, 1983). Given the possibility of less than optimal social interaction during infancy and early childhood, some LD children may not easily evolve these interactional strategies for minimal social participation or for eliciting specific linguistic data. Thus, if excessive resources are expended on trying to process social interaction cues, less energy will be available for the analytic task of discerning relations between the speech stream and objects and events in the context. Another possibility is that LD children may choose conversational strategies that reflect different social goals, as suggested by studies of LD children's performance on persuasive tasks. The net effect may be to elicit linguistic input from parents and peers that may be less transparent or may lead to idiosyncratic paths of language development.

Another approach evolving from the interactionist position that is very compatible with the allocation-of-resources model is the script framework of event representation (Nelson, 1981; Nelson & Gruendel, 1979). Defined as a spatially and temporally organized set of expectations about the actors, actions, and props likely to be present during a given event, scripts serve as a guide to routine social encounters (e.g., dining out, birthday parties, school events). This knowledge then frees up cognitive resources for attending to novel aspects of the event. Nelson and Gruendel (1979) suggest that the conversational turn-taking structure may itself be conceptualized as a kind of social script, albeit a very general one.

These descriptions are reminiscent of the highly routinized interactions in which children learn early words (e.g., "bye-bye"). Nelson and Gruendel (1979) extend this idea, suggesting that it is within the shared scriptal knowledge of mother and child that "the child learns not only the turn-taking aspect of conversational structure, but also the semantics and syntactics of conversational contingencies, such as topic sharing and contingent responding" (p. 91). They suggest that the sophistication of children's skills in exchanging information and maintaining topical coherence can be predicted by the degree to which the dialogue is organized around shared script knowledge.

In light of LD children's difficulties in processing social information and their perhaps qualitatively different history of social experiences, two hypotheses can be generated from this script model of linguistic–pragmatic development. First, incomplete or inefficient learning of particular scripts may mean that some required or optional components are not automatically accessible to LD children. Thus, if the child is less able to gather momentum as he or she proceeds in a social interaction through recognizing script signals, resources that could be spent on learning new linguistic structures or social rules must be diverted.

Second, and possibly more important, LD children may not necessarily be deficient in script knowledge or accessibility. Instead, on the basis of their social experiences, LD children may have constructed rules for expected communicative behavior in particular settings from qualitatively different data. Thus, they may select communicative strategies that meet social goals that are different from those of their peers. For example, Higgins (1981) suggests that the ability to adjust request forms to listener characteristics may reflect the degree to which certain conversational conventions have become scripted (e.g., polite requests to teachers and other powerful adults). Rather than measuring a child's on-line perspective-taking skills, the choice of an appropriate politeness device may merely reflect the activation of a social script for the way one speaks to certain people. In this light, Donahue's (1981) findings that LD boys varied their request forms in different ways than NA boys can be interpreted as evidence for *differing* social scripts.

The source of these differences remains to be determined. However, one possibility is that LD children's perceptions of their social and communicative difficulties lead them to evolve a model for appropriate communicative behavior that accommodates different goals for social interaction. For example, one overriding goal may be to maintain a low-profile style of participation while gathering data and testing hypotheses about what is expected and valued by parents, teachers, and peers. This interpretation is compatible with the metapragmatic hypothesis of View 2.

In sum, View 3 is the most speculative position; there are few relevant data to support it or even to enable us to present more specific hypotheses. However, it has great potential for accounting for individual routes to linguistic and pragmatic development. If linguistic progress can be characterized as a series of solutions to communicative problems, the nature of the social and communicative networks within which LD children learn language deserves greater attention.

Final thoughts

This chapter might be better suited to a volume called *Meanderings in applied psycholinguistics* rather than *Advances*. The arguments put forth to support each of the three views seem to "double back" more than move forward. At this point, the kinds of evidence needed to select one version of one view over another are simply not available. In fact, it is probably not even wise to attempt to disqualify or rule out possible hypotheses generated by each view. Instead, now that a sizable body of research on LD children's linguistic and pragmatic development has accumulated, it is a good time to consider all possibilities of the interactions between linguistic and pragmatic development. It is hoped that an exercise of this sort will enable us to reconsider and refine our research goals, which will in turn lead to more clearly and carefully designed research studies.

Not only is it premature to draw conclusions about these three views, it may also be unnecessary. Rather than being competing hypotheses, they may be equally viable explanations for different subgroups of LD children. It could be speculated that the identification of these subgroups depends, not on their actual language or communicative characteristics at any particular time, but rather on developmental history. For example, View 2 might best describe those children who exhibit an early and persistent history of obvious delay across all language domains. View 3 might fit the temperamentally "difficult" infant who grows into a child with attentional deficits and an ineffective communicative style; the consequent oral language difficulties of this child might be relatively subtle and inconsistent across domains.

To complicate the issue, these views might represent a developmental continuum for some children. However, one major difficulty in the task of tracing the course of developmental changes in linguistic–pragmatic interactions is the possibility that subgroups within the LD population are likely to follow their own developmental timetables. Thus, the inability to identify and examine these subgroups separately may obscure the developmental shifts; this may account in part for the findings supporting View 1 – that linguistic development and pragmatic development seem to be "out of synch." In fact, it has even been suggested that some language therapy formats may actually contribute to these linguistic–pragmatic discrepancies in school-aged children (Steckol, 1983). Therefore, another factor to be included in the equation to identify subgroups may be the kinds of language intervention particular children received.

Obviously, the longitudinal research needed to verify these developmental changes in linguistic–pragmatic interdependencies in various subgroups of LD children would be very difficult to conduct. However, it is hoped that the hypotheses generated in this chapter will, at the least, convince researchers interested in pragmatic development of the importance of including syntactic-semantic measures in their studies. Even now, when it is clearly no longer necessary to persuade psycholinguists that pragmatics is a domain worthy of investigation in its own right, there still seems to be some resistance to the notion that linguistic knowledge may interact with pragmatic development in interesting ways. For example, Ervin-Tripp and Gordon (1986) make the following claim:

The expansion of psycholinguistic research to include pragmatics (the relation of language to social interaction and the functions served by speech) raises very few new linguistic issues. . . . Thus, the basic issues in the child's acquisition of socially appropriate speech are social, not linguistic, and pragmatic research in the future must look less to questions raised by linguistic research than to issues of social development. (p. 92)

At best, this conclusion seems premature in that the data necessary to prove or disprove it have not yet been collected. Furthermore, this view seems incompatible with current psycholinguistic conceptual beliefs that developing language domains are highly interactive. For example, recent work has begun to demonstrate the usefulness of examining trade-offs among lexical access, phonology, and syntactic complexity in explaining both normal and atypical language development (e.g., Bock, 1982; Campbell & Shriberg, 1982; Donahue, 1986b; Kamhi, Catts, & Davis, 1984). It seems clear that identifying where and how linguistic and pragmatic domains intersect will be equally powerful in accounting for individual differences in language learning style.

References

Aram, D., & Nation, J. (1980). Preschool language disorders and subsequent academic difficulties. *Journal of Communication Disorders, 13,* 159–70.

Asher, S., & Renshaw, P. (1981). Children without friends: Social knowledge and social skills training. In S. Asher & J. Gottman (Eds.), *The development of children's friendships* (pp. 273–96). Cambridge University Press.

Bachara, G. H. (1976). Empathy in learning disabled children. *Perceptual and Motor Skills, 43,* 541–2.

Baker, L., Cantwell, D., & Mattison, R. (1980). Behavior problems in children with pure speech disorders and in children with combined speech and language disorders. *Journal of Abnormal Child Psychology, 8,* 245–56.

Bates, E. (1976). *Language and context: The acquisition of pragmatics.* New York: Academic Press.

Bates, E., Benigni, L., Bretherton, I., Camaioni, L., & Volterra, V. (1979). *The emergence of symbols: Cognition and communication in infancy.* New York: Academic Press.

Bates, E., Bretherton, I., Beeghly-Smith, M., & McNew, S. (1982). Social bases of language development: A reassessment. In H. W. Reese & L. P. Lipsitt (Eds.), *Advances in child development and behavior* (Vol. 16, pp. 8–75). New York: Academic Press.

Bates, E., & MacWhinney, B. (1979). A functionalist approach to acquisition of grammar. In E. Ochs and B. Schieffelin (Eds.), *Developmental pragmatics* (pp. 167–211). New York: Academic Press.

Bates, E., & MacWhinney, B. (1982). Functionalist approaches to grammar. In E. Wanner and L. Gleitman (Eds.), *Language acquisition: The state of the art* (pp. 173–218). Cambridge University Press.

Beckwith, L., & Cohen, S. (1980). Interactions of preterm infants with their caregivers and test performance at age two. In T. Field, S. Goldberg, D. Stern, & S. Sostek (Eds.), *High-risk infants and children: Adult and peer interactions* (pp. 155–78). New York: Academic Press.

Bee, H., Barnard, K., Eyres, S., Gray, C., Hammond, M., Spietz, A., Snyder, C., &

Clark, B. (1982). Prediction of IQ and language skill from perinatal status, child performance, family characteristics, and mother–infant interaction. *Child Development, 53,* 1134–56.

Blalock, J. (1982). Persistent auditory language deficits in adults with learning disabilities. *Journal of Learning Disabilities, 15,* 604–9.

Blank, M., Gessner, M., & Esposito, A. (1979). Language without communication: A case study. *Journal of Child Language, 6,* 329–52.

Bloom, L., & Lahey, M. (1978). *Language development and language disorder.* New York: Wiley.

Bock, J. K. (1982). Toward a cognitive psychology of syntax: Information processing contributions to sentence formulation. *Psychological Review, 89,* 1–47.

Bruner, J. (1975). The ontogenesis of speech acts. *Journal of Child Language, 2,* 1–19.

Bryan, J., Bryan, T., & Sonnefeld, J. (1982). Being known by the company one keeps: The contagion of first impressions. *Learning Disability Quarterly, 5,* 19–28.

Bryan, J., & Sherman, R. (1980). Immediate impressions of nonverbal ingratiation attempts by learning disabled boys. *Learning Disability Quarterly, 3,* 19–28.

Bryan, J. H., Sherman, R., & Fisher, A. (1980). Learning disabled boys' nonverbal behaviors within a dyadic interview. *Learning Disability Quarterly, 1,* 65–72.

Bryan, T. H. (1974). Peer popularity of learning disabled children. *Journal of Learning Disabilities, 7,* 621–5.

Bryan, T., Donahue, M., & Pearl, R. (1981). Learning disabled children's peer interactions during a small group problem-solving task. *Learning Disability Quarterly, 4,* 13–22.

Bryan, T., Donahue, M., Pearl, R., & Herzog, A. (1984). Conversational interactions between mothers and learning-disabled or nondisabled children during a problem-solving task. *Journal of Speech and Hearing Disorders, 49,* 64–71.

Bryan, T., Donahue, M., Pearl, R., & Sturm, C. (1981). Learning disabled children's conversational skills. *Learning Disability Quarterly, 4,* 250–9.

Campbell, T., & Shriberg, L. (1982). Associations among pragmatic functions, linguistic stress, and natural phonological processes in speech-delayed children. *Journal of Speech and Hearing Research, 25,* 547–53.

Cantwell, D., & Baker, L. (1977). Psychiatric disorder in children with speech and language retardation. *Archives of General Psychiatry, 34,* 583–91.

Caparulo, B., & Cohen, D. (1983). Developmental language studies in the neuropsychiatric disorder of childhood. In K. Nelson (Ed.), *Children's language* (Vol. 4, pp. 423–63). Hillsdale, NJ: Erlbaum.

Caro, D., & Schneider, P. (1982). Creating referents in text: A comparison of learning disabled and normal adolescents' texts. *Proceedings of the Wisconsin Symposium for Research in Child Language Disorders.* Madison: University of Wisconsin Bookstore.

Carrow-Woolfolk, E., & Lynch, J. (1982). *An integrative approach to language disorders in children.* New York: Grune & Stratton.

Chapman, J., & Boersma, F. (1979). Learning disabilities, locus of control and mother attitudes. *Journal of Educational Psychology, 71,* 250–8.

Cohen, S., Parmelee, A., Sigman, M., & Beckwith, L. (1982). Neonatal risk factors in preterm infants. *Applied Research in Mental Retardation, 3,* 265–78.

Cook-Gumperz, J. (1977). Situated instructions: Language socialization of school-age children. In S. Ervin-Tripp and C. Mitchell-Kernan (Eds.), *Child discourse* (pp. 103–21). New York: Academic Press.

Cosgrove, J., & Patterson, C. (1977). Plans and the development of listener skills. *Developmental Psychology, 13,* 557–64.

Cromer, R. (1974). Receptive language in the mentally retarded: Processes and diagnostic distinctions . In R. Schiefelbusch & L. Lloyd (Eds.), *Language perspectives: Acquisition, retardation, and intervention.* Baltimore, MD: University Park Press.

Curtiss, S. (1981). Dissociations between language and cognition. *Journal of Autism and Developmental Disorders, 11,* 15–30.

Dale, P. (1980). Is early pragmatic development measurable? *Journal of Child Language, 7,* 1–12.

Davies, P., & Stewart, A. (1975). Low birth-weight infants: Neurological sequelae and later intelligence. *British Medical Bulletin, 31,* 85–91.

Denckla, M., & Rudel, R. (1976a). Naming of object drawings of dyslexic and other learning disabled children. *Brain and Language, 3,* 1–16.

Denckla, M., & Rudel, R. (1976b). Rapid "automatized" naming (R.A.N.): Dyslexia differentiated from other learning disabilities. *Neuropsychologia, 14,* 471–9.

Denckla, M., Rudel, R., & Broman, M. (1981). Tests that discriminate between dyslexic and other learning-disabled boys. *Brain and Language, 13,* 118–29.

Donahue, M. (1981). Requesting strategies of learning disabled children. *Applied Psycholinguistics, 2,* 213–34.

Donahue, M. (1984a). Learning disabled children's comprehension and production of syntactic devices for marking given versus new information. *Applied Psycholinguistics, 5,* 101–16.

Donahue, M. (1984b). Learning disabled children's conversational competence: An attempt to activate the inactive listener. *Applied Psycholinguistics, 5,* 21–35.

Donahue, M. (1986a). Linguistic and communicative development in learning disabled children. In S. Ceci (Ed.), *Handbook of cognitive, social and neuropsychological aspects of learning disabilities* (pp. 263–89). Hillsdale, NJ: Erlbaum.

Donahue, M. (1986b). Phonological constraints on the emergence of two-word utterances. *Journal of Child Language, 13,* 263–89.

Donahue, M., & Bryan, T. (1983). Conversational skills and modeling in learning disabled boys. *Applied Psycholinguistics, 4,* 251–78.

Donahue, M., & Pearl, R. (1984). Conversational interactions of mothers and their preschool children who had been at perinatal risk. *Proceedings from the Wisconsin Symposium on Research in Child Language Disorders,* Madison: University of Wisconsin Bookstore.

Donahue, M., Pearl, R., & Bryan, T. (1980). Conversational competence in learning disabled children: Responses to inadequate messages. *Applied Psycholinguistics, 1,* 387–403.

Donahue, M., Pearl, R., & Bryan, T. (1982). Learning disabled children's syntactic proficiency during a communicative task. *Journal of Speech and Hearing Disorders, 47,* 397–403.

Donahue, M., & Prescott, B. (1983). *Young learning disabled children's conversational episodes in dispute episodes with peers.* Chicago Institute for the Study of Learning Disabilities.

Dunn, G., Pearl, R., & Bryan, T. (1981). *Learning disabled children's self-evaluations.* Unpublished manuscript, Chicago Institute for the Study of Learning Disabilities.

Eisenberg, A., & Garvey, C. (1981). Children's use of verbal strategies in resolving conflicts. *Discourse Process, 4,* 149–70.

Ervin-Tripp, S., & Mitchell-Kernan, C. (Eds.). (1977). *Child discourse.* New York: Academic Press.

Ervin-Tripp, S., & Gordon, D. (1986). The development of requests. In R. Schiefelbusch (Ed.), *Language competence: Assessment and intervention* (pp. 61–95). San Diego, CA: College-Hill Press.

Feagans, L., & Appelbaum, M. (1986). Validation of language subtypes in learning disabled children. *Journal of Education Psychology, 78,* 358–64.

Feagans, L., & Short, E. (1984). Developmental differences in the comprehension and production of narratives by reading disabled and normally achieving children. *Child Development, 55,* 1727–36.

Feagans, L., & Short, E. (1985). *Referential communication and reading performance in learning disabled children over a three-year period.* Unpublished manuscript, University of North Carolina at Chapel Hill.

Fey, M., Leonard, L., & Wilcox, K. (1981). Speech style modification of language disordered children. *Journal of Speech and Hearing Disorders, 46,* 91–6.

Field, T., Goldberg, S., Demsey, J., & Shuman, H. (1979). Speech disturbance and minimal brain dysfunction: A five-year follow-up of respiratory distress syndrome. In T. Field, A. Sostek, S. Goldberg, & H. Shuman (Eds.), *Infants born at risk.* New York: Spectrum.

Field, T., Goldberg, S., Stern, D., & Sostek, A. (1980). *High-Risk infants and children: Adult and peer interactions.* New York: Academic Press.

Fletcher, J., Satz, P., & Scholes, R. (1981). Developmental changes in the linguistic performance correlates of reading achievement. *Brain and Language, 13,* 78–90.

Fry, M., Johnson, C., & Muehl, S. (1970). Oral language production in relation to reading achievement among select second graders. In D. J. Bakker & P. Satz (Eds.), *Specific reading disability.* Rotterdam University Press.

Gallagher, T. (1977). Revision behaviors in the speech of normal children developing language. *Journal of Speech and Hearing Research, 20,* 303–18.

Garrett, M., & Crump, W. (1980). Peer acceptance, teacher references, and self-appraisal of social status among learning disabled students. *Learning Disability Quarterly, 3,* 42–8.

Garvey, C. (1975). Requests and responses in children's speech. *Journal of Child Language, 2,* 41–63.

Gazdar, G. (1980). Pragmatic constraints on linguistic production. In B. Butterworth (Ed.), *Language production* (Vol. 1, pp. 49–68). New York: Academic Press.

German, D. (1979). Word-finding skills in children with learning disabilities. *Journal of Learning Disabilities, 12,* 176–81.

Gleitman, L., & Wanner, E. (1982). Language acquisition: The state of the art. In E. Wanner & L. Gleitman (Eds.), *Language acquisition: The state of the art* (pp. 3–38). Cambridge University Press.

Goldberg, S., Brachfeld, S., & DiVitto, B. (1980). Feeding, fussing, and play: First year medical problems. In T. Field, S. Goldberg, D. Stern, & A. Sostek (Eds.), *High-risk infants and children: Adult and peer interactions* (pp. 133–53). New York: Academic Press.

Gottman, J. (1983). How children become friends. *Monographs of the Society for Research in Child Development, 48*(3, Serial No. 201).

Gottman, J., Gonso, J., & Rasmussen, B. (1975). Social interaction, social competence and friendship in children. *Child Development, 46,* 709–18.

Greenfield, P., & Smith, J. (1976). *The structure of communication in early language development.* New York: Academic Press.

Grice, H. (1975). Logic and conversation. In P. Cole & J. Morgan (Eds.), *Syntax and semantics: Vol. 3. Speech acts* (pp. 41–58). New York: Seminar Press.

Haber, L. (1981, April). *Does learning disabled equal language disabled?* Paper presented at the Chicago Linguistics Society Regional Meeting, Chicago.

Hall, P., & Tomblin, J. (1978). A follow-up study of children with articulation and language disorders. *Journal of Speech and Hearing Disorders, 43,* 227–41.

Higgins, E. (1981). Role-taking and social judgment: Alternative developmental perspectives and processes. In J. Flavell & L. Ross (Eds.), *Social-cognitive development: Frontiers and possible futures* (pp. 119–53). Cambridge University Press.

Hornby, P. (1971). Surface structure and the topic–comment distinction: A developmental study. *Child Development, 42,* 1975–88.

Hresko, W. (1979). Elicited imitation ability of children from learning disabled and regular classes. *Journal of Learning Disabilities, 12,* 456–61.

Idol-Maestas, L. (1980). Oral language responses of children with reading difficulties. *Journal of Special Education, 14,* 385–404.

Ironsmith, M., & Whitehurst, G. (1978). The development of listener skills in communication: How children deal with ambiguous information. *Child Development, 49,* 348–52.

Johnson, D., & Myklebust, M. (1967). *Learning disabilities: Educational principles and practices.* New York: Grune & Stratton.

Kamhi, A., Catts, M., & Davis, M. (1984). Management of sentence production demands. *Journal of Speech and Hearing Research, 27,* 329–38.

Kamhi, A., & Johnston, J. (1982). Towards an understanding of retarded children's linguistic deficiencies. *Journal of Speech and Hearing Research, 25,* 435–45.

Keenan, E. (1974). Conversational competence in children. *Journal of Child Language, 1,* 163–83.

Kotsonis, M., & Patterson, C. (1980). Comprehension-monitoring skills in learning disabled children. *Developmental Psychology, 16,* 541–2.

Keogh, B. K., Major-Kingsley, S. M., Omori-Gordon, H., & Reid, H. P. (1982). *A system of marker variables for the field of learning disabilities.* Syracuse, NY: Syracuse University Press.

Knight-Arrest, J. (1984). Communicative effectiveness of learning disabled and normally achieving ten- to thirteen-year-old boys. *Learning Disability Quarterly, 7,* 237–45.

Lassman, F., Fish, R., Vetter, D., & La Benz, E. (1980). *Early correlates of speech, language, and hearing.* Littleton, MA: PSG Publishing.

Leifer, J., & Lewis, M. (1984). Acquisition of conversational response skills by young Down syndrome and nonretarded children. *American Journal of Mental Deficiency, 88,* 610–18.

Lempert, H. (1984). Topic as starting point for syntax. *Monographs of the Society for Research in Child Development, 49*(5, Serial No. 208).

Leonard, L. (1982). The nature of specific language impairment in children. In S. Rosenberg (Ed.), *Handbook of applied psycholinguistics* (pp. 295–328). Hillsdale, NJ: Erlbaum.

Leonard, L. (1983). Speech selection and modification in language-disordered children. *Topics in Language Disorders, 4*(1), 28–37.

Leonard, L., Camarata, S., Rowan, L., & Chapman, K. (1982). The communicative functions of lexical usage by language-impaired children. *Applied Psycholinguistics, 3,* 109–27.

Lieberman, J., Moore, S., & Hutchinson, E. (1984, November). *What's the difference between language-impaired and learning-disabled children?* Paper presented at the American Speech-Language-Hearing Association Convention, San Francisco.

Liles, B. (1985a). Cohesion in the narratives of normal and language-disordered children. *Journal of Speech and Hearing Research, 28,* 123–33.

Liles, B. (1985b). Production and comprehension of narrative discourse in normal and language-disordered children. *Journal of Communication Disorders, 18,* 409–27.

McKinney, J. D. (1984). The search for subtypes of specific learning disability. *Journal of Learning Disabilities, 17,* 43–50.

McKinney, J., & Feagans, L. (1984). Academic and behavioral characteristics: Longitudinal studies of learning disabled children and average achievers. *Learning Disability Quarterly, 7,* 251–65.

MacWhinney, B., & Price, D. (1980). The development of the comprehension of topic–comment marking. In D. Ingram, F. Peng, & P. Dale (Eds.), *Proceedings of the First International Congress for the Study of Child Language, 1,* 121–44.

MaGee, P., & Newcomer, P. (1978). The relationship between oral language skills and academic achievement of learning disabled children. *Learning Disability Quarterly, 1,* 63–7.

Meline, T. (1978, November). *Referential communication by normal- and deficient-language children.* Paper presented at the Meeting of the American Speech-Language-Hearing Association, San Francisco.

Messick, C., & Newhoff, M. (1979, November). *Request forms: Does the language-impaired child consider the listener?* Paper presented at the Meeting of the American Speech-Language-Hearing Association, Atlanta, GA.

Moran, M., & Byrne, M. (1977). Mastery of verb tense markers by normal and learning disabled children. *Journal of Speech and Hearing Research, 20,* 529–42.

Morehead, D., & Ingram, D. (1976). The development of base syntax in normal and linguistically deviant children. In D. Morehead & A. Morehead (Eds.), *Normal and deficient child language* (pp. 209–38). Baltimore, MD: University Park Press.

Nelson, K. (1973). Structure and strategy in learning to talk. *Monographs of the Society for Research in Child Development, 38*(1–2, Serial No. 149).

Nelson, K. (1981). Social cognition in a script framework. In J. Flavell & L. Ross (Eds.), *Social cognitive development* (pp. 97–118). Cambridge University Press.

Nelson, K., & Gruendel, J. (1979). At morning it's lunchtime: A scriptal view of children's dialogues. *Discourse Processes, 2,* 73–94.

Newport, W., Gleitman, L., & Gleitman, H. (1977). Mother I'd rather do it myself. In C. Ferguson & C. Snow (Eds.), *Talking to children* (pp. 109–49). Cambridge University Press.

Nippold, M., Leonard, L., & Anastopoulos, A. (1982). Development in the use and understanding of polite forms in children. *Journal of Speech and Hearing Research, 25,* 193–202.

Noel, N. M. (1980). Referential communication abilities of learning disabled children. *Learning Disability Quarterly, 3,* 70–5.

Orton, A. (1937). *Reading, writing and speech problems in children.* New York: Norton.

Owen, R. W., Adams, P. A., Forrest, T., Stolz, L. M., & Fisher, S. (1971). Learning disorders in children: Sibling studies. *Monographs of the Society of Research in Child Development, 36*(4, Serial No. 144).

Paul, R. (1985). The emergence of pragmatic comprehension: A study of children's understanding of sentence-structure cues to given–new information. *Journal of Child Language, 12,* 161–79.

Pearl, R., & Cosden, M. (1983). Sizing up a situation: Learning disabled children's understanding of social interactions. *Learning Disability Quarterly, 5,* 371–3.

Pearl, R., Donahue, M., & Bryan, T. (1981). Learning disabled and normal children's responses to non-explicit requests for clarification. *Perceptual and Motor Skills, 53,* 919–25.

Pearl, R., Donahue, M., & Bryan, T. (1985). The development of tact: Children's strategies for delivering bad news. *Journal of Applied Development Psychology, 6,* 141–9.

Pearl, R., Donahue, M., & Bryan, T. (1986). Social relationships of learning disabled children. In J. Torgesen & B. Wong (Eds.), *Psychological and educational perspectives on learning disabilities* (pp. 193–224). New York: Academic Press.

Petersen, G., & Sherrod, K. (1982). Relationship of maternal language development and language delay of children. *American Journal of Mental Deficiency, 86,* 391–8.

Prinz, P. (1977, October). *Comprehension and production of requests in normal and language disordered children.* Paper presented at the Boston University Conference on Language Development, Boston.

Prinz, P., & Ferrier, L. (1983). "Can you give me that one?": The comprehension, production and judgment of directives in language-impaired children. *Journal of Speech and Hearing Disorders, 48,* 44–54.

Rees, N. (1978). Pragmatics of language: Applications to normal and disordered language development. In R. Schiefelbusch (Ed.), *Bases of language intervention.* Baltimore, MD: University Park Press.

Rosenberg, S. (1982). The language of the mentally retarded: Development, processes and intervention. In S. Rosenberg (Ed.), *Handbook of applied psycholinguistics* (pp. 329–92). Hillsdale, NJ: Erlbaum.

Roth, F., Spekman, N. (1985, June). *Story grammar analyses of narratives produced by learning disabled and normally achieving students.* Paper presented at the University of Wisconsin Symposium on Research in Child Language Disorders, Madison, WI.

Rudel, R., Denckla, M., & Broman, M. (1981). The effect of varying stimulus context on word-finding ability: Dyslexia further differentiated from other learning disabilities. *Brain and Language, 13,* 130–44.

Rumelhart, M. (1983). When in doubt: Strategies used in response to interactional uncertainty. *Discourse Processes, 6,* 377–402.

Schery, T. (1985). Correlates of language development in language-disordered children. *Journal of Speech and Hearing Disorders, 50,* 73–83.

Schneider, P. (1982). Formal operations skills vs. explanations. *Psycholinguistics Newsletter, Northwestern University, 8,* 16–23.

Scholom, A., & Schiff, G. (1980). Relating infant temperament to learning disabilities. *Journal of Abnormal Child Psychology, 8,* 127–32.

Scranton, T., & Ryckman, D. (1979). Sociometric status of learning disabled children in an integrative program. *Journal of Learning Disabilities, 12,* 402–7.

Semel, E., & Wiig, E. (1980). *Clinical evaluation of language functions.* Columbus, OH: Merrill.

Shatz, M. (1978). Describing the developing conversationalist: A review of *Child discourse. Contemporary Psychology, 23,* 718–20.

Shatz, M. (1982a). Learning the rules of the game: Four views of the relation between social interaction and syntax acquisition. In W. Deutsch (Ed.), *The child's construction of the language* (pp. 17–38). New York: Academic Press.

Shatz, M. (1982b). On mechanisms of language acquisition: Can features of the communicative environment account for development? In E. Wanner & L. Gleitman (Eds.), *Language acquisition: The state of the art* (pp. 102–27). Cambridge University Press.

Shatz, M., Bernstein, D., & Shulman, M. (1980). The responses of language disordered children to indirect directives in varying contexts. *Applied Psycholinguistics, 1,* 295–306.

Shatz, M., & Gelman, R. (1973). The development of communication skills: Modifications in the speech of young children as a function of listener. *Monographs of the Society for Research in Child Development, 38*(5, Serial No. 152).

Siegel, S. (1982). Reproductive, perinatal, and environmental factors of the cognitive and language development of preterm and full-term infants. *Child Development, 53,* 963–73.

Silliman, E. (1984). Interactional competencies in the instructional context: The role of teaching discourse in learning. In G. Wallach & K. Butler (Eds.), *Language learning disabilities in school-age children* (pp. 288–317). Baltimore, MD: Williams and Wilkins.

Skarakis, E., & Greenfield, P. (1982). The role of new and old information in the verbal expression of language-disordered children. *Journal of Speech and Hearing Research, 25,* 462–7.

Snow, C. (1977). The development of communication between mothers and babies. *Journal of Child Language, 4,* 1–22.

Snow, C., & Cancino, H. (1985, June). *Conversation and narrative: The differential development of language skills.* Keynote address presented at the Wisconsin Symposium on Research in Child Language Disorders, Madison, WI.

Snyder, L. (1978). Communicative and cognitive abilities and disabilities in the sensorimotor period. *Merrill-Palmer Quarterly, 24,* 161–80.

Snyder, L. (1984a). Communicative competence in children with delayed language development. In R. Schiefelbusch & J. Pickar (Eds.), *Communicative competence: Acquisition and intervention.* Baltimore, MD: University Park Press.

Snyder, L. (1984b). Developmental language disorders: Elementary school age. In A. Holland (Ed.), *Language disorders in children* (pp. 129–58). San Diego, CA: College-Hill Press.

Snyder, L., & Downey, P. (1983). Pragmatics and information processing. *Topics in Language Disorders, 4,* 75–86.

Snyder-McLean, L., & McLean, J. (1978). Verbal information gathering strategies: The child's use of language to acquire language. *Journal of Speech and Hearing Disorders, 43,* 306–25.

Spekman, N. (1981). A study of the dyadic verbal communication abilities of learning disabled and normally achieving fourth and fifth grade boys. *Learning Disability Quarterly, 4,* 139–51.

Steckol, D. (1983). Are we training young language-delayed children for future academic failure? In H. Winitz (Ed.), *Treating language disorders* (pp. 1–9). Baltimore, MD: University Park Press.

Stein, N., & Glenn, C. (1979). An analysis of story comprehension in elementary school children. In R. Freedle (Ed.), *New directions in discourse processing* (Vol. 2, pp. 53–120). Norwood, NJ: Ablex.

Strominger, A., & Bashir, A. (1977, November). *A nine-year follow-up of language delayed children.* Paper presented at the Meeting of the American Speech-Language-Hearing Association, Chicago.

Torgesen, J. K. (1977). Memorization processes in reading disabled children. *Journal of Educational Psychology, 69,* 571–8.

Torgesen, J., & Dice, C. (1980). Characteristics of research on learning disabilities. *Journal of Learning Disabilities, 13,* 531–5.

Tulkin, S., & Covitz, F. (1975, April). *Mother–infant interaction and intellectual functioning at age six.* Paper presented at the biennial meeting of the Society for Research in Child Development, Denver, CO.

U.S. Office of Education. (1977). Assistance to states for education of handicapped children: Procedures for evaluating specific learning disabilities. *Federal Register, 42,* 65082–5.

Vellutino, F. R. (1979). *Dyslexia: Theory and research.* Cambridge, MA: MIT Press.

Vogel, S. (1975). *Syntactic abilities in normal and dyslexic children.* Baltimore, MD: University Park Press.

Watson, L., Martin, J., & Schaffer, F. (in press). Form, content, and function of the spontaneous communications of autistic students. *Australian Journal of Human Communication Disorders.*

Werner, E. E., Bierman, J. M., & French, F. (1971). *The children of Kauai.* Honolulu: University of Hawaii Press.

Whalen, C., Henker, B., Collins, B., McAuliffe, S., & Vaux, A. (1979). Peer interactions in a structured communication task: Comparisons of normal and hyperactive boys and of methylphenidate and placebo effects. *Child Development, 50,* 388–401.

Whitehouse, C. (1983). Token test performance by dyslexic adolescents. *Brain and Language, 18,* 224–35.

Whitehurst, G., & Sonnenschein, S. (1981). The development of informative messages in referential communication: Knowing when vs. knowing how. In W. P. Dickson (Ed.), *Children's oral communication skills* (pp. 127–41). New York: Academic Press.

Wiig, E., & Semel, E. M. (1974). Logico-grammatical sentence comprehension by learning disabled adolescents. *Perceptual and Motor Skills, 38,* 1331–4.

Wiig, E., & Semel, E. M. (1975). Productive language abilities in learning disabled adolescents. *Journal of Learning Disabilities, 8,* 578–86.

Wiig, E., & Semel, E. (1984). *Language assessment and intervention for the learning disabled.* Columbus, OH: Merrill.

Wilcox, M. J., & Webster, E. (1980). Early discourse behavior: An analysis of children's responses to listener feedback. *Child Development, 51,* 1120–5.

Williams, F. (1976). *Explorations of the linguistic attitudes of teachers.* Rowley, MA: Newbury House.

Wolf, M. (1981). The word retrieval process and reading in children and aphasics. In K. Nelson (Ed.), *Children's language* (Vol. 3, pp. 437–93). Hillsdale, NJ: Erlbaum.

Wong, B., & Roadhouse, A. (1978). The Test of Language Development (TOLD): A validation study. *Learning Disability Quarterly, 1,* 48–61.

Wong, B. Y. L., & Wong, R. (1980). Role-taking skills in normal achieving and learning disabled children. *Learning Disability Quarterly, 3,* 11–18.

Wulbert, M., Inglis, S., Kriegsmann, E., & Mills, B. (1975). Language delay and associated mother–child interactions. *Developmental Psychology, 11,* 61–70.

5   Deafness and language development

Stephen P. Quigley and Peter V. Paul

The major purpose of this chapter is to discuss the effects of deafness on the development of English. The language development of deaf children is considered in relation to the type of input to which they are exposed in infancy and early childhood, namely, Oral English, Manually Coded English, or American Sign Language. Also discussed is the contention that the language acquisition process of some deaf children should be viewed from either a bilingual or an English-as-a-second-language (ESL) framework. A representative, rather than exhaustive, sample of research regarding these issues is presented, and some conclusions are inferred from the evidence.

Definition of deafness

To depict the effects of deafness on English language development, it is important to define the population under consideration (Quigley & Kretschmer, 1982). Typically, the ability to hear is measured in decibels (dB) across a range of frequencies from 125 to 8000 hertz (Hz). The degree of an individual's hearing impairment (i.e., hearing threshold level) is represented on the audiogram as the average loss across the speech frequencies (500, 1000, and 2000 Hz). Five categories of hearing impairment have been established and are illustrated in Table 1. It can be seen that *hearing impairment* is a generic term representing all degrees of hearing loss, with deafness corresponding to the extreme or profound category of impairment. An individual is considered deaf if hearing impairment is so great that vision, rather than audition, becomes the *major* link to receptive language development. There is considerable evidence that the shift from audition to vision occurs at approximately 90 dB or in the extreme category of hearing impairment (see the discussions in Conrad, 1979; Quigley & Paul, 1984a; Ross, Brackett, & Maxon, 1982).

Another significant variable to consider in defining deafness is the age at onset of hearing impairment. This chapter is concerned with individuals who suffered a *prelinguistic*, profound ($\geq$ 90-dB) hearing impairment (i.e., before or at 2 years

180

Table 1. *Relation of degree of hearing impairment in better ear to educational needs*

Degree of impairment	Educational needs
Slight 27 to 40 dB	Does not typically require special class and/or school placement May need lip reading and speech instruction May need amplification May need assistance in language and/or reading
Mild 41 to 54 dB	May need special class and/or school placement Requires instruction in lip reading and speech Requires instruction in the use of hearing aids Requires special assistance in language and/or reading
Moderate 55 to 69 dB	May require special class and/or school placement Requires instruction in lip reading and speech Requires instruction in the use of hearing aids Requires special instruction in language and/or reading
Severe 70 to 89 dB	Requires a full-time special education program with special instruction in language and reading Comprehensive support services Training in lip reading, speech, and the use of residual hearing
Profound (deaf) 90 dB and greater	Requires a full-time special education program with special instruction in language and reading Comprehensive support services Training in lip reading, speech, and the use of residual hearing Usually requires the use of sign communication

Source: Adapted from Moores (1982) and Quigley and Paul (1984a).

of age). Children deafened before or at the age of 2 years may not have established an auditorially based internalized language, which is developed through aural–oral interactions with significant others (Lennenberg, 1967; Slobin, 1979). The linguistic and communication aspects of these children are different from those deafened after the age of 2.

Other descriptive variables of importance are etiology, type of impairment, and the hearing status of the deaf individual's parents. In addition, variables of importance in describing the normal hearing population, for example, intelligence (IQ) and socioeconomic status (SES), are also applicable to the deaf population. The importance of defining deafness with respect to these variables cannot be over-emphasized. As stated by Quigley and Kretschmer (1982), "Much of the confusion in research and practice in the education of deaf children arises from incomplete descriptions of the populations under consideration and from generalization of findings to dissimilar populations" (p. 5).

Language, reading, and writing

It is well documented in the literature that most deaf students fail to acquire reading and writing skills commensurate with those of their hearing counterparts (Cooper & Rosenstein, 1966; Quigley, Wilbur, Power, Montanelli, & Steinkamp, 1976; Trybus & Karchmer, 1977). The ability of the average 18-year-old deaf student to read and write standard English is nearly equivalent to that of the average 9- or 10-year-old normally hearing student, and this level of achievement has remained virtually unchanged since the early 1900s (Moores, 1982; Quigley & Kretschmer, 1982; Quigley & Paul, 1984a).

A number of linguistic variables contributing to this low level of achievement have been delineated. Among these are difficulties with various aspects of vocabulary knowledge (Paul, 1984; Rosenstein & MacGinitie, 1969; Walter, 1978), syntactic structures (Quigley et al., 1976), and idiomatic and other metaphorical extensions (Conley, 1976; Iran-Nejad, Ortony, & Rittenhouse, 1981; Payne, 1982). One of the major inferences that can be drawn from these studies is that poorly developed English literacy skills can be attributed largely to inadequate primary language development.

The importance of an internalized language base has led Pearson and Johnson (1978) to assert "that linguistic competence is an absolute prerequisite for reading comprehension. Such an assertion is almost tautological, since language is the medium of comprehension" (p. 19). For hearing children, English literacy skills are superimposed on internalized auditory verbal experiences. The nature of the internalized language form of deaf children is related to the particular language and communication system to which they are initially exposed. This is more likely to be a visual than an auditory system.

Language and communication systems

The most controversial and enduring issue in the education of deaf students is the form of language and communication that should be used by and with the students in the home and school environments (Moores, 1982; Quigley & Kretschmer, 1982). There are two distinct languages, American Sign Language and English, and two distinct communication forms, oral and manual, that can be used. These languages and forms can be combined in a variety of ways to produce a number of systems or approaches, which can be classified into three general categories: Oral English (OE), Manually Coded English (MCE), and American Sign Language (ASL). These categories are probably representative of most of the linguistic input to deaf students during their formative years (Quigley & Paul, 1984a). Due to the nature and number of these categories, describing the primary language development of deaf students is much more complicated than describing the development of normally hearing students.

Oral English

The approaches within the OE category entail the use of spoken English in the instruction of deaf children. Traditionally, the two approaches employed that rely solely on oral communication are the Aural–Oral and the Acoupedic Methods. There are variations of these approaches as well as overlapping aspects (Ling, 1984; Moores, 1982). Also included in the OE category is Cued Speech, which employs manual (hand) cues to supplement spoken English.

Aural–Oral. The major focus of this approach is on the development of the auditory *and* visual senses of the deaf child in the context of an intensive speech-training program (Ling, 1976, 1984; Ling & Ling, 1978). A great deal of emphasis is placed on the early and consistent use of amplification and auditory training and on the development of adequate speech-reading (lip-reading) skills. Some Aural–Oral approaches employ multisensory (auditory–visual–tactile or auditory–visual–oral) techniques and others emphasize unisensory methods (i.e., the use of audition or residual hearing) (Moores, 1982).

Acoupedics. The major impetus for this approach can be traced to the development of the Acoustic Method by Goldstein (1939). This method has been referred to as the Aural Method, Acoustic Method, Unisensory Method, and Auditory Method (Moores, 1982). The use of speech reading is minimized, whereas the use of amplification and auditory training techniques are heightened to help deaf children utilize their residual hearing as fully as possible (Pollack, 1964, 1970, 1984). Within this perspective, the Acoupedic Method emphasizes the primacy of audition over vision. In recent years, there has been a substantial decline in the use of an exclusive unisensory method; however, many of the techniques have been incorporated in Aural–Oral approaches (e.g., see the discussion in Sanders, 1982).

Cued Speech. Whether Cued Speech (CS) should be placed in the OE or MCE category is open to debate. It probably should be considered a separate system. Nevertheless, since the major purpose of CS is to enable the deaf child to perceive the spoken signal in an unambiguous manner (Cornett, 1967), it appears to fit best in the OE category. This placement, incidentally, is acceptable to the creator of the system (Cornett, 1984).

In CS, eight handshapes (manual cues) are employed in four positions on or near the facial area. The combination of handshapes and positions is used to represent the phonetic elements of speech that cannot be differentiated solely by speech reading (e.g., *m, p,* and *b*). The handshapes are devoid of meaning unless used in conjunction with spoken English. The simultaneous use of the handshapes and speech is supposed to provide a visibly intelligible message to the deaf child. According to Cornett (1984), "[Cued Speech] . . . has enjoyed a steady but slow growth since its inception, culminating in a rapid acceleration beginning in 1979" (p. 5). It is estimated that CS is used in approximately 350 locations in the United States; however, in more than 300 of these locations, the program contains five children or fewer.

Manually Coded English

Manually Coded English refers to the variety of contrived systems that use signs and finger spelling separately or in combinations to represent standard English manually. In educational settings, all MCE systems are *supposed* to be used simultaneously with speech (Wilbur, 1979). The various systems differ mainly in their rules for selecting and constructing their manual aspects and in how closely these aspects represent the structure (syntax) of standard English.

Finger spelling. In this approach 26 handshapes correspond to the 26 letters of the written English alphabet. Thus, it is possible to spell words manually in the air in much the same way that one writes words on paper with the written alphabet. In educational settings, the simultaneous use of finger spelling and speech is known as the Rochester Method, named after the Rochester School for the Deaf, where it originated (Quigley, 1969; Scouten, 1967). Some researchers consider the Rochester Method to be an oral multisensory approach (e.g., Scouten, 1967). The use of finger spelling in the other MCE approaches is limited, for the most part, to the conveying of proper names and places and for some English words for which there are no sign equivalents (Wilbur, 1979). As an educational tool, the Rochester Method is not widely used (Baker & Cokely, 1980; Jordan, Gustason, & Rosen, 1979; Wilbur, 1979).

Seeing Essential English. During the 1960s, Seeing Essential English (SEE I) was one of the earliest attempts to provide by the use of signs a close manual approximation of the structure of English (Anthony, 1966). SEE I was developed for educators as well as for normally hearing parents of deaf children. Existing ASL-like signs are used as a base; however, new sign movements and/or markers have been invented to represent the inflectional system of English and those English words for which there are no clear, unambiguous ASL-like sign equivalents, that is, for which there is no one-to-one correspondence between the ASL sign and the English word. It should be remembered that, *for any two languages,* one-to-one correspondences are rare. Thus, new sign movements have been contrived to represent elements (e.g., pronouns, affixes) that would have been finger-spelled previously (Moores, 1982; Wilbur, 1979). Typically, finger spelling is not employed in this system except to represent proper names.

In SEE I, English words are categorized into three groups: basic, compound, and complex. The basic word category consists of whole word forms or root words. Since there is no one-to-one correspondence between ASL signs and English words, three criteria were arbitrarily established for selecting a sign to represent a word: sound, spelling, and meaning. If any two of the three criteria are similar for two or more English words, the same sign is employed for each word. For example, the English word *run* has several common meanings: to go by moving the legs rapidly, to take part in a contest or race, and to become loosened and ravel (*Webster's new twentieth century dictionary*, 1983). The same sign is used to represent each of the meanings since the *sound* and *spelling* of the word remain the same regardless of the particular meaning being expressed.

Signing Exact English. Signing Exact English (SEE II) was derived from SEE I. There is much overlap between the two sign systems in relation to general vocabulary and the use of affixes (Bornstein, 1973; Wilbur, 1979). In addition, both systems employ the two-out-of-three principle described earlier. The major difference between SEE I and SEE II is the manner in which a root word is operationally defined. This difference affects the manner in which compound and complex words are signed. For example, in SEE II, the word *butterfly* is formed by a sign that is the same as that used by ASL signers. SEE I, however, treats *butterfly* as two root words and uses one ASL sign for *butter* and another for *fly*. A similar pattern exists for complex words, resulting in a greater number of affix sign markers for SEE I than for SEE II. Gustason, Pfetzing, and Zawolkow (1975) reported that the sign vocabulary of SEE II consists of 61% ASL signs, 18% modified ASL signs, and 21% newly invented signs.

Signed English. Signed English (SE) was designed for use with preschool- and elementary-school-aged students (Bornstein, 1973, 1974). The intention of SE is to provide a semantic approximation to the typical language environment of the normally hearing child. Signed English consists of sign words and sign markers. Each of the various sign words (or signs) corresponds to the meaning(s) of one lexical entry in a dictionary of standard English. The 14 sign markers represent a portion of the most commonly used inflections of English in young normally hearing children (Brown, 1973). Finger spelling is used for a number of English words for which there are no sign equivalents in this system.

Pidgin Sign English. Pidgin Sign English (PSE) is not a contrived sign system similar to the others previously discussed. Its structure is purportedly similar to a pidgin spoken by two hearing speakers each of whom is unfamiliar with the other's language (Cokely, 1983). Typically, a pidgin form adheres to the word order of the majority-culture language. The structure of the pidgin varies with a speaker's competence in the unfamiliar language. The major function of a pidgin is to communicate in context (Cokely, 1983).

In PSE, the two languages involved are ASL and English. The blend of ASL and English is slightly more complicated than spoken-only pidgins because PSE is a combination of the signs of ASL and the syntax of spoken English. Keeping in mind that English, the majority-culture language, is a spoken language, a pidgin may be the use of ASL-like signs in an English word order. The signs are labeled ASL-like owing to the elimination of certain syntactic aspects, for example, the directional elements of verbs (see Baker & Cokely, 1980, for further discussion). PSE, or any other pidgin, is difficult to define because of wide variation among its users (Wilbur, 1979; Woodward, 1973). For example, deaf PSE signers may use more ASL grammatical structures than hearing PSE signers (Lee, 1982).

It should be emphasized that any pidgin form is a reduced, imperfect representation of either of the two languages involved. It may also contain structures not present in either language. A pidgin is a *form* of communication, not a bona fide language. For a second generation of users, however, it usually attains the status of a language. PSE has been known as Ameslish (American Sign English), Siglish (Sign English), Signed English, and Manual English (Bragg, 1973).

American Sign Language

American Sign Language is a signed language, whereas the manual approaches discussed previously are signed systems or codes designed to represent the grammar of English. It should be emphasized that ASL differs from English in two important ways: form and grammar. Concepts are executed with sign and other gestural movements and in a grammar different from that of standard English. Although the language status of ASL has been questioned (Schlesinger & Namir, 1978), most investigators have asserted that it is a bona fide linguistic system (Klima & Bellugi, 1979; Lane & Grosjean, 1980; Wilbur, 1979). As an educational tool, ASL has not been systematically tried with deaf students.

Relation of the approaches to English

The primary purpose of the OE and MCE approaches is to teach standard English as a first language so as to provide a basis for the later development of adequate English literacy skills (Bornstein, 1973; Maxwell, 1983; Mitchell, 1982). This is assuming, of course, that the secondary language development of English (i.e., reading and writing) is highly dependent on the primary development. One of the critical issues is the adequacy of the representation of spoken English, and historically this has been the most controversial issue in the education of deaf students (Quigley & Kretschmer, 1982).

Theoretically, it is possible to place the most common approaches on a continuum ranging from least representative to most representative of the morphology of English (Baker & Cokely, 1980; Wilbur, 1979). This is illustrated in Table 2.

Table 2. *Relation of Oral English and Manually Coded English approaches to the structure of standard English*

	Structure of standard English				
Category	Least representative				Most representative
Oral English					Aural–Oral, Acoupedics, Cued Speech
Manually Coded English	Pidgin Sign English	Signed English	Signing Exact English	Seeing Essential English	Finger spelling

Source: Adapted from Quigley and Paul (1984a).

The approaches of OE, including CS, are most representative of standard English grammar owing to the intensive use of English in its spoken form. The manner in which the *manual component* of the MCE approaches is used to represent an English word determines their placement on the continuum. In this view, the system that provides the closest representation of a word is highly likely to provide the most accurate representation of the syntax of English.

Consider the word *slowly* as an example. It is possible to use one ASL-like sign or manual movement to represent the whole word, as in PSE (Wilbur, 1979; Woodward, 1973). Two manual movements can also be used, one for *slow* (ASL-like sign) and one for -*ly* (contrived sign marker), as in SEE II (Gustason, Pfetzing, & Zawolkow, 1980). Finally, one manual marker for each letter can be used, as in finger spelling (Scouten, 1967). Within this theoretical framework, finger spelling should be considered most representative of English in the manual form, followed by SEE I, SEE II, SE, and PSE.

Relation of American Sign Language to English

As discussed previously, ASL differs from English in two important ways: form and grammar (Lane & Grosjean, 1980; Liddell, 1980). It is essential to remember that English is a spoken language, whereas ASL is a signed language. Typically, signed languages are executed without the accompaniment of speech. Since ASL, like any other minority language, coexists in a majority-language culture, its grammar is influenced by that of the majority language, in this case, English. This influence is manifested, for example, by the use of finger-spelled signs (signing JB for job) and the use of adjectives before nouns (the sign for BIG and then the sign for HOUSE). It should be reemphasized that a description of the grammatical development of ASL is still different from that of English.

It is possible that the primary language of some deaf children is ASL (Lane & Grosjean, 1980). For these children, ASL might be employed as an instructional approach to teaching English literacy skills in a bilingual or ESL program (Quigley & Paul, 1984b). This requires, at the least, that a teacher be competent in ASL *and* some representation of spoken English. The point here is not only that ASL is different from spoken English but also that it is different from the signed codes designed to represent the structure of English (Stokoe, 1975; Wilbur, 1979). Essentially, the codes attempt to modify the signs of ASL so that they conform to the grammar of English. The use of ASL-like signs in an English word order is not ASL, and furthermore the meanings of some signs of the codes may not reflect their original meanings in the context of ASL. Consider the following sentence as an example: *I am looking for a chair.* In some systems, the phrase *looking for* can be depicted with two ASL signs, LOOK and FOR. In ASL, the sign LOOK means "to watch" or "to see," whereas FOR means "with a purpose" (Sternberg, 1981). Clearly, the semantics of these ASL signs are different as used in the above sentence. ASL signers express the concept *looking for* by using signs that mean "to search" or "to hunt." Additional differences between ASL and the MCE approaches and between signed and spoken languages can be found in other sources (Stokoe, 1975; Wilbur, 1979). A major problem for educational researchers is to describe the manner in which a signed language (e.g., ASL) can be used to teach the grammar of a spoken language (e.g., English).

Instructional use of Oral English, Manually Coded English, and American Sign Language

When employed consistently and in conjunction with a good amplification system, the OE approaches provide an adequate representation of spoken English (Ling, 1984). This condition, however, may exist only in incontestably intensive oral programs – for example, Central Institute for the Deaf, St. Joseph's Institute for the Deaf, and Clarke School for the Deaf (Moog, Geers, & Calvert, 1981; Ogden, 1979). In addition, these approaches may be educationally successful with only select deaf students. Since fewer than 50% of speech sounds are visible on the lips (Jeffers & Barley, 1971), it is difficult to use oral approaches with most deaf children whose primary mode of receiving information is vision not audition (Quigley & Kretschmer, 1982; Quigley & Paul, 1984a). Consequently, it may be difficult for most deaf children to develop language owing to the ambiguity of the oral approaches.

This has led to the construction of the MCE approaches and the subsequent claim that, in conjunction with speech, these are more representative of English than are the oral approaches (Mitchell, 1982; Ross & Calvert, 1984). This assertion is not empirically justified. There is increasing evidence that the MCE systems and spoken English may be incompatible (e.g., Kluwin, 1981a; Marmor & Pettito,

1979; Reich & Bick, 1977). Since the systems require a number of manual movements to represent, for example, the derivational and inflectional components of English grammar, it is extremely difficult for many practitioners to adhere to the structure of English in a manual manner. The users of the systems may be exposing deaf students to some esoteric form of PSE.

The shortcomings of the OE and MCE approaches have led several researchers to argue that ASL should be used as a pedagogical tool in teaching English (Bockmiller, 1981; Brennan, 1975; Erting, 1981; Stokoe, 1975). Furthermore, they seem to assume that ASL is the only linguistic system that *all* prelingually deaf students can learn in a natural manner, and this in turn would provide a well-developed cognitive base for the later acquisition of a second language, notably English.

Oralism and the development of English

Research on the use of OE approaches with deaf students is discussed with respect to three areas: Cued Speech, the Acoupedic Method, and the Aural–Oral Method. In general, the findings indicate that, when these approaches are employed in a systematic, appropriate manner, favorable results can be obtained in relation to speech and language development in English. It should be reemphasized that these approaches have been successful primarily with select deaf students. Because only limited data are available, Lane's (1976) assertion is still relevant, namely, that there is a need for "well documented research, demonstrating the value and need for oral methods" (p. 137).

Cued Speech

Most data on the use of CS concern deaf students in countries other than the United States. There have been no investigations comparing this method with other instructional approaches. Studies were specifically designed to assess the effects of CS on the speech reception abilities of deaf students, although one of these also investigated the corresponding expressive (i.e., speech and language) development.

Two studies evaluated the use of CS with a group of deaf students in Vancouver, British Columbia, in Canada (Clarke & Ling, 1976; Ling & Clarke, 1975). Ling and Clarke (1975) tested 12 hearing-impaired students who were between the ages of 7 and 11 years and had been exposed to CS for at least 1 year. Seven of the subjects were deaf as defined in this chapter, and one had a pure tone average of less than 70 dB in the better unaided ear. The researchers presented cued (i.e., cues and speech) and noncued (i.e., speech only) phrases and sentences at slow and normal rates. The subjects were required to write their responses, which were analyzed with respect to number of words, phrases, and sentences correct. The phoneme errors of the subjects were also analyzed.

In general, the scores on the cued materials were superior to those on the non-cued materials. Cued words were easier to recognize than cued phrases, which were easier to recognize than cued sentences. Apparently, the subjects processed the stimuli in word units and experienced difficulty in proceeding beyond the word length. It was reported that the difference between cued and noncued stimuli increased with the degree of hearing impairment. Nevertheless, the overall performance of the subjects was poor, especially for cued sentences, in which only 9% of the responses were correct. No significant difference was reported between the rates of presentation.

In a follow-up study conducted 1 year later, Clarke and Ling (1976) replicated the experiment with 8 of the original 12 students. Only one of the students did not have a profound hearing impairment (90 dB) in the better unaided ear. In general, the results were similar to those reported earlier. For example, no significant difference was observed for the rate of presentation. As expected, the scores on the cued materials were significantly superior to those on the noncued materials. Specifically, cued phrases were slightly easier to recognize than cued sentences.

The major difference in the findings of the two studies was revealed by the analyses of phoneme errors produced by the subjects. In the initial study, the researchers stated that no consistent patterns of errors emerged. In the second study, however, the analyses revealed an improvement in the recognition of vowels and consonants. It was observed that the errors were also distributed in a more consistent manner, thus making it beneficial to employ similar analyses in establishing a remedial program for the students.

Nicholls and Ling (1982) investigated the effects of CS on the speech reception abilities of deaf students in Sydney, Australia. Eighteen students, between the ages of 10 and 17 years and exposed to CS for at least 4 years, served as subjects. The researchers designed and presented stimuli in seven test conditions: audition; lip reading; audition and lip reading; cues; audition and cues; lip reading and cues; and audition, lip reading, and cues. The speech productions of the subjects were also assessed. High speech reception scores for key words in sentences and syllabic stimuli were obtained for the lip reading plus cues and the audition, lip reading, plus cues conditions, and these were significantly better than for all other conditions. It was also found that the speech production skills of the subjects did not correlate with the use of CS. Nicholls and Ling argued that CS did not negatively affect the lip-reading ability or the use of residual hearing of the subjects, and they concluded "that more widespread use of Cued Speech would be merited, particularly as an oral option for those children who have very limited residual hearing, are totally deaf, or who are failing to make adequate progress in more conventional programs" (p. 268).

In a more recent study, Mohay (1983) evaluated the effects of CS on the language development of deaf children. Language development was operationally defined according to four criteria: (1) the amount of production of cues, (2) the number of noncued gestures and words, (3) the range and complexity of vocabulary development, and (4) the length and structure of spoken utterances. Three young children served as subjects; two were deaf and one was severely hearing impaired. The subjects had been previously enrolled in an oral program and had transferred to a CS program. The most notable effects of CS were reported for the subjects' spoken utterances. After the children were introduced to CS, their use of word combinations (i.e., two or three words) began to increase. Mohay suggested, however, that this might be attributed to other factors, namely, an increase in the linguistic and cognitive development of the children. It was concluded that the effects of CS on the language development of deaf children should be further investigated.

Acoupedic

Since the 1960s, the Acoupedic Method and its variations have been employed selectively in the United States and Europe, and currently they are experiencing a decline (Moores, 1982). The research literature contains reports dealing mainly with habilitative procedures, that is, with the instruction of speech and auditory perception. Limited data, however, can be found regarding the use of these procedures among children with congenital or acquired hearing impairments.

Eisenberg and Santore (1976), for example, reported on the progress of a 12-year-old deaf student whose IQ ranged from average to above average on nonverbal scales. In regular education classrooms since the age of 5 years, the receptive and expressive language skills of this student had been approximately 4 to 5 years below the hearing norms as measured by the Peabody Picture Vocabulary Test (Dunn, 1959), the Illinois Test of Psycholinguistic Abilities (Kirk, McCarthy, & Kirk, 1968), and the Detroit Tests of Learning Aptitude (Baker & Leland, 1958). Before exposure, he was unable to comprehend speech material by means of audition alone (i.e., with hearing aids). In addition, the researchers remarked that the student was dependent solely on speech reading for communicative purposes.

After 2½ years of therapy, the speech discrimination scores of the subject increased from 0 to 56% at 60 dB hearing level. The researchers argued that the student learned to use his residual hearing more effectively in the perception of speech. Although his discrimination of phonetically balanced words improved, it was not reported whether there was a concurrent improvement in the various language measures.

In a more recent study, Long, Fitzgerald, Sutton, and Rollins (1983) reported the accomplishments of a 4½-year-old deaf girl who had been exposed to the auditory–verbal approach since the age of 13 months. The development of language was assessed through the use of the REEL (Receptive–Expressive Emergent Language; reference not cited) scale and the Developmental Sentence Analysis (DSA; L. Lee, 1974). With respect to the normative data for normally hearing children on the REEL Scale, the deaf girl performed below age level from 15 to 20½ months of age, on age level from about 22 to 26 months of age, and above average from 31 months of age to the present. Analyses of language samples using the DSA substantiated this growth in language ability. The results indicated that the child produced "complete, adult-like sentences 76% of the time" (p. 35) from the age of 4 to the present. The researchers argued that a normal rate of language development can be achieved through the Acoupedic Method, which requires early identification of the hearing impairment and consistent unisensory stimulation (audition only) to maximize the use of the deaf child's residual hearing. This should be coupled with the intense involvement of parents and teachers to provide a normal language-learning environment similar to that provided for normal-hearing children.

The importance of developing the auditory skills of deaf children in early infancy for speech perception was also investigated by Ling, Leckie, Pollack, Simser, and Smith (1981). These investigators were interested in ascertaining the improvement in the reception of syllables when the ability to lip-read was supplemented by the use of residual hearing. Twenty-four deaf students between the ages of 8 to 16 years inclusive served as subjects. The students attended a regular public school with support from skilled resource teachers. They also received intensive unisensory training in the use of audition in special programs before 3 years of age. Specifically, the students were required to use hearing alone during part of their early training sessions.

Ling et al. (1981) presented stimuli under three conditions: audition only (A), vision (lip reading) only (L), and audition–vision (AL). As expected, the L condition produced significantly superior scores than the A condition. Also, as expected, the AL condition produced significantly better scores than either the A or L condition alone. The researchers concluded that the scores of the students under both the A and AL conditions were superior to those previously reported for other deaf students in multisensory programs (e.g., see the review in Erber, 1972), and this was attributed to the early training of the students in the use of audition alone.

Boothroyd (1984) ascertained the extent to which acoustical information was accessible to students with various degrees of sensorineural hearing impairments at Clarke School for the Deaf in Northampton, Massachusetts. The subjects were 138 students between the ages of 11 and 19 years. The hearing impairments of the students ranged from 53 to 123 dB. Speech contrast tasks were administered, and, as expected, the scores decreased as the degree of hearing impairment increased. In addition, the scores correlated significantly with the intelligibility of the students' speech and with the recognition of phonemes in monosyllabic words even when the degree of hearing impairment was statistically controlled. Boothroyd concluded that deaf students with hearing losses as high as 105 to 114 dB were able to perceive segmental and suprasegmental contrasts in a connected speech context. Finally, the researcher argued that the scores may have been better if earlier and more effective intervention in the use of auditory mode had been present in the oral training of these students.

Aural–Oral

As a multisensory approach, Aural–Oral is probably the most widely used of the oral methods (Moores, 1982). There is some evidence that a combined (i.e., audition and vision) approach is likely to produce more favorable results than a unisensory (or auditory) approach in the development of speech in deaf children (e.g., Hack & Erber, 1982; Novelli-Olmstead & Ling, 1984; Sanders, 1982). It should be reemphasized that this approach requires that both audition and vision be utilized as fully as possible. In some instances, the early training of the students may be in the use of audition alone in some sessions (e.g., see Ling et al., 1981).

To evaluate the effects of this method on speech and language development, it is important to ascertain that the students are (1) deaf as defined earlier, (2) exposed only to this method, and (3) enrolled in comprehensive oral programs or, as in some cases, integrated into regular education programs. According to the second criterion, deaf students in total communication (TC) programs do not qualify. Indeed, some studies have shown that the oral abilities of these students are not equal to those in indisputably oral programs (e.g., see the discussion in Ross & Calvert, 1984). Furthermore, it has been argued that the oral components (i.e., speech, speech reading, and auditory training) of TC programs are not adequately implemented (Ling, 1976; Ling & Ling, 1978; Ross & Calvert, 1984).

Mavilya and Mignone (1977) investigated the aural–oral development of deaf children at the Lexington School for the Deaf in Lexington, New York. Three deaf children were studied from birth to 5 years of age. The various stages of speech development were charted and compared with those available for normal-hearing peers. It was reported that the deaf children began to babble at 6 months of age. Hearing children enter the babbling stage at 4 to 5 months of age (Cruttenden, 1979). Like hearing children, however, these deaf children produced one- and two-word utterances at approximately 24 months of age. By 2½ years of age, the three deaf children used speech to communicate among themselves as well as with their instructor and parents. Like normal-hearing children they reached the three-to four-word milestone around age 3, and their speech began to approximate that of an adult speaker around age 5. The researchers concluded that the use of good Aural–Oral techniques can help some deaf children to develop speech and language at rates comparable to those of normal-hearing children.

Geers and Moog (1978) assessed the spontaneous and elicited language of orally trained deaf students, some of whom had been integrated in regular classrooms. The students were between the ages of 4 and 15 years. Several of them had hearing impairments of less than 90 dB. The researchers administered the DSA and the Carrow Elicited Language Inventory (CELI; Carrow, 1974) to nonintegrated deaf students. For these students, the most rapid development of language was reported to occur between the ages of 4 and 9 years. Nevertheless, the scores of more than half of the students on the DSA were inferior to the norms of the average 3-year-old normal-hearing child. Likewise, on the CELI, more than half of the students produced more errors than the norms associated with the average 3-year-old normal-hearing child.

The researchers retested 14 students; some remained at Central Institute for the Deaf and some were integrated into regular classrooms. The integrated students outperformed the nonintegrated students on the assessment of spontaneous language (DSA). The nonintegrated deaf students, however, produced significantly fewer errors on the CELI. Whether the performance of the integrated deaf students was on the same grade level as that of normal-hearing peers was not reported.

In another study, Doehring, Bonnycastle, and Ling (1978) examined the language comprehension abilities of 21 hearing-impaired students who were between the ages of 6 and 13 years inclusive and enrolled in regular public school classrooms. Of relevance here are the performances of the 10 students classified as profoundly hearing impaired (90 dB). A number of language- and reading-related tasks were administered. The deaf students performed at or above the grade level of normal-hearing peers on reading-related tasks but below grade level on four of the five language-related measures. The researchers argued that the poor scores on the language tasks could be attributed to the inappropriateness of the tasks for deaf students. The success of the students on the reading-related tasks, however, was explained as follows: "The auditory–oral training of these children seems to have enabled them to acquire many of the oral reading skills needed in classes for normally hearing children" (p. 407). Indeed, the investigators also asserted that the auditory–oral training of the deaf students was the reason that their performance was superior to that of the severely impaired students.

More recently, Hack and Erber (1982) assessed the perception of vowels by 16 deaf and 2 severely impaired students with good (G), intermediate (I), and poor (P) word recognition skills. The investigators presented 10 vowels through three modalities: audition (amplification only), vision (speech reading only), and combined (amplification and speech reading). In the audition mode, the G group performed better than the I group, which outperformed the P group. On the whole, however, the auditory vowel reception of the best group (G) was still poor. All three groups were very similar in their ability to identify vowels visually. In fact, there were little differences between the audition and vision scores of the G and I groups. In addition, the combined scores (AV) of these groups were similar and represented an improvement over both the A and V modes. The P group also achieved higher scores for the AV mode than for the A or V mode alone; however, their AV scores were significantly inferior to those of the G or I groups. The AV scores of the group with poor word recognition skills represented a small increase in vowel recognition in relation to those obtained by V alone.

The findings of Hack and Erber (1982) suggest that speech reception in communication is enhanced when both audition and vision are employed. Although speech reception is important for the development of language comprehension skills, speech production may be equally important (Novelli-Olmstead & Ling, 1984). A considerable body of evidence has shown that there is a reciprocal relation between speech reception and speech production (e.g., Bennett & Ling, 1977; Ling, 1976; Winitz, 1975).

The relation between speech reception and speech production was investigated by Novelli-Olmstead and Ling (1984). Fourteen deaf students who were between the ages of 5 and 7 years and enrolled in self-contained classes in a large oral program in Canada served as subjects. The researchers created seven matched pairs, and each subject of the pair was randomly assigned to one of two groups: speakers (S) and listeners (L). The speaking subject of each pair was required to listen to and produce certain speech sounds. The listening subject was required to listen to the same sounds and respond by pointing to objects or pictures that represented them. The researchers constructed an auditory discrimination test and used speech production tests devised by Ling (1976). The subjects received training twice daily for 30 sessions. Pre- and posttest results indicated that the S group significantly increased their scores on both the speech production and auditory discrimination tasks. The L group, however, demonstrated only a slight gain in speech production and no gain in auditory discrimination scores. The researchers concluded that speech and auditory training are likely to be more effective in the development of speech and language than the use of auditory training alone.

Manually Coded English and the development of English

During the 1970s, a meteoric rise of TC occurred in the education of deaf children (Moores, 1982; Quigley & Kretschmer, 1982). Briefly, in relation to form of communication, TC is a philosophy that permits the use of any of the MCE systems, ASL, and speech either in isolation or in some combined fashion (Gannon, 1981). The use of ASL in the classroom, however, has not been extensively documented. It appears that many educators have not included ASL in the theoretical framework of TC. At present, it is safe to conclude that some form of sign communication is present in most educational approaches in the United States (Gallaudet Research Institute, 1985; Jordan et al. 1979; Ross & Calvert, 1984).

Most of the MCE approaches have been employed in instructional situations for at least 15 years, yet there is little evidence for producing competence in English literacy skills (Baker & Cokely, 1980; Quigley & Paul, 1984a). In addition, the data on most of the approaches should be interpreted with caution since wide discrepancies have been reported between the idealized conceptions and the practitioners' use of the systems (Kluwin, 1981a; Marmor & Pettito, 1979; Reich & Bick, 1977). It is believed that those who participated in the studies discussed here adhered as closely as possible to the principles of the particular system under investigation.

Pidgin Sign English

Before the influx of the sign systems, deaf persons and hearing persons with a knowledge of some ASL-like signs attempted to communicate with each other by using the ASL signs in an English word order, that is, a form of PSE (Bragg, 1973). The following is a simplified example. Consider the English sentence *I want the red car.* If the car has been mentioned earlier, one way to sign this sentence in ASL (ignoring nonmanual cues) is CAR RED I WANT. If the deaf person wishes to communicate this idea to an English-speaking person with a knowledge of signs, she or he may sign I WANT THE RED CAR or I WANT RED CAR (Baker & Cokely, 1980; Humphries, Padden, & O'Rourke, 1980). The latter expression is also acceptable by the grammar of ASL.

PSE, as well as ASL, has been influenced by the other MCE systems. This can be seen, for example, by the use in PSE of contrived sign markers representing a portion of English morphology, *-ing, -ed,* and *-s.* A current view of PSE is that it combines some of the grammatical aspects of ASL and some aspects of the MCE systems and generally employs these in the word order of English (Baker & Cokely, 1980; Cokely, 1983; Maxwell, 1983; Wilbur, 1979). It should be emphasized that PSE as discussed here is *not* similar to the form of signing produced by an inconsistent use of some of the other MCE systems (e.g., Kluwin, 1981a; Marmor & Pettito, 1979). Within this conceptual framework, the studies included in this category are those whose participants executed ASL-like signs and some contrived sign markers in an English word order or used simultaneous communication.

Griswold and Cummings (1974) examined the expressive signed vocabulary of 19 deaf children from the ages of 2 to 5 years. These children were exposed to TC in the preschool and home environments. The researchers reported a number of words and expressions executed by two or more children. As expected, the vocabulary of these children was smaller than that reported for normally hearing children of similar ages. The deaf children, however, signed nouns, verbs, some prepositions, numbers, and specific question words in the same proportions as those found in the language of hearing children. They differed from hearing children in the proportional use of connections, articles, and auxiliary and modal verbs. It has been argued that these differences can be attributed to the nature of the sign systems; that is, the systems do not represent these aspects of English manually (e.g., Gustason et al., 1975).

Some support for this hypothesis was provided by the work of Crandall (1978) on the developmental order of manual English morphemes. Twenty pairs of normally hearing mothers and their young deaf children were studied. The sign systems of the mothers were labeled manual English. This consisted of using some ASL-like signs and some contrived markers from both SEE II (Gustason et al., 1975) and a basic text on manual communication (O'Rourke, 1973) in an English word order. Results indicated that the order of the first six morphemes signed by the young deaf children was similar to the order spoken by hearing children (Brown, 1973). Crandall also found a relation between the amount of exposure to the manual morphemes from the mothers and their children's productions. This finding emphasizes the importance of the home environment, which has been deemed an essential factor in the language development of deaf children (Moores, 1982; Quigley & Kretschmer, 1982; Quigley & Paul, 1984a).

There have been a few, more recent investigations charting certain aspects of the primary development of English through PSE (e.g., Weber & Weber, 1981). The major shortcoming is that the children in these studies did not meet the definition of deaf as defined in this chapter, making it difficult to generalize the results to the deaf student population. Nevertheless, the major purpose of these studies was to demonstrate that the use of signs in conjunction with speech does not prohibit but rather enhances the development of speech, speech reading, and the use of residual hearing in young hearing-impaired children.

Limited data are available regarding the effects of the primary development of PSE on the secondary language development of English. The work of Brasel and Quigley (1977) serves as an example. These researchers designed a study to explore the interaction of type and form of communication approach and intensity of early communication input. Eighteen deaf students between 10 and 19 years of age were categorized into each of four communication groups: manual English (i.e., PSE), ASL (labeled average manual), intensive oral (IO), and average oral (AO). The parents of the PSE and ASL groups were deaf, whereas those of the IO and AO groups had normal hearing. The students in the IO group received intensive oral training in both the home and school environments, whereas the AO students had parents who were uninvolved with their children's education. Furthermore, the oral training of the AO children was probably not much better than that found in most TC programs (Ross & Calvert, 1984).

The scores of the PSE group were significantly superior to those of the others on most of the language-related subtests of the Stanford Achievement Test (SAT; Madden, Gardner, Rudman, Karlsen, & Merwin, 1972) and the syntactic structures of the Test of Syntactic Abilities (TSA; Quigley, Steinkamp, Power, & Jones, 1978). The performances of the ASL and IO groups were nearly identical, whereas that of the AO group was significantly inferior to all the others on most variables. The two manual groups combined outperformed the two oral groups. The researchers inferred two general conclusions from their data: (1) The early use of manual communication is superior to the early use of oral communication in developing English literacy skills for most deaf children, and (2) the *form* of manual communication is important; that is, the best results seem to be obtained with the form that attempts to represent English manually.

In a more recent study, Maxwell (1983) investigated the relation between the written productions of seven deaf students (ages 14 to 15 years) and the instructors' use of signs and sign markers in a TC program. The TC program had been implemented in the school only 2 years previously. Thus, the subjects received their initial exposure to the markers when they were 12 to 13 years of age. Three stories were signed by an instructor, and the subjects were asked to write what they remembered. Their written English was analyzed in terms of propositions (i.e., content), morphology, and syntax.

In general, little connection was found between the subject's written work and their recall of the signs and markers. It was argued that the English word–sign correspondences were not known by the subjects. For example, "no student wrote cried but several wrote synonymous shouted or yelled. No student wrote anything like the phrase 'no wonder'" (p. 107). On the basis of analyses of propositions, Maxwell concluded that the subjects comprehended the stories despite their inability to produce the morphological and syntactic structures.

These results should be interpreted with caution. In relation to the subjects' reading levels (third to fifth grade on the SAT; Madden et al., 1972), the content of the stories was relatively easy to recall. Also, the subjects' comprehension was somewhat inaccurate with respect to certain information provided by morphological and syntactic use, for example, verb tense and noun–verb agreement.

The benefits of using signing (probably in a pidgin form) in a TC program has been documented by Delaney, Stuckless, and Walter (1984). They reported that the secondary language achievements of the present TC students were superior to those of previously enrolled students exposed to Aural–Oral only or to a combination of Aural–Oral and TC methods. The performance of the TC-only group was equal to that of the best group in the Brasel and Quigley study (1977). Like other researchers, Delaney et al. (1984) suggested that the superior achievement of TC-only students might have been due to factors other than the implementation of TC, for example, improvements in the curricula and involvement of parents and school personnel.

Signed English

The effects of SE on the primary language development of English has been investigated mainly by Bornstein and his associates, who studied certain aspects of syntactic and semantic growth. Bornstein, Saulnier, and Hamilton (1980), for example, conducted a 4-year longitudinal study of 18 severe to profound hearing-impaired students enrolled in residential and day schools. The mean better ear hearing impairment of the group was 88 dB, and the mean chronological age was approximately 4 years. Three measurements were employed annually to test the primary language development of each student: the Peabody Picture Vocabulary Test (Dunn, 1959), the Northwestern Syntax Screening Test (L. Lee, 1969), and a Signed English Morphology Test designed by the researchers.

After 4 years, the findings indicated that receptive vocabulary and syntactic growth took place in a manner similar to that of hearing children but at a slower rate. The rate of growth in vocabulary, for example, was reported to be one-half that observed for hearing children of comparable ages. The expressive abilities were equivalent to a 3- to 4-year-old average-hearing child. The receptive growth in English morphology paralleled the development observed in hearing children. The results of expressive ability in morphology revealed, however, that only half of the students could execute three inflections appropriately: regular plural, possessive, and *-ing*.

Bornstein and Saulnier (1981) conducted a follow-up study 1 year later. Using two rating scales, instructors were asked to rate the extent and frequency of use of the sign markers by their students. Compared with the previous investigation, there was an increase in the frequency of use; however, the students at about 10 years of age were executing only half of the 14 markers.

Bornstein (1982) has remarked that the results of these investigations have not met his expectations. Despite this lack of success, a number of SE readers and materials have been developed (Bornstein & Saulnier, 1984; Collins-Ahlgren, 1974a; Roy, 1975; Saulnier, 1975). Essentially, the SE signs have been placed above the English text. Whether the procedure affects the reading comprehension ability of deaf students has not been reported. There is some evidence, however, that the placement of ASL-like signs above the English text results in an improvement of reading comprehension (Robbins, 1983).

In contrast, Gardner and Zorfass (1983) reported very positive effects of SE in a TC program. The researchers studied the language development of one severely to profoundly hearing-impaired boy (i.e., in the 80- to 90-dB range) from age 13 months to 3 years. The spoken and signed productions of the child were analyzed separately. Specifically, the relations between the two modalities were examined.

The results indicated that the hearing-impaired child executed signs (mean length of utterance, 1) exclusively at the age of 15 months. His vocalizations were not meaningful; however, the sounds were rhythmic and intonational, and these aspects are essential for the later development of speech (deVilliers & deVilliers, 1978). At approximately 17 months, speech development was independent of sign development. Five months later, speech and signs were executed simultaneously; however, signs were dropped or not used for words that were known in the speech mode. By 2 years of age, the child used speech as his primary mode for reception and expression. Signs were produced only for new and unfamiliar words. At 3 years of age, the *oral* language development of this child was comparable to that of hearing peers. The researchers concluded that the use of signs in a TC environment enabled the child to attach meanings to sounds.

Since the degree of hearing impairment of the child was similar to that reported for the subjects in the studies by Bornstein and his associates, the findings are impressive. It can be argued, however, that the results are related to the specific nature of the hearing impairment of the subject in the Gardner and Zorfass study. For example, the contour of the loss was flat, that is, a relatively straight line on the audiogram from 250 to 8000 Hz. This configuration is most conducive to amplification (Sanders, 1982). In fact, it was reported that the child utilized two ear-level hearing aids very effectively. Apparently, the primary mode of this child was audition – not vision – resulting in good oral language development.

Signing Exact English

SEE II, like SE, has been heavily promoted with how-to materials on teaching the system to deaf children, hearing parents, and instructors of the deaf (Gustason, 1983; Gustason et al., 1980). The main rationale is that the deaf child must see (i.e., through signs) English exactly as it is spoken to understand the structures and become competent in reading and writing. Yet in spite of this seemingly sound theoretical position, a perusal of the research literature yielded only one study evaluating the effects of this approach on the language development of deaf students (Babb, 1979). Clearly, a huge gap exists between theory and research, which is indicative of an approach being adopted owing to its promotion or popularity rather than its verified effectiveness (Quigley & Paul, 1984b; Ross & Calvert, 1984).

Babb (1979) examined the academic achievement (SAT), syntactic knowledge (TSA), and written language ability of 36 deaf children exposed to SEE II for approximately 10 years. The design of his study was similar to that employed by Brasel and Quigley (1977). Eighteen deaf students were exposed to this approach at school only, and the rest received exposure in the home and school environments. The scores of the groups were compared with one another, with those of a hearing comparison group, with those of the subjects in the Brasel and Quigley study, and with the normative national achievement data for hearing-impaired students (DiFrancesca, 1972).

In general, the group exposed to SEE II in the home and at school performed better than the group that received instruction in SEE II only at school and as well as the manual English group in the Brasel and Quigley study. The school-only SEE II group's scores were similar to those of the AO group in the Brasel and Quigley study, and their SAT scores were similar to the national norms reported for hearing-impaired students. This investigation, along with others discussed earlier, reiterated the importance of the home environment.

Seeing Essential English

One of the earliest investigations involving the use of the signs of SEE I was undertaken by Schlesinger and Meadow (1972). The interactions of four deaf children and their parents were observed. Three of the children were exposed to at least some SEE I signs. Analyses of language samples and tests of grammatical competence (Menyuk, 1963) revealed that the vocabulary and syntactic development of the deaf children were similar to – albeit slower than – those reported for young hearing children. One subject, exposed to the SEE I morphological markers at the age of 3 years, began to execute them at age 4 years. These researchers concluded, as have others, that early and consistent communication between the deaf child and parents is essential for normal English language development. It should be reemphasized, however, that the rate of development was slower than that of hearing children of similar ages.

The similar but slower development of English in deaf children exposed to SEE I has been substantiated by more recent studies. Raffin (1976) and Raffin, Davis, and Gilman (1978) assessed the acquisition of some of the most common English morphemes: past tense, -*ed*; third person singular present indicative, -*s*; present progressive, -*ing*; present perfect, -*en*; plural, -*s* on nouns; possessive, -'*s*; comparative, -*er*; and superlative, -*est*. The test instrument for both studies was that developed by Raffin (1976). Forty-eight sentences were presented in a simultaneous manner, that is, with speech and signs from the SEE I lexicon. The subjects in the Raffin study were between the ages of 6 and 12 years, whereas those in the Raffin et al. study were between 5 and 11 years old. In general, the results showed that the order of acquisition of English morphemes by a deaf child is nearly similar to that of hearing children at a younger age (Brown, 1973). The researchers concluded that, if deaf children are consistently exposed to a morpheme-based sign code, they will be capable of evaluating the grammaticality of inflectional English morphemes.

Additional support for the findings of Raffin et al. can be found in a study by Gilman, Davis, and Raffin (1980). The subjects were 14 deaf and 6 severely hearing-impaired ($\geq$80 dB) students whose ages ranged from 8 to 12 years and whose exposure to SEE I ranged from 2 to 4 years. To be included in the study, the students were required to exhibit at least a first-grade reading ability as measured by the Metropolitan Reading Inventory and the Stanford Reading Inventory (references not cited). A 40-sentence, 4-item multiple-choice, written test accompanied by illustrations was constructed by the investigators and administered individually to each child. There were five different sentences for each of the eight morphemes discussed previously. The researchers were interested in the effects of sex, age, hearing impairment, reading level, years of exposure to SEE I, and consistency of teacher's use.

As in the previous studies, the order of difficulty of the morphemes revealed a developmental pattern followed by younger hearing children (Brown, 1973), except for the past tense, -ed. In addition, the students used appropriately seven of the eight morphemes on the written test beyond the chance level. No significant effects were observed for length of exposure to SEE I; however, the students with the longest exposure (i.e., 4 years) did obtain the highest scores. This result, along with significant findings reported for sex and reading level, were stated to be confounded by the teacher consistency factor, which was significant. In general, the students associated with teachers using SEE I consistently significantly outperformed those with teachers using SEE I inconsistently. The consistency factor was deemed to be the major determinant of the ability to use the morphemes in view of the finding that students with fewer years of exposure to SEE I under a consistent teacher scored higher than those with longer exposure under an inconsistent teacher.

Finger spelling

Few educational programs employ the simultaneous use of finger spelling and speech (i.e., the Rochester Method, or RM) exclusively, and most that do use it with junior-high- and high-school-aged students (Baker & Cokely, 1980; Quigley, 1969). With respect to elementary-aged deaf students, Hester (1963) reported data on the use of the RM in a residential school in the Southwest. Comparisons were made between deaf students exposed to the method and those who were enrolled before the implementation of the approach. Superior reading scores were found for the students taught by the RM.

Quigley (1969), conducting a longitudinal survey and an experimental study, reported similar findings. Deaf students from nine residential schools were surveyed. The comparison was between students exposed to the RM and those exposed to simultaneous communication of speech and signs (i.e., some form of PSE). The RM students generally produced significantly better scores than the others on various language-related subtests of the SAT. No significant differences, however, were found on measures of written language ability. It should be emphasized that an increase of only one and a half grade levels was observed for the RM students (mean age approximately 18 years) at the completion of the 5-year survey. In addition, the reading level of these students was approximately seven grades below that expected of their hearing-age counterparts.

In the experimental study, Quigley compared the language comprehension ability of 16 selected (i.e., above-average IQ) deaf children exposed to the RM with matched children exposed to an oral method (i.e., Aural–Oral or Auditory–Visual–Oral). At the inception of the study, the ages of the deaf children ranged from 3½ to 4½ years, and each group was selected from a residential school. The RM group outperformed the oral group on measures of reading (SAT scores) and written language. Quigley concluded that the use of the RM with young deaf children may be an effective educational approach; however, it is not a panacea.

More recent investigations have focused on the processing of finger spelling by deaf students. Stuckless and Pollard (1977), for example, examined the abilities of 19 deaf students at the Rochester School for the Deaf (Rochester, New York) to process finger spelling and print. The students were assigned to three groups on the basis of level of competence in English. The groups received two presentations: 10 sentences in a finger-spelled mode (no accompanying speech) and a matched set of 10 sentences in a print mode. After each sentence, they were required to write their responses. The numbers of correct words were analyzed.

For the total group, the overall score on the presentation in the print mode was significantly higher than that in the finger-spelling mode. In-depth analyses revealed that 18 of the 19 students correctly wrote more printed than finger-spelled words. In addition, the ability to process print and/or finger spelling was significantly related to the English competence level of the students. The group of students regarded "as being of superior general academic and English ability relative to other deaf students" (p. 476) obtained the highest and most satisfactory results on the finger-spelled (92% correct) and print (99% correct) words.

Looney and Rose (1979) studied the effects of using finger spelling to teach the past-tense inflectional suffixes of English. Twenty-four deaf students between the ages of 8 and 15 years served as subjects. To be included in the study, the subjects were required to demonstrate the ability to express some basic kernel patterns of English through writing and finger spelling. The subjects were assigned to one of three groups: RM, print, and control. The two treatment groups were exposed to systematic instruction of inflectional suffixes in their respective mode, that is, through RM or print. The receptive and expressive abilities of the groups were evaluated. The results of pre- and posttests revealed significant gains for both treatment groups but not for the control group. No significant differences were reported between the two treatment groups. Looney and Rose concluded that both finger spelling and print can be employed effectively to teach certain morphological structures of English. This is in contrast to the findings of Stuckless and Pollard (1977) and others (e.g., White & Stevenson, 1975), which seem to indicate that deaf students receive more information from print than from any of the other communication modes.

American Sign Language

Research on ASL is considered in relation to three areas: the primary development of ASL, the issue of bilingualism and second-language learning, and the effects of ASL on the development of English. Within these perspectives, the following questions are addressed: (1) Is development in a signed language analogous to development in a spoken language? (2) What is the first language of most deaf children? (3) Should ASL be taught as a first language for *all* deaf children and then be used to teach English as a second language? The scientific study of ASL began with the seminal work of Stokoe (1960), and descriptions of its grammar appeared in the later 1970s (e.g., Baker & Cokely, 1980; Klima & Bellugi, 1979; Lane & Grosjean, 1980; Liddell, 1980; Siple, 1978). It is expected that the use of ASL in bilingual or ESL programs for deaf students will attract the attention of investigators in the 1980s (Luetke-Stahlman, 1983; Quigley & Paul, 1984b).

Primary development of American Sign Language

The acquisition of ASL has been studied in relation to the components established for spoken languages, that is, phonology, syntax, semantics, and pragmatics. A number of studies have delineated, for example, certain linguistic aspects: markedness (McIntire, 1977), classifiers (Kantor, 1980; Luetke-Stahlman, 1984), and iconicity (Orlansky & Bonvillian, 1984). One investigation even concluded that deaf children have an innate predisposition for expressing themselves within the structure of ASL regardless of exposure to a contrived signed code (Livingston, 1983). Succinctly stated, the major inference drawn from a sample of these studies is that the developmental stages of a signed language are analogous to and parallel those of a spoken language.

Stokoe (1960) investigated the linguistic parameters of the formation of a sign, which he classified as *dez* (handshape), *tab* (location), and *sig* (movement). The study of these parameters is termed cherology, which is analogous to the study of phonemes or phonology. Since Stokoe's work, a fourth element, orientation, has been added (Wilbur, 1979, 1980), which refers to the direction in which the palm(s) is (are) facing, namely, up, down, toward the signer's body, or to the side(s). The four parameters are executed simultaneously to form a sign in much the same way that distinctive features are combined to produce consonants and vowels in spoken languages.

With respect to handshapes, McIntire (1977) reported that unmarked elements are acquired before marked ones. He followed the development of signs in one deaf child from the ages of 13 to 21 months. Initially, pointing and grasping handshapes were acquired; for example, A, S, L, and C (similar to finger-spelled shapes), with the more complex handshapes appearing later, for example, H, W, and X. The substitution errors produced by this child involved similar cheremic elements, and this is analogous to those produced by hearing children with similar phonemic elements.

The first words of hearing children have been reported to emerge between the ages of 10 and 13 months (Dale, 1976; deVilliers & deVilliers, 1978). A broader age range can be gleaned from studies on the appearance of the first signs of deaf children, from approximately 7 or 8 months (Hoffmeister & Wilbur, 1980; Orlansky & Bonvillian, 1985) to 13 months (Schlesinger & Meadow, 1972). There is increasing evidence that iconicity does not play a major role in the acquisition of the initial signs (e.g., Orlansky & Bonvillian, 1984) or of signs in general (e.g., Markowicz, 1980).

Orlansky and Bonvillian (1984), for example, conducted a longitudinal study of the acquisition of ASL signs by 13 children with a median age of 10 months at the inception of the investigation. Seven of the children had two deaf parents, three had one deaf parent, and one had a deaf mother in a single-parent household. Most of the parents had attended Gallaudet College, and the three hearing parents were fluent in ASL. Analyses of the initial 10 signs acquired by the subjects revealed that approximately 31% could be described as iconic, that is, a strong resemblance between the sign and its referent. A second analysis performed at 18 months showed the proportion of iconic signs to be approximately 34%. The researchers concluded that the role of iconicity in the child's acquisition of sign language may not be as important as previously assumed. Just as the relation between a word and its referent is essentially arbitrary, it was argued that the relation between a sign and its referent is also arbitrary and must be learned.

Research on the syntactic, semantic, and pragmatic aspects of ASL revealed further evidence for the parallels between signed and spoken languages, in this case, between ASL and English. For example, the developmental stages in the acquisition of negation (Hoffmeister & Wilbur, 1980) and semantic relations (Newport & Ashbrook, 1977) in ASL are similar to those reported for hearing children learning English (Bloom, Lightbown, & Hood, 1975; Brown, 1973). The same is true for the acquisition of classifiers, which may appear as syntactic forms and may also reflect certain semantic properties of their noun referents (Kantor, 1980). In addition, the use of classifiers is one linguistic aspect that seems to differentiate levels of competency in ASL (Luetke-Stahlman, 1984). In the domain of pragmatics, Kantor (1982) reported that deaf mothers, like hearing-speaking mothers, modified the structure of their language to facilitate communication with their children; that is, they used more simple and direct structures.

The major thrust of the research on ASL is to demonstrate that it is a bona fide language with developmental stages that parallel those of a spoken language. The current concern is not with the language status of ASL, but with its instructional use in the education of deaf children. As discussed previously, ASL itself is not usually employed as a teaching approach per se, although its lexicon has been the basis for the majority of signs utilized in several of the contrived sign systems.

Bilingualism and English as a second language

The issues of bilingualism and ESL in the education of deaf children are shrouded in controversies and confusion. The source of some confusion is attributed to the lack of differentiation between ASL and the contrived signed codes (e.g., Luetke-Stahlman, 1983). It should be clear that, in this case, there are only *two* languages:

ASL and some representation of spoken English in an oral and/or manual form. The greatest controversies concern the answers to the following questions: (1) What *is* the first language of the deaf child? (2) What *should* be the first language of the deaf child?

First language: ASL or English? It is a gross understatement that it is difficult to assess the nature of the first language of *most* deaf children (e.g., Luetke-Stahlman & Weiner, 1982). Nevertheless, as previously discussed, the language development of deaf children should be considered in relation to the type of input from their parents in early infancy and childhood. Within this perspective, it may be concluded that the first language of most deaf children ranges from low to high competency in some form of English since most have English-speaking, hearing parents (King, 1981; Moores, 1982; Quigley & Kretschmer, 1982).

It appears that only deaf children with deaf parents would most likely be exposed to ASL. Approximately 3% of deaf children have two deaf parents, with an additional 6% having at least one deaf parent (Rawlings & Jensema, 1977). Not all deaf children of deaf parents, however, may be exposed to ASL; some deaf parents may use a form of PSE (e.g., Brasel & Quigley, 1977; Collins-Ahlgren, 1974b; Schlesinger & Meadow, 1972), and some, OE (e.g., Corson, 1973).

Several investigators have proposed that ASL should be the first language of all deaf children (see discussions in Bockmiller, 1981; Charrow & Wilbur, 1975; Maxwell, 1983), and English should be taught as a second language. There are three general arguments for ASL usage. First, most deaf children will learn ASL either by the time their formal education is completed or during adulthood (Baker & Cokely, 1980; Erting, 1981). Second, there is a gross incompatibility between the use of the contrived signed codes and spoken English, resulting in exposure to an impoverished representation of English (e.g., Kluwin, 1981a; Marmor & Pettito, 1979) or no representation at all (Kluwin, 1981b), overloads on short-term memory and neurological processing (Mitchell, 1982; Wilbur, 1979), and limited results in the development of English literacy skills (see the reviews of Quigley & Kretschmer, 1982; Quigley & Paul, 1984a). Third, some researchers have argued that deaf children may be predisposed to the structure of ASL despite training in or exposure to a signed code (e.g., Livingston, 1983; Suty & Friel-Patti, 1982).

With respect to the last assertion, Livingston (1983) described the spontaneous signing behavior of six deaf children of hearing parents with no ability in ASL or SE. The ages of the subjects ranged from 6 to 16 years. They were enrolled in a large public day school and were exposed to SE after the age of 6 years. It was reported that "at the time of the study all teachers on staff were hearing and none other than the researcher and the two Deaf paraprofessionals possessed near-native ASL competence" (p. 199).

A total of 3,500 signed utterances were transcribed and analyzed. Analyses revealed that the subjects used some grammatical structures that were and some that were not representative of SE. The unrepresentative structures resembled either a pidgin form of SE or some of the structures of ASL. Thus, some of the grammatical forms found in the subjects' signing behavior could not be attributed to the signing model to which they were exposed. In fact, it was reported that they "acquired greater facility in the use of ASL grammatical processes than in those of Signed English . . . even though all signing . . . is in Signed English" (p. 282).

These findings seem to support the assertion that, in lieu of a systematic language input, deaf children generate a gesture-based symbol system that resembles ASL and is independent of and more sophisticated than the input provided by parents and/or teachers (Erting, 1981; Suty & Friel-Patti, 1982; Wilcox, 1984). This is a radical extension of the hypothesis proposed by Goldin-Meadow (1975) asserting the existence of an innate language capacity in deaf children. This was manifested in her subjects' developing a gesture-based communication system despite being raised in an oral (i.e., an impoverished or lacking language) environment. If deaf children possess an innate capacity for language, it may be argued that they are more likely to develop a visual–gestural representation of this capacity. The findings of Goldin-Meadow are more in accordance with psycholinguistic theory than are those of Livingston (Slobin, 1979).

Deaf children, like hearing children, have a *need* to communicate and will develop a symbol system that meets this need. It is possible that such a symbol system may be esoteric in form (e.g., Tervoort, 1975). Furthermore, a predisposition to ASL, as suggested by Livingston, is an argument for sign universals in the form of ASL. Clearly, this position is atheoretical (e.g., Markowicz, 1980). The innate-language hypothesis suggests a predisposition to language in general, not to any specific language such as ASL. The specific language depends on the culture in which the child is raised. Finally, it should be emphasized that, although the innateness hypothesis may have some merit, it may not be an all-or-nothing phenomenon (Armstrong, 1984; Schlesinger, 1982).

From another perspective, some researchers have concluded that English is a second language for deaf students on the basis of their performances on secondary language measurements of English. These researchers also assumed that the signed system of these students was ASL. Odom and Blanton (1970), for example, compared the performances of deaf and hearing students on a reading test administered in English, sign, and nonsense word order. The most important conclusion of the study was that the deaf, when compared with the hearing subjects, understood the material better when it conformed to the grammar and word order of sign language. A closer inspection of the sentences in sign revealed, however, a number of sentences in a word order similar to English. In addition, there were no significant differences in the performances of the hearing subjects on the sign and English versions of the test. Apparently, there was some similarity between the two versions. It is possible that the sign version may have been a form of PSE.

In another study, Charrow and Fletcher (1974) compared the performances on an ESL test of two groups of deaf students (one with deaf parents and the other hearing) with each other and with a group of hearing students learning English as a second language. Of interest here is the hypothesis that the performance of the ESL learners would be more similar to that of deaf students with deaf parents than to that of deaf students with hearing parents. Like previous investigators, these researchers *assumed* that the language of deaf students of deaf parents is homogeneous and also different from that of deaf students with hearing parents. There was no clear evidence to support the hypothesis that English is a second language for these students. Nevertheless, Charrow and Fletcher argued that deaf students learn some aspects of English as they would a second language but not other aspects.

From these investigations, it must be concluded that no substantial evidence yet exists to support the assertion that ASL is or should be the first language for *all* deaf children. Arguing for its use in the classroom on the basis of negative evidence, that is, the lack of success of other methods, does not make a strong case. Inferring from the research on bilingualism and second-language learning, there is a case for the instructional use of ASL and the teaching of English as a second language with at least *some* deaf children for whom ASL *is* a first language (Quigley & Paul, 1984b). This raises the all-important question, How can a signed language (i.e., ASL) be employed to teach a spoken language (i.e., English)?

Instructional use of ASL. Despite the importance of this issue, very few data exist on the manner in which ASL can be employed to teach English as a second language, particularly reading and writing skills. This can be attributed to the past and future perspectives of the role of ASL in the education of deaf children, leading one researcher (Lane, 1980) to state "that ASL will not make much headway as the vehicle of instruction, . . . we will not see much bilingual education of the deaf" (p. 158). It may also be that, since attempts to write a grammar of ASL have been made only recently, its role in a bilingual or ESL situation has yet to be explored. This may mean that the results of the few earlier studies on the use of ASL should be interpreted with caution.

In relation to instructional use, the approach of some researchers has been to compare and contrast the structures of ASL and English (Crutchfield, 1972; Jones, 1979). In this manner, the instructor can demonstrate similarities of grammatical acceptability and unacceptability in both languages. In addition, the instructor should be cognizant of the nonmanual aspects of ASL (e.g., raised eyebrows), which serve certain syntactic functions, for example, yes–no question and relative clause. There is some evidence that deaf students fail to include the nonmanual aspects of ASL in their writing of English (Jones, 1979). In general, these approaches to the problem of errors appear to resemble the contrastive analysis approach employed with hearing ESL learners (e.g., see the discussion in Richards, 1974). There is a need to consider other approaches, namely, error or noncontrastive analyses, that focus on developmental strategies, and in conjunction, these methods should contribute to the understanding of the process of second-language learning and teaching.

American Sign Language and the development of English

Like the data on its instructional use, the effects of having learned ASL in early childhood on the subsequent learning of English literacy skills have not been investigated in detail. Using as subjects students from residential and/or day schools, most of the early studies compared the performances of deaf students having deaf parents with those of deaf students having hearing parents (e.g., Charrow & Fletcher, 1974; Meadow, 1968; Quigley & Frisina, 1961; Stuckless & Birch, 1966). With respect to language, reading, and overall academic achievement, it was found that deaf students with deaf parents performed significantly better than those with hearing parents. In addition, Meadow (1968) reported higher self-image scores for deaf students with deaf parents. Balow and Brill (1975) found that even having only one deaf parent can produce positive effects on educational and psychological factors. In general, the superiority of deaf students with deaf parents was attributed to the early and consistent exposure to manual communication, which, in retrospect, could be labeled ASL.

It can be inferred from these early studies that deaf parents are also more accepting of their deaf children than are hearing parents, and this acceptance manifests in the use of sign language. There is no question that parental acceptance is related to the school achievement of deaf children; however, this relation may occur in situations where deaf parents used *speech* with their deaf children (Corson, 1973; Messerly & Aram, 1980). Furthermore, the findings of Brasel and Quigley (1977) discussed earlier demonstrated that the *type* of manual communication is a critical factor. For the purposes here, it is emphasized that deaf children exposed to manual English performed better than the group exposed to ASL on most measures. This seems to call into question the superiority of ASL over all other forms of manual communication.

Summary

The purpose of this chapter has been to delineate the effects of deafness on the development of English language skills. Descriptions of language development should take into account three important issues: (1) an operational definition of deafness, (2) the nature and extent of linguistic input, and (3) the nature of the communication mode, that is, manual or oral (Quigley & Kretschmer, 1982; Quigley & Paul, 1984a). Within this perspective, the language acquisition of deaf students is charted in each of three categories: Oral English, Manually Coded English, and American Sign Language.

Oral English

Few deaf students are instructed in the various approaches of OE. Early and consistent intervention, augmented with adequate instruction in speech, speech reading (lip reading), and the use of residual hearing, can produce systematic progress in speech and language development. In general, the language development of most of these students is similar in manner to but slower in rate than that of normally hearing peers.

The use of CS may improve speech reception abilities; however, reception beyond the word level presents considerable difficulty (e.g., Clarke & Ling, 1976). The best results were obtained when CS was employed in conjunction with speech reading and auditory cues (Nicholls & Ling, 1982). More research is needed to assess the effects of this method on language development (Mohay, 1983).

The most salient finding of the limited studies on the Acoupedic Method is the importance of exploiting the residual hearing of the deaf child (Boothroyd, 1984; Pollack, 1970, 1984). In most oral multisensory programs, this aspect has not received adequate attention (Ling, 1976, 1984; Ross & Calvert, 1984). Indeed, some researchers argue that it is the most important aspect of an intensive oral program and that it contributes immensely to the development of language comprehension skills (Ling, 1984; Ross & Calvert, 1984). Favorable results were obtained when both auditory and speech-reading training were emphasized (e.g., Ling et al., 1981).

Adopting the procedures of the Acoupedic Method and placing equal emphasis on the development of speech and speech-reading skills have produced impressive results for some deaf students instructed by the Aural–Oral Method (e.g., Moog et al., 1981; Ogden, 1979). A large number of these students performed at grade level when compared with hearing-age peers. Typically, favorable results were obtained in indisputably comprehensive oral education programs in which both parents and teachers were intensely involved. It should be emphasized that most of these deaf students were more select in IQ and SES than those in other programs. The adequate language comprehension abilities of these students were attributed to their well-developed oral skills, that is, in speech, speech reading, and the use of residual hearing (e.g., Doehring et al., 1978). Although these students were primarily visually oriented, they may have been using their residual hearing more effectively than students in other programs (Ross & Calvert, 1984).

Manually Coded English

Since about 1970, the majority of education programs for deaf students have employed one or more of the approaches of MCE (Jordan et al., 1979; Maxwell, 1983). The use of these approaches reflects the widely held assumption that through them deaf students will develop the ability to read and write at a level commensurate with that of their hearing counterparts. There is little evidence to support this contention (Maxwell, 1983; Quigley & Paul, 1984a). One of the major problems is an inconsistent implementation by practitioners (Kluwin, 1981a; Marmor & Pettito, 1979).

However, several studies have shown that, with early intervention and systematic usage, certain aspects of English morphology can be acquired (e.g., Crandall, 1978; Gilman et al., 1980; Looney & Rose, 1979). Typically, the rate of development is slower than that reported for hearing students (Bornstein, 1982). In addition, it was reported that some deaf students have developed good secondary language abilities (e.g., Babb, 1979; Brasel & Quigley, 1977; Delaney et al., 1984). Like those taught successfully by OE approaches, most of these students also appear to possess select characteristics, for example, high IQ, high SES, and highly involved and motivated parents.

Despite the preponderance of usage, limited research data are available on the effects of MCE codes. It is not clear, for example, how complete a match between signs and speech is necessary in order for MCE to be effective (Maxwell, 1983; Mitchell, 1982). In addition, the assertion that deaf students will associate the signs or sign markers with their corresponding written or spoken equivalents in English should be further investigated (Robbins, 1983). Finally, an aspect that has been overlooked in most TC programs and should be explored is the contributions of the oral components to the successful development of language and reading in some deaf students taught by these approaches (Ross & Calvert, 1984).

American Sign Language

The research on ASL is presented with respect to three general areas: (1) the primary development of ASL, (2) the issues of bilingualism and ESL, and (3) the effects of ASL on the development of English. Most of the research has charted the acquisition of ASL by deaf children of deaf parents (e.g., Hoffmeister & Wilbur, 1980). One investigator has suggested that the use of ASL in a bilingual or ESL program will be limited in the future (Lane, 1980), whereas others maintain that it should be attempted initially with deaf children of deaf parents for whom ASL is the native or home language (e.g., Luetke-Stahlman, 1983; Quigley & Paul, 1984b).

The linguistic study of ASL commenced with the work of Stokoe (1960). This work, along with that of others (Lane & Grosjean, 1980; Wilbur, 1979), has demonstrated that ASL meets all the requirements of a language *and* that its grammar is different from that of English. Psycholinguistic studies have indicated that the acquisition of ASL may be analogous to that of spoken languages (e.g., Kantor, 1982; McIntire, 1977). Specifically, deaf children acquiring ASL proceed through stages and exhibit strategies similar to those reported for children learning a spoken language, notably English.

It has been shown that ASL is not the first language of all deaf children with deaf parents (Brasel & Quigley, 1977; Collins-Ahlgren, 1974b; Corson, 1973). Furthermore, the argument that ASL *should* be the first language of all deaf students is supported mainly by negative data, that is, the failure of other approaches (Quigley & Kretschmer, 1982; Quigley & Paul, 1984b). Although ASL should perhaps be used to teach English as a second language to some deaf students, not much is known about the manner in which this can be accomplished (e.g., see Crutchfield, 1972; Jones, 1979).

To assess the effects of ASL on the later development of English, several early investigations employed the paradigm of comparing deaf students of deaf parents with deaf students of hearing parents (Meadow, 1968; Quigley & Frisina, 1961; Stuckless & Birch, 1966). In general, the findings favored deaf students of deaf parents, and this was attributed to the early use of manual communication, which was, in retrospect, presumed to be ASL. A more recent study demonstrated that deaf students exposed to manual English (i.e., PSE) produced significantly higher scores on most educational measures than those exposed to ASL (Brasel & Quigley, 1977). This seems to indicate that the development of English is affected by the *form* of manual communication as well as other operative factors, for example, parental acceptance. Thus, the most essential task for future investigators is to show the manner in which a signed communication system can be employed to teach English literacy skills. This is assuming, of course, that the ability to read and write well is a desirable goal in the education of deaf students.

References

Anthony, D. (1966). *Seeing Essential English*. Unpublished master's thesis, Eastern Michigan University, Ypsilanti.

Armstrong, D. (1984). Scientific and ethical issues in the case for American Sign Language: Review of *The other side of silence* by Neisser. *Sign Language Studies, 43,* 165–84.

Babb, R. (1979). *A study of the academic achievement and language acquisition levels of deaf children of hearing parents in an educational environment using Signing Exact English as the primary mode of manual communication*. Unpublished doctoral dissertation, University of Illinois, Urbana–Champaign.

Baker, C., & Cokely, D. (1980). *American Sign Language: A teacher's resource text on grammar and culture*. Silver Spring, MD: T. J. Publishers.

Baker, H., & Leland, B. (1958). *The Detroit Tests of Learning Aptitude*. Indianapolis, IN: Bobbs-Merrill.

Balow, I., & Brill, R. (1975). An evaluation of reading and academic achievement levels of 16 graduating classes of the California School for the Deaf, Riverside. *Volta Review, 77,* 255–66.

Bennett, C., & Ling, D. (1977). Effects of voiced–voiceless discrimination training upon articulation of hearing-impaired children. *Language and Speech, 20,* 287–93.

Bloom, L., Lightbown, P., & Hood, L. (1975). Structure and variation in child language. *Monographs of the Society for Research on Child Development, 40*(Serial No. 2).

Bockmiller, P. (1981). Hearing impaired children: Learning to read a second language. *American Annals of the Deaf, 126,* 810–13.

Boothroyd, A. (1984). Auditory perception of speech contrasts by subjects with sensori-neural hearing loss. *Journal of Speech and Hearing Research, 27,* 134–44.

Bornstein, H. (1973). A description of some current sign systems designed to represent English. *American Annals of the Deaf, 118,* 454–63.

Bornstein, H. (1974). Signed English: A manual approach to English language development. *Journal of Speech and Hearing Disorders, 39,* 330–43.

Bornstein, H. (1982). Towards a theory of use for Signed English: From birth to adulthood. *American Annals of the Deaf, 127,* 26–31.

Bornstein, H., & Saulnier, K. (1981). Signed English: A brief follow-up to the first evaluation. *American Annals of the Deaf, 126,* 69–72.

Bornstein, H., & Saulnier, K. (1984). *The Signed English starter: A beginning book in the Signed English system.* Washington, DC: Kendall Green, Gallaudet College Press.

Bornstein, H., & Saulnier, K., & Hamilton, L. (1980). Signed English: A first evaluation. *American Annals of the Deaf, 125,* 467–81.

Bragg, B. (1973). Ameslish – Our American heritage: A testimony. *American Annals of the Deaf, 118,* 672–4.

Brasel, K., & Quigley, S. (1977). The influence of certain language and communication environments in early childhood on the development of language in deaf individuals. *Journal of Speech and Hearing Research, 20,* 95–107.

Brennan, M. (1975). Can deaf children acquire language? An evaluation of linguistic principles in deaf education. *American Annals of the Deaf, 120,* 463–79.

Brown, R. (1973). *A first language: The early stages.* Cambridge, MA: Harvard University Press.

Carrow, E. (1974). *Carrow Elicited Language Inventory.* Austin, TX: Learning Concepts.

Charrow, V., & Fletcher, J. (1974). English as the second language of deaf children. *Developmental Psychology, 10,* 463–70.

Charrow, V., & Wilbur, R. (1975). The deaf child as a linguistic minority. *Theory into Practice, 14,* 353–9.

Clarke, B., & Ling, D. (1976). The effects of using Cued Speech: A follow-up study. *Volta Review, 78,* 23–34.

Cokely, D. (1983). When is a pidgin not a pidgin? An alternate analysis of the ASL–English contact situation. *Sign Language Studies, 38,* 1–24.

Collins-Ahlgren, M. (1974a). *Julie goes to school in Signed English.* Washington, DC: Gallaudet College Press.

Collins-Ahlgren, M. (1974b). Teaching English as a second language to young deaf children: A case study. *Journal of Speech and Hearing Disorders, 39,* 486–500.

Conley, J. (1976). The role of idiomatic expressions in the reading of deaf children. *American Annals of the Deaf, 121,* 381–5.

Conrad, R. (1979). *The deaf school child: Language and cognitive function.* New York: Harper & Row.

Cooper, R., & Rosenstein, J. (1966). Language acquisition of deaf children. *Volta Review, 68,* 58–67.

Cornett, R. O. (1967). Cued Speech. *American Annals of the Deaf, 112,* 3–13.

Cornett, R. O. (1984). Book review: Language and deafness. *Cued Speech News, 17(3),* 5.

Corson, H. (1973). *Comparing deaf children of oral deaf parents and deaf parents using manual communication with deaf children of hearing parents on academic, social, and communication functioning.* Unpublished doctoral dissertation, University of Cincinnati, Cincinnati, OH.

Crandall, K. (1978). Inflectional morphemes in the manual English of young hearing impaired children and their mothers. *Journal of Speech and Hearing Research, 21,* 372–86.

Crutchfield, P. (1972). Prospects for teaching English Det + N structures to deaf students. *Sign Language Studies, 1,* 8–14.

Cruttenden, A. (1979). *Language in infancy and childhood: A linguistic introduction to language acquisition.* New York: St. Martin's Press.

Dale, P. (1976). *Language development: Structure and function* (2d ed.). New York: Holt, Rinehart & Winston.

Delaney, M., Stuckless, E. R., & Walter, G. (1984). Total communication effects: A longitudinal study of a school for the deaf in transition. *American Annals of the Deaf, 129,* 481–6.

deVilliers, J., & deVilliers, P. (1978). *Language acquisition.* Cambridge, MA: Harvard University Press.

DiFrancesca, S. (1972). *Academic achievement test results of a national testing program for hearing impaired students,* United States, Spring 1971 (Series D, No. 9). Washington, DC: Gallaudet College, Office of Demographic Studies.

Doehring, D., Bonnycastle, D., & Ling, A. (1978). Rapid reading skills of integrated hearing impaired children. *Volta Review, 80,* 399–409.

Dunn, L. (1959). *Peabody Picture Vocabulary Test* (original ed.). Circle Pines, MN: American Guidance Service.

Eisenberg, D., & Santore, F. (1976). The verbotonal method of aural rehabilitation: A case study. *Volta Review, 78,* 16–22.

Erber, N. (1972). Auditory, visual and auditory–visual recognition of consonants by children with normal and impaired hearing. *Journal of Speech and Hearing Research, 15,* 413–22.

Erting, C. (1981). An anthropological approach to the study of the communicative competence of deaf children. *Sign Language Studies, 32,* 221–38.

Gallaudet Research Institute (1985). *Gallaudet Research Institute Newsletter* (J. Harkins, Ed.), Gallaudet College, Washington, DC.

Gannon, J. (1981). *Deaf heritage.* Washington, DC: Gallaudet College Press.

Gardner, J., & Zorfass, J. (1983). From sign to speech: The language development of a hearing-impaired child. *American Annals of the Deaf, 128,* 20–4.

Geers, A., & Moog, J. (1978). Syntactic maturity of spontaneous speech and elicited imitations of hearing impaired children. *Journal of Speech and Hearing Disorders, 43,* 380–91.

Gilman, L., Davis, J., & Raffin, M. (1980). Use of common morphemes by hearing impaired children exposed to a system of manual English. *Journal of Auditory Research, 20,* 57–69.

Goldin-Meadow, S. (1975). *The representation of semantic relations in a manual language created by deaf children of hearing parents: A language you can't dismiss out of hand.* Unpublished doctoral dissertation, University of Pennsylvania, Philadelphia.

Goldstein, M. (1939). *The Acoustic Method for the training of the deaf and hard of hearing child.* St. Louis, MO: Laryngoscope Press.

Griswold, E., & Cummings, J. (1974). The expressive vocabulary of preschool deaf children. *American Annals of the Deaf, 119,* 16–28.

Gustason, G. (1983). *Teaching and learning Signing Exact English.* Los Alamitos, CA: Modern Signs Press.

Gustason, G., Pfetzing, D., & Zawolkow, E. (1975). *Signing Exact English* (rev. ed.). Rossmor, CA: Modern Signs Press.

Gustason, G., Pfetzing, D., & Zawolkow, E. (1980). *Signing Exact English* (1980 ed.). Los Alamitos, CA: Modern Signs Press.

Hack, Z., & Erber, N. (1982). Auditory, visual, and auditory–visual perception of vowels by hearing-impaired children. *Journal of Speech and Hearing Research, 25,* 100–7.

Hester, M. (1963). Manual communication. *Proceedings of the International Congress on Education of the Deaf of the 41st Meeting of the Convention of American Instructors of the Deaf* (pp. 211–22). Washington, DC: U.S. Government Printing Office.

Hoffmeister, R., & Wilbur, R. (1980). The acquisition of sign language. In H. Lane & F. Grosjean (Eds.), *Recent perspectives on American Sign Language* (pp. 61–78). Hillsdale, NJ: Erlbaum.

Humphries, T., Padden, C., & O'Rourke, T. (1980). *A basic course in American Sign Language.* Silver Spring, MD: T.J. Publishers.

Iran-Nejad, A., Ortony, A., & Rittenhouse, R. (1981). The comprehension of metaphorical uses of English by deaf children. *Journal of Speech and Hearing Research, 24,* 551–6.

Jeffers, J., & Barley, M. (1971). *Speech reading (lip reading).* Springfield, IL: Thomas.

Jones, P. (1980). Negative interference of signed language in written English. *Sign Language Studies, 24,* 273–9.

Jordan, I., Gustason, G., & Rosen, R. (1979). An update on communication trends at programs for the deaf. *American Annals of the Deaf, 124,* 350–7.

Kantor, R. (1980). The acquisition of classifiers in American Sign Language. *Sign Language Studies, 28,* 193–208.

Kantor, R. (1982). Communicative interaction: Mother modification and child acquisition of American Sign Language. *Sign Language Studies, 36,* 233–82.

King, C. (1981). *An investigation of similarities and differences in the syntactic abilities of deaf and hearing children learning English as a first or second language.* Unpublished doctoral dissertation, University of Illinois, Urbana–Champaign.

Kirk, S., McCarthy, J., & Kirk, W. (1968). *The Illinois Test of Psycholinguistic Abilities* (rev. ed.). Urbana: University of Illinois Press.

Klima, E., & Bellugi, U. (1979). *The signs of language.* Cambridge, MA: Harvard University Press.

Kluwin, T. (1981a). The grammaticality of manual representations of English in classroom settings. *American Annals of the Deaf, 126,* 417–21.

Kluwin, T. (1981b). A rationale for modifying classroom signing systems. *Sign Language Studies, 31,* 179–87.

Lane, H. (1976). Thoughts on oral advocacy today . . . with memories of the society of oral advocates. *Volta Review, 78,* 136–40.

Lane, H. (1980). A chronology of the oppression of sign language in France and the United States. In H. Lane & F. Grosjean (Eds.), *Recent perspectives on American Sign Language* (pp. 119–61). Hillsdale, NJ: Erlbaum.

Lane, H., & Grosjean, F. (Eds.). (1980). *Recent perspectives on American Sign Language.* Hillsdale, NJ: Erlbaum.

Lee, D. (1982). Are there signs of diglossia? Re-examining the situation. *Sign Language Studies, 35,* 127–52.

Lee, L. (1969). *Northwestern Syntax Screening Test.* Evanston, IL: Northwestern University Press.

Lee, L. (1974). *Developmental Sentence Analysis.* Evanston, IL: Northwestern University Press.

Lenneberg, E. (1967). *Biological foundations of language.* New York: Wiley.

Liddell, S. (1980). *American Sign Language syntax.* The Hague: Mouton.

Ling, D. (1976). *Speech and the hearing impaired child: Theory and practice*. Washington, DC: Alexander Graham Bell Association for the Deaf.

Ling, D. (1984). Early oral intervention: An introduction. In D. Ling (Ed.), *Early intervention for hearing-impaired children: Oral options* (pp. 1–14). San Diego, CA: College-Hill Press.

Ling, D., & Clarke, B. (1975). Cued Speech: An evaluation study. *American Annals of the Deaf, 120,* 480–8.

Ling, D., Leckie, D., Pollack, D., Simser, J., & Smith, A. (1981). Syllable reception by hearing impaired children trained from infancy in auditory–oral programs. *Volta Review, 83,* 451–7.

Ling, D., & Ling, A. (1978). *Aural habilitation: The foundations of verbal learning in hearing-impaired children*. Washington, DC: Alexander Graham Bell Association for the Deaf.

Livingston, S. (1983). Levels of development in the language of deaf children: ASL grammatical processes, SE structures, and semantic features. *Sign Language Studies, 40,* 193–286.

Long, N., Fitzgerald, C., Sutton, K., & Rollins, J. (1983). The auditory–verbal approach: Ellison, a case study. *Volta Review, 85,* 27–30, 35.

Looney, P., & Rose, S. (1979). The acquisition of inflectional suffixes by deaf youngsters using written and fingerspelled modes. *American Annals of the Deaf, 124,* 765–9.

Luetke-Stahlman, B. (1983). Using bilingual instructional models in teaching hearing-impaired students. *American Annals of the Deaf, 128,* 873–7.

Luetke-Stahlman, B. (1984). Classifier recognition by hearing-impaired children in residential and public schools. *Sign Language Studies, 42,* 39–44.

Luetke-Stahlman, B., & Weiner, F. (1982). Assessing language and/or system preferences of Spanish-deaf preschoolers. *American Annals of the Deaf, 127,* 789–96.

McIntire, M. (1977). The acquisition of American Sign Language hand configurations. *Sign Language Studies, 16,* 247–66.

Madden, R., Gardner, E., Rudman, H., Karlsen, B., & Merwin, J. (1972). *Stanford Achievement Test* (adapted for hearing-impaired students by the Office of Demographic Studies, Gallaudet College, Washington, DC). San Diego, CA: Harcourt Brace Jovanovich.

Markowicz, H. (1980). Myths about American Sign Language. In H. Lane & F. Grosjean (Eds.), *Recent perspectives on American Sign Language* (pp. 1–6). Hillsdale, NJ: Erlbaum.

Marmor, G., & Pettito, L. (1979). Simultaneous communication in the classroom: How well is English grammar represented? *Sign Language Studies, 23,* 99–136.

Mavilya, M., & Mignone, B. (1977). *Educational strategies for the youngest hearing impaired children, 0–5 years of age* (Educational Series, Book 10). New York: Lexington School for the Deaf.

Maxwell, M. (1983). Simultaneous communication in the classroom: What do deaf children learn? *Sign Language Studies, 39,* 95–112.

Meadow, K. (1968). Early manual communication in relation to the deaf child's intellectual, social and communicative functioning. *American Annals of the Deaf, 113,* 29–41.

Menyuk, P. (1963). A preliminary evaluation of grammatical capacity in children. *Journal of Verbal Learning and Verbal Behavior, 2,* 429–39.

Messerly, C., & Aram, D. (1980). Academic achievement of hearing-impaired students of hearing parents and of hearing-impaired parents: Another look. *Volta Review, 82,* 25–32.

Mitchell, G. (1982). Can deaf children acquire English? An evaluation of Manually Coded English systems in terms of the principles of language acquisition. *American Annals of the Deaf, 127,* 331–6.

Mohay, H. (1983). The effects of Cued Speech on the language development of three deaf children. *Sign Language Studies, 38,* 25–47.

Moog, J., Geers, A., & Calvert, D. (1981). Conclusions. *American Annals of the Deaf, 126,* 965–9.

Moores, D. (1982). *Educating the deaf: Psychology, principles, and practices* (2d ed.). Boston: Houghton Mifflin.

Newport, E., & Ashbrook, E. (1977). The emergence of semantic relations in American Sign Language. *Papers and Reports on Child Language Development, 13,* 16–21.

Nicholls, G., & Ling, D. (1982). Cued Speech and the reception of spoken language. *Journal of Speech and Hearing Research, 25,* 262–9.

Novelli-Olmstead, T., & Ling, D. (1984). Speech production and speech discrimination by hearing-impaired children. *Volta Review, 86,* 72–80.

Odom, P., & Blanton, R. (1970). Implicit and explicit grammatical factors and reading achievement in the deaf. *Journal of Reading Behavior, 1,* 47–55.

Ogden, P. (1979). *Experiences and attitudes of oral deaf adults regarding oralism.* Unpublished doctoral dissertation, University of Illinois, Urbana–Champaign.

Orlansky, M., & Bonvillian, J. (1984). The role of iconicity in early sign language acquisition. *Journal of Speech and Hearing Disorders, 49,* 287–92.

Orlansky, M., & Bonvillian, J. (1985). Sign language acquisition: Language development in children of deaf parents and implications for other populations. *Merrill-Palmer Quarterly, 31,* 127–43.

O'Rourke, T. J. (1973). *A basic course in manual communication.* Silver Spring, MD: National Association of the Deaf.

Paul, P. (1984). *The comprehension of multimeaning words from selected frequency levels by deaf and hearing subjects.* Unpublished doctoral dissertation, University of Illinois, Urbana–Champaign.

Payne, J.-A. (1982). *A study of the comprehension of verb–particle combinations among deaf and hearing subjects.* Unpublished doctoral dissertation, University of Illinois, Urbana–Champaign.

Pearson, P. D., & Johnson, D. (1978). *Teaching reading comprehension.* New York: Holt, Rinehart & Winston.

Pollack, D. (1964). Acoupedics: A unisensory approach to auditory training. *Volta Review, 66,* 400–9.

Pollack, D. (1970). *Educational audiology for the limited hearing infant.* Springfield, IL: Thomas.

Pollack, D. (1984). An acoupedic program. In D. Ling (Ed.), *Early intervention for hearing-impaired children: Oral options* (pp. 181–253). San Diego, CA: College-Hill Press.

Quigley, S. (1969). *The influence of fingerspelling on the development of language, communication, and educational achievement in deaf children.* Urbana: University of Illinois, Institute for Research on Exceptional Children.

Quigley, S., & Frisina, D. (1961). *Institutionalization and psychoeducational development of deaf children.* Council for Exceptional Children Research Monograph (Series A, No. 3).

Quigley, S., & Kretschmer, R. E. (1982). *The education of deaf children: Issues, theory, and practice.* Baltimore, MD: University Park Press.

Quigley, S., & Paul, P. (1984a). *Language and deafness*. San Diego, CA: College-Hill Press.

Quigley, S., & Paul, P. (1984b). ASL and ESL? *Topics in Early Childhood Special Education, 3*(4), 17–26.

Quigley, S., Steinkamp, M., Power, D., & Jones, B. (1978). *Test of Syntactic Abilities: Guide to administration and interpretation*. Beaverton, OR: Dormac.

Quigley, S., Wilbur, R., Power, D., Montanelli, D., & Steinkamp, M. (1976). *Syntactic structures in the language of deaf children* (final report). Urbana: University of Illinois. (ERIC Document Reproduction Service, No. ED 119 447)

Raffin, M. (1976). *The acquisition of inflectional morphemes by deaf children using Seeing Essential English*. Unpublished doctoral dissertation, University of Iowa, Iowa City.

Raffin, M., Davis, J., & Gilman, L. (1978). Comprehension of inflectional morphemes by deaf children exposed to a visual English sign system. *Journal of Speech and Hearing Research, 21*, 387–400.

Rawlings, R., & Jensema, C. (1977). *Two studies of the families of hearing impaired children* (Series R, No. 5). Washington, DC: Gallaudet College, Office of Demographic Studies.

Reich, P., & Bick, M. (1977). How visible is visible English? *Sign Language Studies, 14*, 59–72.

Richards, J. (Ed.). (1974). *Error analysis: Perspectives on second language acquisition*. New York: Longman.

Robbins, N. (1983). The effects of signed text on the reading comprehension of hearing-impaired children. *American Annals of the Deaf, 128*, 40–4.

Rosenstein, J., & MacGinitie, W. (Eds.). (1969). *Verbal behavior of the deaf child: Studies of word meanings and associations*. New York: Teachers College Press.

Ross, M., Brackett, D., & Maxon, A. (1982). *Hard of hearing children in regular schools*. Englewood Cliffs, NJ: Prentice-Hall.

Ross, M., & Calvert, D. (1984). Semantics of deafness revisited: Total communication and the use and misuse of residual hearing. *Audiology, 9*, 127–43.

Roy, H. (1975). *Bobby visits the dentist in Signed English*. Washington, DC: Gallaudet College Press.

Sanders, D. (1982). *Aural rehabilitation: A management model* (2d ed.). Englewood Cliffs, NJ: Prentice-Hall.

Saulnier, K. (1975). *Little lost Sally in Signed English*. Washington, DC: Gallaudet College Press.

Schlesinger, H., & Meadow, K. (1972). *Sound and sign: Childhood deafness and mental health*. Berkeley & Los Angeles: University of California Press.

Schlesinger, I. (1982). *Steps to language: Toward a theory of native language acquisition*. Hillsdale, NJ: Erlbaum.

Schlesinger, I, & Namir, L. (Eds.). (1978). *Sign language of the deaf*. New York: Academic Press.

Scouten, E. (1967). The Rochester Method: An oral multi-sensory approach for instructing prelingual deaf children. *American Annals of the Deaf, 112*, 50–5.

Siple, P. (Ed.). (1978). *Understanding language through sign language research*. New York: Academic Press.

Slobin, D. (1979). *Psycholinguistics* (2d ed.). Glenview, IL: Scott, Foresman.

Sternberg, M. (1981). *American Sign Language: A comprehensive dictionary*. New York: Harper & Row.

Stokoe, W., Jr. (1960). *Sign language structure: An outline of the visual communication systems of the American deaf* (Studies in Linguistics, Occasional Paper No. 8). Washington, DC: Gallaudet College Press.

Stokoe, W., Jr. (1975). The use of sign language in teaching English. *American Annals of the Deaf, 120,* 417–21.

Stuckless, E. R., & Birch, J. (1966). The influence of early manual communication on the linguistic development of deaf children. *American Annals of the Deaf, 111,* 452–60; 499–504.

Stuckless, E. R., & Pollard, G. (1977). Processing of fingerspelling and print by deaf students. *American Annals of the Deaf, 122,* 475–9.

Suty, K., & Friel–Patti, S. (1982). Looking beyond signed English to describe the language of two deaf children. *Sign Language Studies, 35,* 153–68.

Tervoort, B. (1975). *Developmental features of visual communication: A psycholinguistic analysis of deaf children's growth in communicative competence.* New York: American Elsevier.

Trybus, R., & Karchmer, M. (1977). School achievement scores of hearing impaired children: National data on achievement status and growth patterns. *American Annals of the Deaf, 122,* 62–9.

Walter, G. (1978). Lexical abilities of hearing and hearing impaired children. *American Annals of the Deaf, 123,* 976–82.

Weber, J., & Weber, S. (1981). Communication skills of a 4-year-old deaf child. Eleven modes of production in the vocal and motor modalities. *Sign Language Studies, 31,* 99–116.

Webster's new twentieth century dictionary (2d ed.). (1983). New York: Simon & Schuster.

White, A., & Stevenson, V. (1975). The effects of total communication, manual communication, oral communication and reading on the learning of factual information in residential school deaf children. *American Annals of the Deaf, 120,* 48–57.

Wilbur, R. (1979). *American Sign Language and sign systems.* Baltimore, MD: University Park Press.

Wilbur, R. (1980). The linguistic description of American Sign Language. In H. Lane & F. Grosjean (Eds.), *Recent perspectives on American Sign Language* (pp. 7–31). Hillsdale, NJ: Erlbaum.

Wilcox, S. (1984). "STUCK" in school: A study of semantics and culture in a deaf education class. *Sign Language Studies, 43,* 141–64.

Winitz, H. (1975). *From syllable to conversation.* Baltimore, MD: University Park Press.

Woodward, J. (1973). Some characteristics of Pidgin Sign English. *Sign Language Studies, 3,* 39–46.

6   Language lateralization and disordered language development

Marcel Kinsbourne and Merrill Hiscock

In its most general form, the question to be discussed in this chapter concerns the relation between the development of a skill and the neural representation of that skill. If a certain pattern of neural organization characterizes normal children, what are the behavioral consequences of deviation from that pattern? Does deviant neural organization imply cognitive deficit? Does deficient cognitive development imply deviant neural organization? Specifically, this chapter concerns the relation between abnormal language development and the cerebral lateralization of language. Especially when defined broadly so as to include reading and writing, abnormal language development has traditionally been attributed to deviant cerebral lateralization (Orton, 1937). We shall examine the empirical and conceptual underpinnings of this attribution and arrive at some conclusions about the importance of cerebral lateralization in various forms of disordered language development.

A framework for evaluating the evidence

If the relation between disordered language development and the cerebral lateralization of language is to be understood, three categories of variables – pathological, behavioral, and developmental – must be considered.

Pathological variables

Much of our present knowledge about the basis in the brain for language development is derived from studies of children who have sustained lateralized brain damage. This source of information, though useful, is not without ambiguities. First, the outcome of such studies quite likely depends on how the children are identified. If the literature is searched for case reports, a particular kind of sampling bias is inevitable: Unusual cases will be overrepresented simply because they are considered noteworthy. Accordingly, a case of aphasia (i.e., language disruption) in association with right-hemisphere damage is more likely to be published than a case of aphasia in association with left-hemisphere damage (Kinsbourne & Hiscock, 1977). Irrespective of whether cases are culled from the

220

published literature or accumulated in a clinical setting, children may be identified on the basis of abnormal cognitive development, neurological abnormality, or both; and the observed association between linguistic and neurological variables is likely to vary as a function of the method of selecting cases. Assume that early cerebral insult usually causes some abnormality of language development. If one begins by identifying children with neurological abnormality, a high proportion will show abnormal language development. However, if one initially identifies children with disordered language, only a small proportion will show any evidence of neurological abnormality. This kind of sampling problem is compounded by differences among clinical settings. The clinical investigator who is not a specialist in childhood aphasia may find a relatively low incidence of language disorder following cerebral damage simply because most children suspected of having language problems are sent elsewhere for evaluation or treatment.

Apart from the difficulty of selecting representative clinical cases, there is the problem of establishing the nature, and in some cases even the existence, of the brain damage in each case. Some useful information concerning prenatal and perinatal brain damage and its implications for subsequent nervous system development has been obtained from a large-scale collaborative study conducted at 15 American medical centers (National Institutes of Health and National Institutes of Neurological Disease and Blindness, 1965). The major findings from this and other studies have been summarized by Towbin (1978), who emphasized the following five conclusions:

1. Hypoxia (inadequate oxygenation) is by far the most frequent cause of cerebral damage in the fetus and neonate. Hypoxia, in turn, may be attributed to a large number of factors associated with pregnancy and delivery.
2. There is an important distinction between damage to the premature fetal or neonatal brain, which affects structures deep within the cerebral hemispheres, and damage to the brain at full term, which affects the cerebral cortex.
3. Brain damage present at birth often has occurred days or weeks before birth. Consequently, one cannot necessarily attribute cerebral dysfunctions apparent after birth to birth injury, that is, to traumatic injury from the extraction of the fetus. Statistically speaking, the numerous dangers of the prenatal environment account for most cerebral damage that becomes apparent after birth.
4. The acute and subacute hypoxic lesions that occur in the fetus or neonate evolve into chronic lesions that are responsible for mental retardation, cerebral palsy, and other cerebral dysfunctions.
5. The duration and intensity of the pathological factors producing hypoxia determine its severity, and its severity determines the extent of the structural damage, which can range from patchy or diffuse neuronal loss to total destruction of the cerebrum.

Of the evidence summarized by Towbin (1978), certain points are particularly relevant to the relation between language disorders and lateralized cerebral damage. Irrespective of whether the cerebral damage is identified about the time of birth or years later, the lesion is more likely to be deep than cortical. In other words, hypoxic damage to the fetus is more common during gestation than at term. Because most early cerebral damage is primarily subcortical, it may be inappropriate to compare lesions in children with the generally cortical lesions that produce aphasia in adults. Towbin (1978) also pointed out that neurological sequelae of prenatal and of perinatal hypoxia often abate or disappear during childhood. In contrast, other indications of cerebral dysfunction may first appear at a later stage of development, that is, when the damaged cerebral region normally would have assumed control of a particular behavior (Goldman, 1974; Kinsbourne, 1973). Thus, a given set of selection criteria, whether derived from neurological, psychological, or linguistic examination, will be differentially sensitive to the effects of early cerebral damage, depending on the age of the child being considered. Even when prenatal or perinatal damage is cortical, the damage may be either focal or diffuse. Towbin (1978) cautioned that, in cases of diffuse neuronal depletion, a loss of neurons as great as 30% may not be evident in postmortem examination even though neuronal loss of this magnitude may lead to substantial disability. Thus, one might suspect that, in children who survive and subsequently show developmental abnormalities, failure to detect a focal cerebral lesion does not imply the absence of significant brain pathology. Moreover, detection of a focal lesion does not preclude neuronal loss elsewhere in the cerebrum.

Behavioral variables

The neuropsychological literature may be confusing or misleading when investigators use vague terms to label behavioral deficits. The word *aphasia,* for example, is used to refer to a host of linguistic deficits ranging from difficulties of articulation and repetition to deficits of auditory comprehension and reading (Goodglass & Kaplan, 1983). Consequently, two studies are not necessarily comparable just because both address the issue of aphasia in children. If one finding is based on a measure of auditory comprehension and the other on a test of object naming, it may not be possible to interpret differences between the respective findings even though both findings are related to childhood aphasia.

Not only do the target behaviors vary from one study to the next, but the source of information about these behaviors often varies as well. In some published reports, the diagnosis of aphasia is based on nothing more substantial than the observation of the examining physician. As we have pointed out previously (Kinsbourne & Hiscock, 1977), there are many reasons for the failure of a hospitalized child to communicate with the physician. Thus, reliance on the doctor's impression may result in nonaphasic children (e.g., emotionally traumatized children) being included in a study of childhood aphasia. Conversely, the physician may overlook the more subtle signs of disordered language and thus fail to diagnose an actual case of aphasia. It is particularly difficult to detect and properly interpret signs of receptive disturbance in a child during a brief bedside examination. The

IQ test is another means of assessing linguistic deficits. Many IQ tests, as well as developmental tests designed for preschool children, are reasonably objective measures that tap various aspects of verbal functioning. However, these tests, having been designed to measure more general cognitive ability, may not be sufficiently sensitive or selective with respect to linguistic deficits. Dennis and Whitaker (1977) noted that the verbal IQ profile of children reflects a number of factors in addition to the presence of language disability and that "verbal IQ measures in nonretarded infantile hemiplegics predict neither how rapidly nor how well language develops" (p. 100). Clearly, sensitive and selective tests of linguistic functions are the best sources of information about language deficits in children.

Developmental variables

It is the developmental dimension that makes the neuropsychology of children so much more difficult than the neuropsychology of adults. The quintessential characteristic of childhood is change; that which is normal at one age may be quite abnormal at another (see Gaddes & Crockett, 1975). Change may be quantitative or qualitative or both. Important developmental changes occur in both the neurological and behavioral realms, and these changes limit one's ability to make general statements about the relation between brain and behavior. One cannot, for example, study the effects of head trauma in 5-year-olds and expect to generalize the results to 2-year-olds (or even 5-year-olds) whose brain damage occurred prenatally. The common causes of brain damage in children vary with age (cf. Woods, 1980a), and even when the same causal agent is implicated, the nature and locus of damage may be entirely different depending on the time at which damage occurred (Towbin, 1978). The ability of the brain to compensate for damage seems to vary with age, and in addition the completeness of recovery will change as a function of the interval between the damage and the time at which behavioral capacity is assessed (St. James-Roberts, 1981).

In short, developmental changes are found at the behavioral and neurological levels of analysis. Such changes, which may be quantitative or qualitative, occur in normal and in neurologically abnormal children. In cases of abnormality, developmental factors influence the nature of the damage, its immediate consequences, and its long-term implications.

Summary

There are various attributes of a brain lesion – etiology, size, locus, and so on – that may influence the relation between brain injury and its behavioral consequences (see Reitan & Davison, 1974). It is seldom possible to match subjects with respect to those attributes, but poor matching (e.g., between left- and right-hemisphere-damaged groups within the same study or between comparable groups in different studies) may lead to spurious conclusions. Prenatal damage is particularly difficult to assess. Damage that occurs in utero may be mistakenly identified as a birth injury, but the consequences of damage to the immature fetal brain are distinctly different from the consequences of damage to the fetal brain at full term. The problem of establishing correspondence between lesion and behavioral impairment is compounded by certain sampling biases that are common in clinical research.

In addition to considerations of brain pathology, we emphasized the need for a precise description of behavioral deficits. Broad clinical terms such as *aphasia* may be operationalized in various ways. For example, two different studies of childhood aphasia cannot be compared directly if aphasia is defined as verbal fluency in one and auditory comprehension in the other. The common measures of linguistic performance range from clinical observations and broad-band tests (such as certain IQ tests) to specific psycholinguistic tests. These measures differ markedly in sensitivity and selectivity for detecting language impairment.

Finally, studies of brain-damaged children can be meaningfully compared and interpreted only if temporal variables are well controlled. The rapidly changing nature of the child's brain and behavioral characteristics necessitates greater attention to the timing of the damage and of the behavioral assessment.

The ontogeny of language lateralization

Equipotentiality and progressive lateralization

The existence of marked functional asymmetries in a largely symmetric organism is sufficiently enigmatic as to have generated considerable myth and superstition (Corballis, 1983). If such asymmetries in the adult arise from a bilaterally symmetric state in infancy, the enigma becomes even more remarkable. What is the process through which the neonatal hemispheres, presumed to be comparable in every way, become differentiated to the extent that one assumes the leading role in manual control as well as complete responsibility for speech? What is the temporal course of this transformation? Traditionally, the doctrines of hemispheric equipotentiality and progressive lateralization have been used to "explain" the presumed evolution of lateralized language (see Dennis & Whitaker, 1977; Woods & Teuber, 1978). The cerebral hemispheres of the neonate, which appear symmetric on casual inspection, were thought likewise to be equivalent in their suitability for subsequent language development (e.g., Marie, 1922, cited in Dennis & Whitaker, 1977). This is referred to as equipotentiality. Equipotentiality was thought to persist at least until the beginning of speech acquisition, after which language continues to develop in the left hemisphere, whereas the right hemisphere becomes increasingly unable to subserve language. This alleged gradual shifting of language representation from a bilateral to unilateral substrate is referred to as progressive lateralization.

Lenneberg (1967) incorporated these principles into a biologically oriented model of language development that gained widespread uncritical acceptance. In an attempt to account for what he perceived to be a universal sequence of milestones in motor and language development, Lenneberg rejected environmental explanations in favor of maturational factors. Then he used aphasia cases to show that, just as there is a lower limit of maturational readiness for language learning, there is also an upper limit. Most cases of adult aphasia considered by Lenneberg (i.e., those described by Russell & Espir, 1961) either recovered within 3 months or left permanent residues. In contrast, there was no evidence of residual impairment in children who acquired aphasia due to unilateral brain injury before the age of 9 years. Lenneberg concluded that aphasias that have not had time to resolve by puberty or those that occur after puberty usually leave some permanent residue. Thus, the upper limit of his putative critical period of maturational readiness seemed to coincide with pubescence.

Lenneberg next related this critical period to the cerebral lateralization of language. For this purpose, he again turned to aphasia data, primarily those of Basser (1962), which suggested that before speech onset left- and right-hemisphere lesions have similar consequences. Speech either develops normally or is delayed somewhat, and the likelihood of either outcome is about the same for left-sided lesions as for right-sided lesions. From this evidence, Lenneberg concluded that the hemispheres remain equipotential during the period before speech onset. Basser's (1962) data for older children implied that unilateral damage occurring after speech onset but before the age of 10 years may cause speech disturbance irrespective of the side damaged, but more commonly with left- than with right-hemisphere lesions (85 vs. 45%, respectively). In these cases, the aphasia clears within 2 years. Lenneberg contrasted these statistics with those for adults in which right-sided lesions lead to aphasia in no more than approximately 3% of cases (Ajuriaguerra, 1957; Zangwill, 1960). Lenneberg cited hemispherectomy cases, in which the lesion was acquired before age 13, during puberty (one case) or during adulthood (Basser, 1962; Hillier, 1954) as further support for his thesis. Most of the early-lesioned patients did not have permanent aphasia irrespective of the hemisphere removed, but those with lesions of adult onset were spared permanent aphasia only if the hemisphere removed was the right one. Individuals who acquired their lesion as an adolescent apparently had a permanent language deficit.

The data reviewed by Lenneberg (1967) thus seem to accord well with an initial equipotentiality of the hemispheres for language that, from the time of speech onset, gradually yields to a bilateral but unequal pattern of language representation in which language gradually becomes concentrated in the left hemisphere while, at the same time, the right hemisphere undergoes a corresponding diminution in its language potential. This progressive lateralization reaches its end point at about the time of puberty, when the fully lateralized adult state is attained.

New evidence and reinterpretation of the old

Lenneberg's seemingly plausible model has since been challenged on various grounds. Krashen (1973), reviewing Basser's (1962) cases and other data, pointed out that evidence in fact fails to support the inference of bilateral language representation beyond the age of 5 years. For children above the age of 5, the incidence of aphasia following right-hemisphere lesions is comparable to the incidence among adults. Kinsbourne and Hiscock (1977) argued that even Krashen's weaker version of the progressive lateralization model is incorrect – that hemispheric specialization exists before speech onset and remains invariant thereafter. Childhood aphasia data reported by Basser (1962) and others were criticized by Kinsbourne and Hiscock (1977) on four methodological grounds: (1) a sampling bias such that uncommon outcomes would be overrepresented in the literature, (2) the tendency for damage to occur in children whose brains previously were abnormal and thus unrepresentative of normal brains, (3) ambiguity regarding the extent of the lesion and, in particular, the possibility of bilateral involvement, and (4) inconsistent and often questionable criteria for defining aphasia. In a series of 58 cases of childhood aphasia reported by Kinsbourne and Hiscock, there were only eight children below the age of 6 years whose aphasia was substantiated and was well documented as being due to unilateral rather than bilateral disease, and all eight had left-sided damage.

Kinsbourne and Hiscock (1977) also questioned the logic of Lenneberg's inference concerning bilateral language in young children. They pointed out that the occurrence of aphasia following right-hemisphere damage could not be used to argue for bilateral language representation, but only that language was represented in the right hemisphere. The concept of bilateral language representation is ambiguous, in any event. It could mean that the linguistic functions of the left hemisphere are duplicated redundantly in the right, in which case unilateral damage, irrespective of side, should not disrupt language. Alternatively, bilateral representation could refer to complementary functions, but then it is not clear which hemisphere is responsible for what, or whether the allocation of specific functions between hemispheres is supposed to be invariant from one child to the next. (Sodium amytal studies of adults show that both duplicative and complementary forms of bilaterality occur in [epileptic] left-handers and that, when the complementary pattern is found, the distribution between hemispheres of skills varies from one person to the next; see Rasmussen & Milner, 1975.) Kinsbourne and Hiscock (1977) concluded that, in the absence of sequential damage to one hemisphere and then to the other, valid inferences about the bilaterality of language are not possible.

Hecaen (1976) attempted to reconcile his own and others' clinical findings with existing evidence of early hemispheric specialization. His own cases of childhood aphasia led him, like Krashen (1973), to affirm the equipotentiality of the cerebral hemispheres in the young child and of progressive lateralization, but with a critical period during which language may develop in the right hemisphere much shorter than that conjectured by Lenneberg (1967). Accepting at face value the anatomical evidence consistent with very early, possibly innate hemispheric specialization (e.g., Wada, Clarke, & Hamm, 1975; Witelson & Pallie, 1973), Hecaen pointed out that compensatory displacement of language to the right hemisphere is not inconsistent with early left-hemisphere dominance for language. He distinguished between normal hemispheric specialization in the young child's brain and the capacity for functional reorganization of the cerebral hemispheres following unilateral injury. Despite the normal tendency for language to develop in the left hemisphere, early damage to that hemisphere's language area could result in reorganization of language representation such that either the right hemisphere or "uncommitted" intact regions of the left hemisphere assume control of at least some linguistic functions. Insofar as this capacity for reorganization is supposed by Hecaen to exist for only a limited period of time during early childhood, the child's ability to recover language following left-hemisphere damage decreases as the child matures (Landsdell, 1969). Diminishing plasticity could account for some of the clinical findings for which a progressive lateralization model was invoked, that is, the diminished ability of older children to recover language following an aphasia-producing left-hemisphere lesion (see Kinsbourne & Hiscock, 1977).

The distinction between normal hemispheric specialization and capacity for reorganization after injury (plasticity) is important. Nonetheless, it is not clear how plasticity can explain a high incidence of aphasia following right-hemisphere lesions in right-handed children. Unless the children with so-called crossed aphasia (i.e., aphasia in association with a right-hemisphere lesion) had sustained earlier left-hemisphere damage that resulted in a shifting of language representation to the right hemisphere, one would not expect to find language disruption following right-hemisphere damage. With respect to Hecaen's (1976) data, this point is moot, for the data do not convincingly demonstrate an association between right-hemisphere damage and aphasia in even the youngest of right-handed children. Hecaen found that two of six children with right-hemisphere damage (compared with 15 of 17 children with left hemisphere lesions) became aphasic. However, since one of the two aphasic children was left-handed and the other had suffered a traumatic injury (in which case bilateral damage is likely), Hecaen's data do not necessarily indicate right-hemispheric or bilateral language in even the youngest of right-handed children.

The contradictions in the childhood aphasia data were resolved by Woods and Teuber (1978). In reviewing the literature from the latter half of the nineteenth century until the modern era, Woods and Teuber (1978) discovered an intriguing dichotomy. Before the 1930s, 35% of the 490 documented cases of childhood aphasia were associated with right-hemisphere lesions. In contrast, only 8% of 270 more recently reported cases were associated with right-hemisphere lesions, and that figure decreased to about 5% when known left-handers were excluded. Woods and Teuber explained that contradiction in terms of the introduction of antibiotics and mass immunization, which occurred during the 1940s and which may have altered substantially the common causes of childhood aphasia. Specifically, they suggested that, before these advances in medicine and public health, aphasias and hemiplegias often resulted from systemic infectious disease. Systemic infections, when severe and untreated, could cause focal cortical lesions as well as diffuse encephalopathy involving both cerebral hemispheres. In these cases the apparent association between aphasia and right-hemisphere damage (left hemiplegia) could be due to the extension of pathology to the left hemisphere. Recent evidence fails to support the claimed bilaterality of language representation in young children. The incidence of aphasia consequent to right-hemisphere lesions seems to be as low in children as in adults. The findings of Basser (1962), on which Lenneberg (1967) based much of his argument for equipotentiality and progressive lateralization, are not really inconsistent with the Woods and Teuber analysis, because as Woods and Teuber pointed out, many of Basser's patients incurred their cerebral damage in the late 1930s or early 1940s.

Woods and Teuber's (1978) own data, which support the thesis of early hemispheric specialization, were derived from the examination of 65 children who had sustained unilateral cerebral lesions after speech acquisition. Although only 26 of the patients were examined by one of the authors, all patients met stated criteria regarding lesion characteristics as well as the presence of aphasia. Of the 34 children with left-hemisphere damage, 25 had either transient or more protracted speech disturbances. However, of the 31 children with right-sided lesions, only four showed any language disturbance, and two of these children were premorbidly left-handed. Thus, the incidence of aphasia following right-hemisphere damage was about 7% for right-handed children, similar to that reported for adults. Although a formal analysis was not performed, Woods and Teuber detected no linear relation between the time required for recovery of normal language and the age at which the damage occurred. The time required for recovery "was variable."

Asymmetries in normal infants and children

Studies of normal children have been instrumental in establishing that hemispheric specialization takes place much earlier in life than previously had been thought. Since the number of such studies has grown rapidly since the mid-1970s, we have selected only a representative sample of studies to summarize. A more detailed review of this literature can be found elsewhere (Kinsbourne & Hiscock, 1983; Hiscock and Kinsbourne, 1987).

Anatomical asymmetries have been found postmortem in the adult cerebrum (e.g., Geschwind & Levitsky, 1968; Wada et al., 1975), one of which involves the temporal speech region (planum temporale) of the left hemisphere, which is usually larger than the homologous region of the right temporal lobe. A similar anatomic asymmetry has been found in the cerebrum of the neonate (Chi, Dooling, & Gilles, 1977; Teszner, Tzavaras, Gruner, & Hecaen, 1972; Wada et al., 1975; Witelson & Pallie, 1973). Among 40 brains examined by postmortem computerized tomography (CT) scan, 15 were of fetuses aged 20 to 42 weeks gestation. The observed tendency for right frontal lobe and left occipital lobe to be the larger of each pair was as significant for them as for 20 brains of adults (Weinberger et al., 1982). Whether these asymmetries are actually related to language dominance is unknown, although an association is often taken for granted (e.g., Galaburda, 1984). Without a better understanding of the implications for language development, if any, of the neuranatomical asymmetries in the neonate, one can only emphasize that there is no obvious qualitative difference between the immature and mature brain in this respect. Thus, one of the historical bases of the equipotentiality argument – the impression that the infant's cerebral hemispheres are physically identical (see Dennis & Whitaker, 1977) – has been shown to be incorrect.

Certain postures and orienting behaviors suggest that the infant's brain is functionally asymmetric. Among these is the tonic neck reflex, an inherently asymmetric posture involving a lateral orienting of the head and correspondingly postural adjustments of all four limbs. Most infants, whether full term or premature, orient more frequently to the right (Gesell, 1938; Gesell & Ames, 1950). This suggests an early prepotency of the left half of the brain, insofar as asymmetric activation produces a contralateral turning tendency (Kinsbourne, 1972). Spontaneous head turning and head turning in response to stimulation also favor the right side (Liederman & Kinsbourne, 1980; Siqueland & Lipsitt, 1966; Turkewitz, Gordon, & Birch, 1965; Turkewitz, Moreau, Gordon, Birch, & Crystal, 1967). In accordance with the intimate, if complex, association between orienting and speaking (Lempert & Kinsbourne, 1985), there is a report of infants' turning being modulated as a function of linguistic characteristics of the situation. MacKain, Studdert-Kennedy, Spieker, and Stern (1983) found that 6-month-old infants detected the correspondence between the acoustic and visual aspects of synchronized consonant–vowel–consonant–vowel (CVCV) disyllables but did so only when looking to the right. This suggested to the authors that two left-hemispheric functions, namely intermodal speech perception and rightward orienting, are mutually facilitative. The various instances of phasic, as well as tonic, turning tendencies in the prelinguistic infant demonstrate not only a general prepotency of the left hemisphere but also a specific prepotency in responding to speech stimuli.

Even though the development of hand preference in the individual infant seems to follow "a variable and unstable course" (Liederman, 1983a), some asymmetries of grasping and reaching can be demonstrated very early in life. Caplan and Kinsbourne (1976) found that 3-month-old infants held an object longer with the right hand than with the left. Hawn and Harris (1983) duplicated this result with 2- and 5-month-old infants, and Petrie and Peters (1980) reported a similar asymmetry with infants as young as 17 days. Petrie and Peters also showed that the stepping reflex is asymmetric for the first month of life; that is, infants tend to lead with the right leg. The right arm is more active than the left within the first 3 months of life (Coryell & Michel, 1978; Liederman, 1983b; von Hofsten, 1982), and early goal-directed reaching and manipulation of objects also seem to favor the right hand. Hawn and Harris (1983) found that 5-month-olds, but not 2-month-olds, reached more quickly for objects with the right hand than with the left. Although Ramsay (1980) failed to find any asymmetry of unimanual manipulation of toys in 5-month-old infants, right-hand contacts were more frequent than left-hand contacts at the age of 7 months. Other investigators have reported that infants move the left arm more than the right (McDonnell, Anderson, & Abraham, 1983) and that they reach more frequently with the left hand than with the right during the first 3 or 4 months of life (e.g., DiFranco, Muir, & Dodwell, 1978), but the preponderance of evidence fails to support those claims. When a significant hand difference is found among young infants, that difference favors the right hand in almost all cases (Young, Segalowitz, Miscek, Alp, & Boulet, 1983). Asymmetry of hand function during bimanual manipulation appears about the age of 1 year (Ramsay, 1980; Ramsay, Campos, & Fenson, 1979) and a right-hand preference for unimanual and bimanual tapping has been observed in children as young as 15 months (Ramsay, 1979). The onset of both unimanual and bimanual handedness has been related to speech milestones (Ramsay, 1980, 1984). Moreover, it has been suggested that the right-hand preference is more marked for symbolic (e.g., pretend play) than for nonsymbolic (e.g., picking up and putting down) movements (Bates, O'Connell, Vaid, Sledge, & Oakes, 1985). Bates et al. (1985) and Oakes (1985) have suggested that degree of right-hand preference during the first 3 years of life is cyclic and that transitory periods of bilaterality are associated with passage into new stages of language development. It is speculated that the newly acquired linguistic abilities draw so heavily on left-hemisphere resources that they interfere with right-hand activity (see Kinsbourne & Hiscock, 1983). Presumably, as these new linguistic processes become more practiced and more highly automatized, surplus left-hemisphere resources for right-hand control become available and the inherent right-hand preference again becomes manifest.

Perceptual asymmetries in infants also have been demonstrated. Entus (1977) used a nonnutritive sucking response to show that infants between the ages of 22 and 140 days could detect transitions from one consonant–vowel (CV) nonsense syllable to another more readily at the right ear than at the left. When pairs of CV syllables were presented in dichotic competition via headphones, infants responded to repetitive stimulation by habituation of sucking. Transitions from one CV to another produced recovery from habituation, and this recovery occurred more often when the transition occurred at the right ear than at the left. This ear asymmetry was reversed when musical stimuli replaced the CV syllables. Even though these findings were not confirmed by Vargha-Khadem and Corballis (1979) on somewhat younger children, subsequent studies using a measure of cardiac habituation did yield asymmetries similar to those reported by Entus (Best, Hoffman, & Glanville, 1982; Glanville, Best, & Levenson, 1977). In a study of premature infants at the age of 36 gestational weeks, Segalowitz and Chapman (1980), using accelerometers to measure limb tremor, found that the amount of left- and right-hand movement depended on the nature of the acoustic stimuli to which the infants had been exposed. Neonates exposed repeatedly to speech showed a disproportionate reduction of right-hand movement as compared with a group exposed repeatedly to music and a control group.

Additional evidence of infant asymmetry can be found in electrophysiological studies. Crowell, Jones, Kapuniai, and Nakagawa (1973) reported that simple repetitive visual stimuli yielded a greater response from the right hemisphere than from the left hemisphere of neonates. From recordings of spontaneous electroencephalograms (EEGs) in 6-month-old infants, Gardiner and Walter (1977) found that power over the right hemisphere was reduced when music was heard. Although these power differences were clearest in a frequency band well below the adult alpha range, the investigators suggested that their task-related shifts were comparable to those found in adults. In contrast, Shucard, Shucard, Cummins, and Campos (1981), who recorded the scalp potentials evoked by probe tones, failed to find asymmetries in either a verbal or a musical condition. Irrespective of experimental condition, females showed greater responses from the left hemisphere and males showed greater responses from the right hemisphere. Davis and Wada (1977, 1978) found greater left-sided than right-sided evoked responses to click stimuli in infants as well as adults and the opposite asymmetry in both groups for brief flashes of light. These investigators attributed the stimulus-specific asymmetries to differences in how structured and unstructured stimuli are processed. They suggested that the left hemisphere is specialized for processing highly structured material (e.g., clicks) that can be readily identified or related to past experience. Identification or referential processing, according to Davis and Wada (1977), is independent of language and may develop before language. However, the work of Molfese and his associates suggests that the left hemisphere of the neonate may be specialized for the analysis of speech-specific acoustic cues. In their early work, Molfese and colleagues (e.g., Molfese, Freeman, & Palermo, 1975), found that evoked responses to speech stimuli were greater over the left temporal region in infants as well as older children and adults, whereas responses to a piano chord and a noise burst were greater over the right temporal region. Subsequent work has indicated a left-hemisphere mechanism in infants for perceiving consonant place-of-articulation information and a right-hemisphere mechanism for discriminating differences in voice onset time (as well as bilateral mechanisms for making both kinds of distinctions) (Molfese & Molfese, 1979, 1980, 1983). These mechanisms resemble those found in adults, although there are some important age-related differences. Even if the exact nature of hemispheric specialization in the infant is not revealed by the diverse electrophysiological data, there is ample evidence of task-related asymmetries.

The infant data, despite certain inconsistencies, show that structural, physiological, and behavioral asymmetries exist very early in life. Although we can only speculate as to how these asymmetries are related to subsequent linguistic development, at least some of the asymmetries are probably precursors of left-hemisphere specialization for language processing. For instance, the relatively high amplitude evoked responses from the left side of the head during the presentation of speech stimuli may reflect a brainstem activation pattern that serves no immediate purpose in the neonate but that will facilitate the processing of language in the left hemisphere when the cerebral cortex has become sufficiently mature to organize behavioral responses to the information contained in speech signals (Kinsbourne & Hiscock, 1983). Accordingly, by the time the infant has reached 6 months of age, this asymmetric activation causes speech perception (and the resultant behavior responses) to occur in the context of rightward turning (MacKain et al., 1983). Other asymmetries in the infant appear to be related to subsequent handedness (Michel, 1981, 1983).

If the infant asymmetries are, in fact, precursors of hemisphere specialization for manual and linguistic functions, the evidence is inconsistent with the principle of equipotentiality insofar as equipotentiality is taken to mean functional equivalence of the hemispheres. (One could still argue that the infant's right hemisphere, though not specialized for manual control and speech, is nevertheless perfectly capable of performing these functions if the left hemisphere becomes incapacitated.) The infant data, however, are not incompatible with a weak form of the progressive lateralization model. A slight or inconsistent asymmetry in the infant could evolve into a marked and consistent asymmetry in the adult. Hand preference, for example, seems to be less marked and stable in the infant than in the adult (see Liederman, 1983b). The question of differential degrees of laterality is difficult to answer using infant data, because the activities available for assessment in the infant (e.g., grasp duration) are quite different from those whose asymmetries are measured in adults (e.g., manual skill). Consequently, investigators have relied on studies of normal children to determine whether the size of asymmetries increases during development.

Dichotic listening studies suggest that the processing of linguistic stimuli is lateralized at the age of 2½ or 3 years (the earliest age at which children can be tested using procedures designed for adults and older children) and that the degree of lateralization remains constant from that age until adulthood. These conclusions are based on the assumption that the magnitude of the right-ear advantage (REA) indexes the degree to which the left hemisphere subserves the processing of linguistic material. In fact, that there is a one-to-one relation between the direction of ear advantage and language lateralization is questionable (e.g., Hiscock & Stewart, 1984; Satz, 1978). Most developmental studies that encompass broad age ranges fail to show any consistent developmental trend in the magnitude of the REA (Berlin, Hughes, Lowe-Bell, & Berlin, 1973; Geffen, 1978; Goodglass, 1973; Hiscock & Kinsbourne, 1977, 1980a; Hynd & Obrzut, 1977; Kimura, 1963, 1967; Kinsbourne & Hiscock, 1977; Knox & Kimura, 1970; Nagafuchi, 1970; Shulman-Galambos, 1977), although a few have yielded positive or ambiguous findings (Bryden & Allard, 1978; Morris, Bakker, Satz, & van der Vlugt, 1984; Satz, Bakker, Teunisson, Goebel, & van der Vlugt, 1975). Similarly, studies of verbal–manual time sharing in children have shown early asymmetries and, generally, a lack of any age-related change in degree of asymmetry (Hiscock, Antoniuk, Prisciak, & von Hessert, 1985; Hiscock & Kinsbourne, 1978, 1980b; Hiscock, Kinsbourne, Samuels, & Krause, 1987; Kinsbourne & McMurray, 1975; Obrzut, Hynd, Obrzut, & Leitgeb, 1980; Piazza, 1977; White & Kinsbourne, 1980). Only a single study by Hiscock (1982) reported an age-related increase in degree of asymmetry. In these studies, children perform a verbal task (e.g., recitation) as they engage in speeded tapping with either the left or right hand. The verbal activity slows right-hand tapping more than left-hand tapping, a finding that is attributed to interference in the left hemisphere between speech control and control of the right hand. Since this asymmetric pattern of interferences is found even in 3-year-old children, the results of these concurrent-task experiments suggest early lateralization of speech control.

Implications of developmental invariance

The evidence against equipotentiality and progressive lateralization with respect to language is strong. If the cerebral hemispheres are in fact differentially specialized for the processing of language at a very early age, we may use that information to evaluate anomalous lateralization as an explanation for disordered language development.

First, the notion of delayed lateralization becomes untenable. Cognitive or linguistic deficiency cannot plausibly be attributed to delayed lateralization if lateralization is not a developmental phenomenon (see Hiscock & Kinsbourne, 1982). The cognitive or linguistic deficiency might be attributable to the absence, incompleteness, or reversal of lateralization, but without the additional implication that the normal pattern of language lateralization will evolve with further maturation.

The second implication of developmental invariance is that anomalous lateralization must be relatively rare in children because it is relatively rare in adults. Since clinical studies of adults (e.g., Annett, 1975; Rasmussen & Milner, 1975) show that only a small minority of right-handers deviate from the norm of left-hemisphere language representation, we would expect that anomalies of language representation are equally infrequent among right-handed children. Nonetheless, whether the incidence of right-hemisphere language in right-handers is 7.5% (Annett, 1975) or only 3% (Rasmussen & Milner, 1975), one could argue that the incidence is high enough to account for a substantial proportion of clinically identified cases of cognitive or linguistic deficit. In other words, the incidence of anomalous language representation in right-handed children could still be quite high in clinical populations even if there were no cases of delayed lateralization. The likelihood of anomalous language lateralization would be much higher among left-handed and ambidextrous children, because a large proportion of adult left-handers are thought to have either right-hemispheric or bilateral language representation (Annett, 1975; Rasmussen & Milner, 1975; Satz, 1979). An elevated incidence of left-handedness has traditionally been held to support the argument that anomalous cerebral organization plays a causal role in various developmental disorders. Thus, dismissing the concept of delayed lateralization does not completely preclude attributing cognitive and linguistic deficits to deviant cerebral lateralization (although, as we shall discuss subsequently, there are other reasons to doubt that anomalies of cerebral lateralization cause language disorders in the otherwise normal brain).

A third implication of invariant lateralization is that the brain may be "prelateralized" for a particular function before that function develops (Kinsbourne & Hiscock, 1977, 1983). As noted previously, asymmetrical lateral orienting is thought to foreshadow unimanual reaching (Michel, 1981, 1983). The prepotency of the left side of the brain, which will ultimately be expressed as right-handedness, is manifested as a rightward orienting tendency before the development of many aspects of handedness. Two corollaries of this principle are especially relevant to the understanding of abnormal behavioral development. The dissociation between the neurological phenomenon of lateralization and the behavioral phenomenon of language development allows a parallel distinction to be made between incomplete lateralization of language and disordered language development. Disordered language development is not necessarily derived from anomalous lateralization. Instead, the neural substrate responsible for language may be immature or defective. This substrate, even though it may be properly located in the left hemisphere, may not be fully functional for reasons such as covert prenatal damage. This possibility, to which we have referred as delayed maturation, is often confused with delayed lateralization, even though the two explanations are readily distinguishable (Hiscock & Kinsbourne, 1980a). The principle that lateralization precedes lateralized behavior has another corollary that is important for understanding behavioral deficit: The early lateralization may be maladaptive if, in compensation for cortical damage, anomalous neural organization of the behavior has been established. If, for example, damage to the left hemisphere causes a shift of language representation to the right, the excellence of this right-hemispheric language capability may be limited less by the inadequacy of that hemisphere to process linguistic material than by the inability of ascending projections from brainstem to activate the right hemisphere at the appropriate times (Kinsbourne, 1980). In other words, the previously established activation pattern, which features activation of the left hemisphere during verbal processing, may preclude optimal activation of the right hemisphere subsequently, when such activation is needed to support verbal processing.

Summary

Even though the principles of hemispheric equipotentiality and progressive lateralization have been firmly established in neurological theory for many decades, current evidence clearly favors a different point of view. The human brain is anatomically and functionally asymmetric long before observable language function emerges. It is probable that at least some of the early asymmetries are precursors of a more mature form of hemispheric specialization for language and manual control, but the significance of the early asymmetries for linguistic and manual development is still a matter of speculation. Studies of childhood aphasia – at least those conducted in the present era – suggest that the consequences of unilateral cerebral damage in young children are similar to those in adults. Language in right-handers is seldom disrupted by damage to the right cerebral hemisphere (Woods & Teuber, 1973). The clinical and experimental evidence for language lateralization substantiates what we have termed the developmental invariance hypothesis.

The developmental invariance of language lateralization constrains laterality-based explanation for disordered language development in at least two ways: The concept of delayed lateralization becomes implausible; and the incidence of anomalous language lateralization in children should be no greater than in adults. Moreover, developmental invariance implies that the brain may be lateralized for a function before that function has an observable impact on behavior. This principle in turn reinforces the distinction between incomplete lateralization and disordered language development; and it raises the possibility that, under certain pathological conditions, early lateralization may even be maladaptive.

The effects of lateralized brain damage

Lesion studies

For adults as well as children, the association between the lateralization of damage and the relative magnitude of verbal and performance IQ is a matter of long-standing dispute (e.g., Annett, 1970, 1975; Klove & Reitan, 1958; McFie, 1961; Reed

& Reitan, 1969; Reitan, 1955; Todd, Coolidge, & Satz, 1977). Woods (1980a) found that the effect of right-hemisphere, but not left hemisphere, lesions on subsequent IQ depends on the age at which the lesion occurred. Starting with a pool of 400 patients with hemiparesis of infantile or childhood onset, he analyzed 50 with cerebral lesions thought to be unilateral and nonprogressive. Twenty-seven had left-hemisphere and 23 had right-hemisphere lesions. Wechsler IQ tests, administered at an average age of 15 years, failed to show any side-of-lesion effects for those children whose hemiparesis was evident before their first birthday. Irrespective of which cerebral hemisphere was damaged, IQ levels were below average and there were no significant differences between verbal and performance IQ. However, among children who developed hemiparesis after the first birthday, left- and right-hemisphere lesions had dissimilar effects on IQ. Left-hemisphere lesions were associated with below-average verbal and performance IQs, but right-hemisphere lesions were associated with average verbal IQ and low performance IQ. Only among patients with late right-hemisphere lesions was there a significant difference between verbal and performance IQ. With one exception, each group of patients had lower mean verbal and performance IQs than normal sibling controls. The exception was that the patients with late right-hemisphere lesions did not differ from their siblings in verbal IQ.

Woods (1980b) augmented his finding with meta-analyses of previous data concerning lateralized brain damage in adults as well as children. From seven published studies in which Wechsler IQ tests were administered to patients with adult-onset brain lesions (Doehring, Reitan, & Klove, 1961; Gersten, Jung, & Brooks, 1972; Klove, 1974; Meier, 1970; Satz, 1966; Vega & Parsons, 1969; Warrington & James, 1967), Woods computed mean verbal and performance IQ as a function of lesion side. For 178 patients with left-hemisphere lesions, the average verbal IQ was 97.2 and the average performance IQ was 85.4. Although significance tests were not performed, the averages seem to be consistent with Woods's own data for patients with hemiparesis occurring after the age of 1 year: Left-hemisphere lesions are associated with relatively low verbal and performance IQ, but right-hemisphere lesions are associated with a selective deficit in performance IQ. A meta-analysis of Wechsler data from patients with childhood-onset lesions yielded results similar to those for Woods's early-lesioned group. From six studies (Fedio & Mirsky, 1969; Fitzhugh & Fitzhugh, 1964, Meier & French, 1966; Meyer & Jones, 1959; Milner, 1969; Reed & Reitan, 1969), Woods calculated mean verbal and performance IQs for 116 patients with left-hemisphere lesions and 95 with right-hemisphere lesions. The left-hemisphere patients had an average verbal IQ of 83.5 and an average performance IQ of 85.2; the right-hemisphere patients had an average verbal IQ of 90.3 and an average performance IQ of 86.8. Woods concluded that these results are comparable to those for his patients with early lesions, namely, that early lesions on either side affect verbal and performance IQs about equally.

On the basis of these findings, Woods (1980a) emphasized the limited effects of right-hemisphere lesions that occur after the first year of life. He suggested that the effects of very early lesions are relatively nonselective because, during the first year of life, "both sides of the brain have the potential for a widespread functional reorganization" (p. 69) but that this potential, especially with respect to left-hemisphere reorganization following right-hemisphere damage, is diminished as the brain matures. The ironic (though not necessarily implausible) aspect of Woods's argument is that the alleged bilateral reorganization, in the youngest children, appears to have been for both verbal and nonverbal performance. If only the damaged hemisphere undergoes reorganization, as in older children and adults, the functions of the intact hemisphere may not be greatly compromised. However, this functional sparing of the healthy hemisphere seems to occur only if the damage is right-sided.

Woods's conclusions can be challenged on two grounds. First, they rest on the assumption that verbal and performance IQs reflect left- and right-hemisphere functions, respectively. However, it seems unlikely that the Wechsler tests, which were not devised for neuropsychological purposes, would yield uncontaminated measures of left- and right-hemisphere capacities (see Hiscock & Mackay, 1985). Perhaps, as Inglis, Lawson, Maclean, and Monga (1982) have suggested, it is possible to use either verbal or nonverbal strategies to accomplish the Wechsler Performance subtests. Data reported by Inglis et al. suggest that women, in particular, tend to use verbal means of solving problems from the Performance subtests. If some patients in Woods's sample tended to rely on verbal mediation for solving problems from the Performance subtests and other patients tended to rely on nonverbal processes, it is easy to understand why both left- and right-hemisphere lesions would lower the average performance IQ. Thus, the nonspecific effects of left-hemisphere lesions, as noted by Woods, might be attributable to characteristics of the Wechsler Performance subtests and not to bilateral cerebral reorganization following left-hemisphere damage. The second objection to Woods's conclusions is that early- and late-childhood lesions are not necessarily comparable. An examination of Woods's list of etiologies reveals no commonality between pre- and perinatal lesions, on the one hand, and postnatal lesions, on the other hand. From the results of the collaborative study described previously (Towbin, 1978), it seems likely that many of Woods's patients with early lesions suffered hypoxic cerebral damage in utero. If the damage occurred when the fetus was immature, the lesion probably would be deep rather than cortical and probably would involve the germinal matrix, which serves as a repository of tissue required for further brain development. Consequently, there is reason to suspect that the damage in the early-lesioned group is less lateralized than that in the group with postnatal damage. If so, the more widespread effects of early damage, relative to late damage, might be attributable to a higher prevalence of bilateral damage in the supposedly unilateral early-lesioned group.

Vargha-Khadem, O'Gorman, and Watters (1985) examined the effects of lesion laterality, age at injury, and severity of damage on expressive and receptive language skills in 54 children with unilateral cerebral lesions. The children were divided into three groups according to age at the time of injury. Those in the prenatal group showed unilateral deficits in size, motor development, or coordination during the first 6 months of life. There was no evidence of perinatal or postnatal episodes that might have been responsible for the abnormalities. Children in the postnatal groups had developed hemiplegia subsequent to a distinct and well-documented episode that usually involved hospitalization. Etiologies were diverse. In the case of the early postnatal group, the incident occurred between the ages of 2 months and 5 years; in the case of the late postnatal group, damage occurred between the ages of 5 and 14 years. All children had IQs of 75 or higher.

At the time of testing, which was at least 2 years postinjury, only one child – a child with left-sided late postnatal damage – was still classified as dysphasic and was receiving speech therapy. Nonetheless, left-hemisphere-damaged children in each of the three groups performed significantly worse than normal controls on a test of object naming (Oldfield & Wingfield, 1964) as well as the Token Test for auditory comprehension (DeRenzi & Vignolo, 1962). Irrespective of the language measure, children with left-hemisphere lesions were significantly more impaired than those with right-hemisphere lesions, and those with late left-hemisphere lesions were especially impaired. Although the object-naming performance of the right-hemisphere–early postnatal group was significantly worse than that of normal controls, no other linguistic deficiency was found for the children with right-hemisphere lesions. Since children with left- and right-sided lesions did not differ significantly in digit span, Vargha-Khadem et al. argue that the poor Token Test performance of children with left-hemisphere damage is attributable to a specific linguistic defect rather than an impairment of memory.

In addition to the unambiguous effect of lesion laterality on language performance, other findings of the Vargha-Khadem et al. study are noteworthy. The first is the relatively great magnitude of linguistic impairment in children with late postnatal damage to the left hemisphere. This suggests that recovery of linguistic function is more complete following early lesions than following later lesions. In other words, the degree of plasticity decreases with increasing age. (Vargha-Khadem & Isaacs, 1985, in a study of verbal learning and memory, failed to find corresponding evidence of plasticity in early lesioned children.) Since the interval between injury and assessment varied across the three clinical groups, one cannot rule out the possibility that the children with later left-hemisphere damage showed greater impairments simply because there was less time for recovery to take place. However, as the investigators note, the postdamage interval was carefully matched between the left- and right-lesioned patients within each group, and there is no evidence of inferior performance among children with late right-hemisphere lesions. Given the difficulty of matching patients with respect to etiology and lesion characteristics, the left-hemisphere–late postnatal group might have happened to have more severe damage than the other groups. However, this explanation is undermined by the finding that the degree of linguistic impairment was unrelated to the extent of structural damage, as rated from CT scans. Furthermore, the CT ratings of left-hemisphere lesions were, on the whole, less abnormal than those of right-hemisphere lesions. Thus, we are unable to reject the investigators' conclusion that the age of the child at the time of damage to the left hemisphere is an important factor in determining subsequent linguistic functioning.

Another notable finding concerns discrepancies between verbal and performance IQ. Although performance IQ tended to exceed verbal IQ in children with left-hemisphere lesions, and verbal IQ tended to exceed performance IQ in children with right-hemisphere lesions, the differences were not marked. Statistical tests of the discrepancy within each group yielded only two significant differences: Performance IQ was greater than verbal IQ in the left-hemisphere–early postnatal and normal control groups. The patterns of IQs did not resemble closely those described by Woods: that is, children in the right-hemisphere–late postnatal group did not have selective deficit of performance IQ and children in the other groups did not show obvious impairment of both verbal and performance IQ. It should be noted, however, that cell sizes were small in the case of postnatal groups, and the criteria for early and late lesions differed from those used by Woods.

This work by Vargha-Khadem, O'Gorman, and Watters shows how conclusions about language impairment following lateralized brain damage may vary according to the criterion of linguistic performance. Only 1 of 28 children with left-hemisphere damage was considered to be dysphasic by clinical criteria, and only one of the three left-hemisphere groups had an average verbal IQ that was significantly lower than its performance IQ. Yet the children with left-hemisphere lesions were distinctly inferior to children with right-hemisphere lesions as well as to normal controls on measures of receptive and expressive language skills.

Residual deficits persisted long after an acute hemisphere lesion indicate the limits of compensatory ability of the intact hemisphere. Acute effects permit inferences about the ability of the undamaged hemisphere to support aspects of language function right away, rather than after a lengthy period of functional reorganization.

A possible clue to a change in right-hemisphere capability with increasing age in childhood is afforded by age-dependent change in the phenomenology of childhood aphasia. Aphasia in the first decade is almost always nonfluent. It features difficulties in articulation and syntax, but not paraphasias or jargon (Brown & Hecaen, 1976; Hecaen, 1983). However, by ages 9 to 11 fluent aphasia begins to occur (Van Dongen & Loonen, 1977). One interpretation would be that below that age the right hemisphere is fully able to decode speech. The child decodes his or her own speech output and, fully cognizant of its impaired quality, suppresses further utterance. If this is correct, then by the second decade, the right hemisphere has lost this ability to decode, at least right at the onset of the cerebral insult.

Early damage of the right hemisphere similarly seems to have enduring effects on children's developing spatial thought. Stiles-Davis, Sugarman, and Nass (1985) studied four children with right-hemisphere damage present before age 1 year in terms of their developing spatial classification skills. These were delayed, whereas no delay was observed when the classification was done in other modes.

Hemispherectomy studies

The surgical procedure of hemispherectomy or hemidecortication, provides a unique opportunity to determine the linguistic potential of the right hemisphere in isolation. One of the most widely publicized cases is that of a man whose diseased left hemisphere had been removed at the age of 5½ years in a successful attempt to abolish right-sided seizures that were intractable to anticonvulsant medication (Smith & Sugar, 1975). When tested at 26 years of age, this man had a verbal IQ of 126 and a performance IQ of 102. On the Peabody Picture Vocabulary Test, his performance exceeded the upper limit of the scale. The remarkable performance of this young man with one hemisphere shows dramatically the potential capacity of the right hemisphere for verbal processing. One should be careful, however, not to overgeneralize these findings. Since the left hemisphere of Smith and Sugar's patient was known to be abnormal from an early age, at least some linguistic functions may have been represented in the right hemisphere long before the hemispherectomy was performed. It does not follow that the right hemisphere of a normal brain would be capable of such a high level of verbal skill if the left hemisphere were removed at age 5 years. Also, as we have pointed out, the verbal IQ is not an ideal measure of left-hemisphere functioning. Perhaps some linguistic deficits would have become apparent had Smith and Sugar's patient undergone more exacting language testing.

The favorable outcome with Smith and Sugar's patient differs strikingly from the results of left hemidecortication in adolescents and adults, for such patients have significant linguistic impairment, especially impairment of voluntary, propositional speech output (St. James-Roberts, 1981; Searleman, 1977). One circumstance thought to favor the development of linguistic competence in the right hemisphere is early removal of the left hemisphere. This has been shown by Dennis and her collaborators (Dennis, 1980a,b,c; Dennis & Kohn, 1975; Dennis & Whitaker, 1976, 1977) in their investigations of children who have undergone hemidecortication very early in life. Children with early decortication of the left hemisphere characteristically are free of clinical signs of aphasia and have verbal IQs comparable to those of right hemidecorticates (e.g., Dennis & Kohn, 1975).

Thus, on first analysis, it seems that a healthy right hemisphere can subserve linguistic functions quite satisfactorily if language is allowed to develop in that hemisphere from the time of early childhood. Dennis and her colleagues addressed a more specific question: whether the isolated right hemisphere, under ideal circumstances, can attain the same level of linguistic competency as the isolated left hemisphere. Their answer is that it cannot, although the linguistic deficits in left-hemidecorticated children often are subtle. In the first study of linguistic performance, Dennis and Kohn (1975) compared four right and five left hemidecorticates, each of whom had had lateralized brain pathology since the first year or two of life. The age at surgery ranged from less than 1 year to 20 years. Patients were administered a sentence comprehension task involving sentences with four voices: active affirmative, passive affirmative, active negative, and passive negative. The patient demonstrated comprehension of a sentence by choosing a picture that correctly portrayed the action described in the sentence. Relative to the right hemidecorticates, the left hemidecorticates showed significantly longer latencies in responding to passive sentences and made fewer correct responses to passive sentences. Irrespective of sentence category, the left and right groups differed in the distribution of response latencies: the left hemidecorticates made fewer correct responses at short latencies. Dennis and Kohn concluded that left and right hemidecorticates differ in overall processing or response time (for some unknown reason) as well as in the ability to comprehend certain syntactic forms. The left-hemidecorticate children were not generally more impaired in cognitive ability; their IQs were comparable to the right hemidecorticates and they outperformed the right hemidecorticates on visuospatial tasks (Kohn & Dennis, 1974).

Subsequent studies by Dennis and her associates (Dennis, 1977, 1980b; Dennis & Whitaker, 1976, 1977; Dennis, Lovett, & Wiegel-Crump, 1981) focused on three children whose hemidecortication was performed before the age of 5 months, that is, before the development of speech. Each of these children was diagnosed as having Sturge–Weber–Dimitri syndrome, a congenital disorder entailing seizures and progressive intellectual deterioration, in which early removal of the diseased hemisphere often leads to a favorable outcome (Hoffman, Hendrick, Dennis, & Armstrong, 1979). Two of the patients were left hemidecorticates and one was a right hemidecorticate. Each of the three children had Wechsler Verbal IQs between 91 and 96. Performance IQs ranged from 87 to 108, with the score of the right hemidecorticate falling between the scores of the two left hemidecorticates. The children were either 9 or 10 years old when the tests were administered.

After administering an extensive set of standardized and experimental language tests to the three children, Dennis and Whitaker (1976) concluded that the linguistic capacity of the right hemisphere is limited in some (not all) respects:

A less complete language capacity has developed in these subjects by the end of the first decade of life in the right hemisphere than in the left, even when language has been acquired under seizure-free and educationally normal conditions. The impairments of right

hemisphere linguistic processing do not reflect a global language breakdown nor a deficiency of verbal cognitive capacity; and they are evident only when particular linguistic
functions are being taxed. Different configurations of language skills have developed in the
two isolated hemispheres: phonemic and semantic abilities are similarly developed, syntactic competence has been asymmetrically acquired. (p. 428)

Children with left and right hemidecortication did not differ in articulating
speech sounds or making phonemic discriminations, in producing words, or in
making semantic distinctions. Dennis and Whitaker concluded that both hemispheres are equally satisfactory substrates for the development of phonemic competence and that both may develop a normal lexicon and normal ability to retrieve
words from that lexicon. In contrast, the investigators found numerous syntactic
deficits in the two children with only a right hemisphere. These children often
performed poorly when appreciation of sentence structure or function words was
critical. For example, performance of the left hemidecorticates was relatively impaired on Part 5 of the Token Test (DeRenzi & Vignolo, 1962), in which the instructions to be executed are syntactically more complex than those in the first four
parts. On the first four parts of the test, in which information load is varied but
syntax remains simple, left and right hemidecorticates showed comparable performance. As in the earlier study (Dennis & Kohn, 1975), the left hemidecorticates
showed impaired comprehension of sentences with passive, but not active voice.
The left hemidecorticates also had difficulty in judging the grammaticality of sentences and in repeating sentences with complex or unusual syntactic form (e.g.,
passives, clefts, and pseudoclefts). They failed to appreciate the implications of
sentences in which the implicative and complement verb could be either positive
or negative, for example, whether the action occurred in the sentence "Mary
didn't manage not to get wet." Other deficits – in using pronouns, in using the
function word by in its temporal application, and in judging the relatedness of
words within a sentence – were described.

Linguistic characteristics of left and right hemidecorticates have been elaborated further in subsequent publications (Dennis, 1980a,b,c; Dennis et al., 1981).
Dennis (1980a) divided six left hemidecorticates into two groups according to the
speed with which they processed passive sentences and then provided evidence
that the syntactic deficits of the respective groups could be attributed to different
factors. Dennis et al. (1981), after examining differences between left and right
hemidecorticates in reading and spelling, concluded that the superior performance
of the right hemidecorticate is related to a greater ability to "manipulate and exploit the rules of English orthography" (p. 87).

Despite the thoroughness with which Dennis and her colleagues studied their
hemidecorticates, many of the phenomena they described may be specific to the
individuals who participated in their investigations. Not only is the sample size
extremely small, but there was substantial divergence in the performance of the
two children with left hemidecortication. As pointed out by Jacobs (1977), hem-

ispherectomy is a procedure that offers the surgeon many choices with respect to the removal or sparing of brain tissue. For instance, the thalamus, the importance of which in linguistic function is well recognized, may either be excised or not. Thus, uncontrolled structural variation may account for at least some of the linguistic differences between the one child with right hemidecortication and the two children with left hemidecortication. Bishop (1983) also noted the variability of performance among Dennis's left hemidecorticates and suggested that, in at least some instances, the poor language performance of members of this group might be attributed to a generally low level of cognitive development. Bishop further pointed out that MW, the sole right hemidecorticate in several of Dennis's studies, outperformed other right hemidecorticates on several linguistic tasks and thus is not representative of right hemidecorticates with respect to linguistic ability. After describing several shortcomings in this series of studies by Dennis and her associates, for example, the absence of a normal control group and an improper use of statistics, Bishop (1983) concludes that "one should be cautious about uncritically accepting these researchers' conclusions as the sole possible interpretation of their findings until the impressionistic data they present is backed up by adequate control data on the same tasks" (p. 206). The conclusions of Dennis and her colleagues are further compromised by some of their own data. In one of the studies involving an expanded sample of six left and four right hemidecorticates (Dennis, 1980a), the three left hemidecorticates classified as "passive proficient" consistently obtained scores that were comparable to those of the right hemidecorticates on various linguistic tasks. Even if left hemidecorticates, on average, are less proficient than right hemidecorticates, on average, the considerable overlap in performance between the two groups implies that the isolated right hemisphere, under ideal conditions, is approximately as good a substrate as the left for the development of language. This interpretation, of course, is opposite to one of the main conclusions of Dennis and her associates (e.g., Dennis & Whitaker, 1976, 1977).

Irrespective of whether a healthy right hemisphere is ever capable of subserving language as well as a healthy left hemisphere, it seems plausible that the linguistic competence of the respective hemispheres may be achieved in different ways, that is, through the use of dissimilar strategies (Dennis, 1980a). Consequently, even when the performance of left and right hemidecorticates is equivalent, the limiting factors may differ. The data of Dennis and her colleagues (e.g., Dennis & Whitaker, 1976) show clearly that, when left hemidecorticates have difficulty in producing or comprehending speech, the difficulty is much more likely to involve the processing of syntactic information than phonemic or semantic information. Commissurotomy (split-brain) studies have also pointed to the syntactic disabilities of the right hemisphere (Gazzaniga & Hillyard, 1973). Zaidel (1976, 1977, 1978), however, on the basis of his own commissurotomy and hemispherectomy data, reached conclusions about right-hemisphere language capacity that diverge somewhat from those of Dennis and her associates as well as those of earlier commissurotomy studies. Although Zaidel's sample size was very small – two split-brain patients and one left and one right hemidecorticate – his own conclusions are strengthened by the similar patterns obtained from the two different kinds of patients. Moreover, his investigations of commissurotomy patients benefited from the use of a contact lens technique that allowed him to present visual stimuli to one hemisphere without restricting the patient's eye movements. Consequently, the right hemisphere of each commissurotomized patient could be presented the same test stimuli as used with the right hemidecorticate. In this way, Zaidel was able to compare results obtained using two dissimilar means of isolating the right hemisphere. His findings agree with those of Dennis and her colleagues insofar as the right hemisphere was not severely handicapped in semantic and lexical performance (Zaidel, 1976). As in Dennis's work, right-hemisphere processing was associated with relatively marked deficits in Token Test performance (Zaidel, 1977). However, unlike Dennis and her associates (e.g., Dennis & Whitaker, 1976), Zaidel (1978) found major deficiencies in the ability of the right hemisphere to perform auditory discriminations. Moreover, syntactic difficulties were attributed to restricted short-term verbal memory rather than a more specific linguistic deficit: "The language system in the right hemisphere is more constrained by informational redundancy, length, and memory than by abstract linguistic variables, such as grammatical or transformational complexity" (Zaidel, 1978, p. 268).

Clearly, the study of hemidecorticates, no matter how directly it addresses the question of right-hemisphere linguistic capability, fails to provide the ultimate answer. Some of the shortcomings of the method have been noted in our review of selected studies; others have been discussed in a comprehensive summary and critique of the hemispherectomy literature by St. James-Roberts (1981). Although St. James-Roberts (1981) evaluates the literature with respect to a somewhat different criterion, namely, whether the evidence supports the hypothesis of greater plasticity in the immature brain relative to the mature brain, many of the criticisms apply equally well to attempts to determine the maximal language capacity of the right hemisphere. Some of the criticisms concern factors potentially within the control of investigators – for example, inclusion of the same patients in different studies; lack of standardization in experimental design, techniques, and measures; and sporadic testing of patients over variable periods of time. Other shortcomings are intrinsic to the study of this population – for example, difficulty in ascertaining the exact onset of brain damage; unsuitability of some patients for testing, which causes a selection bias in favor of more able patients; and variability of hemidecortication effects within, as well as between, left and right hemisphere groups. St. James-Roberts points out the importance of the interval between brain damage and assessment or between surgery and assessment, and argues that favorable outcomes in infantile cases may be attributable to recovery intervals that are lengthy in comparison with those in adult-onset cases (in which the usual etiology is neoplasm and survival time seldom is sufficient to allow long-term follow-up). Even in the Dennis et al. studies, in which age at surgery and at testing were roughly comparable, there are differences that could account for some of the differences between the right and left hemidecorticates. For example, Dennis and Whitaker (1976) report that their right hemidecorticate was 1 year and 3 months older than the two left hemidecorticates when the Token Test was administered. Assuming that Part 5 of the test (the part in which syntactic difficulty is greatest) is the most difficult part, the selective impairment of the two left hemidecorticates on this part might simply reflect the fact that they were younger and less educated than the right-hemidecorticate patient. Admittedly, the differential recovery period cannot account for all of the right-hemisphere deficits found by Dennis and her colleagues, but it is a confounding factor in some instances.

Summary

We have reviewed some recent studies that illustrate current issues and findings regarding the effects of lateralized brain damage on verbal intelligence and language. Among the diverse findings are a few particularly noteworthy observations. The contemporary literature confirms Lenneberg's earlier contention that aphasia acquired during childhood as a consequence of unilateral cerebral damage is reversible, provided that pubescence does not occur before the process of language recovery is complete. However, recovery from clinically obvious aphasia does not preclude the persistence of more subtle linguistic deficits or diminished verbal IQ. The significance of the side of the lesion varies with the choice of dependent variable. Left-hemisphere damage is associated with clinically apparent aphasia-defective performance on objective tests for aphasia and a diminution of both verbal and performance IQ. Right-hemisphere damage clearly has less impact on linguistic performance and may, if sustained after the first year of life, have more limited effect on intellectual ability as well (Woods, 1980a). However, any differential implications of left- and right-sided damage for verbal and nonverbal intelligence remain a matter of controversy. A child's intellectual ability following unilateral injury varies as a function of many factors, which include the age at injury, the time available for recovery between injury and test, and the tests used for the assessment of intellectual ability.

Hemispherectomy cases provide a means of determining the linguistic performance of one cerebral hemisphere in the absence of the other. These cases – particularly those in which one hemisphere is removed during the first year of life – indicate the maximal capacity of a single left or right hemisphere rather than the typical functions of each hemisphere in the intact brain. Whether the isolated right hemisphere can ever subserve language as well as its counterpart remains a contentious issue. When linguistic deficits are observed in patients with only a right hemisphere, the character and severity of those deficits vary across cases and studies. Nonetheless, one important implication of the hemispherectomy literature is clear: Under certain circumstances, the isolated right hemisphere may display an impressive linguistic competence.

Deviant language representation as a causal factor in developmental disorders

There is a vast literature concerning incomplete or otherwise anomalous cerebral lateralization as a putative cause of cognitive or linguistic impairment. Perhaps the most popular claim is that certain learning disabilities stem from some deviation from the norm of left-hemisphere language specialization (Orton, 1937). Since we have reviewed and critiqued this literature in considerable detail elsewhere (Hiscock, 1983; Hiscock & Kinsbourne, 1982; Kinsbourne & Hiscock, 1978, 1981, 1983), we shall provide here only a brief summary of our reasons for doubting the existence of a causal link between anomalous lateralization and behavioral deficit.

As an initial step in establishing a causal relation between anomalous cerebral lateralization and behavioral deficit, one might wish to demonstrate that anomalous lateralization is prevalent in various clinical populations. Do learning-disabled or language-disordered children, for example, show signs of deviant lateralization? Many such claims have been made (e.g., Jones, 1966; Silver & Hagin, 1982), but most reviewers have failed to find the evidence either consistent or convincing (e.g., Benton, 1974; Critchley, 1970; Naylor, 1980; Satz, 1976; Vernon, 1957, 1971; Zangwill, 1962). As Harris (1979) has pointed out, the more direct methods of ascertaining hemispheric specialization cannot be used to study individuals who have no obvious brain pathology. Consequently, our understanding of the relation, if any, between deviant lateralization and behavioral deficit is limited by the dubious reliability and validity of indirect methods such as dichotic listening and visual half-field studies (Hiscock & Kinsbourne, 1982).

What exactly is meant by *anomalous lateralization*? Is the term sufficiently precise to generate testable hypotheses? In our 1982 critique, we enumerated four classes of hemisphere-related models of dyslexia that include a total of nine existing or possible exemplars, each of which could be used to generate one or more predictions. For example, the class of models that we called translocation models included a model in which hemispheric specialization for verbal and spatial functions is reversed; that is, verbal functions are represented in the right hemisphere and spatial functions in the left. This configuration can be used to generate no less than four predicted behavioral outcomes: no deleterious effects, impairment of verbal skills, impairment of spatial skills, or impairment of both verbal and spatial skills. When the translocation models are combined with unilateral-deficit models, it is apparent that anomalous cerebral lateralization has a multitude of possible meanings. Moreover, in the unlikely event that findings fit none of the nine models we described, it probably would not be difficult to construct a tenth model that fit the data satisfactorily in retrospect.

Thus far we have argued that there is no convincing empirical link between anomalous lateralization and behavioral deficit in children and that, in any event, the concept of anomalous lateralization is so vague as to have an almost unlimited number of meanings. Nevertheless, in our opinion, the most compelling argument against anomalous lateralization as a cause or linguistic deficit is derived from studies of normal left-handers. Here we rely on an experiment of nature. It is known from clinical studies that the functional organization of the cerebrum in left-handers frequently deviates from the norm of left-hemisphere speech representation (e.g., Annett, 1975; Rasmussen & Milner, 1975; Satz, 1979). There is great divergence among estimates regarding the incidence of bilateral language in left-handers (cf. Rasmussen & Milner, 1975; Satz, 1979), but different investigators agree that language representation is either right hemisphere or bilateral in 30 to 70% of left-handers (as compared with 3 to 8% of right-handers). Consequently, if deviant language organization per se causes cognitive deficit , a large sample of normal left-handers should contain a sufficient number of disadvantaged individuals to lower the average score on tests of cognitive or linguistic skill (Kinsbourne & Hiscock, 1977). Although it has been reported that left-handers in fact show inferior performance relative to right-handers on certain cognitive tests (e.g., Levy, 1969), evidence from large samples of normal left-and right-handers fails to substantiate those reports (Hardyck, Petrinovitch, & Goldman, 1976; Briggs, Nebes, & Kinsbourne, 1976; Newcombe & Ratcliffe, 1973; Roberts & Engle, 1974). One may conclude, at least tentatively, that there is no substantial cognitive deficit associated with left-handedness. Consequently, there is no reason to assume that deviation from the most prevalent pattern of language representation has any implications for cognitive or linguistic development. It appears that, when the neural substrate is intact, various patterns of language lateralization are equally satisfactory for the development of language and cognitive ability. An elevated incidence of left-handedness in clinical populations (Harris, 1980) appears to be due to an associated difference *other* than anomalous lateralization. Some probably is secondary to prenatal brain damage that alters hand preference while limiting capacity for mental development (Satz, 1977; but see McManus, 1983, for a dissenting view). It could also reflect familial sinistrality as a risk factor for early brain damage causing cognitive deficit. In mental retardation both factors seem to operate (Bradshaw-McAnulty, Hicks, & Kinsbourne, 1984). We have discovered that, in dyslexia, regardless of the dyslexic probands' hand preference, they have significantly more non-right-handed relatives than do normally reading controls (Kinsbourne, 1986). This finding also calls for an explanation over and above the effect of "pathological left-handedness" (Satz, 1972).

It appears that right laterality, left laterality, and ambilaterality, whether for hand preference or for central language representation, are not markers for major differences in developing language skills. It still remains to consider inconsistent laterality. At least at the peripheral level, it can be observed that some children fail to hold constant the hand used for a given activity, and this action has been termed ambiguous handedness (Soper & Satz, 1984). It characterizes some very young normal children (Palmer, 1965) but also subgroups of mentally handicapped children at any age, notably children suffering from infantile autism (Satz et al., 1975). Failure to establish either right- or left-hand preference does have cognitive implications in autism, in that the subgroup without consistent hand preference is in general the lower-functioning subset of the autistic population (Fein, Skoff, & Mirsky, 1981). This does not, however, simply represent a greater degree of maturational delay, because older autistic individuals are just as likely not to have established hand preference as younger ones (Tsai, Jacoby, Stewart, & Beisler, 1982).

An obvious possible interpretation is that autistics can be subdivided into those with unilateral hemisphere damage and those damaged bilaterally (DeLong, 1978) and that the latter, without hand preference, are more disabled because more damaged. However, despite suggestive neuroimaging evidence (Hier, LeMay, & Rosenberger, 1974), neuropathological evidence for any cerebral damage at all in autism is strikingly lacking in the relevant autopsies that have been performed (Darby, 1976; Bauman & Kemper, 1985; Williams, Hauser, Purpura, DeLong, & Swisher, 1980). If, as seems highly likely, a brainstem disorder is responsible for autistic behavior (Damasio & Maurer, 1978), how might that bear on failure to lateralize cortical control of behavior?

There is indirect evidence that ascending influences from the brainstem are instrumental in setting up cerebral laterality. Ipsilateral relations between thalamus and cerebral hemisphere have been well documented (Ojemann, 1977). As has already been noted, asymmetries in infant behavior indicate that brainstem mechanisms must incorporate functional lateral asymmetry, for at that young age cerebral cognitive activity is minimal if present at all. Furthermore, the rightward bias in infant head turning is particularly sensitive to the condition of the infant at birth as determined by Apgar scores (Turkewitz, Moreau, & Birch, 1968). It appears that prenatal or perinatal insult to the nervous system tends to render the child bisymmetric in turning tendency. It is therefore possible that early brainstem malfunction can inactivate a mechanism that facilitates the establishment of cerebral laterality.

Ascending activation can be either deficient or excessive. There is some evidence that in autism certain arousal systems are overactive. In animal experimentation it has been shown that the effects on behavior of lateral cerebral damage can be minimized through sensory stimulation and stimulant drug administration (Wolgin, 1982). It may be that chronic hyperarousal in severe autism antagonizes the establishment of both peripheral and central laterality (Kinsbourne, in press).

Summary

Despite the long-standing popularity of claims that deviant cerebral lateralization is responsible for various cognitive and linguistic disorders in children, empirical support for such claims is unconvincing. Moreover, the concept of deviant lateralization is ambiguous. Studies of normal left-handers suggest that deviation from the norm of left-hemispheric language representation need not have deleterious consequences for cognitive function.

The structural basis for impaired language development

A substantial minority of children suffer from various degrees of inferiority in aspects of speech and language skills, ranging from articulation (e.g., stuttering) to reading (dyslexia). It remains a matter of controversy which of these maladaptive conditions represent specific disorders (presumably of left-hemisphere speech and language mechanisms) and which the lowest end of a normal distribution of verbal skills resulting from genetic diversity. Although stuttering between the ages of 4 and 6 is so frequent as to be regarded as a stage through which many normal children pass, some children continue to stutter, and it is disputed whether this is because they differ from the rest in some organic fashion or because environmental or emotional factors conspire to perpetuate what would otherwise have been a transient defect. With respect to reading acquisition, it is difficult to draw the line between mediocre readers and children who experience such extreme difficulty that they must be regarded as qualitatively different, namely, dyslexic. It is remarkably hard to teach some children to read, and a simple estimate of the number of years by which their reading age lags behind their chronological age may do less than justice to that difficulty. It is when the child remains several years behind in spite of intense and individualized remedial efforts, both in the school system and in special institutions, that the term *dyslexia* is most applicable and the child is a suitable subject for studies of this condition. Nevertheless, it remains difficult to distinguish dyslexics from poor readers (or even younger normal readers at a comparable achievement level) by any qualitative aspect of their reading and writing performance, by measurement of reading-related subskills (Olsen, Kliegl, Davidson, & Foltz, 1985), or indeed by any concomitant pattern of psychometric or neuropsychological test performance. There is thus an understandable focus of investigative attention on possible biological concomitants or markers that might distinguish those children whose language is based on definite, even structural, impairments in language cortex.

The problem is complicated by the fact that nothing definite is known about the neurohistology of individual differences in intellectual skill within the normal population (Hiscock & Mackay, 1985). Although some theorists, whose ideas we shall shortly discuss, find it plausible to suppose that large cortical masses, more densely populated with well-organized neurons, underlie more efficient intellectual performance for whatever function is localized in that cerebral area, there are no data either to support this view or to contradict it. Thus, it might be that the minor evidence of anomalous cortical development that we shall cite is irrelevant to the problem of developmental language disorder. Conversely, however, it might be that even the wide range of language skills in the ostensibly normal population is contributed by brain differences that neuropathologists could readily and reliably discern. There has been widespread reluctance to adopt such a view, because of the large number of children held to be dyslexic and appearing otherwise to be quite normal. It seems gratuitous to label this substantial childhood population brain-damaged solely on rather restricted behavioral grounds. Nonetheless, in a major theoretical article, Geschwind and Galaburda (1985) present an explicit and uncompromisingly brain-based perspective on a wide range of behavioral phenomena, with language function and hand preference as central variables. They summarize their views about the causes of impaired speech and language development in some individuals (dysphasics, dyslexics, stutterers, autistics), relying on evidence for a disproportionate incidence of non-right-handedness ("anomalous dominance") in each. On the basis of preliminary evidence from neuroimaging in vivo (Hier, LeMay, Rosenberger, & Perlo, 1978) and from postmortem studies of cortical cytoarchitectonics (Galaburda, Sherman, Rosen, Aboitiz, & Geschwind, 1985), they relate dyslexia to inferior development of the left temporal planum, by cellular dysgenesis in that area. They imply that this could also be related to the appearance of non-right-handedness. Such left-sided inadequacy results in either or perhaps both of the following: (1) impaired verbal performance, (2) bilateralization of language representation (and weakened right-hand preference). They further suggest that the hypothesized left-hemisphere underdevelopment releases the right hemisphere for corresponding overdevelopment, and this, they further suppose, is apt to lead to the development of superior right-hemisphere cognitive skills. The right hemisphere, according to Geschwind and Galaburda, is not equally subject to these adverse outcomes, for two reasons. First, it matures earlier, reducing the window of time during which it is vulnerable to external damaging factors (assuming that immaturity increases vulnerability). Second, endogenous influences that might similarly constrain the maturation of the right hemisphere have not been suggested.

The theory accounts for a number of hitherto unexplained facts and also instigates a diversity of further claims. The alleged female superiority in verbal skill is accounted for by a relatively low level of testosterone in that sex. Male spatial superiority finds explanation in right-hemisphere hyperdevelopment secondary to the testosterone-related left-sided maturational delay. Allegedly superior right-hemisphere skills of dyslexics of either sex (Gordon, 1980, 1983) would represent an extreme instance of this hemispheric imbalance of development. The greater incidence of left-handedness among males than females and among people with language pathology than among those without is similarly attributed to left-hemisphere impairment, in this instance affecting the left-sided motor control area as well as the language area. Because these two areas are adjacent, there will be some coincidence of language delay and shift to non-right-handedness, but the two would not necessarily be perfectly correlated. Gender differences in the incidence of a wide range of allegedly left-hemisphere-based developmental disorders are also accounted for.

Based as it is on tenuous evidence and pilot data, this far-ranging and imaginative theory should, as the authors repeatedly insist, be treated as a heuristic or blueprint for a program of research rather than as a currently defensible construct. It certainly generates a rich set of testable predictions. Some, however, tend to be irrefutable. The implied reciprocity between verbal and spatial skills does not appear to be evident in the general population. However, one could argue that it is present but obscured by a general cerebral competence factor that controls levels of intellectual potential in both these cognitive domains. Anatomically, the theory generates the prediction that the proportionate anatomical extent of relative hemispheric areas will parallel an individual's relative skill in verbal and spatial domains. And yet Geschwind and Galaburda point out that in the very cases in which structurally apparent neuropathology has been reported and incriminated in the dyslexic deficit, the territory within which these anomalies were found was by no means contracted and would not be expected to appear diminished in bulk radiologically. Thus, a failure to find "reversed asymmetry" (e.g., of right vs. left temporal territory) in dyslexics (see Haslam, Dalby, Johns, & Rademaker, 1981) would not refute the principle of size–skill correlations. Negative findings could simply be attributed to inclusion in the sample of just such cases as Galaburda and colleagues have reported. A prediction that seems explicit and quantifiable arises from the hypothesized role of testosterone in generating the disorder of left-hemisphere development. And yet, if on studying the relationship no simple inverse correlation between testosterone levels and language development were found, this could be, as Geschwind and Galaburda point out, because some individuals are genetically more vulnerable than others to the left-hemisphere arresting effect of testosterone. There would be no externally objective way of determining who those individuals might be. As for the different role of the right hemisphere, this too is open to some ambiguity. Although one consequence of right-hemisphere damage – unilateral neglect of space – appears to be as lateralized in left- as in right-handers (as one would expect from the Geschwind and Galaburda theory), in other respects there is a more balanced distribution of spatial deficit between hemispheres in the left-handed unilaterally brain-damaged group (Bryden, Hecaen, & DeAgostini, 1983). But then one could argue that some of these spatial skills are really ones that either hemisphere could subserve.

Some facts that the theory explains may not be facts at all. The supposed verbal superiority of females is elusive, except in childhood (see Hiscock & Mackay, 1985). The earlier maturation of the right hemisphere on which the theory heavily relies is based on literature that is itself highly speculative (Corballis & Morgan, 1978, and associated commentaries). The idea that impairment of left-hemisphere maturation releases the right hemisphere to perfect its role in spatial processing fits poorly with the language bilateralization that is known to result often from early left-brain damage. Nor does it square with the work of Woods (1980a) cited in an earlier section, which found that early left damage impairs skills proper to both hemispheres. Does "disinhibiting" the right hemisphere release it to enhance its spatial role or to assume a compensatory verbal role? If both these alternatives are possible, there is a need for some guidelines in making objective predictions of when the one consequence is to be expected and when the other.

In the context of previous approaches, the Geschwind and Galaburda theory exemplifies a strong form of the pathological left-handedness model (Satz, 1972, 1973). The left-handers so classified are regarded as genotypic dextrals who manifest a sinistral phenotype because of minor but strategically located left-hemisphere damage. That same damage is held responsible for a wide range of anomalies of left-hemisphere development, which manifest more than chance association with non-right-handed phenotype. Whereas in the past theorists have thought mainly in terms of gross structural damage of the left hemisphere, particularly damage sustained perinatally, bringing about the pathological left-handed state, it is not logically restricted to that kind of pathogenesis, and Geschwind and Galaburda broaden the range of possibilities by stressing not only prenatal adverse influences from the exterior, but also the body's own testosterone as a potentially toxic agent.

A second point of similarity between the Geschwind–Galaburda theory and previous theories is the assumption that brain pathology underlies abnormal language development. Geschwind and Galaburda firmly align themselves with those who regard dyslexia and other developmental language disorders as organic disease entities. From their findings of well-defined abnormalities in each of four consecutive brains of dyslexics coming to autopsy, they infer that such changes should be demonstrable in the wide range of dyslexic individuals. If one accepts prevalent estimates of dyslexia as approaching 5% of the childhood population, this is indeed more childhood neuropathology than most have bargained for. In any case, evidence that the foci of cellular cerebral dysgenesis found in dyslexics' brains are of pathological significance awaits the examination of control brains of normally reading individuals.

Third, the authors align themselves with the view that, whereas right-handedness is genetically determined, left-handedness is not. Instead, there is a continuum of non-right-handedness varying in the extent of deviation from the right-handed prototype. This view corresponds to that of Annett (1970). That those deviations are caused by pathological influences was proposed by Bakan (1971). Although Geschwind and Galaburda disclaim as extreme a view as Bakan's, if testosterone is regarded as a pathological influence, it is difficult to see any difference in principle between the two approaches.

Perhaps the most poorly documented of all links in the argument is the view that testosterone exerts the critical effect on left-hemisphere maturation that is attributed to it. That it does so is inferred mainly from the gender differences in incidences of language disorders and in patterns of cognitive skill. The notion that endocrine influences can modify the development of the cortical network does receive support from other areas of research, but this particular mechanism is speculative. At any rate, a distinction should be made between this claim and the general biological approach that Geschwind and Galaburda espouse, because the latter may well remain valid even if the influence of testosterone cannot be confirmed.

Summary

As an alternative to attributing developmental disorders of cognition and language to anomalous cerebral organization (e.g., anomalous lateralization), one may speculate that these disorders stem from a defect in the neural substrate itself. Even if mental functions are represented in the usual sites within the cerebral cortex, the structure of the brain at some of these sites may be abnormal. Taking this approach, Geschwind and Galaburda (1985) have constructed a comprehensive biological model for the development of handedness and language function as well as other behavioral characteristics. According to this model, the left hemisphere is especially vulnerable to damage from various factors, including endogenous testosterone. Both left-handedness and linguistic disabilities are linked to underdevelopment of the language region of the left hemisphere with concomitant overdevelopment of the right hemisphere.

The Geschwind–Galaburda model explains various extant observations and provides numerous testable hypotheses. However, some of the observations are of dubious validity, and some of the hypotheses seem framed in such a manner as to be irrefutable. The model incorporates older concepts – such as pathological left-handedness and the presence of neuropathology in dyslexia – that remain controversial. The validity of Geschwind and Galaburda's model hinges on the putative influence of testosterone on left-hemisphere development, yet their general approach may prove useful even if the particulars of their argument prove to be wrong.

References

Ajuriaguerra, J. de (1957). Language et dominance cerebrale. *Journal Francais d'Oto-Rhino-Laryngologie, 6*, 489–99.

Annett, M. (1970). A classification of hand preference by association analysis. *British Journal of Psychology, 61*, 303–21.

Annett, M. (1975). The reliability of difference between the hands in motor skill. *Neuropsychologia, 12*, 527–31.

Bakan, P. (1971). Handedness and birth order. *Nature, 229*, 195.

Basser, S. (1962). Hemiplegia of early onset and the faculty of speech with special reference to the effects of hemispherectomy. *Brain, 85*, 427–60.

Bates, E., O'Connell, B., Vaid, J., Sledge, P., & Oakes, L. (1985). *Language and hand preference in early development.* Paper presented to the Society for Research in Child Development, Toronto.

Bauman, M., & Kemper, T. L. (1985). Histoanatomic observations of the brain in early infantile autism. *Neurology, 35*, 866–74.

Benton, A. L. (1974). Clinical neuropsychology of childhood: An overview. In R. M. Reitan & L. A. Davison (Eds.), *Clinical neuropsychology: Current status and applications* (Vol. 13, p. 417). Washington, DC: Winston.

Berlin, C. I., Hughes, L. F., Lowe-Bell, S. S., & Berlin, H. L. (1973). Dichotic right ear advantages in children 5–13. *Cortex, 9*, 394–402.

Best, C. T., Hoffman, H., & Glanville, B. B. (1982). Development of infant ear asymmetries for speech and music. *Perception and Psychophysics, 35*, 75–85.

Bishop, D. V. (1983). Linguistic impairment after left hemidecortication for infantile hemiplegia? A reappraisal. *Quarterly Journal of Experimental Psychology: Human Experimental Psychology, 35A*, 199–207.

Bradshaw-McAnulty, G., Hicks, R. E., & Kinsbourne, M. (1984). Pathological left-handedness and familial sinistrality in relation to degree of mental retardation. *Brain and Cognition, 3*, 349–56.

Briggs, G. G., Nebes, R. D., & Kinsbourne, M. (1976). Intellectual differences in relation to personal and family handedness. *Quarterly Journal of Experimental Psychology, 28*, 591–601.

Brown, J. W., & Hecaen, H. (1976). Lateralization and language representation: Observations on aphasia in children, left-handers, and "anomalous" dextrals. *Neurology (Minneapolis), 26*, 183–8.

Bryden, M. P., & Allard, F. A. (1978). Dichotic listening and the development of linguistic processes. In M. Kinsbourne (Ed.), *Asymmetrical function of the brain* (pp. 392–404). Cambridge University Press.

Bryden, M. P., Hecaen, H., & DeAgostini, M. (1983). Patterns of cerebral organization. *Brain and Language, 20*, 249–62.

Caplan, P. J., & Kinsbourne, M. (1976). Baby drops the rattle: Asymmetry of duration of grasp by infants. *Child Development, 47*, 532–4.

Chi, J. G., Dooling, E. C., & Gilles, F. H. (1977). Gyral development of the human brain. *Annals of Neurology, 1*, 86–93.

Corballis, M. C. (1983). *Human laterality.* New York: Academic Press.

Corballis, M. C., & Morgan, M. J. (1978). On the biological basis of human laterality: I. Evidence for a maturational left–right gradient. *Behavioral and Brain Sciences, 2*, 261–336.

Coryell, J., & Michel, G. (1978). How supine postural preferences of infants can contribute toward the development of handedness. *Infant Behavior and Development 1*, 245–57.

Critchley, M. (1970). *The dyslexic child.* London: Heinemann.

Crowell, D. H., Jones, R. H., Kapuniai, L. E., & Nakagawa, J. K. (1973). Unilateral cortical activity in newborn humans: An early index of cerebral dominance. *Science, 180*, 205–8.

Damasio, A. R., & Maurer, R. G. (1978). A neurological model for childhood autism. *Archives of Neurology, 35*, 777–86.

Darby, J. K. (1976). Neuropathologic aspects of psychosis in childhood. *Journal of Autism and Child Schizophrenia, 6*, 339–52.

Davis, A. E., & Wada, J. A. (1977). Hemispheric asymmetries in human infants: Spectral analysis of flash and click evoked potentials. *Brain and Language, 4*, 22–31.

Davis, A. E., & Wada, J. A. (1978). Speech dominance and handedness in the normal human. *Brain and Language, 5*, 42–55.

DeLong, G. R. (1978). A neuropsychologic interpretation of infantile autism. In M. Rutter & E. Schopler (Eds.), *Autism: A reappraisal of concepts and treatment*. New York: Plenum.

Dennis, M. (1977a). Cerebral dominance in three forms of early brain disorder. In M. Blaw, I. Rapin, & M. Kinsbourne (Eds.), *Topics in child neurology* (pp. 189–212). New York: Spectrum.

Dennis, M. (1977b). Impaired sensory and motor differentiation with corpus callosum agenesis: A lack of callosal inhibition during ontogeny? *Neuropsychologia, 14*, 455–9.

Dennis, M. (1980a). Capacity and strategy for syntactic comprehension after left or right hemidecortication. *Brain and Language, 10*, 287–317.

Dennis, M. (1980b). Language acquisition in a single hemisphere: Semantic organization. In D. Caplan (Ed.), *Biological studies of mental processes* (pp. 159–85). Cambridge, MA: MIT Press.

Dennis, M. (1980c). Strokes in childhood. I: Cummunicative intent, expression, and comprehension after left hemisphere arteriopathy in a right-handed nine-year-old. In R. Rieber (Ed.), *Language development and aphasia in children* (pp. 45–67). New York: Academic Press.

Dennis, M., & Kohn, B. (1975). Comprehension of syntax in infantile hemiplegics after cerebral hemidecortication: Left-hemisphere superiority. *Brain and Language, 2*, 475–86.

Dennis, M., Lovett, M., & Wiegel-Crump, C. A. (1981). Written language acquisition after left or right hemidecortication in infancy. *Brain and Language, 2*, 475–86.

Dennis, M., & Whitaker, H. A. (1976). Language acquisition following hemi-decortication: Linguistic superiority of the left over the right hemisphere. *Brain and Language, 3*, 404–33.

Dennis, M., & Whitaker, H. A. (1977). Hemispheric equipotentiality and language acquisition. In S. J. Segalowitz & F. A. Gruber (Eds.), *Language development and neurological theory* (pp. 93–106). New York: Academic Press.

DeRenzi, E., & Vignolo, L. A. (1962). The Token Test: A sensitive test to detect disturbances in aphasics. *Brain, 85*, 655–78.

DiFranco, D., Muir, D., & Dodwell, P. C. (1978). Reaching in very young infants. *Perception, 7*, 385–92.

Doehring, D. G., Reitan, R. M., & Klove, H. (1961). Changes in patterns of intellectual test performance associated with homonymous visual field defects. *Journal of Nervous and Mental Disease, 123*, 227–33.

Entus, A. K. (1977). Hemispheric asymmetry in processing of dichotically presented speech and non-speech stimuli by infants. In S. J. Segalowitz & F. A. Gruber (Eds.), *Language development and neurological theory*. New York: Academic Press.

Fedio, P., & Mirsky, A. F. (1969). Selective intellectual deficits in children with temporal lobe or centrencephalic epilepsy. *Neuropsychologia, 7*, 287–300.

Fein, D., Skoff, B., & Mirsky, A. F. (1981). Clinical correlates of brainstem dysfunction in autistic children. *Journal of Autism and Developmental Disorders, 11*, 303–15.

Fitzhugh, L. C., & Fitzhugh, K. B. (1964). Relationships between WB and WAIS performance of Ss with longstanding cerebral dysfunction. *Perceptual and Motor Skills, 10*, 539–43.

Gaddes, W. H., & Crockett, D. J. (1975). The Spreen–Benton Aphasia Tests, normative data as a measure of normal language development. *Brain and Language, 2*, 257–80.

Galaburda, A. M. (1984). Anatomical asymmetries. In N. Geschwind & A. L. Galaburda (Eds.), *Cerebral dominance: The biological foundations* (pp. 11–25). Cambridge, MA: Harvard University Press.

Galaburda, A. M., Sherman, G. F., Rosen, G. D., Aboitiz, F., & Geschwind, N. (1985). Developmental dyslexia: Four consecutive patients with cortical anomalies. *Annals of Neurology, 18*, 222–33.

Gardiner, M. F., & Walter, D. O. (1977). Evidence of hemispheric specialization from infant EEG. In S. Harnad, R. W. Doty, L. Goldstein, J. Jaynes, & G. Krauthamer (Eds.), *Lateralization in the nervous system* (pp. 481–502). New York: Academic Press.

Gazzaniga, M. S., & Hillyard, S. A. (1973). Attention mechanisms following brain bisection. In S. Kornblum (Ed.), *Attention and performance* (Vol. 4, pp. 221–38). New York: Academic Press.

Geffen, G. (1978). The development of the right ear advantage in dichotic listening with focused attention. *Cortex, 14*, 11–17.

Gersten, J. W., Jung, A., & Brooks, C. (1972). Perceptual deficits in patients with left and right hemiparesis. *American Journal of Physiological Medicine, 51*, 79–85.

Geschwind, N., & Galaburda, A. M. (1985). Cerebral lateralization. Biological mechanisms, association and pathology: I. A hypothesis and a program for research. *Archives of Neurology, 42*, 428–59.

Geschwind, N., & Levitsky, W. (1968). Human brain: Left–right asymmetries in temporal speech regions. *Science, 161*, 181–7.

Gesell, A. (1938). The tonic neck reflex in the human infant. *Journal of Pediatrics, 13*, 455–64.

Gesell, A., & Ames, L. B. (1950). Tonic neck reflex and symmetrotonic behavior. *Journal of Pediatrics, 35*, 165–78.

Glanville, B. B., Best, C. T., & Levenson, R. A. (1977). Cardiac measure of cerebral asymmetries in infant auditory preception. *Developmental Psychology, 13*, 55–9.

Goldman, P. S. (1974). An alternative to developmental plasticity: Heterology of CNS structures in infants and adults. In D. G. Stein, J. J. Rosen, & N. Butters (Eds.), *Plasticity and recovery of function in the nervous system*. New York: Academic Press.

Goodglass, H. (1973). Developmental comparisons of vowels and consonants in dichotic listening. *Journal of Speech and Hearing Research, 16*, 744–52.

Goodglass, H., & Kaplan, E. (1983). *The assessment of aphasia and related disorders*. Philadelphia: Lea & Febiger.

Gordon, H. W. (1980a). Cognitive asymmetry in dyslexic families. *Neuropsychologia, 18*, 645–56.

Gordon, H. W. (1980b). Right hemisphere comprehension of verbs in patients with complete forebrain commissurotomy: Use of dichotic method and manual performance. *Brain and Language, 11*, 76–86.

Gordon, H. W. (1983). Learning disabled are cognitively right. In M. Kinsbourne (Ed.), *Topics in Learning Disabilities* (Vol. 3, pp. 29–39). Gaithersburg, MD: Aspen Systems.

Hardyck, C., Petrinovitch, L., & Goldman, R. (1976). Left handedness and cognitive deficit. *Cortex, 12*, 266–79.

Harris, A. J. (1979). Lateral dominance and reading disability. *Journal of Learning Disabilities, 12*, 57–63.

Harris, L. J. (1980). Left-handedness: Early theories, facts and fancies. In J. Herron (Ed.), *Neuropsychology of left-handedness*. New York: Academic Press.

Haslam, R. H. A., Dalby, J. T., Johns, R. D., & Rademaker, A. W. (1981). Cerebral asymmetry in developmental dyslexia. *Archives of Neurology, 38*, 679–82.

Hawn, P. R., & Harris, L. J. (1983). Hand differences in grasp duration and reaching in two- and five-month-old human infants. In G. Young, S. J. Segalowitz, M. Carter, & S. E. Trehub (Eds.), *Manual specialization and the developing brain* (pp. 331–48). New York: Academic Press.

Hecaen, H. (1976). Acquired aphasia in children and the ontogenesis of hemispheric functional specialization. *Brain and Language, 3*, 114–34.

Hecaen, H. (1983). Acquired aphasia in children: Revisited. *Neuropsychologia, 21*, 581–7.

Hier, D. B., LeMay, M., & Rosenberger, P. B. (1974). Autism and unfavorable left–right asymmetries of the brain. *Journal of Autism and Developmental Disorders, 9*, 153–9.

Hier, D. B., LeMay, M., Rosenberger, P. B., & Perlo, V. P. (1978). Development dyslexia: Evidence for a subgroup with reversal of cerebral asymmetry. *Archives of Neurology, 35*, 90–2.

Hillier, W. F. (1954). Total left hemispherectomy for malignant glioma. *Neurology, 4*, 718–21.

Hiscock, M. (1982). Verbal–manual timesharing in children as a function of task priority. *Brain and Cognition, 1*, 119–31.

Hiscock, M. (1983). Do learning disabled children lack functional hemispheric specification? *Topics in Learning and Learning Disabilities, 3*, 14–28.

Hiscock, M., Antoniuk, D., Prisciak, K., & von Hessert, D. (1985). Generalized and lateralized interference between concurrent tasks performed by children: Effects of age, sex and skill. *Developmental Neuropsychology, 1*, 29–48.

Hiscock, M., & Kinsbourne, M. (1977). Selective listening asymmetry in preschool children. *Developmental Psychology, 13*, 217–24.

Hiscock, M., & Kinsbourne, M. (1978). Ontogeny of cerebral dominance: Evidence from time-sharing asymmetry in children. *Developmental Psychology, 16*, 70–82.

Hiscock, M., & Kinsbourne, M. (1980a). Asymmetries of selective listening and attention switching in children. *Developmental Psychology, 16*, 70–82.

Hiscock, M., & Kinsbourne, M. (1980b). Asymmetry of verbal–manual timesharing in children: A follow-up study. *Neuropsychologia, 18*, 151–62.

Hiscock, M., & Kinsbourne, M. (1982). Laterality and dyslexia: A critical review. *Annals of Dyslexia, 32*, 177–228.

Hiscock, M., & Kinsbourne, M. (1987). Specialization of the cerebral hemispheres: implications for learning. *Journal of Learning Disabilities, 20*, 130–43.

Hiscock, M., Kinsbourne, M., Samuels, M., & Krause, A. E. (1987). Dual task performance in children: Generalized and lateralized effects of memory encoding upon the rate and variability of concurrent finger tapping. *Brain and Cognition, 6*, 24–40.

Hiscock, M., & Mackay, M. (1985). Neuropsychological approaches to the study of individual differences. In C. Reynolds and V. Willson (Eds.), *Methodological and statistical advances in the study of individual differences* (pp. 117–76). New York: Plenum.

Hiscock, M., & Stewart, C. (1984). The effect of asymmetrically focused attention upon subsequent ear differences in dichotic listening. *Neuropsychologia, 22*, 337–51.

Hoffman, H. J., Hendrick, E. B., Dennis, M., & Armstrong, D. (1979). Hemispherectomy for Sturge–Weber syndrome. *Child's Brain, 5*, 233–48.

Hynd, G. W., & Obrzut, J. E. (1977). Effects of grade level and sex on the magnitude of the dichotic ear advantage. *Neuropsychologia, 15*, 689–92.

Inglis, J., Lawson, M., Maclean, A. W., & Monga, T. N. (1982). Sex differences in the cognitive effects of unilateral brain damage. *Cortex, 18*, 257–76.

Jacobs, J. (1977). An external view of neuropsychology and its working milieu. In S. J. Segalowitz & F. A. Gruber (Eds.), *Language development and neurological theory* (pp. 155–63). New York: Academic Press.

Jones, R. K. (1966). Observations on stammering after localized cerebral injury. *Journal of Neurology, Neurosurgery and Psychiatry, 29*, 192–5.

Kimura, D. (1963). Speech lateralization in young children as determined by an auditory test. *Journal of Comparative and Physiological Psychology, 16*, 355–8.

Kimura, D. (1967). Functional asymmetry of the brain in dichotic listening. *Cortex, 3*, 163–7.

Kinsbourne, M. (1972). Eye and head turning indicates cerebral lateralization. *Science, 176*, 539–41.

Kinsbourne, M. (1973). School problems. *Pediatrics, 52*, 697–710.

Kinsbourne, M. (1980). A model for the ontogeny of cerebral organization in non-right-handers. In J. Herron (Ed.), *Neuropsychology of left-handedness*, (pp. 177–83). New York: Academic Press.

Kinsbourne, M. (1986, October). *Sinistrality and risk for immune diseases and learning disorders*. Paper presented at the meeting of the Child Neurology Society, Boston, MA.

Kinsbourne, M. (in press). Cerebral–brainstem interactions in infantile autism. In E. Schopler and G. Mesibov (Eds.), *Neurobiological theories of arousal and autism*. New York: Plenum.

Kinsbourne, M., & Hiscock, M. (1977). Does cerebral dominance develop? In S. J. Segalowitz & F. A. Gruber (Eds.), *Language development and neurological theory*. New York: Academic Press.

Kinsbourne, M., & Hiscock, M. (1983). Asymmetries of dual task performance. In J. B. Hellige (Ed.), *Cerebral functional asymmetry: Theory, measurement and application*. New York: Praeger.

Kinsbourne, M., & McMurray, J. (1975). The effect of cerebral dominance on timesharing between speaking and tapping by preschool children. *Child Development, 46*, 240–2.

Klove, H. (1974). Validation studies in clinical neuropsychology. In R. M. Reitan & L. A. Davison (Eds.), *Clinical neuropsychology: Current concepts, status and applications*. Washington, DC: Winston.

Klove, H., & Reitan, R. M. (1958). Effects of dysphasia and spatial distortion on Wechsler–Bellevue results. *Archives of Neurology and Psychiatry, 80*, 708–31.

Knox, C., & Kimura, D. (1970). Cerebral processing of nonverbal sounds in boys and girls. *Neuropsychologia, 8*, 227–37.

Kohn, B., & Dennis, M. (1974). Selective impairments of visuo-spatial abilities in infantile hemiplegics after right hemidecortication. *Neuropsychologia, 12*, 505–12.

Krashen, S. D. (1973). Lateralization, language learning and the critical period: Some new evidence. *Language Learning, 23*, 63–74.

Landsdell, H. (1969). Verbal and nonverbal factors in right-hemisphere speech: Relation to early neurological history. *Journal of Comparative and Physiological Psychology, 69*, 734–8.

Lempert, H., & Kinsbourne, M. (1985). Possible origin of speech in selective orienting. *Psychological Bulletin, 97*, 62–73.

Lenneberg, E. H. (1967). *Biological foundations of language*. New York: Wiley.

Levy, J. (1969). Possible basis for the evolution of lateral specialization of the human brain. *Nature, 224*, 614–15.

Liederman, J. (1983a). Mechanisms underlying instability in the development of hand preference. In G. Young, S. Segalowitz, C. M. Carter, & S. Trehub (Eds.), *Manual specialization and the developing brain* (pp. 71–89). New York: Academic Press.

Liederman, J. (1983b). Is there a left-sided precocity during early manual specialization? In G. Young, S. J. Segalowitz, C. M. Carter, & S. E. Trehub (Eds.), *Manual specialization and the developing brain* (pp. 321–9). New York: Academic Press.

Liederman, J., & Kinsbourne, M. (1980). The mechanism of neonatal rightward turning bias: A sensory or motor asymmetry? *Infant Behavior and Development, 3*, 223–38.

McDonnell, P. M., Anderson, V. E. S., & Abraham, W. C. (1983). Asymmetry and orientation of arm movement in three- to eight-week-old infants. *Infant Behavior and Development, 6*, 287–98.

McFie, J. (1961). The effects of hemispherectomy on intellectual functioning in cases of infantile hemiplegia. *Journal of Neurology, Neurosurgery and Psychiatry, 24*, 240–9.

MacKain, K., Studdert-Kennedy, M., Spieker, S., & Stern, D. (1983). Infant intermodal speech perception is a left hemisphere function. *Science, 214*, 1347–9.

McManus, I. C. (1983). Pathologic left-handedness: Does it exist? *Journal of Communication Disorders, 16*, 315–44.

Meier, M. J. (1970). Objective behavioral assessment in diagnosis and prediction. In A. L. Benton (Ed.), *Behavioral change in cerebral–vascular disease*. New York: Harper & Row.

Meier, M. J., & French, L. A. (1966). Longitudinal assessment of intellectual functioning following unilateral temporal lobectomy. *Journal of Clinical Psychology, 22*, 22–7.

Meyer, H., & Jones, H. F. (1959). Patterns of cognitive test performance as functions of the lateral localization of cerebral abnormalities in the temporal lobe. *Journal of Mental Science, 103*, 758–72.

Michel, G. F. (1981). Right handedness: A consequence of infant supine head orientation preference? *Science, 212*, 385–7.

Michel, G. F. (1983). Development of hand-use preference in infancy. In G. Young, S. J. Segalowitz, C. M. Carter, & S. Trehub (Eds.), *Manual specialization and the developing brain*. New York: Academic Press.

Milner, B. (1969). Residual intellectual and memory deficits after head injury. In E. Walker, W. Caveness, & M. Critchley (Eds.), *The late effects of head injury*. Springfield, IL: Thomas.

Molfese, D. L., Freeman, R. B., & Palermo, D. (1975). The ontogeny of brain lateralization for speech and non-speech stimuli. *Brain and Language, 2*, 356–68.

Molfese, D. L., & Molfese, V. J. (1979). Hemisphere and stimulus differences as reflected in the cortical responses of newborn infants to speech stimuli. *Developmental Psychology, 15*, 505–11.

Molfese, D. L., & Molfese, V. J. (1980). Cortical responses of preterm infants to phonetic and nonphonetic speech stimuli. *Developmental Psychology, 16*, 574–81.

Molfese, D. L., & Molfese, V. J. (1983). Hemispheric specialization in infancy. In G. Young, S. J. Segalowitz, C. M. Carter, & S. E. Trehub (Eds.), *Manual specialization and the developing brain*. New York: Academic Press.

Morris, R., Bakker, D., Satz, P., & van der Vlugt, H. (1984). Dichotic listening ear asymmetry: Patterns of longitudinal development. *Brain and Language, 22*, 49–66.

Nagafuchi, M. (1970). Development of dichotic and monaural hearing abilities in young children. *Acta Otolaryngologia, 69*, 409–14.

National Institutes of Health and National Institutes of Neurological Disease and Blindness (1965). *Collaborative study of cerebral palsy, mental retardation, and other neurologic and sensory disorders of infancy and childhood* (Research Profile No. 11, Public Health Service Publication No. 1370). Bethesda, MD.

Naylor, H. (1980). Reading disability and lateral asymmetry: An information processing analysis. *Psychological Bulletin, 87*, 531–45.

Newcombe, F., & Ratcliffe, G. (1973). Handedness, speech lateralization and ability. *Neuropsychologia, 11*, 399–407.

Oakes, L. (1985). *The relationship between early handedness and language development.* Unpublished manuscript.

Obrzut, J. E., Hynd, G. W., Obrzut, A., & Leitgeb, J. L. (1980). Time sharing and dichotic listening asymmetry in normal and learning-disabled children. *Brain and Language, 11*, 181–94.

Ojemann, G. A. (1977). Asymmetric function of the thalamus. *Annals of the New York Academy of Sciences, 299*, 380–96.

Oldfield, R. C., & Wingfield, A. (1964). The time it takes to name an object. *Nature (London), 202*, 1031–2.

Olsen, R. K., Kliegl, R., Davidson, B. J., & Foltz, G. (1985). Individual and developmental differences in reading disability. In T. G. Waller (Ed.), *Reading research: Advances in theory and practice.* New York: Academic Press.

Orton, S. T. (1937). *Reading, writing and speech problems in childhood.* New York: Norton.

Palmer, R. D. (1965). Development of differentiated handedness. *Psychological Bulletin, 62*, 257–72.

Petrie, B. N., & Peters, M. (1980). Handedness: Left/right differences in intensity of grasp response and duration of rattle holding in infants. *Infant Behavior and Development, 3*, 215–21.

Piazza, D. M. (1977). Cerebral lateralization in young children as measured by dichotic listening and finger tapping tasks. *Neuropsychologia, 15*, 417–25.

Ramsay, D. S. (1979). Manual preference for tapping in infants. *Developmental Psychology, 15*, 437–42.

Ramsay, D. S. (1980). Onset of unimanual handedness in infants. *Infant Behaviour and Development, 3*, 377.

Ramsay, D. S. (1984). Onset of duplicated syllable babbling and unimanual handedness in infancy: Evidence for developmental change in hemispheric specialization: *Developmental Psychology, 20*, 64–71.

Ramsay, D. S., Campos, J. J., & Fenson, L. (1979). Onset of bimanual handedness in infants. *Infant Behavior and Development, 2*, 69–75.

Rasmussen, T., & Milner, B. (1975). Clinical and surgical studies of the cerebral speech areas in man. In K. J. Zulch, O. Creutzfeldt, & G. Galbraith (Eds.), *Otfrid Foerster symposium on cerebral localization.* New York: Springer-Verlag.

Reed, J. C., & Reitan, R. M. (1969). Verbal and performance differences among brain-injured children with lateralized motor deficits. *Perceptual and Motor Skills, 29*, 747–52.

Reitan, R. M. (1955). Certain differential effects of left and right cerebral lesions in human adults. *Journal of Comparative and Physiological Psychology, 48*, 474–7.

Reitan, R. M., & Davison, L. A. (1974). *Clinical neuropsychology: Current status and applications.* New York: Winston/Wiley.

Roberts, J., & Engle, A. (1974). Family background, early development, and intelligence of children 6-11 years. In *National Center for Health statistics, data from national health survey* (Series II, No. 142, DHEW No. [HRA] 75–1624). Washington, DC: U. S. Government Printing Office.

Russell, W. R., & Espir, M. L. (1961). *Traumatic aphasia: A study of aphasia in war wounds of the brain.* New York: Oxford University Press.

Satz, P. (1966). Specific and nonspecific effects of brain lesions in man. *Journal of Abnormal Psychology, 71,* 65–70.

Satz, P. (1972). Pathological left-handedness: An explanatory model. *Cortex, 8,* 121–35.

Satz, P. (1973). Left-handedness and early brain insult: An explanation. *Neuropsychologia, 11,* 115–17.

Satz, P. (1976). Cerebral dominance and reading disability: An old problem revisited. In R. M. Knights & D. J. Bakker (Eds.), *The neuropsychology of learning disorders.* Baltimore, MD: University Park Press.

Satz, P. (1978). Laterality tests: An inferential problem. *Cortex, 13,* 208–12.

Satz, P. (1979). A test of some models of hemispheric speech organization in the left- and right-handed. *Science, 203,* 1131–3.

Satz, P., Bakker, D. J., Teunisson, J., Goebel, R., & van der Vlugt, H. (1975). Developmental parameters of the ear asymmetry: A multivariate approach. *Brain and Language, 2,* 171–85.

Searleman, A. (1977). A review of right hemisphere linguistic capabilities. *Psychological Bulletin, 84,* 503–8.

Segalowitz, S. J., & Chapman, J. S. (1980). Cerebral asymmetry for speech in neonates: A behavioral measure. *Brain and Language, 9,* 281–8.

Shucard, J. L., Shucard, D. W., Cummins, K. R., & Campos, J. J. (1981). Auditory evoked potentials and sex-related differences in brain development. *Brain and Language, 13,* 91–102.

Shulman-Galambos, C. (1977). Dichotic listening performance in elementary and college students. *Neuropsychologia, 15,* 577–84.

Siqueland, E. R., & Lipsitt, L. P. (1966). Conditioned head turning in human newborns. *Journal of Experimental Child Psychology, 4,* 356–7.

Silver, A. A., & Hagin, R. A. (1982). A unifying concept for the neuropsychological organization of children with reading disability. *Journal of Developmental and Behavioral Pediatrics, 3,* 127–32.

Smith, A., & Sugar, O. (1975). Development of above normal language and intelligence 21 years after hemispherectomy. *Neurology, 25,* 813–18.

Soper, H. V., & Satz, P. (1984). Pathological left-handedness and ambiguous-handedness: A new explanatory model. *Neuropsychologia, 22,* 511–15.

St. James-Roberts, I. (1981). A reinterpretation of hemispherectomy data without functional plasticity of the brain: I. Intellectual function. *Brain and Language, 13,* 31–53.

Stiles-Davis, J., Sugarman, S., & Nass, R. (1985). The development of spatial and class relations in four young children with right hemisphere damage: Evidence for an early spatial constructive deficit. *Brain and Cognition, 4,* 388–412.

Teszner, D., Tzavaras, A., Gruner, J., & Hecaen, H. (1972). Etude anatomique de l'asymétrie droite–gauche du planum temporale. *Revue Neurologie, Paris, 126,* 444–62.

Todd, J., Coolidge, F., & Satz, P. (1979). The Wechsler Adult Intelligence Scale Discrepancy Index: A neuropsychological evaluation. *Journal of Consulting and Clinical Psychology, 45,* 450–4.

Towbin, A. (1978). Cerebral dysfunctions related to perinatal organic damage. *Journal of Abnormal Psychology, 87,* 617–35.

Tsai, L., Jacoby, C. G., Stewart, M. A., and Beisler, J. M. (1982). Unfavorable left–right asymmetries of the brain and autism: A question of methodology. *British Journal of Psychiatry, 140*, 312–19.

Turkewitz, G., Gordon, E. W., & Birch, H. G. (1965). Head turning in the human neonate: Spontaneous patterns. *Journal of Genetic Psychology, 107*, 143–8.

Turkewitz, G., Moreau, T., & Birch, H. G. (1968). Relation between birth condition and neuro-behavioral organization in the neonate. *Pediatric Research, 2*, 243–9.

Turkewitz, G., Moreau, T., Gordon, E. W., Birch, H. G., & Crystal, D. (1967). Relationships between prior head positions and lateral differences in responsiveness to somesthetic stimulation in the human neonate. *Journal of Experimental Child Psychology, 5*, 548–61.

Van Dongen, H. R., & Loonen, M. C. B. (1977). Factors related to prognosis of acquired aphasia in children. *Cortex, 13*, 131–6.

Vargha-Khadem, F., & Corballis, M. C. (1979). Cerebral asymmetry in infants. *Brain and Language 8*, 1–9.

Vargha-Khadem, F., & Isaacs, E. (1985, May). *The effects of early vs. late cerebral lesions on verbal learning and memory in children.* Paper presented at the meeting of the Society for Research in Child Development, Toronto.

Vargha-Khadem, F., O'Gorman, A. M., & Watters, G. V. (1985). Aphasia and handedness in relation to hemispheric side, age at injury and severity of cerebral lesion during childhood. *Brain, 8*, 677–96.

Vega, A., & Parsons, O. A. (1969). Relationships between sensorimotor deficits and WAIS verbal and performance scores in unilateral brain damage. *Cortex, 5*, 229–41.

Vernon, M. D. (1957). *Backwardness in reading.* Cambridge University Press.

Vernon, M. D. (1971). *Reading and its difficulties.* Cambridge University Press.

von Hofsten, C. (1982). Eye–hand coordination in the newborn. *Developmental Psychology, 18*, 450–61.

Wada, J., Clarke, J., & Hamm, A. (1975). Cerebral hemispheric asymmetry in humans. *Archives of Neurology, 32*, 239–46.

Warrington, E. K., & James, M. (1967). An experimental investigation of facial recognition in patients with cerebral lesions. *Cortex, 3*, 317–26.

Weinberger, D. R., Luchins, D. J., Morihisa, J., & Wyatt, R. J. (1982). Asymmetrical volumes of the right and left frontal and occipital regions of the human brain. *Annals of Neurology, 11*, 97–9.

White, N., & Kinsbourne, M. (1980). Does speech output control lateralization over time? Evidence from verbal–manual time sharing tasks. *Brain and Language, 10*, 215–33.

Williams, R. S., Hauser, S. L., Purpura, D. P., DeLong, R., & Swisher, C. N. (1980). Autism and mental retardation: Neuropathological studies performed in four retarded persons with autistic behavior. *Archives of Neurology, 37*, 749–53.

Witelson, S. F., & Pallie, W. (1973). Left hemisphere specialization for language in the newborn: Neuroanatomical evidence of brain asymmetry. *Brain, 96*, 641–6.

Wolgin, D. L. (1982). Motivation, activation and behavioral integration. In R. L. Isaacson & N. E. Spear (Eds.), *The expression of knowledge.* New York: Plenum.

Woods, B. T. (1980a). The restricted effects of right-hemisphere lesions after age one: Wechsler test data. *Neuropsychologia, 18*, 65–70.

Woods, B. T. (1980b). Observations on the neurological basis for initial language acquisition. In D. Caplan (Ed.), *Biological studies of mental processes* (pp. 149–58). Cambridge, MA: MIT Press.

Woods, B. T., & Teuber, H. L. (1973). Early onset of complementary specialization of cerebral hemispheres in man. *Transactions of the American Neurological Association, 98*, 113–15.

Woods, B. T., & Teuber, H. L. (1978). Changing patterns of childhood aphasia. *Annals of Neurology, 32*, 239–46.

Young, G., Segalowitz, S. J., Miscek, P., Alp, I. E., & Boulet, H. (1983). Is early reaching left-handed? Review of manual specialization research. In S. J. Segalowitz, C. M. Carter, & S. E. Trehub (Eds.), *Manual specialization and the developing brain.* New York: Academic Press.

Zaidel, E. (1976). Auditory vocabulary of the right hemisphere following brain bisection or hemidecortication. *Cortex, 12*, 191–211.

Zaidel, E. (1977). Unilateral auditory language comprehension on the Token Test following cerebral commissurotomy and hemispherectomy. *Neuropsychologia, 15*, 1–18.

Zaidel, E. (1978). Auditory language comprehension in the right hemisphere following cerebral commissurotomy and hemispherectomy: A comparison with child language and aphasia. In A. Caramazza & E. B. Zurif (Eds.), *Language acquisition and language breakdown: Parallels and divergencies.* Baltimore, MD; Johns Hopkins University Press.

Zangwill, O. L. (1960). *Cerebral dominance and its relation to psychological function.* London: Oliver & Boyd.

Zangwill, O. L. (1962). Dyslexia in relation to cerebral dominance. In J. Money (Ed.), *Reading disability.* Baltimore, MD: Johns Hopkins University Press.

7 Language changes in healthy aging and dementia

Jennifer Sandson, Loraine K. Obler, and Martin L. Albert

The ultimate goal of the study of language in healthy and abnormal aging is the maximization of communication potential. Although it may seem tactful or humane, it is actually only destructive to deny the existence of difficulties or differences. Maximizing communication potential may involve teaching new strategies for talking and listening either to older and demented patients or to their younger or healthy relatives. In either case, these strategies should be based on the nature of the changes that characterize language in healthy aging and dementia.

This chapter contains two main sections covering language in dementia and in healthy aging. We first discuss language changes in dementia of the Alzheimer's type, looking especially at naming, comprehension, syntax, and discourse. We then present a view of the typical patterns of language deterioration found at different stages of Alzheimer's dementia. Language changes in other cortical dementias and in subcortical dementia are also addressed. In the section on language changes in healthy aging we contrast the relatively subtle changes that occur in the normal elderly with the more dramatic changes of Alzheimer's disease. Changes in naming, comprehension, and discourse are considered in the context of the sensory and neuropsychological changes associated with healthy aging. In a third short section, we address the question of changing neural organization for language with age.

Dementia

Dementia is an acquired loss of intellectual functioning that leads to an incapacity for reasonably independent activity (Alexander & Geschwind, 1984). Approximately 5% of Americans over the age of 65 suffer from severe dementia, and an additional 10% are probably mildly demented (Albert, 1984). These figures, however, encompass dementias of many different etiologies. Approximately 20% of patients with dementia have a treatable disease (Alexander & Geschwind, 1984),

This research was supported by the Veterans Administration Medical Research Service, NIH Grant No. NS06209, and the Seidel Fund for the Study of Dementia.

264

etiologies ranging from depression or delirium to nutritional and metabolic disorders. This section focuses on the progressive dementias and, as a heuristic device, categorizes them as cortical or subcortical syndromes.

Cortical dementias

Cortical dementias are characterized by changes in high-level functions such as language, perception, and planned movements. They include such syndromes as senile dementia of the Alzheimer's type (SDAT), Pick's disease, and multi-infarct dementia (MID). Although the pathology of these syndromes is known to affect the outer layers of brain matter, it is likely that deeper subcortical structures are also involved. Before describing the language changes associated with the cortical dementias, we must consider the context of neurological and neurobehavioral changes in which they occur.

SDAT is an age-related disease affecting women twice as often as men and reducing life expectancy by approximately 50% (Alexander & Geschwind, 1984). During the initial evaluation, often prompted by an unusual physical or social stress, the patient's family complains that the patient is forgetful, apathetic, anxious, or confused. Further neurological examination in the early stages generally reveals impairment of visuospatial abilities (e.g., difficulty in drawing a cube or a house) and topographic skills (e.g., difficulty in returning from the restroom). At this stage, measures of anatomical or physiological functioning such as a computerized tomography (CT) scan and an electroencephalogram (EEG) often appear normal, although the possibility of atrophy is sometimes suggested by enlarged ventricles and sulci.

On evaluation, the relative preservation of social skills is often particularly striking. The Information, Vocabulary, Digit Span, and Comprehension subtests of the WAIS-R (Wechsler, 1981) are also relatively preserved, even when patients can no longer care for themselves. In general, the more novel, dependent on new learning, abstract, or speed-related a task, the greater is the impairment (Lezak, 1983). Patients with SDAT thus do particularly poorly on Performance subtests such as Digit Symbol or Block Design. Visuospatial problems are often manifested by disorganization, segmentation, pull to salient aspects of a stimulus, and perseveration. Memory loss, contrary to myth, affects both old and new information, although immediate memory span is likely to be disproportionately good.

The differential diagnosis between SDAT and Pick's disease is particularly difficult to make before microscopic analysis at autopsy. Patients with Pick's disease experience a gradual onset of forgetfulness, impaired comprehension, difficulty in coping with novelty, and confusion. However, the pattern is more likely to be one in which personality changes (apathy, paranoia, irritability, silliness, social disinhibition, and poor judgment) precede the deterioration of memory and visuospatial skills.

Multi-infarct dementia, sometimes called stroke-related dementia, is character-ized by impaired attention, impaired ability to learn new material, and impaired ability to manipulate acquired knowledge. These symptoms occur in the context of each patient's unique pattern of focal deficits. The cardinal signs suggesting a diagnosis of MID are (1) abrupt onset (e.g., sudden tingling, numbness, weak-ness of limb or face, slurred speech, (2) focal neurological signs and symptoms (e.g., reflex changes, visual neglect, motor abnormalities), (3) stepwise decline with periods of plateau, (4) hypertension, and (5) history of stroke. One or more small strokes are often observable on the CT scan.

Language changes in dementia of the Alzheimer's type. This subsection high-lights the experimental literature on naming, comprehension, and discourse. The literature is then reconsidered in terms of the overall evolution of language changes in SDAT.

Confrontation naming. The inability to name objects or actions to command is a conspicuous early symptom of SDAT. Here we explore the confrontation naming deficit from the perspective of a simple information-processing model with mul-tiple stages. These stages, usually believed to occur sequentially, include visual perception, conceptual recognition, lexical access, and activation of a motor pro-gram for speech. Naming deficits would, of course, result from disruption at one or more processing stages. The precise stage or stages at which this disruption occurs in patients with SDAT is currently the focus of considerable controversy.

One prominent theory attributes the anomia of SDAT to an underlying percep-tual deficit. Barker and Lawson (1968), for example, found longer reaction times on a picture-naming task for a group of 100 demented patients than for controls. This discrepancy was greatly reduced when the object's perceptual salience was increased by a demonstration of its function. The possibility that this demonstra-tion provided additional semantic as well as perceptual information, however, was not considered.

Rochford (1971) presented aphasic and demented subjects (of mixed etiology and type) with two sets of stimuli: (1) eight line drawings of objects and (2) eight parts of the examiner's body. Errors on the object-naming task were scored as cor-rect recognition (e.g., for *book,* "what you read"), misrecognition (e.g., for *whale,* "vegetable marrow"), unclassifiable, and no response. More than half (53%) of the aphasic patients' errors but only 15% of the demented patients' er-rors were scored as either no response or correct recognition. The demented pa-tients produced a significantly greater proportion (55%) of misrecognitions than the aphasic patients. Although the majority of these misrecognitions were judged to be perceptually similar to the target (e.g., for *anchor,* "hammer"), the percent-age that were also semantically related was not computed. The demented patients, but not the aphasics, also performed significantly better on naming the more perceptually salient body parts than on naming the pictured objects, further supporting a perceptual locus for their naming difficulty.

Recognizing that the nature of a naming disorder probably changes with its severity, Horner and Heyman (1982) presented 26 clinically diagnosed SDAT patients (4 mildly anomic, 10 moderately anomic, and 12 severely anomic) with pictures from the Boston Naming Test (Kaplan, Goodglass, & Weintraub, 1976). Errors were classified as phonological, semantically related, semantically unrelated, visually related, circumlocutory, and null. Visually and semantically related errors and circumlocutions all occurred with equal frequency in the mildly anomic subjects. Nearly 60% of the mildly anomic patients' errors were corrected following a semantic cue. Visually related errors were the most common in the mildly anomic group and were much less likely to be corrected after semantic cuing. In the severely anomic subjects, visually related, semantically unrelated, and circumlocutory errors were equally frequent. Very few errors were corrected after cuing. These data suggest that perceptual deficits influence naming errors, particularly in SDAT patients who are moderately anomic. It is interesting, however, that the visually related errors in all three groups were often "incomplete" (a detail being named instead of the general configuration) rather than "erroneous" (e.g., for *pyramid*, "roof"). Some of the errors that appear to be visually related to the target, then, may actually reflect underlying cognitive or linguistic distortion rather than a purely perceptual failure.

Our laboratory (Obler, Nicholas, Albert, & Woodward, 1985) has explored in detail the nature of naming errors and the effectiveness of semantic and phonological cuing in both healthy and demented subjects (e.g., Nicholas, Obler, Albert, & Goodglass, 1985). Our results with demented patients (in preparation) support the hypothesis that most naming errors are attributable not to perceptual distortion but to difficulty with lexical access or retrieval.

The stimuli for this study were 63 easily imagable actions, ranging in difficulty from *sleeping* to *knighting,* which comprised the Action Naming Test (Obler & Albert, 1979). The subjects were 10 patients with mild to moderate SDAT, 10 age- and education-matched controls, and the 10 poorest-performing healthy 70-year-olds from a longitudinal study being conducted in our laboratory. Subjects were instructed to name the action in the picture and encouraged to use only one word. Semantic cues designed to facilitate recognition (e.g., "It's at a theater" for *applauding*) were provided in response to obvious misperceptions or lack of any response. Subjects still unable to name the action were given a phonological cue consisting of the first phoneme, consonant cluster, or syllable of the target word. Accurate responses before phonological cuing were scored as correct. Multiple responses (such as "apron, no fins" for *flippers*) were all coded, and any single responses could be multiply coded (e.g., semantically and perceptually related). Examples of each scoring category are listed in Table 1.

As expected, subjects with SDAT produced significantly fewer correct re-

Table 1. *Action Naming Test scoring system*

Error type	Definition
No response	Either silence or a comment such as "I don't know" or "I can't remember."
Augmented correct	Target word plus additional words such as "marching in a parade" for *marching*
Semantically related	Members of the same category, the name of the superordinate category, or actions found in the same context as the target (e.g., "exploding" for *erupting*)
Phonologically related	Both sound and syllable substitutions (e.g., "prongs" for *tongs*)
Perceptually related	Misperceptions or actions resembling the target (e.g., "ballooning" for *parachuting*)
Whole–part or part–whole	Responses in which the name of an entire action is given instead of just a part, or the name of a part of the action is given instead of the whole (e.g., "kneeling" for *proposing*)
Off target	Circumlocutions such as "down on his hands and knees" for *crawling*

Source: Reprinted with permission from Nicholas, Obler, Albert, and Goodglass (1985).

sponses than either control group. The most frequent error type produced by subjects with SDAT was circumlocution, whereas that of the healthy elderly was a semantically related response. Demented subjects actually produced a significantly lower percentage of semantically (21%) and perceptually (11.5%) related errors than the controls. The demented subjects were aided by phonological cues to the same extent as the elderly controls. They did, however, display an initial tendency to respond impulsively to these cues (e.g., replying "jug of water" to the cue *ju* for *juggling*). Semantic cues were too infrequent to allow comparison.

In summary, these results imply that the ability to access the lexicon may be particularly impaired in SDAT. The low proportion of visually related errors argues against a purely perceptual locus, whereas the high rate of circumlocutions argues against a purely conceptual locus. The ability to respond correctly as often as the healthy elderly to phonological cues indicates that the lexicon itself is largely intact. The use of circumlocutions is, in fact, an obvious compensatory strategy for coping with impaired lexical access or retrieval.

A third possible locus for the anomia of SDAT is suggested by the naming study of Bayles and Tomoeda (1983). In this study, 20 pictures from the Peabody Picture Vocabulary Test (Dunn & Dunn, 1981) were presented to 29 subjects with SDAT

(11 mild and 18 moderate), 8 subjects with MID, 24 subjects with subcortical syndromes (11 with Huntington's disease and 13 with Parkinson's disease), and 33 healthy elderly controls.

The moderately impaired Alzheimer's group, but not the subjects with mild SDAT or subcortical syndromes, made significantly more errors than controls. Errors were classified into five non-mutually exclusive categories: no response, unrelated response, visually related response, semantically associated response (includes circumlocutions), and visually and semantically associated response. Semantically associated misnamings were the most common error type for all groups. The moderately impaired SDAT group made 97 errors (out of 360 total responses): 19.6% of these errors were no response, 9.3% were unrelated, 61.9% were semantically associated, and 33.0% were visually similar. Most of the visually similar errors (71%), however, were also semantically associated. Of the subjects whose errors were semantically associated, 40% named items from the same superordinate category as the target, 20% named the target's function, 8.5% named a part of the target, 16.7% named a superordinate, 6.7% named an attribute, and 8.3% a related context. Error analyses were not performed for the healthy controls.

The semantically related nature of most errors further argues against a purely perceptual basis for naming impairment in SDAT. The pattern of relatedness seen in the semantically associated errors is suggestive of a systematic disturbance in semantic organization in SDAT. Some of the discrepancies between this study and the study conducted by our laboratory, particularly the absence of a naming deficit in the early SDAT group, may be attributable to differences in stimulus difficulty. The Peabody Picture Vocabulary Test is designed for use with children and thus may not be sensitive to the subtle changes that take place in patients with mild SDAT. Other discrepancies may have resulted from categorizing circumlocutions as semantic errors in this study but not in ours.

Changes in semantic representation and their effects on word production were experimentally probed with a free-association paradigm specifically chosen to minimize difficulties with lexical access in a study by Gewirth, Shindler, and Hier (1984). (The need to search for elusive target items is theoretically eliminated by allowing the subjects to retrieve whatever lexical items they are able to access.) Responses were scored as syntagmatic (words from a different grammatical class than the target, e.g., "down" associated with "sit"), paradigmatic (words from the same grammatical class that are related in meaning, e.g., "table" for "kitchen"), idiosyncratic, and identical. Patients with SDAT produced significantly fewer paradigmatic, but not syntagmatic, responses than controls. Paradigmatic responses were also found to decrease as a function of dementia severity, whereas syntagmatic responses tended to increase. Paradigmatic responses were also replaced by null, perseverative, and idiosyncratic associations. This increasing tendency away from paradigmatic associations further supports a semantic/

conceptual locus in naming impairment, possibly due to a loss of the semantic markers that describe specific lexical features.

Difficulties at each stage of the naming process were simultaneously explored in patients with SDAT by manipulating the difficulty of semantic encoding, lexical access, and articulation (Kirshner, Webb, & Kelly, 1984). Twelve patients with SDAT and 12 age- and education-matched controls were presented with 40 items at each of four levels of perceptual difficulty: actual objects, black and white photographs, line drawings, and cross-hatched drawings. Each level of perceptual degradation was intended to make semantic encoding progressively more difficult. In addition, half of the items were of low frequency (difficult to access from the lexicon) and half were of high frequency (easy to access). Half of the items had long names that were hard to articulate, and half had short names that were easy to articulate.

The effects of both perceptual degradation and word frequency were significant for the demented subjects, but not for the controls. Error analysis revealed a disproportionate number of perceptual errors in the two more difficult conditions for both groups. The demented patients, as expected, made more total errors, but the controls made proportionately more perceptual errors. There was no effect of word length for either group.

In conclusion, it appears that each of the first three levels of the naming model contribute to the anomia of SDAT. (There is so far no evidence for impairment of motor programs for speech.) Evidence for a perceptual locus includes the small but significant percentage of naming errors across studies that are related to the target only in appearance and the effect of perceptual saliency on naming performance. Evidence for a locus at the lexical level includes a disproportionate number of circumlocutions and the ability to utilize phonological cues. Finally, there seems to be a consistent core of semantic errors that conform to a pattern of conceptual deterioration.

There are many possible explanations for apparent contradictions observed across studies, including (1) differences in criteria for diagnosing SDAT, (2) differences in severity, (3) individual differences, and (4) effects of test demands. The diagnosis of SDAT remains a diagnosis of exclusion that is rarely certain in life. It seems likely that studies conducted before the availability of the CT scan contain more subjects with dementia of other etiology. With respect to severity, it has been suggested (e.g., Auerbach, Obler, & Firnhaber-White, 1982; Seltzer & Sherwin, 1983) that there may be a subset of SDAT patients, particularly those whose onset is late in life, in which language skills are disproportionately preserved until late in the course of the illness. The interaction between language changes and individual factors such as age, duration of illness, education, occupation, and current environment remains unexplored. Finally, the relative difficulty of each of the four stages of processing in our model is not constant across tasks. Greater difficulty at any stage will, of course, increase the likelihood of attributing naming errors to that locus.

Comprehension. Linguistic comprehension for sentence- and narrative-length materials is difficult to study in SDAT because of the inevitable interaction of linguistic factors with general cognitive deterioration. Patients with SDAT, unlike healthy controls, err on tasks of single-word comprehension. Single-word comprehension is thus a promising perspective from which to study both the effects of SDAT on language and the normal organization of semantic representations for meaning.

The systematic dissolution of semantic representations is strikingly demonstrated in the longitudinal study of a 62-year-old demented woman with probable SDAT reported by Schwartz, Marin, and Saffran (1979). The subject had a naming deficit so severe that she was able to name only 1 of 70 objects from a series of 35 pictured pairs of household items belonging to the same superordinate category (e.g., *fork* and *knife*). Despite her anomia, the subject, WLP, was able to pantomime the use of the pictured objects so well that paired items could be differentiated by unpracticed raters. On a written multiple-choice naming test, however, WLP did quite poorly, rarely getting both items from the same category correct. Her errors, the consistent selection of semantic distractors from the same category as the target, suggested that verbal labels were gradually becoming overextended.

In an attempt to document this change and explore nonlinguistic parallels, WLP was then presented with pictures of dogs, cats, and birds. Her task was to sort each picture into one of two category piles, first labeled with words and then with pictures. The results confirmed a change in WLP's semantic and conceptual boundaries that, unexpectedly, seemed to differ for linguistic and pictorial labels. When the task was to sort the pictures into categories labeled by words, WLP correctly sorted all of the dog pictures into the dog pile, where she also placed most of the cats and one bird. When the piles were labeled with photographs, WLP consistently matched both cats and dogs with the cat sample. In summary, WLP's knowledge about both pictorial and linguistic information deteriorated in a systematic fashion, such that category boundaries blurred and basic-level terms became overextended. The specific attributes that were lost or altered, however, were not identical for the two types of information. This dissociation suggests that representations for verbal and pictorial information may be independent.

The possibility that semantic changes in dementia might be hierarchical, affecting specific attribute and associative information before more global knowledge, was also explored by Warrington (1975). The procedure consisted of presenting three demented subjects (of uncertain etiology) with pictures of 20 objects and 20 animals. Superordinate-level information was probed by inquiring for each, "Is it an animal?" Similar questions were then used to probe for basic-level information (e.g., "Is it a bird?") and attribute- and associative-level information (e.g., "Is it bigger than a bread box?" "Is it found in England?"). All three subjects performed almost perfectly for the most global questions, intermediate but better than chance for the basic-level questions, and at or below chance for the attribute- and associative-level questions. Identical results were obtained for verbal stimuli.

The hierarchical disruption of representation for meaning is supported by the results of a larger group study conducted by Martin and Fedio (1983). In this study, subjects with SDAT were administered two types of comprehension task: (1) one requiring subjects to rate target words according to a seven-point scale ranging from *very unpleasant* to *very pleasant* and (2) a symbol-referent task requiring subjects to read words from four categories (objects, actions, modifiers, and emotions) and match them with the appropriate picture from an array. On the rating task, which Martin and Fedio maintain required only global knowledge about a word's referents, the demented subjects did not differ from age- and education-matched controls. On the symbol-referent task the demented subjects made more errors than controls on all categories except the purportedly more global emotional terms.

In conclusion, converging evidence suggests that semantic representations are somehow disturbed in SDAT. Changes in representations appear to be hierarchical, affecting attribute- and associative-level information before superordinate information. This pattern of dissolution is parallel to the pattern of semantic errors seen on naming tasks, where the greatest number of semantically associated errors are the names of items from the same superordinate category.

Syntax. There is some evidence from both the experimental and clinical literature for a possible dissociation between syntax and semantics in SDAT. This evidence consists of reports of disproportionate sparing of syntactic abilities. WLP, the patient studied by Schwartz, Marin, and Saffran (1979), was able, for example, to transform active declarative target sentences spoken by the examiner into corresponding questions and plural, past-tense, and passive sentences. WLP's comprehension of syntactic structures was tested through multiple-choice picture identification. Comprehension of both passive and active sentences, as well as of comparative adjectives and terms of spatial location, was largely intact. In addition, written production of orally presented homophones was significantly more biased by syntactic (e.g., the /sea/) than by semantic (e.g., ocean, /sea/) contexts.

Syntax was disproportionately spared in an even more severely demented, largely noncommunicative woman studied by Haiganoosh Whitaker (1976). In this case, speech was almost entirely restricted to echoing the examiner and, even then, was produced only when direct eye contact had been established. Despite the severity of her deficits, syntactic anomalies, for example,

E: There are two chair in this room.

were spontaneously corrected in the echoed utterances:

S: two chairs in this room

Stimuli presented in a British dialect, similarly, were spontaneously echoed in the subject's native American dialect. Semantic anomalies (e.g., "The apple was eaten by a stone"), however, were echoed without correction:

S: Apple was eaten by a stone.

Discourse. For oral discourse to communicate ideas or needs, speech must convey information in a coherent manner that conforms to certain implicit rules of social interaction. Clinicians often note that the spoken discourse of patients with SDAT fails to convey the intended message. In this subsection we explore two factors that impede the use of discourse for communication in SDAT: emptiness of content and impaired pragmatics.

Our laboratory has examined in detail those aspects of discourse that contribute to the empty speech of SDAT (Nicholas, Obler, Albert, & Helm-Estabrooks, 1985). The subjects were 19 patients with mild to moderately severe SDAT, 24 patients with aphasia due to focal lesion (16 Wernicke's and 8 anomic), and 30 elderly controls. (Anomic aphasia is characterized by word-finding difficulty in the context of fluent grammatical speech. Wernicke's aphasia is characterized by impaired auditory comprehension and fluent speech with word or sound substitutions.) Each subject was shown a copy of the Cookie Theft Picture (Figure 1) from the Boston Diagnostic Aphasia Examination (Goodglass & Kaplan, 1983) and asked to describe what was happening in the picture. Responses were tape-recorded and then transcribed for analysis.

Definitions of the language measures tabulated are listed in Table 2. Table 3 contains the raw counts for each measure for the four groups. Each group produced an average of at least 75 words, the SDAT subjects producing the most and the anomic aphasics the least. There were, however, no significant group differences on total number of words, comments, empty phrases, or judgments. Control subjects produced the greatest number of themes, all other groups producing approximately four of eight. To determine whether changes in discourse could be largely attributed to word-finding difficulty, we also explored correlations between our language measures and Boston Naming Test scores. Naming scores were found to correlate negatively with content elements and positively with indefinite terms. The discourse samples of good and poor namers, however, could not be distinguished within any subject group.

Demented subjects, in comparison with controls, produced significantly more deictic terms, semantic paraphasias, pronouns without antecedents, and repetitions. The demented subjects also tended to produce more empty phrases, indefinite terms, and conjunctions than the controls. The demented subjects were not significantly different from the anomic aphasics on any measure, although they

Figure 1. Cookie Theft Picture. (From Goodglass and Kaplan, 1983; reprinted by permission of Lea & Febiger.)

tended to produce more of most measures except indefinite terms, literal paraphasias, and content elements. In contrast, the demented subjects produced significantly fewer neologisms and literal and verbal paraphasias and more empty phrases, indefinite terms, and conjunctions than the Wernicke's aphasics.

The discourse of patients with SDAT, then, is significantly "more empty" than that of healthy elderly controls. It shares characteristics with the discourse of anomic aphasics (especially in the early stages of SDAT) and with the discourse of Wernicke's aphasics (especially in the later stages). This "emptiness," as indicated by low correlations with naming scores, cannot be attributed to impaired naming.

Changes in discourse in SDAT are not limited to increases in the use of language measures indicating "emptiness." The discourse of patients with SDAT, in addition to being uninformative, often also violates implicit rules of social interaction that are necessary for conversation. Hutchinson and Jensen (1980) systematically compared samples of conversation between an examiner and 10 subjects from an Idaho nursing home, five with senile dementia and five with normal intellectual functioning. The discourse of the demented subjects evidenced fewer utterances during each subject's turn as a speaker and contained more directives

Table 2. *Linguistic measures for discourse analysis*

Measure	Definition
Total number of words	Number of words produced
Empty phrases	Filler phrases such as "and so on and so forth" and "something like that"
Indefinite terms	Words without direct referents, such as "thing," "somebody," and "stuff"
Deictic terms	For example, "this," "here," "that"
Pronouns without antecedents	"He" or "she" without previous identification
Comments on the task	For example, "I know the word but I can't say it"
Neologisms	Nonwords with no apparent relation to the target
Literal paraphasias	Nonwords phonologically related to the target
Verbal paraphasias	Real words with no apparent relation to the target
Semantic paraphasias	Incorrect real words related to the target in meaning
Verbal/phonological paraphasias	Incorrect real words related to the target in sound
Conjunctions	For example, "but," "or," "so"
"And"	Number of "ands" produced
Repeated words or phrases	Number of repetitions
Personal judgments about the picture	For example, "The mother is careless"
Content elements	"Mother," "washing," "sink overflowing," "boy," "stealing cookies," "stool tipping," "girl," and "mother's inattention"

Source: Adapted from Nicholas, Obler, Albert, and Helm-Estabrooks (1985).

that the examiner do something; moreover, these subjects were less likely to continue appropriately with either their own or the examiner's topic after one conversational turn. The following typical discourse sample demonstrates an inappropriate change of conversational topic:

S: And she was my horse and I would harness her and hitch her up. I would always pat her and smooth her hair and pet her so she's like me. I didn't want her to be afraid that I'd hurt her, but I never did. I never did whip her. She was a nice horse. We liked her.
E: Did you train her?
S: Well, my flowers you folks brought me today . . . Aren't they beautiful.

One mechanism the authors suggest might underlie this broad range of conversational violations is increasing egocentrism (exclusive reference to the speaker's viewpoint). Increasing egocentrism could mislead a speaker to assume that his or

Table 3. *Raw count means for each measure in discourse analysis*

Measure	Control	Anomic	Wernicke's	SDAT
Total words	85.3	78.6	94.0	103.4
Empty phrases	0.5	0.8	0.6	1.5
Indefinite phrases	0.7	2.1	1.3	1.7
Deictic terms	2.6	4.9	7.6	6.4
Pronouns without antecedents	0.4	0.6	1.2	1.3
Comments	1.0	0.6	1.6	1.1
Neologisms	0.0	0.0	2.4	0.5
Literal paraphasias	0.1	0.3	1.6	0.2
Verbal paraphasias	0.0	0.0	2.7	0.4
Semantic paraphasias	0.3	0.6	1.5	1.4
Verbal and phonological paraphasias	0.1	0.0	1.3	0.2
Conjunctions	1.0	0.6	0.8	2.5
"Ands"	3.1	2.8	3.6	5.3
Repetitions	0.9	2.4	6.6	5.2
Judgments	0.3	0.3	0.6	0.4
Content themes	6.7	5.8	3.4	4.8

Source: Reprinted with permission from Nicholas, Obler, Albert, and Helm-Estabrooks (1985).

her words convey more information than they actually do. This mistaken assumption could easily result in the type of pragmatic violations reported both in this study and by our laboratory.

Perseveration in dementia of the Alzheimer's type. The term *perseveration* is generally used to describe any continuation or recurrence of an experience or activity without the appropriate stimulus. It is often among the symptoms reported in many forms of neurological disease. Its observation on tests requiring attention and flexibility has traditionally been associated with frontal-lobe lesion. Perseveration is also common, however, in a range of dementing illnesses, where it is found on a variety of both verbal and nonverbal tasks. It occurs in patients with MID, normal pressure hydrocephalus, Parkinsonian dementia, and, most frequently, SDAT.

One variety of perseveration, verbal intrusion (the inappropriate recurrence of a verbal response from a preceding test, item, or procedure), has been found to be a diagnostic indicator of SDAT in two groups of subjects: elderly nursing home residents and patients referred for neurological evaluation of possible dementia (Fuld, Katzman, Davies, & Terry, 1982). In the first group, the occurrence of intrusions correlated significantly with decreased levels of the enzyme choline acetyltransferase in brains examined at autopsy. Levels of this enzyme are often low in patients with verified SDAT. In the second group, intrusions were significantly more common among patients ultimately diagnosed as having SDAT than among subjects whose dementia was of another etiology.

Shindler, Caplan, and Hier (1984) compared the occurrence of perseverations (repetitions from an immediately preceding test response) and intrusions (repetitions after intervening stimuli) in aphasic and demented subjects on three tasks: visual confrontation naming, word association, and vocabulary definition. Interestingly, the generation of animal names was excluded from analysis because of the frequency with which intrusions were produced by healthy controls. The healthy controls, all older than 50, produced no perseverations and only one intrusion on any of the other tasks analyzed. Intrusions occurred in 55% of subjects with SDAT, 40% of subjects with MID, and 20% with hydrocephalus. Perseverations, however, occurred most often in patients with hydrocephalus (33%), only rarely in SDAT (9%), and not at all in MID. Intrusions were very common in Wernicke's aphasia (83%), and common in Broca's aphasia (50%) and anomic aphasia (38%). Perseverations were also more common in aphasia than in dementia.

Verbal intrusions are common in SDAT and appear to be important in differential diagnosis. Other varieties of perseveration (e.g., Sandson & Albert, 1984), which may also contribute to diagnosis, are only now being explored in our laboratory. Preliminary results suggest that perseveration may have an unexpectedly significant underlying role in many of the language deficits of SDAT.

Evolution of language changes in SDAT. We have so far considered changes in different linguistic abilities relatively separately. In the demented patient, as in the aphasic, however, language changes present a unified picture with much co-occurrence and interaction of deficits. We have also considered language changes at only one point in time. Language changes in the demented patient, unlike those in the aphasic patient, are continuously evolving. In order to demonstrate this global pattern of interacting changes, Obler and Albert (1984) described the most characteristic changes that occur at the mild, moderate, and severe stages of SDAT. This pattern of changes is summarized below.

Mild to moderate Alzheimer's disease. Language changes in the early and moderate stages of SDAT are most likely to be manifest in tasks of naming. Patients with SDAT are impaired in tasks of confrontation naming, for both pictured objects and actions, and in tasks of word list generation. The confrontation naming tasks yield long latencies and errors that tend to be descriptions of or otherwise semantically related to the target. Naming is facilitated by phonological cues, and errors are usually spontaneously corrected. Word list generation protocols are often contaminated by intrusions and may contain out-of-category responses as well.

Naming difficulties may also be manifest in spontaneous speech that, although still informative, is characterized by pauses, occasional word substitutions, digressions, and wordiness. Mildly demented patients frequently cover their mouths with their hands as they are talking and use such terms as "perhaps" and "maybe," which indicate their uncertainty. If asked to tell a tale such as "Little Red Riding Hood," these patients often claim not to remember it and, once started, may produce elements from other tales or confuse the order of events.

Comprehension at the sentence and narrative levels is relatively spared in mild SDAT. Questions about sentences and simple passages are generally answered correctly, although errors are easily elicited by longer or more complex texts. Performance on repetition tasks is unimpaired for single words and reasonably short high-probability sentences. Repetition of sentences composed of low-frequency words (e.g., "Limes are sour") is more difficult.

Automatic sequences, such as the alphabet or the numbers from 1 to 21, are easily initiated but may run over or contain omissions. Idioms are generally well explained, although proverbs are often interpreted literally or incompletely. There is some difficulty in establishing and maintaining set on metalinguistic tasks such as changing a prefix to produce the opposite of a given target (e.g., transforming "literate" to "illiterate").

Although purely spontaneous writing may be difficult to initiate, early SDAT patients are still able to write a paragraph-length description of a picture. Spelling errors generally involve the addition, deletion, or perseveration of individual letters. There are occasional word substitutions. Reading aloud is still largely intact, but comprehension of more difficult texts is clearly diminished.

Middle- and middle-to-late-stage SDAT. By the middle stage, patients with SDAT begin to sound like patients with Wernicke's aphasia. Naming has become quite poor with many circumlocutions, semantic and literal paraphasias, misperceptions, and augmentations. Neither semantic nor phonological cues are very likely to facilitate the correct response. Word list generation is also severely impaired, patients generally producing one or two responses and then perseverating or losing set.

Discourse is notable for rushed, fluent speech with a pressed quality, emptiness, grammatical errors, and clang associations. Responses to questions tend to be tangential, apparently guided by one or two substantive words appreciated out of context. It is no longer possible for the patient to tell a coherent story. Yes–no responses, however, are still reliable in conversation.

By the middle stage, repetition of high-probability sentences longer than six words is also difficult, containing errors of omission, combination, and nonsense words. Patients now need prompting in order to start automatic speech series and are likely to omit items or stop before the end. It is difficult to establish set for such tasks as idiom interpretation or morphological opposites, although correct responses can sometimes be elicited within a multiple-choice format.

Written descriptions are now limited to a single sentence or phrase or, in some cases, to the patient's name and address. Written picture descriptions contain spelling errors, word substitutions, and paragrammatisms, as well as evidence of misperception. Reading aloud is interspersed with sound and word substitutions and nonsense words. Comprehension of written material is poor.

Late-stage SDAT. Patients in the late stages of SDAT lose the rushed quality of their speech and become nonfluent or, by the end stage, even mute. Speech is sometimes produced, however, even when there is no listener. When there is speech, it is likely to contain instances of perseveration, echolalia (repetition of another person's utterances), palalalia (repetition of one's own utterances), and clang associations. Late-stage SDAT patients often appear to have no comprehension of spoken language. Some patients respond better to gestures. Formal testing is not possible in the late stages of SDAT.

Language changes in other cortical dementias. Language changes in other varieties of cortical dementia are largely unexplored. Language changes in MID reflect the pattern of focal strokes in the individual patient. These small strokes may or may not result in one of the classical aphasic syndromes described earlier.

About 66% of patients with Pick's disease experience language changes, which, in fact, are likely to be the first cognitive symptom. Initial language changes may include anomia, circumlocutions, and verbal paraphasia (Alexander & Geschwind, 1984). As the disease progresses, speech often becomes more telegraphic and disorganized. Echolalia, palalalia, and verbal stereotypy are not infrequent (Cummings & Duchen, 1981). Patients late in the course of Pick's disease are often largely or completely mute.

The evolution of language changes in one patient with verified Pick's disease over the course of his 12-year illness was described by Holland, McBurney, Moossy, and Reinmuth (1985). The patient's first symptoms included word-finding difficulties, paraphasias, and the substitution of low-frequency words for common ones. These difficulties became progressively more severe, leading eventually to mutism and an aversion for oral speech. The subject was able to communicate by writing messages for several years after the onset of his mutism and was able to read the messages written by others. Writing too, however, gradually became more telegraphic and disorganized. There was no spontaneous attempt to use gesture for communication. Formal attempts to teach the patient sign language were unsuccessful. Nonlinguistic cognitive functioning, including calculation and memory of names and dates, was relatively spared until very late in the course of the disease.

Subcortical dementia

The term *subcortical dementia* has been applied to the cognitive changes that occur in progressive syndromes involving the basal ganglia (and other diencephalic and mesencephalic structures) such as Parkinson's disease, Huntington's disease, and progressive supranuclear palsy (PSP; e.g., Albert, Feldman, & Willis, 1974; Cummings & Benson, 1983). The behavioral characteristics of subcortical dementia include (1) a mild memory impairment (often manifest as "forgetting to remember"), (2) striking slowness (both in motor activity and in information processing), (3) defective ability to make abstractions and manipulate acquired knowledge, and (4) personality changes (e.g., apathy with outbursts of irritability).

The spontaneous speech of patients with subcortical illnesses is often dysarthric, characterized by slowed initiation, low volume, disturbances of rhythm and pitch, and a tendency for acceleration over the course of a phrase or sentence. In addition, patients with subcortical dementias tend to be mildly impaired on tests of confrontation naming. Their performance on word list generation tasks is poor and does not improve when they are provided unlimited time. Discourse tends to be sparse but appropriate in content.Proverb interpretation, however, is often concrete. Writing is micrographic and may contain letter repetitions or omissions of letters or affixes. Reading comprehension of longer passages may be mildly impaired.

I. Lebrun (personal communication) describes two cases of PSP with unusual disorders of repetition.(PSP affects many subcortical structures including the pallidum, substantia nigra, superior colliculus, and midbrain reticular formation.) In the first patient, speech was never spontaneously initiated. Latencies in response to questions were very long, and speech was often preceded by movements of the mouth and face. Once initiated, responses were slow, monotone, and slurred and contained frequent sound substitutions and stutter-like repetitions. Many responses were also echolalic, containing repetitions that were both verbatim and appropriately altered for tense. These echolalic sentences were sometimes repeated two or three times. Apart from inappropriate repetition, choice of lexical items and syntax appeared to be normal. The second patient differed from the first in the striking selectivity and quantity of his repetition deficit, involving only function words, which were sometimes repeated as many as 50 times each.

Language in healthy aging

Language changes in the elderly, both healthy and demented, must be considered in the context of the sensory and cognitive changes that accompany them. This section briefly addresses the issues of presbycusis and general cognitive changes in aging that appear to be most relevant to the topics of naming, comprehension, and discourse.

Presbycusis

Hearing loss with age (presbycusis) appears to be an inevitable consequence of aging in an industrialized society with its concomitant noise levels (Hayes & Jerger, 1984). Presbycusic changes may be either peripheral or central. There are observable anatomical changes in the ear with aging. In the outer ear, for example, there are atrophic changes in the supporting wall of the ear canal, and in the middle ear calcification of cartilage frequently leads to reduced joint space. Anatomical changes in the inner ear include (1) degeneration of hair cells, primarily in the basal region of the cochlea associated with high frequencies; (2) degeneration of nerve cells; (3) atrophy of the stria vascularis; and (4) thickening of the basilar membrane.

These peripheral changes are most often manifested by a slowly progressing bilateral hearing loss, affecting high frequencies before low frequencies, especially in men. These changes generally begin to affect speech comprehension some time in the seventh decade.

There are many reports of decreased speech comprehension in the elderly, however, that cannot be attributed to peripheral hearing changes. Pestalozza and Shore (1955), for example, found that comprehension of phonemically balanced syllables was 20 to 40% worse for subjects older than 60 than for subjects younger than 50, even when the degree of peripheral hearing loss was controlled for. Jerger (1973) confirmed this result by testing the word comprehension of 2,162 subjects with peripheral loss. He found comprehension decreases with age that were accelerated after the fifth decade. Similar tasks involving synthetic sentences (e.g., Jerger & Hayes, 1977), rather than words, reveal age effects as early as the fourth decade.

In conclusion, almost all older people suffer from some degree of hearing loss with both peripheral and central components. The precise locus of the central components, which might originate at any level from the eighth nerve to the cortex, remains undetermined. Changes in the auditory system must always be considered in any attempt to explain linguistic deficits with aging.

Neuropsychological changes

Language changes in the elderly must also be considered in the context of changes in more global neuropsychological processes such as memory and attention. Most tests of cognitive functioning, however, have not been normed on an elderly population. One explanation for the lack of normative studies with aging is the difficulty of defining a healthy elderly population. Does one, for example, exclude subjects with common systemic illnesses such as hypertension or diabetes, each of which has been demonstrated to have an effect on neuropsychological abilities? Another explanation for the lack of norms is the difficulty of finding a suitable methodology. Cross-sectional studies tend to exaggerate age effects because of cohort differences, whereas longitudinal studies minimize differences due to selective attrition, as less healthy subjects drop out of the research program. Cross-sequential studies, following several cohort groups over time, are, like longitudinal studies, limited by time constraints.

Despite these difficulties, there is a growing literature on changes in cognitive functioning with age. One strategy reported in this literature is to compare the performance of the elderly with that of different groups of brain-damaged populations. Elderly subjects, for example, have been reported by some clinicians to exhibit visuospatial deficits similar to those of patients with focal right-hemisphere lesions and by other clinicians to exhibit patterns of deficits similar to those of patients with damage limited to the frontal lobes. This approach to neuropsychological changes with age can be valuable in that it provides information about the cognitive capacities and styles of the elderly. However, it should not be interpreted as providing literal information about actual neurological changes.

Similarities and differences between performances of a group of patients with right-hemisphere damage and a group of healthy elderly controls were explored by Kaplan (1980). Emphasizing that the same neuropsychological performance can be achieved in many different ways, Kaplan stressed the importance of qualitative (or process) analysis when exploring subtle changes due to aging or disease. When constructing three-dimensional block designs from a two-dimensional model, for example, older subjects and subjects with right-hemisphere damage are more likely than young healthy subjects to work from right to left. Older subjects and patients with right-hemisphere disease are also more likely to distort the basic configuration of the design while preserving the internal details. Older people similarly tend to distort the general configuration while preserving isolated internal features when copying a complex design such as the Rey–Osterreith Complex Figure (Osterreith, 1944), their errors often implying that verbal labels have been applied to parts of the picture.

Farver (1975), as reported by Hochanadel and Kaplan (1984), administered a series of tests associated with functioning of the right and left parietal lobes to a group of healthy elderly subjects. No impairment was found on tasks such as right–left orientation, verbal finger identification, and arithmetic, which are generally associated with the left parietal lobe. As predicted, age-related changes were found on recall of stick designs, three-dimensional block designs, clock construction, and visual finger identification, tasks generally associated with functioning of the right parietal lobe. On closer analysis, however, most errors were found to consist of right–left reversals (echopraxia), imitation, and segmentation, symptoms more commonly associated with the frontal lobes than the right parietal lobe.

Qualitative analysis of neuropsychological performance reveals that older people sometimes employ different strategies than younger controls. Some of these strategies resemble those utilized by patients with focal right-hemisphere lesions, and others those utilized by patients with frontal-lobe damage. The use of these strategies does not necessarily imply that older people begin to suffer from either right-hemisphere or frontal-lobe damage.

In addition to those changes that resemble focal types of brain damage, there are other cognitive changes associated with healthy aging. These changes have been categorized into four areas: (1) changes in memory (both for new and remote information), (2) difficulty with abstraction and complex conceptualization, (3) mental inflexibility, and (4) general behavioral slowing (Lezak, 1983). Like sensory changes, general cognitive changes must always be considered in any attempt to explain linguistic changes in aging.

Language strategies

Despite the sensory and cognitive changes outlined above, the healthy elderly seem to perform well on real-life language tasks. Our laboratory attempted to explore strategies elderly subjects might use to compensate for the sensory and cognitive changes of aging (Obler, Nicholas, Albert, & Woodward, 1985). We hypothesized that older subjects might differentially benefit from lip- or face-reading cues or from lexical and semantic predictability. We thus presented healthy good-hearing (pure tone hearing better than 35 dB at 2 kHz) subjects from four decades (ages 30–9, 50–9, 60–9, 70–9) with two sets of stimuli. In the first condition, subtests from the Boston Diagnostic Aphasia Examination (testing general information, repetition, paragraph recall, repetition of sentences with grammatical and semantic anomalies, sentence completion, and comprehension of passive and active sentences) were presented over speech babble at 70 dB with and without a video accompaniment to engage lip or face reading. The level of the signal intensity was varied relative to a constant noise level in order to maintain subjects just above a level of discomfort. In the second condition, subjects identified final words that either were or were not semantically predictable in sentences presented over speech babble.

Overall performance, as predicted, decreased with age on both tasks and was facilitated for all ages by both semantic redundancy (high predictability) and video accompaniment. The facilitory effects of the video and semantically predictable conditions, however, were not greater for the older than for the younger adults. The strategies older adults use to compensate for sensory and cognitive deficits in everyday language tasks remain largely unexplored.

Naming

Older adults often complain of a difficulty in producing intended words. This intuition has been confirmed in the laboratory, but only for subjects in the eighth decade (e.g., Goodglass, 1980). Our laboratory has completed a detailed study of lexical access for both nouns and verbs across the adult life span (Nicholas, Obler, Albert, & Goodglass, 1985).

Subjects were recruited from the community through advertisements in local newspapers and posters placed in senior citizen centers. Respondents were

Table 4. *Boston Naming Test scoring*

Error type	Example
No response	"This is a hard one"
Augmented correct	"*propeller* on an airplane"
Semantically related	"harness" for *yolk*
Phonologically related	"prong" for *tongs*
Perceptually related	"flower" for *pinwheel*
Whole–part, part–whole	"clock" for *pendulum*
Off target	"artistic thing for flowers" for *pendulum*

Source: Reprinted with permission from Nicholas, Obler, Albert, and Goodglass, (1985).

screened in order to exclude subjects whose language functioning might be complicated by any of the following factors: history of neurological or psychiatric disorder, history of alcoholism, uncorrected hearing or vision problems, bilingualism, or sinistrality. The subjects were divided into four age groups (30–9, 50–9, 60–9, 70–9), each containing at least 19 men and 19 women.

The Boston Naming Test (Kaplan, Goodglass, & Weintraub, 1976) and the Action Naming Test (Obler & Albert, 1979) were administered to all subjects. The Boston Naming Test consists of 85 line drawings of objects ranging in frequency from *tree* to *trellis,* which can be named with a one-word response. If a subject had difficulty in naming an object, semantic and phonological cues were provided in the same manner as in the Action Naming Test. Responses were coded according to the same system employed for the Action Naming Test. Examples of each scoring category are listed in Table 4.

Correctness scores and number of attempts per item are summarized in Table 5 and reflect significant age effects for both tests. The correctness effect results from a small decrement in performance from the fourth to the sixth decade, a slightly larger decrement from the sixth to the seventh decade, and a larger and significant decrement from the seventh to the eighth decade.

The results of error analyses are summarized in Table 6. The most frequent error type for both tests was a semantically related noun or verb. In the Boston Naming Test, comments were the second most frequent error type, followed by circumlocutions in the three oldest groups and by whole–part responses in the youngest group. On the Action Naming Test, perceptually related responses were the second most frequent error type, followed by comments, whole–part responses, and circumlocutions. Phonologically related responses were rare in all groups.

Younger subjects produced significantly more semantically related, semantically and perceptually related, and phonologically related responses than older subjects, whereas older subjects produced significantly more circumlocutions and

Table 5. *Boston Naming Test and Action Naming Test scores*

Scoring category	Test[a]	Decade			
		30s	50s	60s	70s
Number correct	BNT	75.9 (6.4)	75.7 (5.7)	73.6 (6.8)	67.6 (8.4)
	ANT	59.3 (2.8)	59.0 (2.6)	58.3 (3.0)	56.2 (3.6)
Range of scores	BNT	56–85	59–83	55–83	52–80
	ANT	53–63	52–63	50–62	46–62
Percent correct	BNT	89.3	89.0	86.4	79.5
	ANT	94.3	93.8	92.8	89.1
Percentage of total	BNT	72.3 (9.9)	67.5 (12.2)	62.3 (14.4)	52.3 (15.8)
attempts correct on first try	ANT	84.4 (7.5)	80.9 (9.9)	78.9 (12.0)	71.7 (12.0)
Attempts per item	BNT	1.1 (.09)	1.2 (.11)	1.2 (.14)	1.3 (.19)
	ANT	1.1 (.06)	1.1 (.07)	1.1 (.11)	1.2 (.11)
Number of	BNT	96.6 (7.2)	100.7 (9.2)	104.0 (12.0)	110.9 (16.1)
total attempts	ANT	67.3 (3.7)	69.1 (4.2)	70.1 (6.6)	72.3 (6.6)
Percent correct after	BNT	50.0 (50.0)	40.0 (49.0)	17.9 (32.6)	45.5 (31.0)
semantic cue	ANT	—	—	—	—
Percent correct after	BNT	81.0 (22.4)	83.9 (20.2)	76.4 (25.7)	76.2 (16.2)
phonemic cue	ANT	66.7 (47.1)	87.5 (29.8)	96.4 (12.9)	84.9 (30.)

Note: Numbers in paretheses represent standard deviations.
[a]BNT, Boston Naming Test; ANT, Action Naming Test.
Source: Reprinted with permission from Nicholas, Obler, Albert, and Goodglass (1985).

augmented correct responses. Semantic and phonological cues were equally facil-itory for all age groups.

In summary, error analysis reveals a greater tendency for circumlocution in the context of a lower proportion of semantically related errors and equal responsivity to phonological cues in the healthy elderly. All these findings suggest that lower correctness scores with age can be largely attributed to increasing difficulty in accessing (or retrieving from) an intact lexicon. This pattern of responses resem-bles a pattern that is also observed, to a much greater degree, in patients with SDAT. The healthy elderly subjects in this study, unlike patients with SDAT, did not produce errors suggestive of a disturbance at either the perceptual or the con-ceptual recognition stages of the naming process.

One way to explore the intactness of semantic representations while minimizing the need for lexical access is to ask subjects to define rather than retrieve target words. Vocabulary skills, unlike naming, have generally been found to remain un-changed (or even improve) across the life span (e.g., Kramer & Jarvik, 1979). Botwinick and Storandt (1974), however, report subtle changes on the WAIS Vo-cabulary subtest (Wechsler, 1958) when the standard scoring system is expanded

Table 6. *Boston Naming Test and Action Naming Test: error types*

Error type	Test[a]	Decade			
		30s	50s	60s	70s
Percentage of correct	BNT	2.0 (2.0)	2.0 (3.0)	3.5 (3.0)	4.0 (4.0)
responses with augmentation	ANT	1.0 (1.0)	1.0 (2.0)	1.0 (3.0)	2.0 (4.0)
Semantic[b]	BNT	38.9 (11.8)	31.2 (10.7)	32.4 (12.9)	29.2 (10.8)
	ANT	50.9 (22.1)	43.9 (19.1)	36.2 (16.4)	37.7 (15.7)
Perceptual[b]	BNT	6.8 (5.2)	8.0 (8.1)	7.7 (6.9)	8.4 (6.9)
	ANT	16.9 (14.6)	18.8 (14.3)	23.1 (18.1)	22.5 (12.4)
Circumlocution[b]	BNT	6.6 (6.4)	10.3 (7.9)	13.0 (14.5)	13.9 (8.4)
	ANT	3.0 (6.2)	3.4 (8.1)	4.4 (8.0)	7.5 (9.1)
Whole–part[b]	BNT	8.2 (7.9)	9.0 (7.4)	11.3 (12.9)	10.6 (6.3)
	ANT	3.5 (7.0)	5.9 (11.3)	4.4 (7.7)	2.9 (5.8)
Phonological[b]	BNT	6.6 (7.4)	5.8 (5.7)	4.4 (4.0)	3.4 (3.2)
	ANT	—	—	—	—
Comments[b]	BNT	16.9 (10.8)	19.9 (12.2)	12.1 (10.5)	23.4 (11.8)
	ANT	7.5 (16.9)	5.7 (7.0)	9.6 (11.6)	8.0 (8.4)
All other[b] responses	BNT	15.4 (8.4)	16.6 (8.1)	12.3 (7.0)	12.9 (8.2)
added together	ANT	14.9 (12.3)	16.9 (15.2)	17.0 (12.1)	16.7 (11.8)
Nouns[b]	BNT	—	—	—	—
	ANT	12.2 (15.8)	19.5 (14.8)	20.1 (20.4)	17.9 (12.8)

[a] BNT, Boston Naming Test; ANT, Action Naming Test.
[b] Percentage of noncorrect attempts.
Source: Reprinted with permission from Nicholas, Obler, Albert, and Goodglass (1985).

qualitatively. The qualitative scoring system consists of six possible scores, which differentiate superior synonyms, good explanations, inferior synonyms, poor explanations, descriptions and usages, and illustrations. Young adults produced significantly more superior synonyms and significantly fewer poor explanations. The older subjects were more likely than the younger subjects to define words with good multiword explanations. This result has many possible explanations, which include increased loquaciousness and differences in perceived task demands as well as changes in the representation of word meanings.

The discrepancy between confrontation naming and vocabulary skills in aging has been explored through the use of two types of priming task (Bowles & Poon, 1985). The first task involved presenting letter strings preceded by primes (related, unrelated, or neutral) and requiring a lexical decision. There were no age effects on this task for accuracy, reaction time, or type of prime, suggesting that the ability to access the lexicon (assumed to be orthographically organized) does not change with age. The second task tested word retrieval by presenting definitions for which subjects were to generate a one-word label. Definitions were preceded by one of six prime types: the word itself, the first two letters of the word, an orthographically related prime, a neutral prime consisting of XXXXXX, an un-related word, or a semantically related word. On this task, young subjects were correct significantly more often for all prime types except identity and orthograph-ically related. This suggests that the ability to access semantic representations (as-sumed to be conceptually organized), or perhaps the ability to move from those representations to the lexicon, is impaired with age. In conclusion, this study dem-onstrates a dissociation between the ability to access an orthographically orga-nized lexicon and the ability to access (or move on from) a conceptually organized network or word representations with age.

Comprehension

It is particularly difficult to find a pure metric of linguistic comprehension in the healthy elderly. Tasks of comprehension difficult enough to yield age differences are almost invariably confounded by both general neuropsychological (e.g., mem-ory, attention) and sensory (e.g., presbycusis, cataracts) demands.

At the one-word level, comprehension has been tested by such tasks as defining vocabulary words (e.g., Botwinick & Storandt, 1974) and matching pictures with their referents (e.g., Martin & Fedio, 1983). Age effects on such tasks are incon-sistent and often attributable to factors other than comprehension. The future use of semantic primes to explore changes in word relations is promising.

Studies utilizing stimuli at the sentence and narrative levels typically find dif-ferences with age, but these differences are also often attributed to general cog-nitive factors. Cohen (1979), for example, tested three aspects of comprehension in young and old subjects with high and low levels of education. The three tasks involved making inferences based on short passages, detecting anomalies within short passages, and recalling a somewhat longer passage. The older adults with both high and low educational levels were significantly worse than the younger controls at answering questions requiring inferences based on the presented facts. Their performance for verbatim questions requiring only the reproduction of sur-face meaning was unimpaired. The older adults were also significantly worse at judging passages as "right" or "wrong" depending on whether they contained a mistake or events that could not be true. Their errors consisted of false detections rather than misses and usually involved either accessing incorrect information or imposing a value judgment (e.g., judging a story about a woman making her hus-band sandwiches for lunch as wrong because lunch should be a hot meal). For the story-recall task, subjects were read a 300-word passage and asked to recall it aloud. Older subjects recalled significantly fewer of both total propositions and summary (gist) propositions.

Cohen concluded that comprehension of spoken narratives is impaired by di-minished cognitive capacity. Diminished capacity makes it more difficult to carry out simultaneously the registration of surface meaning and other processes of in-tegration, construction, and reorganization that may be unimpaired in isolation.

Linguistic factors alone were not thought to be contributory. However, the precise role of linguistic factors in narrative comprehension might be better tested within a reading paradigm where factors of memory and speed are at least somewhat controlled by the subject.

Discourse

Older people, especially in non-Western societies, are often the most admired storytellers. To young Americans, however, the discourse of the elderly often seems long-winded and tangential. Obler (1980) reported a series of studies on written and oral discourse designed to analyze these stylistic differences systematically.

In the studies of written discourse, 18 male Parkinsonian patients in their fifties and sixties and 18 hospitalized nonneurological controls were initially asked to describe the Cookie Theft Picture. The healthy 50-year-olds differed from the Parkinsonian patients and the older controls in their use of a more abbreviated style, with more sentences, fewer words per theme, and fewer embeddings. This result was replicated for 50- to 70-year-olds in a second study with 106 nonhospitalized male volunteers. Somewhat unexpectedly, the 30- to 40-year-olds in the second study resembled the 70-year-olds more than the 50-year-olds.

In a study of oral discourse, three groups of older subjects (55–64, 65–74, and 75 +) were asked to recall aloud a narrative passage from the Wechsler Memory Scale (Wechsler, 1945) both immediately and after a brief delay. Paraphrasing and the use of indefinite terms increased with age in both conditions. Comments and questions also increased with age but only on immediate recall, perhaps because the subjects thought they should have been able to recall more material than they did. It is interesting that comments and questions, indefinite terms, and filler phrases were the elements that most distinguished the tales told by particularly renowned storytellers from those told by other storytellers in an Arab village near Jerusalem (Obler, 1978).

In conclusion, the written narratives of older subjects are more likely to contain well-structured full sentences, complex syntax, indefinite terms, questions, comments, and judgments than are narratives produced by younger subjects. The pattern of oral discourse appears to be similar. These differences may be viewed negatively as a reflection of disinhibition or press of speech, as seen in Wernicke's aphasia, or positively as the maturation of a talent for storytelling. Most likely, they provide the structure needed to cope with other, less global language and cognitive changes.

Changing neural organization for language with age

The evidence we have reviewed so far demonstrates patterns of change in language behavior in the healthy elderly. Are these language changes reflective of changes in neural organization? A hypothesis of increasing left-hemisphere specialization for language across the adult life span (Brown & Jaffe, 1975) has been investigated both experimentally and clinically. The experimental studies provide information about whether language functions become more or less left-hemisphere-lateralized with age. The clinical studies, although less systematic, address the question of increasing specialization for language in the left hemisphere.

Experimental studies have employed both dichotic listening and tachistoscopic techniques. Dichotic listening involves presenting auditory stimuli through earphones for recall or recognition. This information, because of the predominance of crossed pathways in the auditory system, is then assumed to be processed by the contralateral hemisphere. Borod and Goodglass (1980), for example, presented subjects between the ages of 24 and 79 with binaural verbal (digits) and nonverbal (nursery rhyme tunes) stimuli, carefully controlling for order of report. Although the expected effects of ear (right ear better than left for digits, left ear better than right for tunes) and age (young subjects better than old for both stimuli) were obtained, neither set of stimuli was more or less lateralized with age.

Tachistoscopic studies involve the brief presentation of information to one visual field for processing by the contralateral hemisphere. Obler, Woodward, and Albert (1984) tachistoscopically administered verbal and nonverbal stimuli for same–different judgments to subjects from three age groups. The verbal stimuli consisted of two-letter syllables, one above the other, presented in upper and lower case. The nonverbal stimuli were the upper and lower halves of faces. The expected effects of visual field (right visual field better than left for syllables, left better than right for faces) and age were again obtained, also in the absence of any interaction effect.

The evidence from experimental studies with healthy subjects, then, seems to indicate that there are no changes in interhemispheric lateralization for language with age. It is not yet technically feasible to measure intrahemisphere specialization experimentally in healthy subjects. The issue of changes in intrahemispheric organization, however, can be approached by an exploration of the differences in the effects of left-hemisphere damage on language across the life span. Obler, Albert, Goodglass, and Benson (1978) examined the relation between age and aphasia syndrome in a sample of right-handed men at the Boston Veterans Administration Medical Center over a 7-year period. Only patients with a classical pattern of language deficits attributable to a single cerebral event were considered. The mean age of patients with Broca's (nonfluent) aphasia, 51 years, was significantly younger than the mean age, 63 years, of patients with Wernicke's (fluent) aphasia. The possibility that this difference is due to changes in the vascular system, resulting in a tendency for more posterior strokes with age, rather than to changes in neural organization for language, however, has not yet been resolved.

In conclusion, language changes with age are not associated with increasing (or decreasing) left-hemisphere dominance for language. The possibility of increasing specialization within the left hemisphere across the life span is suggested by changing patterns of aphasia. It is likely that advances in technology will soon make it possible to investigate this question in a healthy elderly population.

Conclusion

Because the study of language in aging and dementia is in its infancy, research has so far been directed toward the description of observed changes. This approach has been extremely valuable in clarifying the nature of language changes across the life span, in healthy aging and in dementia. Now that the foundation has been laid, there are two new directions research efforts can follow. The first is theoretical and involves developing a model to explain neurobiological and linguistic mechanisms of language changes associated with age. This work must integrate descriptive information with knowledge from theoretical linguistics, aphasiology, and the neurosciences. The second direction is clinical and involves developing programs for improved communication. These programs can benefit from our knowledge about the nature of specific deficits in the context of normal sensory, cognitive, and linguistic changes with age.

References

Albert, M. L. (1978). Subcortical dementia. In R. Katzman, R. Terry, & K. Bick (Eds.), *Alzheimer's disease, senile dementia, and related disorders*. New York: Raven Press.

Albert, M. L. (1984). Preface. In M. L. Albert (Ed.), *Clinical neurology of aging* (pp. vi–vii). New York: Oxford University Press.

Albert, M. L., Feldman, R. G., & Willis, A. L. (1974). The "subcortical dementia" of progressive supranuclear palsy. *Journal of Neurology, Neurosurgery, and Psychiatry, 37*, 121–30.

Alexander, M., & Geschwind, N. (1984). Dementia in the elderly. In M. L. Albert (Ed.), *Clinical neurology of aging*. (pp. 254–76). New York: Oxford University Press.

Auerbach, S., Obler, L. K., & Firnhaber-White, R. (1982). *Two clinical patterns of Alzheimer's disease*. Paper presented at the annual meeting of the Gerontological Society of America, Boston.

Barker, M., & Lawson, J. (1968). Nominal aphasia in dementia. *British Journal of Psychiatry, 114*, 1351–6.

Bayles, K., & Tomoeda, C. (1983). Confrontation naming impairment in dementia. *Brain and Language, 19*, 98–114.

Borod, J., & Goodglass, H. (1980). Hemispheric specialization and development. In L. K. Obler & M. L. Albert (Eds.), *Language and communication in the elderly* (pp. 91–103). Lexington, MA: Heath.

Botwinick, J., & Storandt, M. (1974). Qualitative vocabulary responses and age. *Journal of Genetic Psychology 125*, 303–8.

Bowles, N., & Poon, L. (1985). Aging and retrieval of words in semantic memory. *Journal of Gerontology, 40*, 71–7.

Brown, J. W., & Jaffe, J. (1975). Hypothesis on cerebral dominance. *Neuropsychology, 13*, 107–10.

Cohen, G. (1979). Language comprehension in old age. *Cognitive Psychology, 11*, 412–29.

Cummings, J., & Duchen, L. (1981). The Kluver–Bucy syndrome in Pick's disease: Clinical and pathological correlations. *Neurology, 31*, 1415–22.

Cummings, J., & Benson, D. F. *Dementia: A clinical approach*. Boston: Butterworth, 1983.

Dunn, L., & Dunn, L. (1981). *Peabody Picture Vocabulary Test*. New York: American Guidance Service.

Fuld, P., Katzman, R., Davies, P., & Terry, R. (1982). Intrusions as a sign of Alzheimer dementia: Chemical and pathological verification. *Annals of Neurology, 11*, 155–9.

Gewirth, A., Shindler, A., & Hier, D. (1984). Altered patterns of word associations in dementia and aphasia. *Brain and Language, 21*, 307–18.

Goodglass, H. (1980). Naming disorders in aphasia and aging. In L. K. Obler & M. L. Albert (Eds.), *Language and communication in the elderly* (pp. 37–45). Lexington, MA: Heath.

Goodglass, H., & Kaplan, E. (1983). *The assessment of aphasia and related disorders*. Philadelphia: Lea & Febiger.

Hayes, D., & Jerger, J. (1984). Neurotology of aging: The auditory system. In M. L. Albert (Ed.), *Clinical neurology of aging* (pp. 362–80). New York: Oxford University Press.

Hochanadel, G., & Kaplan, E. (1984). Neuropsychology of normal aging. In M. L. Albert (Ed.), *Clinical neurology of aging* (pp. 231–44). New York: Oxford University Press.

Holland, A., McBurney, D., Moossy, J., & Reinmuth, O. M. (1985). The dissolution of language in Pick's disease with neurofibrillary tangles: A case study. *Brain and Language, 24*, 36–58.

Horner, J., & Heyman, A. (1982, October). *Aphasia associated with Alzheimer's dementia*. Paper presented to the International Neuropsychological Society, Pittsburgh, PA.

Hutchinson, J., & Jensen, M. (1980). A pragmatic evaluation of discourse communication of normal and senile elderly in a nursing home. In L. K. Obler & M. L. Albert (Eds.), *Language and communication in the elderly*. Lexington, MA: Heath.

Jerger, J. (1973). Audiological findings in aging. *Advances in Oto-Rhino-Laryngology, 20*, 115–24.

Jerger, J., & Hayes, D. (1977). Diagnostic speech audiometry. *Archives of Otolaryngology, 103*, 216–22.

Kaplan, E. (1980). Changes in cognitive style with aging. In L. K. Obler & M. L. Albert (Eds.), *Language and communication in the elderly* (pp. 121–32). Lexington, MA: Heath.

Kaplan, E., Goodglass, H., & Weintraub, S. (1976). *Boston Naming Test,* experimental ed. Boston: VA Medical Center.

Kirshner, H., Webb, W., & Kelly, M. (1984). The naming disorder of dementia. *Neuropsychologia, 22*, 23–30.

Kramer, N., & Jarvik, L. (1979). Assessment of intellectual changes in the elderly. In A. Raskin & L. Jarvik (Eds.), *Psychiatric symptoms and cognitive loss in the elderly*. Washington, DC: Hemisphere.

Lezak, M. (1983). *Neuropsychological assessment*. New York: Oxford University Press.

Martin, A., & Fedio, P. (1983). Word production and comprehension in Alzheimer's disease: The breakdown of semantic knowledge. *Brain and Language, 19*, 124–41.

Nicholas, M., Obler, L. K., Albert, M. L., & Helm-Estabrooks, N. (1985). Empty speech in Alzheimer's disease, healthy aging, and aphasia. *Journal of Speech and Hearing Research, 28*, 405–10.

Nicholas, M., Obler, L. K., Albert, M. L., & Goodglass, H. (1985). Lexical access in healthy aging. *Cortex, 21,* 595–606.

Obler, L. K. (1978). *Tale-telling conventions of three elderly Palestinians.* Paper presented at MESA meeting, Ann Arbor, MI.

Obler, L. (1980). Narrative discourse style in the elderly. In L. K. Obler & M. L. Albert (Eds.), *Language and communication in the elderly* (pp. 75–90). Lexington, MA: Heath.

Obler, L. K., & Albert, M. L. (1979). *Action Naming Test,* experimental ed. Boston: VA Medical Center.

Obler, L. K., & Albert, M. L. (1984). Language in aging. In M. L. Albert (Ed.), *Clinical neurology of aging* (pp. 245–53). New York: Oxford University Press.

Obler, L. K., Albert, M. L., Goodglass, H., & Benson, D. F. (1978). Aphasia type and aging. *Brain and Language, 6,* 318–22.

Obler, L. K., Nicholas, M., Albert, M. L., & Woodward, S. (1985). On comprehension across the adult lifespan. *Cortex, 21,* 273–80.

Obler, L. K., Woodward, S., & Albert, M. (1984). Changes in cerebral lateralization in aging? *Neuropsychologia, 22,* 235–40.

Osterreith, P. (1944). Le test de copie d'une figure complexe. *Archives de Psychologie, 30,* 206–356.

Pestalozza, G., & Shore, I. (1955). Clinical evaluation of presbycusis on basis of different tests of auditory function. *Laryngoscope, 65,* 1136–63.

Rochford, G. (1971). A study of naming errors in dysphasic and in demented patients. *Neuropsychologia, 9,* 437–43.

Sandson, J., & Albert, M. L. (1984). Varieties of perseveration. *Neuropsychologia, 22,* 715–32.

Sarno, M. (1980). Language rehabilitation outcome in the elderly aphasic patient. In L. K. Obler & M. L. Albert (Eds.), *Language and communication in the elderly* (pp. 191–204). Lexington, MA: Heath.

Schwartz, M., Marin, O., & Saffran, E. (1979). Dissociations of language functions in dementia: A case study. *Brain and Language, 7,* 277–306.

Seltzer, B., & Sherwin, I. (1983). A comparison of clinical features in early- and late-onset primary degenerative dementia. *Archives of Neurology, 40,* 143–6.

Shindler, A., Caplan, L., & Hier, D. (1984). Intrusions and perseverations. *Brain and Language, 23,* 148–58.

Warrington, E. (1975). The selective impairment of semantic memory. *Quarterly Journal of Experimental Psychology, 27,* 635–57.

Wechsler, D. (1945). A standardized memory scale for clinical use. *Journal of Psychology, 19,* 87–95.

Wechsler, D. (1958). *The measurement and appraisal of adult intelligence.* Baltimore, MD: Williams & Wilkins.

Wechsler, D. (1981). *WAIS-R manual.* New York: Psychological Corporation.

Whitaker, H. (1976). A case of the isolation of the language function. In H. Whitaker & H. Whitaker (Eds.), *Studies in neurolinguistics* (Vol. 2). New York: Academic Press.

Index